RADICAL

RELEVANCE

Toward a Scholarship of the Whole Left

EDITED BY

LAURA GRAY-ROSENDALE

AND STEVEN ROSENDALE

STATE UNIVERSITY OF NEW YORK PRESS

Published by
STATE UNIVERSITY OF NEW YORK PRESS
ALBANY

© 2005 State University of New York

For information, address
State University of New York Press,
90 State Street, Suite 700, Albany, NY 12207

Production, Laurie Searl
Marketing, Anne M. Valentine

Library of Congress Cataloging-in-Publication Data

Radical relevance : toward a scholarship of the whole left / edited by Laura Gray-Rosendale and Steven Rosendale.
    p. cm.
Includes bibliographical references and index.
ISBN 0-7914-6273-0 (alk. paper) — ISBN 0-7914-6274-9 (pbk. : alk. paper)
    1. Radicalism. 2. Right and left (Political science) I. Gray-Rosendale, Laura. II. Rosendale, Steven.
HN49.R33R33   2005
303.48'4—dc22   2003070439

10 9 8 7 6 5 4 3 2 1

RADICAL RELEVANCE

CONTENTS

INTRODUCTION

TOWARD A SCHOLARSHIP OF
THE "WHOLE LEFT"

Steven Rosendale

THE ESSAYS IN THIS VOLUME PRESUPPOSE A DISSATISFACTION WITH THE CONDITION of the contemporary left in the United States, and with the role of the academic left within that condition. Despite marked differences in the analyses presented by each thinker represented here, most agree upon a broad portrait of the American left as sadly diminished in numbers, efficacy, and presence in public political discourse. Whatever measure one uses—membership in left organizations, electoral results, influence in public debate, and so on—the American left is currently more notable for its weakness than its vitality as a force in American society. The familiar debates about the relative virtues of the old left versus the new left are beginning to give way to a more pressing question about radical and progressive movements for social change in America: "what's left?"

The precise answer to that question remains a subject of debate in this volume; indeed, the approaches to the problem represented in *Radical Relevance* range so widely that it would be futile to attempt a detailed synthesis here. The essays presented here do, however, share an interest in identifying broad external factors in the diminishment of the left: the historical suppression of traditional left organizations; the failure of potentially viable historical models for the "good society" (exemplified variously by certain periods in Chinese communism, the Soviet Union prior to the Hitler-Stalin pact, or prior to the Moscow show trials, or prior to the fall of the Soviet bloc, or as never historically realized); the homogenization of national political discourses under the two-party system (exemplified and exacerbated by the aftermath of the 2000 presidential election, during which Al Gore's narrow defeat in Florida was frequently blamed on votes lost to Ralph Nader's Green Party); and the virtual elimination of left

VII

discourses from public debate in the major media (exemplified by the stunningly univocal nationalism and suppression of dissenting voices in the major media outlets during the terrorist attacks of September, 2001, and the ensuing—and by now years-long—U.S. military operations abroad).

In addition to their agreement regarding the importance of expansive external factors such as these, an internal criticism of the left also emerges as a strong theme in all of the essays contained in this volume. Each essay, that is, scrutinizes problems intrinsic to left organizations and discourses for their contribution to the reduction of left influence. Although each essay builds a distinctive portrait of these problems, all participate in the recent resurgence of attention to the left's potential culpability in its own diminishment. Among recent texts to explore this issue is Harvey Teres's 1996 book *Renewing the Left*, which offers a useful distillation of several related issues that continue to occupy the center of debate in the essays collected here. Teres's introduction to that book builds a powerful indictment of the left for failing to address "certain perennial internal problems" in left organizations, problems that have predictably led to the left's failure to achieve its aims (or even sustain member support). Reflecting upon his own experience with radical groups in the early 1970s, Teres suggests that their failure was due to the left's stubborn attraction to "sectarian and even authoritarian trends"—to the "odor of orthodoxy" that permeated both the political goals and the entire culture of the left. Richard Flacks supports a similar indictment of left organizational goals and ideological rigidity in *Making History: The American Left and the American Mind*. Flacks argues that for left activists in both the old and new American lefts, "organizational commitment tended to undermine activist effectiveness rather than aiding it" (200). He cites two reasons for this difficulty:

> First, the organizational need for ideological consensus and closure contradicted members' continuous discovery that the society they had to deal with was more complex than any organizationally serviceable ideology could encompass. Second, the organizations' orientation toward the development of their power fundamentally conflicted with the members' efforts to act in either principled or effective terms. (200)

In the accounts given by both Teres and Flacks, the left's historical devotion to centrist organizations forged in an atmosphere of ideological rigidity thus predictably gave way to a contemporary left characterized by the disintegration of major left organizations, the failure (or rejection) of Marxism and other focalizing discourses, and the correlative dispersal of left constituents across a large number of minor activist groups.

Flacks finds much to admire in the decentralization of the left, but this organizational shift has also introduced a set of urgent problems. First, while Flacks is suspicious of the ability of rigid "focusing ideologies" to account for the complexity of American social reality, the more recent dispersal of left focus into discrete issue-groups fails to reflect the actual interdependence of social categories like race, class, gender, and others. Even more importantly, the fragmentation of the organized left into dozens of issue-domains and independent organizations has resulted in a kind of internal balkanization of the left that has inevitably reduced its political clout. Contemporary advocacy groups tend to maintain a relatively narrow focus and constituency, and this focus can sometimes aid groups in achieving specific goals. However, no single group carries a sufficiently large constituency to effect comprehensive change, and coordination of the various goals and resources of individual groups has proven extremely difficult in the absence of a unified left culture. Indeed, one is more likely to observe competitive relations between left groups than effective cooperation: Fred Rose's recent sociological study of environmental, peace, and labor groups, *Coalitions Across the Class Divide*, for example, exposes how the "struggle for political advantage between several just causes" (1) has historically hampered the efficacy of each of these advocacy groups. Flacks usefully formulates the defining tension that has still to be negotiated by the decentralized, fragmented left:

> The problem is to create sufficient structure to facilitate coordination; sharing of resources and information; mutual clarification of vision, strategy, and program; the maintenance of collective memory and identity—while avoiding the encapsulation, rigidity, intellectual deceit and distortion, interpersonal abuse and personal alienation that have been the plagues of the organized left throughout its history. (277)

How can the academic left contribute to the negotiation of these difficult demands? The essays that comprise this book differ, sometimes sharply, in their prescriptions for addressing the condition Flacks describes. Many thinkers on the left would agree that the drive toward diversity in university curricula includes a healthy desire to bring otherwise marginalized voices and issues into the center of inquiry, and that important advances (for example, in institutional recognition of interest groups and issues through the establishment of programs in ethnic, women's, and environmental studies) have been made under the auspices of diversity discourses. However, it is also apparent to most contributors to this volume that the discourses of diversity that permeate academic social-justice initiatives have largely failed to truly coordinate the broad range of issues and organizations that make up the contemporary left. Although the emphasis on diversity is ostensibly in line with progressive criticism of monolithic understandings of Western culture, diversity discussions have generally not, unfortunately, provided grounds for left intellectuals to articulate a shared agenda for social change. For an increasing number of left scholars, enthusiasm for the apparent pluralism of diversity initiatives needs to be tempered by a realization that, in an arena of limited resources, all too often diversity discussions devolve into struggles for political advantage between equally valid causes. Academic leftists are all too often oddly forced, against their better judgments, to draw difficult lines about which identity category or issue-domain counts more when curricular decisions or funding for student advocacy groups are at stake: Should a diverse curriculum mean supporting ethnic and racial diversity over gender or class diversity? Is it possible to articulate race, class, and gender issues together with equally urgent environmental ones? Which issue-domain should gain primacy, why, who gets to decide, and what are the consequences? Even with institutional resources now available to traditionally left groups concentrating on rectifying gender, race, class, ethnicity, environmental, and disability inequities, the bureaucratization of diversity has in practice led left intellectuals to fight against each other for a slice of the pie. In practice, the diversity concept too often parades in the guise of an inclusive pluralism that masks the actual internal divisions between discrete interest groups. To date, the radical alternative—a true articulation of joint agendas for social change in curricula, funding of student groups, hiring decisions, and more—has remained largely unthinkable in scholarly research and in the everyday lives of left intellectuals in the academy.

The scholars represented in *Radical Relevance* all share a common desire to change this situation by looking squarely at the fragmentation of American movements for social change, by thinking rigorously about what critical scholarship might contribute to the task of renewing (or creating) a more unified and efficacious left, and by examining the left's possibly inadequate dealings with many marginalized groups. Representing a diverse range of theoretical perspectives within several textual disciplines, the essays collected here each assess historical, practical, or speculative models for a "whole left"—a left not divided but rather constituted by a broad range of interests, including issues of class, environment, gender, sexuality, disability, race, and ethnicity.

What the outcome of this emerging effort to rethink the left will be is uncertain, but the scholarship collected in *Radical Relevance* does suggest that a relatively small cluster of very large issues will likely be central to the ongoing project. These issues are generally reflected in the subsection titles for *Radical Relevance*: "Legacies of Marxism," "Left Coalitions Beyond the Triad," and "The Academic Left, Critical Theory, and the Global Context." This division into subsections is meant to suggest the primary thrust of the essays contained therein rather than an absolute demarcation: in fact, many of the essays investigate several of the large topics identified in the section titles simultaneously, and can usefully be read in conjunction with essays from other sections. Indeed, all of the essays in the collection are most profitably understood not in isolation but in relation to each other—as a complex and mutually enriching exchange of ideas that, considered together, clarify the situation of the intellectual left in the textual disciplines better than any individual essay could alone.

As they "rethink" the role of intellectual discourse in addressing left fragmentation, many of the contributions to *Radical Relevance* attend to the legacy of prior left discourses and practices, especially Marxism. Some essays are explicitly and thoroughly critical of the practical and theoretical history of American Marxism, regarding these histories more as a cautionary lesson than a current resource. Others find a partially usable past in lost histories of Marxist attempts to comprehend social categories outside of class, in the speculative articulation of categories in Marxism-feminism, or in the lessons afforded by attempts to articulate theoretical bases for coalition within specific disciplines. Essays in the first section, "Legacies of Marxism," provide perspectives on the resources for the contemporary left available in new literary-historical research on left culture, in the critical analysis of specific literary texts and traditions, and in attempts to articulate Marxist rhetorical theories.

Alan Wald begins this section with "Black Nationalist Identity and Internationalist Class Unity: The Political and Cultural Legacy of Marxism." In this essay, Wald is concerned to recover a largely repressed history in which the U.S. communist movement emerges as a partially worthy model for left cooperation across the issue-domains of class, race, and ethnicity. Wald contends that U.S. communism comprised by far the most sustained and coherent left-wing American cultural movement of the twentieth century—a movement far more successful at enlisting and sustaining the principled allegiance of oppressed racial and ethnic minorities across several decades than has been properly recognized. While considerable attention has already been devoted to the impact of the Great Depression on writers and artists during the 1930s, Wald demonstrates that the central role of African American, communist culture-workers extended far into subsequent decades as well—a cultural history that has largely been obscured by the legacy of 1950s anticommunism. Emerging from the communist-led radical cultural tradition were among the most prominent U.S. writers of the 1940s and 1950s, along with scores of lesser-known figures who made signal contributions in a wide range of cultural sites, including film, popular culture, science fiction, detective and mystery fiction, modern poetry, theater, television, and children's literature. The surprising, unrecognized extent of interacting African American contributions to communist-led American culture that Wald briefly sketches in this chapter suggests that the traditional left's ability to enlist the sympathies, interests, and allegiances of varying interest groups may be seriously underestimated by a contemporary left more influenced by anticommunist historiography than it ought to be.

Complementing the broad historical sketch Wald provides, Barbara Foley's "Race, Class, and Communism: The Young Ralph Ellison and the 'Whole Left'" offers a closely focused analysis of how the history of U.S. anticommunism has distorted the contemporary left's grasp of its own history. Like Wald, Foley's focus is upon the historical record regarding the CPUSA's ability to incorporate the interests of identity groups like racial minorities. Glossing her innovative work on Ralph Ellison's career, Foley offers a close analysis of the composition history of Ellison's most influential work, *Invisible Man*. While Ellison's biting portrayal of the CPUSA as manipulative and racist in *Invisible Man* is usually understood as a fair representative of Ellison's own relation to the American communism, Foley's reexamination of the historical record shows that Ellison actually had a sustained and overwhelmingly positive relationship to the left for at least eight years. Documenting this relationship and tracing the successive drafts of *Invisible Man* that illustrate Ellison's changing representation of communism between 1945 and 1952, Foley complicates the entrenched view of *Invisible Man* as an "anticommunist" novel, and demonstrates that the hostility toward American communism manifested in the novel is properly attributed to sources other than Ellison's own experience with the CPUSA. More than a specialist's revision of Ellison's biography, Foley's essay reveals that the reductiveness of our received cultural histories of the 1940s and 50s has obscured an inclusive history of American communism that might serve as a relevant contemporary model for left coalition.

Wald and Foley each argue that the contemporary left's fragmentation is at least in part due to its neglect of positive precedents available in the actual cultural history of American Marxism. Victor Villanueva's "Toward a Political Economy of Rhetoric (or A Rhetoric of Political Economy)" applies a similar critique to the discipline of rhetoric itself. Sketching a brief disciplinary history of rhetoric in the United States, Villanueva suggests that contemporary rhetorical theory generally fails to conceive of discursive practices as integrally connected with political economy. Villanueva proposes a return to the discourses of political economy as a corrective to what he describes as rhetorical theory's overinvestment in the purely "superstructural" functions of discourse. The need to radically revise rhetorical theory in order to accommodate the Gramscian perspective that Villanueva favors, however, is only a necessary rather than sufficient step toward rhetorical theory's potential contribution to unifying the left. Rhetorical theory, Villanueva concludes, is presently only beginning a rigorous discussion about the intersecting theories of discourse, power relations, and economy.

Like the work described above, essays in the second section, "Left Coalitions Beyond the Triad," insist upon the importance of efforts to develop coherent theoretical and practical models that can facilitate the coordination of multiple issue-domains. The common theme of this group of essays is a close focus upon the need to expand the established triad of race, class, and gender—to develop scholarly discourses that can better accommodate the pressing issues of ethnicity, environment, and disability that have in recent decades engaged the expanded sensibilities of left constituents.

Scott Richard Lyons's "The Left Side of the Circle: American Indians and Progressive Politics" reveals how the leftist community has in many ways failed to adequately address Native Americans' needs and experiences. Lyons traces his own role as a member of the Anishaabe and as a teacher of Native American students at Leech Lake Tribal College. In doing so, he exposes the actual material conditions faced every day by many people who make their homes on reservations, conditions that too often fail to get discussed by leftist scholars. Lyons also investigates the suspect history of "progressive politics" and its relationship to Native peoples. Lyons exposes the troubling 1980 exchange between American Indian Movement leader Russell Means and the Revolutionary Communist Party, an exchange that makes clear the rhetorical tactics that the left has utilized historically in order to assimilate Indian people. In the end, Lyons remains somewhat skeptical about whether people on the left are willing to give up the comfort of their political identities in an effort to create the coalitions that would adequately address these concerns. Yet Lyons has hope that strides can be made. He closes with several specific recommendations— namely that we should better "affirm and respect the sovereignty of indigenous nations" and "the Whole Left should bring this commitment to sovereignty and respect into the university curriculum" (82). Lyons's essay demands that leftists not make the American Indian an "add-on," yet one more marginalized group. Instead, Lyons contends that leftist scholars need to start "by locating their work not on the 'frontier' but on *Indian land*, not as 'pioneers' but as *settlers*" (74). The first people, he articulates, need to be made the first priority of all leftists.

Michael Bennett's "Reconciling Red and Green" offers a similarly expanded model of issue-articulation on the American left, this time through a discussion of the connections between multi-issue activism and scholarship. Bennett traces his own journey as an activist in antiapartheid, antiglobalization, and environmental movements, as well as his parallel journey as a scholar from African American studies to ecocriticism (the study of the mutually constitutive relationship between culture and the environment). In sketching his own development into an urban, socialist, antiracist, feminist ecocritic, Bennett suggests that the ecocritical focus on issues of environmental justice offers a useful model for the integration of these multiple issue-domains. Bennett directly challenges the left's proclivity to sideline environmental issues, and dismantles the left's three main contentions against ecocriticism: "1) Ecocriticism is all about wilderness and wildlife and so is irrelevant for understanding the sociopolitical dimensions of humans and their habitations; 2) Ecocritics only care about the Thoreauvian tradition of nature writing and thus are unable to say anything interesting about most of our culture; 3) The environmental movement is the domain of privileged white males who are uninterested in issues of race, class, and gender" (87). In the end he reveals the positive ways in which both the environmental justice and the antiglobalization movements can build coalitions around confronting the ecological plight of the poor and of communities of color.

Brenda Jo Brueggemann, Wendy L. Chrisman, and Marian E. Lupo's "A Monstrous Emerge-agency: Cripping the Whole Left" argues that "disability" should be a key term that rebuilds the familiar traditional triangle of difference composed of the categories of race, class, and gender. After providing a close analysis of the concept of disability as an identity category, the authors examine the impacts on radical theory that might result from taking disability seriously as a theoretical construct as well as an advocacy issue. The authors contend that, in refiguring the critical space of difference, the concept of disability can offer a variety of crucial insights that might usefully reform a number of other radical discourses, correcting an inadequate theorization of social categories like class, gender, and race in ways that might bolster possibilities for coordination of left concerns. Tracing a series of "classroom moments" that throw these ideas into relief, the authors suggest the kinds of new pedagogical choices that must be made in order to better highlight the connections between different forms of oppression as well as to better denaturalize the concept of disability itself.

 ⸱ Like the essays that precede it, Derek Owens's "What the Left Left Out" concentrates upon the limitations of the "left triumvirate" of race/class/gender. Owens suggests that despite progressive efforts to widen the purview of left discourse and activism, the left has still typically "left out" serious attention to environmental issues. Central to Owens's argument is a critique of the left's anthropocentric humanism, which while clearly providing a motive force for progressive social change, has also largely obscured the environmental systems in which human societies and cultures participate, and the environmental health upon which they depend. Tracing some of the reasons for and consequences of this conspicuous blind spot in left discourses, Owens argues that "sustainability" might usefully serve as a corrective metaphor that, far from simply *superadding* an environmental dimension to existing left concern, might serve as a useful—if not essential—reorganizing term on the left. Owens contends that left intellectuals must, "if they are to remain relevant in an age of catastrophic local and global environmental crises, embrace orchestrating metaphors like 'sustainability,' 'conservation,' 'preservation,' and 'survival' as viable catalysts for furthering the objectives of progressive teaching and learning" (134).

Essays in the final section, "The Academic Left, Critical Theory, and the Global Context," provide especially focused and explicit explorations of a third theme: the role of the academic left within the context of the growing globalization of the political arena. Despite marked differences, each essay deals with a phenomenon that Fredric Jameson calls the "paradox of totalization," in which the social critic's apparent power to change conditions decreases as her grasp of the scale of those conditions grows. How to maintain a focus on the global context of oppression while avoiding becoming intimidated by questions of scale (or the opposite danger, an inappropriately optimistic sense of the importance of scholarship and pedagogy in addressing the larger context) is an issue that exercises each of the thinkers in this section.

Henry A. Giroux's "Globalizing Dissent and Radicalizing Democracy: Politics, Pedagogy, and the Responsibility of Critical Intellectuals" begins this section. In this essay, Giroux suggests that the political potentiality of the academic left has been largely hamstrung by a limited sense of the true range of pedagogical sites. Giroux explores what it means to make the pedagogical more political by refusing to reduce pedagogy to "schooling," suggesting that left intellectuals expand their sense of the sites in which education actually takes place. Giroux argues that we must focus on the actual educational force of culture, reclaiming sites like television and other mass media from neoliberalism, and constantly reaffirming the responsibility of intellectuals in addressing those pedagogical practices that are actually central to a pervasive dominant cultural politics. Drawing from emerging, innovative forms of activism, what Giroux finally tenders in this essay is a provocative working model for reconnecting learning to social change, and theory to a variety of concrete public spheres in order to "take on the task of regenerating both a renewed sense of social and political agency as well as a critical subversion of dominant power itself" (149).

Noah De Lissovoy and Peter McLaren's "Toward a Contemporary Philosophy of Praxis" also suggests that intellectual discourses and practices can and must intervene in the fragmentation of the left within global as well as smaller contexts. These authors focus on how the concept of imperialism, rearticulated and redeployed, can help to specify the particularity of "globalization" in a way that explains the linkages between multiple forms of oppression. Without denying the crucial differences between class, race, gender, and other oppressions, De Lissovoy and McLaren trace the affinities between them. Ultimately, the authors contend that these categories (race, class, gender) do not simply *describe* forms of oppression, but are actually *used* to reproduce an economy of violence that structures continuing cultural and economic exploitation. De Lissovoy and McLaren analyze recent events as a crystallization of these processes, but they also contend that these events provide an occasion for the elaboration of an "anti-imperialist pedagogy." The centerpiece of this pedagogy is the naming of, not a single root of exploitation (for example, understanding all oppression as ultimately class-based), but rather a nexus and coherence of multiple forms of oppression under imperialism. Their hope is to make possible a strategy of liberatory education that can bring together various left movements in coordinated struggle. By redefining pedagogical practices and intellectual discourses about pedagogy, they seek to enact a different logic of production of meaning and relationships, one that in initiating forms of sociality not premised on exploitation could project a path toward the construction of an authentically socialist counter-future.

In contrast to the relative optimism of these essays, Wendy S. Hesford's "Global/Local Labor Politics and the Promise of Service Learning" cautions that, given the institutional realities of the American academy, intellectual discourses that purport to work on behalf of leftist political agendas are easily co-opted by conservative, corporate interests. Hesford begins by setting the context for this assertion through a discussion of Bill Readings's *The University in Ruins*, which argues that economic globalization and the subsequent decline of the status of the nation-state as a reproducer of national culture has led to a shift in the university's sense of mission. Hesford suggests that the university no longer envisions itself as a producer of cultural capital but functions instead as a bureaucratic consumer-oriented corporation defined by the needs of global economy. Examining the current trend toward service-learning programs in American universities, Hesford balances her admiration for the progressive intent of such initiatives with a critical view of their ultimate social implications. Indeed, service-learning initiatives might, she suggests, be more properly understood through a series of more critical questions: How are we to understand the gendered labor politics of service learning in the context of global capitalism and the corporate university, namely the trend toward client-oriented education? Is the current interest in service learning simply nostalgia for the university system's now defunct claim to a national cultural mission separate from that of capital? Does the push to institutionalize service learning represent a resurgent nationalism? And if so, how is this resurgent nationalism shaped by the feminization and/or privatization of service? Is service learning functioning as an alibi for the corporate university? Hesford considers how a global analysis of the "corporate university" might help teachers develop programs that counter rather than comply with the exploitation of student, faculty, and local/global labor.

Like Hesford's essay, Evan Watkins's contribution advocates a close and even skeptical scrutiny of left intellectual discourses within the academy. Watkins begins his chapter, "Between School and Work: Classroom and Class," by offering an overview of the contemporary academic left's uneasy relationship to communities outside the institution, weighing alternately how we perceive ourselves and how people working outside the walls of academe perceive us. Watkins's aim is to suggest a more exacting degree of attention to the terminology that typically structures debates over the public role of education, especially the left's own advocacy of idealistic, democratizing forms of education over against the ostensibly increasing trend toward viewing education as job training—the "vocationalizing" of the university. Watkins suggests that much discourse on the public role of education—on the left as well as the right—is too constrained by such dichotomies, and contends that it is the responsibility of critical intellectuals to resist the attractions of discourses that hold out only a false promise of unity on the intellectual left.

Mark Wood's "Another World Is Possible" offers an enthusiastic appraisal of critical pedagogy's potential relation to international movements for global justice. Noting an increasingly ecumenical spirit of cooperation among diverse international movements for social change, Wood argues that critical pedagogy can and must encourage student activism in ways that can highlight structural connections between class, identity, and ecological issues that once may have seemed disconnected. Reiterating the basic critical mission of the left intellectual, Wood implores the academic left to renew its commitment to "clarify the conflicting perspectives that compromise the movement for global justice," to "help forge a counterhegemonic culture of international solidarity by teaching our students about other cultures and by linking our students to students, organizations, and movemenets around the world that are working to build a just mode of socioeconomic organization," to help students "analyze capitalist social relations" in complex ways, and to encourage students to "develop the pedagogical skills they need to teach others what they know and the organizational skills they need to teach others what they know and the organizational skills they need to mobilize friends, co-workers, and community members in the fight for global justice" (126–217).

In the closing piece of the volume, "Feminism(s) and the Left: A Discussion with Linda Martín Alcoff," Laura Gray-Rosendale invites Linda Martín Alcoff to consider the potential of feminism's relation to the left. Alcoff outlines the current state of feminist studies in the United States, describing how she views the history of the specific relationship between the women's movement and the left, and how this relationship has played itself out in her own life and scholarship. In her conversation with Gray-Rosendale Alcoff cites a variety of difficulties in historical efforts to integrate feminism and the left, including internal sexism in left organizations, inadequate attention in many left movements to the development of plausible, nonreductionist accounts of women's oppression, and the dilution of truly radical feminist agendas in favor of partial gender reforms for the middle class. Despite the troubled historical relationship between feminism and the left, Alcoff sees genuine progress in strides taken by labor unions during recent years and in the emergence and growth of new organizational models in antiglobalization, antiwar, as well as other movements.

In closing, let me return to the portrait of the contemporary left proposed by Richard Flacks in *Making History: The American Left and the American Mind*. Flacks's indictment of the American left stems in part from his sense that the social reality now faced by the left is a highly complex one, one not easily comprehended by the ideologies that have traditionally served the organizational needs of centralized left groups. Equally problematic, Flacks suggests, is the failure of left organizations to appeal to the full range of interests (political and more) that are likely to motivate potential left constituents. This difficulty, it must be recognized, has not been resolved by the decentralization of the left. As Flacks has it, single-issue advocacy groups and theories are no more effective than the organized left at integrating the multiple and complex investments that together make up the human life of left constituents.

Flacks acknowledges the existence of a "rather well-established intellectual left in America," but this fact offers, in his view, little hope for the renewal of the left:

> Instead, the intellectual left . . . seems increasingly to be reproducing the established institutional and cultural structures. Such organization as now exists among radical intellectuals is entirely specialized. Such groupings, networks, journals, and conferences provide frameworks of support for sustaining professional careers and intellectual work within particular disciplines. But they do not cross-fertilize very much—and like the diffused and fragmented left as a whole, they do not advance an alternative vision. Moreover, internally, such groups increasingly resemble the formal character of conventional professional organizations, failing to encourage an atmosphere in which the practice of individuals is reflected on, or in which members can find intellectual or emotional community. (282)

Flacks's influential book closes by calling for the formation of a "collective intellectual" left that can begin to correct the fragmented situation of today's activist intellectuals and restore the left's historic functions "of socialization, of cultural renewal, of prophecy" (279). The potential of such a network of social movements is suggested by historical precedents, including that of the American Popular Front in the 1930s. During this period, the communist-led American left was transformed from a narrowly sectarian group to a movement encompassing a variety of radical and liberal political groups in common cause against fascism. As cultural historian Michael Denning has shown in *The Cultural Front*, the time of the American Popular Front evidenced what was a radical change in the left's formerly limited appeal and public relevance. As a result of this coalition across what had previously been seen as divergent political investments, the left was for a short time able to exercise what Denning calls a "powerful, indeed an unprecedented, impact on U.S. culture" (xvii).

The challenge facing the intellectual left today is how to create a new *and sustainable* "cultural front" that can heal the fragmented situation of contemporary left interests. Before the intellectual left can hope to make a real contribution to this effort, however, it must squarely face its tendency to focus myopically upon narrowly circumscribed issues and disciplinary discourses. As Flacks has it:

> what is needed—in every milieu that is linked to the left tradition—is that at least some members consciously operate in terms of the "gentle power of reason," fostering an atmosphere in which ideas can be freely expressed and tested, in which individual needs can be voiced without fear of recrimination, and criticism offered without the taint of condemnation, and in which local action can be openly discussed in its global, historical relevance. (283)

Can the intellectual left in the United States begin to open the peripheries of specialization through the "gentle power of reason"? Can it begin to articulate an appealing and coherent shared agenda for social change across disciplinary, identity, and issue-domain boundaries? The answers to these questions are, of course, uncertain, but the essays in *Radical Relevance* suggest that the intellectual left continues to build upon earlier efforts to move toward precisely such a project. Although the scholarship proffered in this volume comes out of a wide and differentiated array of disciplines, theoretical stances, and political interests, all of the essays converge upon a common project that must continue to urgently occupy our intellectual, creative, and political lives: envisioning the interdependence of left causes in an effort to move toward the realization of a "whole left."

WORKS CITED

Denning, Michael. *The Cultural Front: The Laboring of American Culture in the Twentieth Century*. London: Verso, 1996.

Flacks, Richard. *Making History: The American Left and the American Mind*. New York: Columbia UP, 1988.

Rose, Fred. *Coalitions across the Class Divide: Lessons from Labor, Peace, and Environmental Movements*. Ithaca: Cornell UP, 2000.

Teres, Harvey. *Renewing the Left: Politics, Imagination, and the New York Intellectuals*. New York: Oxford UP, 1996.

I

LEGACIES OF MARXISM

CHAPTER ONE

BLACK NATIONALIST IDENTITY AND INTERNATIONALIST CLASS UNITY: THE POLITICAL AND CULTURAL LEGACY OF MARXISM

ALAN WALD

ONE METHOD OF EXPANDING AND RENEWING THE UNITED STATES LEFT IS FOR activists and scholars to revisit pivotal episodes of the past when our predecessors broke free from narrower visions and practices to forge fresh alliances and perspectives. An example of such an achievement can be found in the manner in which the U.S. communist movement forged a relationship with Black American militants and cultural workers. This occurred mainly between the early 1920s until the late 1950s, when the U.S. communist movement became indubitably a significant pole of attraction in African American political and cultural life. Only a few prominent African American poets, fiction writers, playwrights, and critics—such as novelist Richard Wright—publicly boasted of membership in the Communist Party. Yet it seems likely that Margaret Walker, Lance Jeffers, Claude McKay, John Oliver Killens, Julian Mayfield, Alice Childress, Shirley Graham, Lloyd Brown, John Henrik Clarke, William Attaway, Frank Marshall Davis, Lorraine Hansberry, Douglas Turner Ward, Audre Lorde, W. E. B. DuBois, and Harold Cruse were among those organizationally affiliated in individualized ways. A list of other African American cultural workers who were, to varying degrees and at different points, fellow travelers (that is, ideological supporters without necessarily having conventional formal affiliation) would probably include Ralph Ellison, Chester Himes, Sterling Brown, Langston Hughes, Paul Robeson, Theodore Ward, Countee Cullen, James Baldwin (as a teenager), Richard Durham, Alain Locke, Willard Motley, Rosa Guy, Sarah Wright, Jessie Fausett, Owen Dodson, Ossie Davis, Dorothy West, Marion Minus, Robert Hayden, Waring Cuney, and Lonne Elder III.

For five decades, students of the left have had access to the reasons why some Black cultural and intellectual figures were eventually dismayed by communism, through novels such as Chester Himes's *The Lonely Crusade* (1947), Ralph Ellison's *Invisible Man* (1952), and Richard Wright's *The Outsider* (1953), reinforced by Harold Cruse's brutal polemic *The Crisis of the Negro Intellectual* (1967). Less available were richly documented, independently critical, yet compelling explanations of just how and why the communist movement wielded the attractive power that it did, despite all of the obvious disadvantages of being regarded as a "communist" for Blacks[1] as well as whites.

Then, during the 1980s, two scholarly works began to promote a rethinking of the relationship of Blacks to Reds: Mark Naison's *Communists and Harlem during the Depression* (1983), and Robin D. G. Kelley's *Hammer and Hoe: Alabama Communists during the Great Depression* (1990). Next came four new books in 1998 and 1999 by Mark Solomon, William J. Maxwell, Bill V. Mullen, and James Edward Smethurst, that represented a quantum leap forward in our ability to understand what was achieved by this symbiotic relationship. They also instruct us about what has been lost in the assaults upon the legacy of Communist-led antiracist struggles by McCarthyites, Cold War Liberals, and overzealous leftist critics of Stalinism, as well as by the contemporary communist movement's incapacity to understand and fairly represent its own remarkable history in the 1930s and 1940s. The focus of three of the books is on culture, but all four together provide a wealth of new detail and conceptual propositions that need to be critically assimilated by those committed to building an interracial movement for social transformation.

In what follows, the arguments of this new scholarship will be recapitulated and critically assessed in order to emphasize the relevance of the Afro-Marxist tradition to the construction of a unified leftist social movement in the new millennium. For example, we will explore the ways in which national identity and class issues can be integrated, and the crucial part that must be played by Euro-American opposition to "white chauvinism" as any part of such an alliance. We will also examine the significance of the "Black ideology" produced by white exclusionism, and the necessary response of "humanizing" white/Black relations and redressing grievances in such a manner as to facilitate African Americans' self-liberation. Finally, we will interrogate cultural issues such as the need for an antiracist leftist culture distinct from liberalism (which extends a hand while perpetuating racist structures), and especially one that sees the value of Black self-determination for all oppressed groups.

NATIONAL LIBERATION AND SOCIALISM

The indispensable foundation for appreciating this body of new scholarship is Mark Solomon's stunning narrative of the absorption of revolutionary Black Nationalists and other Black radicals into the post-World War I communist movement. His highly nuanced and finely researched *The Cry Was Unity* treats the consequences of this commingling for the development of communist ideology and activity from the early 1920s through the first year of the Popular Front. Solomon, a retired history professor from Simmons College, is in a unique situation to assess the experience. He has been a participant in the antiracist and radical movement since he was a teenager in the early Cold War years, and is the author of an earlier published doctoral dissertation from Harvard University called *Red and Black: Communism and Afro-Americans, 1929–1935* (1988).

Solomon's approach is deftly elaborated in a short introduction explaining his motivations for recreating the story of how the communist movement "broke free from isolation and ideological abstractions to achieve a significant place in the battle for racial justice" (xviii). In contrast to recent liberal discussions, such as President Clinton's "conversation on race," Solomon pledges to review the early history of the antiracist left because the pivotal issues then were neither tactical nor sentimental; they involved the basic character of American society. Capitalism's cornerstone was seen to have been laid by slavery and fortified by racism. Therefore, the achievement of equality implied the ultimate transformation of the nation's economic and social foundation (xviii).

On the one hand, Solomon's book seeks to elaborate the theory of national oppression and the road to liberation worked out by U.S. communists, Black and white, in their first decade and a half. On the other hand, his aim is equally to explore the practical activities against which the evolving theory was tested as this heroic, interracial organization rose up against white supremacism "with unprecedented passion as an indispensable requirement for achieving social progress" (xviii).

Most impressive is the way that Solomon triangulates the development of communist theory and practice by examining Black Marxist activists and theorists, the national Communist Party institutions, and the influence of Comintern (Communist International) policy. In contrast to those who favor the "top down" or "bottom up" approach to communist historiography, Solomon presents us with what might be called a "force field" approach in which different elements gain hegemony at various points and under certain circumstances. That Comintern hegemony might be shown to be paramount over a period of decades and at moments of crisis does not negate how important it was for a group of Black Party women in Harlem to raise an issue (unknown to the Soviet Party) for debate and discussion. Without that latter—the local vitality—the attractiveness of the Party would be inexplicable, which certainly seems to be the case in many extant hostile narratives of Party history.

In rich detail, Solomon's book covers the period of nearly two decades from the founding of Cyril Briggs's magazine *The Crusader* after World War I to the launching of the Party-led National Negro Congress in 1936. Thus he follows communist policy through three phases: from the view of a "colorblind" class outlook, to the theory of nationality, to the broad-based "Negro-labor alliance."

The overall structure of the book is divided into three components, recalling the traditional Hegelian triad. The initial five chapters review the efforts of the first Black communists to formulate a policy, their interaction with a vision of the Communist International, and the development of a theory (the view of African Americans as "a nation within a nation") as well as an organization (the American Negro Labor Congress) to realize this project.

Part II presents another six chapters, this time focused on the 1929–1933 era of the ultrarevolutionary "Third Period." Solomon convincingly demonstrates his rather disconcerting view that unrealistic visions, aspirations, and demands frequently motivated the most heroic projects. From this perspective he discusses Party practice in the Deep South and its struggles against eviction, hunger, and lynching. The book marches to a climax at the beginning of the Popular Front when, at last, in Solomon's judgment, the foundation of Black-Labor unity is established. This is achieved through the success of People's Front policy in Harlem and the creation of the National Negro Congress, a multiracial organization under Black leadership. Within this daunting framework, Solomon presents many discrete episodes worthy of at least a brief survey.

PIONEER AFRICAN AMERICAN COMMUNISTS

From the very first sentences of the introductory chapter, Solomon meticulously corrects the record of previous writings on Blacks and communism with the kind of scrupulous research only possible from the pen of a scholar committed to learning what really happened because the record matters for life and death struggles. For example, contrary to earlier studies claiming that no Blacks were present at the founding of the U.S. communist movement—and an alternative version that two attended—Solomon documents that only Otto Huiswood, born in the Dutch West Indies (now called Surinam) was present. Huiswood would have been joined by his comrade from the left wing of the Socialist Party, Arthur P. Hendricks, who was born in British Guiana, but Hendricks had just died of tuberculosis (possibly Huiswood's presence was not noticed by some who wrote reports on the meeting due to his light color.) Although the two militants, and many who would join them, were Caribbean-born, Solomon views the pioneer cadre of U.S. Black communism as a genuine Harlem-based alliance of immigrants from colonized nations and U.S.-born men and women. The former tended to have a greater class and anti-imperialist awareness, and a more "assertive psychological makeup" (4), along with a greater degree of formal education.

It is significant that, initially, Black revolutionists tended to gravitate around their own institutions, especially the People's Educational Forum in Harlem. One group—Huiswood, Richard B. Moore, Lovett Fort-Whiteman, and Grace Campbell—soon joined the new communist movement when the left wing of the Socialist Party was purged. Another group—Frank Crosswaith, A. Philip

Randolph, and Chandler Owen—remained with the Socialists. An additional important figure, Cyril Briggs, also from the Caribbean (he was born on the island of Nevis), was a journalist for Harlem's *Amsterdam News*. Briggs was much inspired by the Easter Rebellion in Ireland and committed to the prospects of a decolonized Africa. He launched *The Crusader* in December 1918, a dynamic organ of the "New Negro Crowd" that advocated "a renaissance of Negro culture and power throughout the world" (6). Over the next six months Briggs's journal began drawing the links between capitalism and imperialism, as well as "projecting a shared proletarian identity between Black and white workers as the counterweight to the dominant system" (7). According to Solomon, Briggs "merged Black Nationalism with revolutionary socialism and introduced the twentieth century global revolutionary tide to America" (7).

One of Briggs's signal contributions was that he devoted himself to solving the riddle of overcoming the contradiction between a separate Black national destiny and achieving unity with Euro-American workers. The first organizational expression of this perspective was Briggs's formation of the African Blood Brotherhood (ABB) in the fall of 1919, which was led by Caribbean-born radicals (with many World War I veterans in its ranks) and would grow to a membership of about 3,500. The ABB was clearly independent of the communist movement at the outset. The various communist factions were too busy vying for the Moscow franchise to pay attention, and Briggs was simultaneously influenced by an Afrocentric movement called the Hamitic League, as well as by the rituals (passwords, secrecy, oaths) of the Irish Sinn Fein. By 1921, when the ABB declared *The Crusader* its public organ and also gained some notoriety for its association with the armed resistance of Blacks against whites in Oklahoma, its leadership had evolved to pro-communism.

According to correspondence located by Solomon in Comintern archives, Briggs was recruited to the Party by Caribbean poet Claude McKay. This was facilitated by McKay's having introduced Briggs to a couple of Euro-American communists with a special interest in Black Liberation—the famous cartoonist from Texas, Robert Minor, and the Jewish American firebrand, Rose Pastor Stokes. These two were affiliated with the "Goose Caucus," which advocated parallel communist parties, one to be legal and aboveground, while the other party would remain secret and underground. Still, more important than organizational affiliation, is the manner in which Briggs creatively projected Afro-Marxist strategies and visions for liberation.

Blending a strong "sense of African identity and national culture with Leninist internationalism," he formulated arguments to combine a struggle for an "independent Negro State" (which might be in Africa, although not necessarily) in the process of fighting for a "universal Socialist Cooperative Commonwealth" (13). Briggs admitted that the independent Black state might not be the ideal route, but that it was understandably necessary in light of the need for "peoples of African descent" to "reclaim their distinct political and

cultural heritage" (13). To put it bluntly, "the Negro has been treated so brutally in the past by the rest of humanity that he may be pardoned for now looking at the matter from the viewpoint of the Negro than from that of a humanity that is not humane" (13). The liberation of African Americans and the
struggle for socialism worldwide was theorized by Briggs as an alliance in which
a distinct Black agenda remained viable and central.

With Briggs's communist membership, this program was further clarified
so as to provide a clear alternative to the politics of middle-class reform organizations. Briggs promoted a dramatic switch in the objectives of the African
American liberation movement away from assimilation into the bourgeois order
and toward a goal of socialist transformation. He also urged that the class composition of Black leadership be proletarian and no longer middle-class, and that
African Americans ally with Euro-American workers instead of white liberals.

Briggs and his comrades were well aware that racism was widespread in the
Euro-American working class and that historically Blacks had been betrayed
by false white friends. Thus he held that the left was obligated to aggressively
educate against white supremacism in order to facilitate an alliance. Analogous
notions of African American autonomy and alliances also carried over to the
predominant attitude of Briggs and his associates toward the Russian revolution. Solomon observes that

> The embrace of communism carried with it a promising connection with
> Soviet power as indispensable ally, patron, and spiritual guide. For the new
> black Communists the Soviets were an exhilarating source of strength, pride,
> hope and respect for Black interests. Heretofore anonymous men and women
> would now have an international stage where they would be taken seriously
> and where power was manifest and at the disposal of the Black liberation strug-
> gle. The greatness of Bolshevik power—as an anti-imperialist force, as liber-
> ator of labor, as cleanser and avenger of racism, as faithful ally—became an
> ardent belief and defining point of the African Blood Brotherhood. (16)

Finally, Briggs certainly believed that, in the long run, Euro-American workers would come to recognize their commonality of interests with Blacks. Yet he
also held that, if Blacks were to devote themselves to the class struggle, there
had to be an "acid test of white friendship"—which was the acceptance by Euro-
Americans of the right of Black armed self defense, even if such defense resulted
in the killing of whites (17).

A NATION WITHIN A NATION

Solomon argues that the pro-communist evolution of the African Blood Brotherhood profoundly affected the American communists. A result was the ultimate transformation of the left-wing "color blind" view of race that prevailed
in the early 1920s in both the Communist Labor Party and the Communist Party,

most of which fused into the United Communist Party (UCP) in 1920.[2] Leaders of the UCP did listen to and learn from the ABB, and their publications and resolutions began to resemble ABB ideas, with one exception—the Euro-Americans omitted the need to fight racism within their political party itself.

It is also true that the May 1921 convention that finally unified all communist factions did not reflect the new alliance in the composition of its delegates nor in resulting resolutions. Still, Solomon quotes from internal discussion documents (written under pseudonyms) that show a rich understanding of the complex strategic issues that needed to be addressed. For example, there was now a recognition that the Black population could not be won over by abstract ideological professions of good will; communists would have to respond specifically to the "Black ideology" that had developed due to white racist exclusionism. They would also have to "humanize" their political dealings with African Americans and fight aggressively for specific reforms (such as voting rights in the South) crucial to allowing Blacks to create their own conditions for developing activity and consciousness.

Simultaneously, Briggs was involved in a bitter battle with Black nationalist leader Marcus Garvey. Solomon talks candidly of Briggs's collaboration with the Federal government's case against Garvey's Universal Negro Improvement Association (which continually published the claim that Briggs was actually a European, until Briggs took legal action). Moreover, destruction of the Garvey movement became the obsession of *The Crusader*.[3] In this clash, Solomon sees central themes in the U.S. Black radical tradition. Briggs held to the view that "racial consciousness alone was not enough to win freedom in the modern world, where power was based partially on race but centrally on corporate, class, national and military forces"; thus he championed alliances with progressive forces around a common interest in socioeconomic restructuring (28).

Although anticolonialist and antiimperialist, in his determination to create a separate African-based territory, Garvey refused alliances with forces aimed at challenging those very seats of power. Believing that, in the last analysis, white workers would side with white bosses against Blacks, Garvey alternatively attempted to negotiate with governments and even white supremacist forces who likewise favored separation of the races. Nevertheless, the communists would continue to see the ranks of the Garvey movement as a radicalized milieu from which potential recruits might be garnered.

TOWARD SELF-DETERMINATION

In a chapter called "The Comintern's Vision," Solomon explains how the Leninist notion of the necessary alliance of working class and national liberation movements as "a linked social process" was closer to that of the former ABB members than the ideas of early Euro-American communists such as John Reed. At the 1922 Fourth Congress of the Comintern, in response to presentations by

McKay and Huiswood, a multinational Negro Commission was set up under Huiswood's direction (and with McKay as a guest participant). This body viewed the African diaspora peoples in the framework of colonialism with Black Americans poised to play a key role in a global struggle requiring communist backing of all movements of Blacks opposed to capitalism and imperialism. This perspective probably set the stage for the slogan of "Self-determination in the Black Belt" (which was a region of the South with majority Black population) adopted by U.S. communists six years later. Although McKay departed from the conference en route to a stance as an independent radical (eventually converting to Catholicism before his death), Huiswood would become the first Black member of the Central Committee of the U.S. Party, now headquartered in Chicago.

A new figure emerging to prominence by the mid-1920s was Lovett Fort-Whiteman, an African American who had studied at Tuskegee and who was closely associated with Robert Minor. Fort-Whiteman pursued earlier efforts to get the Comintern to back U.S. Black communists in internal U.S. policy by forwarding the first concept of an American Negro Labor Congress. Fort-Whiteman also developed the argument that Blacks perceive oppression as stemming from race more than class, and that such persecution had bonded Blacks of all economic strata together. Marxism had to be recast to address this unique psychology, and practical work required a dual focus on both the South and problems specific to the great migration in the North (such as the housing crisis in urban ghettos).

Thus, in preparing for the 1925 American Negro Labor Congress (ANLC), Huiswood, Moore, and others pleaded for the involvement of Black communists on all Party committees responsible for the gathering, for the Party not to push itself aggressively, and for literature that took into account the special psychology of the Black proletariat. This was ignored, and the event—which had only thirty-three accredited delegates—had a majority white audience who were entertained by Russian ballet and theater groups but no Black artists.

For the next year the organization stumbled along until a shake-up in which Moore replaced Fort-Whiteman as leader, and the latter departed for the Soviet Union (where he would teach for a while and then be imprisoned and die in a labor camp).[4] This led to a less sectarian phase of community and union work. Followers of Lovestone, including Fort-Whiteman, now favored dumping the NLC in favor of direct Party recruitment. However, the advent of the Comintern's Third Period, following the Sixth Congress, ended any hope for a broader political strategy, due to its campaign against "social fascism" and in favor of a "United Front from Below."

Solomon is especially critical of the Third Period for its ideological rigidity; he believes that the political line was really about Stalin's fight to dominate the Soviet Party and the Comintern, one that would be "ultimately drenched in Soviet blood" (68). He is also distressed by evidence of Party members (in the early years almost all white and largely foreign-born) speaking an alien political language and occasionally using "internationalism" to undermine racial priorities. Moreover, he is dismayed at what he sees as arrogant and thoughtless efforts to substitute workers for the traditional middle-class leaders, accompanied by a blindness to the resentment expressed by African Americans aspiring to assemble their own agendas.

At the Sixth Congress of the Comintern no veteran Black communists were present. Instead, the U.S. was represented by a young African American student at the Lenin school, Harry Haywood. Haywood was influenced by a Siberian named Charles Nasanov who had lived in the U.S. and saw U.S. Blacks as an oppressed nation with the right to self-determination. He and Haywood shared the view that historical circumstances (slavery, betrayal of Reconstruction, imperialism) had prevented Blacks from joining whites in a single nation, resulting in a distinct cultural and psychological makeup. Garveyism was regarded as an expression of authentic national strivings that would arise again—only next time communists should be in the leadership. Such an approach broke free at last from class-reductionist dogmas that relegated the antiracist struggle to second place. Rather, the Black movement was regarded as inherently revolutionary yet also an indispensable ally of the working class. Haywood had no support in the early stages of the debate, but gradually it became evident that the Comintern leadership favored an alteration in Party policy toward African Americans. The amended resolution provided "an ostensible middle ground . . . based on the concept of a racial *and* national question—with *national* switching places with *racial* in parentheses" (77).

When the official resolutions appeared in 1928 and 1930, they explained a difference in the communist policy in the North and South of the U.S. In the North, where Blacks were a national minority, the struggle would be for social and political equality; in the South, where Blacks held a majority in certain regions (the Black Belt), the African American nationality had the right to secede and form a separate republic if it so desired. However, if a revolution were successful in the larger nation, communists would urge the Black population to remain as part of the larger state entity. (If Blacks did opt to secede, Euro-Americans might reside in the Black republic with minority rights.)

Nevertheless, Solomon's opinion is that the nation thesis was flawed. While Lenin was accurate in recognizing nationalist feelings among the Black population, he thought that these would be undermined by the expansion of the capitalist economy (industrialization, migration) because the economy was inseparable from that of the larger nation. Communist defenders of the nation thesis such as James Allen believed that capitalism, having advanced as far as it would, was imprisoning the African American peasantry in the region with no escape except through social revolution.[5]

Yet Solomon is impressed with the effects of "self-determination" on Party practice. In everyday life it meant that communists believed in the right of oppressed people to choose their own future, and the Party throwing itself wholeheartedly into antiracist struggles. As a concept it meant the end of sub-ordinating race to class and the beginning of paying close attention to all issues—cultural as well as political—that affected African America. Solomon concludes that "national oppression" is the appropriate terminology for describing what happened to Black Americans.

There were contradictions, of course, to carrying out such a policy under the delusions of the Third Period. Communists held that revolution was on the agenda, so they crudely exposed liberal compromisers as social fascists, and they marched in parades under slogans urging defense of the USSR. Yet such fervent belief enabled the same communists, Euro-American and Black, to brave police clubs—and bullets—as they organized election rallies, antilynching protests, resistance to evictions and police brutality, and funerals for martyred comrades in the streets of Harlem.

Likewise, the communists' revolutionary dual union, the National Miners Union (NMU), took strong antiracist actions. In Pennsylvania, the NMU convinced Black miners to join striking white miners, and in Kentucky it convinced white miners to desegregate the strike kitchen. Most famously, the communist-led National Textile Workers Union emphasized antiracism in its leadership of the Gastonia Strike in North Carolina. This was followed by a heroic campaign to organize the South, an effort that Solomon believes had been hampered by the Communist Party's adherence to an earlier theory (when Jay Lovestone was in the leadership of the Party) holding that the rural South was a reserve of reaction. The new efforts resulted in the creation of a union of sharecroppers in Alabama, as well as impressive organizing activities in the face of murderous harassment in Tennessee, Louisiana, Mississippi, and elsewhere.

The Party's steadfast opposition in the 1930s to any form of racial segregation, at a time when it was tolerated by liberals and other progressives, was also an outgrowth of its assessment of the Party's failure to make gains in the 1920s. Solomon says that the Party came to the conclusion that "racial segregation and the savaging of black identity represented both an institutional foundation for American capitalism and its weak point." Thus the toleration of any form of racism only bolstered capitalism and "wounded its most potent foes." The Party had to create an internal culture qualitatively different from other radical or liberal movements that "extended a hand to blacks while allowing in its own structures the very circumstances that engendered inequality" (128).

Hence the Party promoted a view of race chauvinism as the ultimate evil. Anti-Black racism served the ruling class; Euro-Americans could only purify themselves of its stink by personally engaging in militant "struggles against Negro oppression," which would also be a step toward dismantling the legitimate distrust by Blacks of whites (131). Moreover, one could not expect Blacks to unite with communists without taking steps to counter the special oppression of Blacks. One Jewish Party leader, Israel Amter, demanded that all white communists should be prepared to violently avenge any insult against Blacks, even at the risk of death.

The center of CP and Young Communist League life became the interracial dance, even when it antagonized the larger community. A more theatrical approach was the occasional mass trial of a Party member accused of racist behavior; this was carried out for purposes of public education. Solomon compellingly recapitulates the antiracist arguments developed by communists, who tried to go beyond older appeals to "morality, abstract justice, and 'healing' through 'understanding.'" Instead, communists emphasized changing power relationships in the interests of all the dispossessed. Rather than appealing to sentimentality and guilt, the effort was to win over white workers on the basis of their own needs. This was possible because working class whites could never achieve what they wanted as long as racial division persisted. Instead of being "pitied or patronized," Blacks were to be "welcomed as indispensable allies in the battle to change the world" (146). This meant that whites should respect Black history and culture, as well as understand that the prerequisite for unity was Black self-organization and autonomous leadership.

A LEGACY OF STRUGGLE

Among the most inspiring aspects of Solomon's research is his chronicle of the efforts of Party members to fight racism on every front, starting with campaigns against hunger and eviction. He provides portraits of many female and male activists, vignettes of martyrdom, and descriptions of heroism by Blacks and whites. The result of such selfless work was that thousands of Blacks joined unemployment councils, and hundreds applied for Communist Party membership as well as signed up for the Party's legal defense auxiliary, International Labor Defense. Simultaneously, an interracial culture emerged. In the late 1920s "Negro Weeks" were launched by Briggs to celebrate revolutionary heroes such as Toussaint L'Ouverture and Denmark Vesey. Whites did go into Black communities and serve on Black publications, but usually in subordinate positions under the supervision of Black communists. What was expected of these whites was a record of fighting racism and respecting the abilities of Blacks.

In the early 1930s, the American Negro Labor Congress (ANLC), which regarded anticapitalism as a basis of the antilynching movement, collapsed and was followed by the League of Struggle for Negro Rights (LSNR). The new Party-led organization saw the campaign against lynching as the major manifestation of national oppression within its larger agenda of demands for justice. Nevertheless, as an organization that was openly pro-communist, the LSNR was somewhat in competition for space with the Party itself, and the Unemployed Councils occupied available space, too. Even when the LSNR developed its own leadership with Langston Hughes as honorary president and an official membership of ten thousand, it did not reach much beyond the Party's influence.

In contrast, the Party's response to the Scottsboro case (when nine Black youths were framed on rape charges in Alabama) was a breakthrough vindicating communists' claims to sincerity about antracism. Throughout the country activists, white and Black, gave their all to the slogan "They shall not die!" Such activity was possible because they were imbued with the belief that the fate of the defendants was linked inextricably to their own lives. Nevertheless, Solomon is harshly critical of the CP's sectarian policy toward middle-class allies—he even endorses criticisms of the "United Front from Below" policy made by the expelled Lovestone group. However, he refutes the claims that the communists wanted the nine youths to die as martyrs, and he believes that charges about the communists' inflammatory conduct toward the courts "were overstated and deflected attention from a racist judicial system" (203).

There was constant Party-led antiracist activity throughout the early 1930s. The candidacy of African American James Ford on the CP presidential electoral ticket, the running of dozens of other Black communist candidates, and the defense of Angelo Herndon, charged with insurrection for leading a demonstration in Atlanta, were important developments. There were also numerous strikes in which the Party played a role and where race issues were important— St. Louis, Chicago, San Joaquin Valley, San Francisco, Birmingham, Louisiana, and so forth. Moreover, Harlem became a centerpiece for antiracist activity, especially when U.S.-born Black Party leader James Ford took control and Briggs and Moore were eased out. The latter tended to emphasize race issues more emphatically and were sometimes accused of blaming white workers more than the bosses; but they defended themselves by insisting that forging unity should be more of a white responsibility than a Black one.

Solomon's biggest criticism of the Party in this era is its conviction that it deserved sole leadership of the Black movement due to its possession of the correct revolutionary program. As long as the Party spoke of establishing "hegemony over the Negro liberation struggle itself," it would often antagonize those who questioned or opposed it and would negate its own claims to be fighting for self-determination (205). Thus Solomon ends the book with a chapter and a half devoted to the development of the Popular Front, which he regards as a positive advance away from this posture.

In his view, the dropping of Third Period sectarianism primarily meant the opportunity to work with liberals and Socialists cooperatively, as well as taking a friendlier attitude toward churches and professional organizations. Some of the tactical flexibility was shown in holding together an alliance against the invasion of Ethiopia and in the CP's intervention into the 1935 "Harlem Riot" (272).

The culminating event for Solomon is the founding of the National Negro Congress, launched in Chicago in 1936. It was preceded by broad discussions and impressive organizational groundwork under the leadership of John P. Davis, a nonpublic communist. The perspective was for "a multiracial organization under Black leadership, working to build a Negro-labor alliance and advance civil rights on a wide front." At the same time, Solomon cites internal CP material to show that Davis had the view that the CP should control the NLC to "guarantee its breadth and democratic character" (303). This raises a question—one that Solomon never clearly answers—about the exact nature of the Party's understanding of "self-determination" when it came to trusting an independent Black leadership. In any event, the organization was launched with over eight hundred delegates from 551 organizations that claimed to represent as many as three million people. In a striking effort to demonstrate sincerity about the new unity, the Party's old Socialist rival, A. Philip Randolph, was elected president.

THE BLACK CULTURAL FRONT

William Maxwell's 254-page *New Negro, Old Left: African-American Writing and Communism between the Wars* (including a handsome thirteen-page insert of photographs and illustrations) puts cultural flesh on the organizational and political scaffolding constructed by Solomon. It also reconfigures the entire terrain of 1920s and 1930s left-wing cultural production in startlingly new ways. Maxwell's focus is on the movement of a number of African American writers from a background of "New Negro" and "Harlem Renaissance" experiences toward the communist movement in the interwar period. His unique orientation emphasizes a mutual indebtedness, a two-way channel "between radical Harlem and Soviet Moscow, between the New Negro renaissance and proletarian literature" (1). This interchange is the reason why the explanation for such a development "cannot be pursued without acknowledging both modern Black literature's debt to Communism and Communism's debt to modern Black literature" (1). Moreover, the importance of the Harlem-Moscow transit in Black cultural history also explains the reason why the disillusionment of a handful of African American leftists was expressed so fervently after the 1930s and has received so much attention.

Maxwell's emphasis on "Black volition" and the "interracial education of the Old Left" corresponds to Solomon's research; but Maxwell aims to enhance our understanding of African American and "white" modern literature as well as radicalism. Included among the misrepresentations of the relationship of "New Negro" (the term for militants in the Harlem Renaissance days) and "old left" refuted by Maxwell are the preeminent readings of novels by Wright and Ellison that view the relationship of the left to African Americans as one of manipulation; Black nationalist interpretations of the faults of earlier Black writing that are usually attributed to the malign influence of the white left; the claims of Black feminist and "vernacular" critics that the communist tradition posited a hostility to Black folk materials; and the ironic exclusion of the Black left relationship from recent arguments in literary theory about "mulatto modernism." Maxwell's objection to these earlier treatments of the Black left cultural relation is *not* due to a disagreement with the dismay of some of the critics about the Left's illusions in the Stalin regime—a dismay that Maxwell shares. His dissent is caused by the failure of these earlier critics to recognize that the association had a great impact on changing the culture and politics of both the U.S. communist movement and the Black left.

Maxwell's effort to recuperate African American agency in the relationship is based on his observation that Black pro-communists were independently zealous in their support of what they took to be Soviet policy in and beyond the USSR; that neither Black nor white literary communists took "dictation from Moscow"; and that earlier narratives of this symbiotic relationship have been too immersed in the Cold War fixation on evidence of "white seduction and betrayal of Black mouthpieces" (5). Moreover, what Maxwell calls "Black Communist initiative" (5) is supported by the most compelling trend in historical and literary scholarship of the recent era, such as the aforementioned books by Kelley and Naison.

This is a trend to which Maxwell wants to make additions and corrections, primarily by extending the time line backwards from the 1930s. To Maxwell, the 1920s comprise the crucial moments when historical forces such as the Great Migration of Blacks to urban centers and the Harlem Renaissance's pioneering of "Black routes into international modernity" produced a "Black working class protagonist" by means of which socialism might be African-Americanized through joining Marxism to the "vernacular culture of the descendants of African slaves" (6–7). The resulting negotiations between Black militants moving toward communism and the communist institutions themselves can best be traced through literary-cultural expressions, especially the advent of "proletarian literature" and the Party's construction of a view of African America as a nation within a nation.

Maxwell's first and by far longest chapter begins the revision of the post-World War I cultural landscape through an examination of the poet-lyricist Andy Razaf, whose writings are used to present him "as a partial product and gauge of the place of Black bolshevism within the cultural field of the Harlem Renaissance" (15). Maxwell's view contrasts with those of Harold Cruse, George Hutchinson, and others, who hold that an attraction to communism destroyed the potential evolution of the Renaissance—or else that the Renaissance came about by displacing post-World War I Black militancy. Razaf, however, expresses an important trend of mostly Caribbean immigrants around *The Crusader* who saw the new Black Renaissance within a field of class relationships affected by the international crisis of capitalism and the impact of the Russian Revolution.

Indeed, part of the attraction to Moscow was based on a conviction that the Soviet leadership would assist the "special interests" of U.S. Blacks in relation to the left; *The Crusader* view was that, with the Harlem Renaissance as a cultural center, the new urban African Americans (including Caribbean immigrants) would continue the struggle launched by Black World War I veterans, escalating it even into the international arena. Razaf, who had a special feeling for the experience of "service" work (he had held jobs such as operating an elevator), wrote first for Cyril Briggs's *Crusader* and then for midtown music publishers. Maxwell sees the efforts of Howard University professor Alain Locke to promote his interpretation of the Renaissance as partly in competition with the pro-Bolshevik trend; he also regards the version fostered by the group around W. E. B. DuBois, which privileged spirituals as the Black musical achievement, as missing the boat in its failure to appreciate Razaf's focus on blues, jazz, films, broadcasting, and vaudeville.

Chapter two returns initially to *The Crusader* to examine its favorite poet, Claude McKay, and his book *The Negroes in America* (1923), as an example of the way in which Blacks shaped Communist policy. From the perspective now established, Maxwell provides compellingly fresh interpretations of McKay's poems "If We Must Die" and "The White City." McKay's experiences in the USSR are also recounted, after which Maxwell offers an important interpretation of McKay's long-neglected one-hundred-page Marxist treatise on Black America. In particular, McKay viewed white workers as having developed a white supremacist "race-consciousness" on their own, as a way to defend their privilege and also as a response to having assimilated a complex social psychology of Black sexuality rooted in the agricultural labor of early colonies in the South. McKay's antidotes to racism involve "the modern upsurge of Black culture" (including sports) and "white feminism" (which needs to recognize that the "protective" role of white men against alleged Black rapists is premised on misogyny). Maxwell's case is strong that "McKay's pre-echo of more recent, more exclusively academic work in African-American history, whiteness studies, cultural studies, and a post-Soviet Marxism without guarantees is valuable for its challenges as well as its flattering symmetries" (88). Moreover, Maxwell provides evidence of the little-known text's influence on the Bolshevik leadership (especially Trotsky) and the role of its author's ideas in preparing for the Black Belt Nation thesis.

The third chapter shifts to McKay's co-editor on the Marxist *Liberator*, the Jewish American writer Mike Gold, especially Gold's "anti-minstrel show," *Hoboken Blues* (1927), which reinforces from another angle a blending of communist proletarian literature and the Harlem Renaissance. Maxwell observes that Gold's manifesto "Towards Proletarian Art" parallels Alain Locke's "New Negro" perspective of drawing sustenance from the common people and soil. He also notes that, under Gold's editorship, *The Liberator* offered McKay's poetry collection *Harlem Shadows* as a subscription premium, characterized as a work of proletarian internationalism. Moreover, Maxwell believes that Gold's 1923 book *The Life of John Brown* is "an oblique reference" to his and McKay's collaboration. Using careful textual analysis of primary documents, Maxwell shows that Gold's famous Puritanical attacks on Harlem cabaret culture in the 1930s communist press were similar to those of DuBois, and that Gold held a positive view of certain Black-specific cultural traditions rooted in spirituals, writings by Frederick Douglass, and perhaps noncommercial jazz.

This is a crucial corrective to those (especially Hutchinson, North, and Cruse) who misread select conjunctural writings of Gold as the defining anti-Renaissance moment of the left. It is also a useful entrée to Maxwell's reading of Gold's *Hoboken Blues* (1927) as an effort to temporarily elude white identity and participate in the Harlem Renaissance. Although Maxwell pulls no punches in noting paternalistic and ineffective aspects of the drama, he makes a powerful case that the play is antiminstrel in that it "embraces the identification of African Americans with pre-industrial values yet rejects the moment of censure and the imprisonment of these values within a rigidly racialized and rapidly fading arcadian memory" (119). In mulling over Gold's surprising celebration of a nonproletarian protagonist, Maxwell considers the views expressed on "the race question" in light of McKay's opinions, and Maxwell concludes that "McKay's simultaneous possession of the garlands of revolutionary and New Negro poetry is the standard of aesthetic achievement that Gold's play covets, a play that poses Sam's [the Black protagonist's] renaissance in Harlem as a lesson in proletarian revolution and a lesson to proletarian art" (120).

That later (in *The Hollow Men*, 1941) Gold would counterpoise proletarianism as the negation of decadent New Negroism cannot erase the view here and in other places of a "considerable harmony" that paved the way for a "depression-era re-emergence of the position in the renaissance field that spliced New Negro and working-class insurrection, a position that took a low profile during the second half of the 1920s but never vanished . . ." (122). Moreover, Maxwell observes that a less selective examination of Gold's achievement than that offered by Gold-bashers suggests that his proletarianism was a "'normal' modernism" in its "scramble of interracial attraction and aversion" (123). Once again, we have evidence that the Left's theory and practice (in this instance, Gold's view of proletarian art) evolved from a multifaceted dialogue with the cultural renaissance in Harlem.

Chapter four is a turning point in the book, not only for its shift to the 1930s but also for its introduction of a gender critique of the tendency of communism to masculinize the very prospect of interracial radicalism. Maxwell's focus is on the effort by the Left to deconstruct the "triangular lynch myth" that involves a Black male rapist, a white female victim, and the white male protector; this in turn produced a homosocial "anti-lynch triangle" premised on the interracial bonding of male proletarians against a misogynist view of white female accusers. Maxwell traces the function of such triangular mythologies (right and left), culminating in a consideration of Langston Hughes' Scottsboro writings. He concludes by considering the corrective work of Black communist Louise Thompson, whose "reportage" managed to write "a way through Scottsboro's paired triangles against the exclusions of both the rape-lynch and the anti-lynch trios" (149).

The fifth chapter is the first of two focused on Richard Wright. Here Maxwell claims that Wright's views of a Black southern nation, following communist theory, resembled that of novelist Zora Neale Hurston's anthropological approach influenced by the work of Franz Boaz. This analysis is a continuation of Maxwell's method of challenging oversimplified oppositions. Maxwell also effectively reconstructs Wright's career as a communist and the particular attraction of Stalin as a member of an oppressed minority group. He then compares a number of texts by Hurston and Wright from the late 1930s to demonstrate the degree to which they shared sympathy for the rural Black folk under assault from the Great Migration.

The final chapter compares the "antibuddy" narratives of Wright's famous *Native Son* and his radical friend Nelson Algren's novel *Somebody in Boots*. These narratives of failed male bonding comprise sympathetic but informative critiques of the communist project of interracialism. But Maxwell's fresh and cogent contextualized rethinking of the novels is now enriched by a continuous backward look at previous discussions of the Harlem Renaissance-Marxist connections, the "interracial triangles" of the cultural discourse around Scottsboro, and the debate around rural southern folk culture.

This is a book that demands the attention not only of those who wish to be informed about the history of the African American left, the Harlem Renaissance, and proletarian literature, but also those seeking to gain an understanding of the potential relevance of contemporary critical arguments from scholars such as Eric Lott, David Roediger, Pierre Bourdieu, Eve Sedgewick, Hazel Carby, George Hutchinson, Michael North, Michael Rogin, Robyn Wiegman, and others. Indeed, the book is so rich and pithy, so full of complex allusions (very often expressed through humorous "signifying" on phrases familiar mainly to those working in the fields), that its most important weakness may be that it is written in a style that will limit accessibility to the very large and diversified audience that the book deserves. Yet careful readings and rereadings of *New Negro, Old Left* are worth the effort, for this is without doubt a pathbreaking and clarifying advance in our understanding of African American literature, modernity, and the left.

What is especially sound and convincing in this achievement stems from Maxwell's thorough grounding in prior scholarship—his working through the arguments of predecessors in order to correct and advance them. This approach is most evident in Maxwell's insistence on rigorously historicizing and contextualizing conventional bifurcations and oppositions in order to demonstrate that, in the world of living cultural practice, various texts and careers do not fit into the prevailing narratives that have previously dominated the discourse of the Black-left interaction. Repeatedly Maxwell demonstrates how selective quotations—from Mike Gold in relation to the Harlem Renaissance, from Wright in relation to Hurston—create false paradigms.

Yet Maxwell's method is not to reverse these paradigms, only to rethink them in terms of the actual aims, activities, and views of the protagonists. Often this requires our holding several contradictory opinions in mind at the same time—for example, in regard to Gold's opinions about jazz and Black culture, or the profound misogyny of much of the most admirable antiracist discourse. We come away from the experience with a more authentic apprehension of the ambiguities of cultural practice even at the expense of losing some of those little boxes by means of which we had neatly classified earlier relationships, as well as the breadth and unitary nature of left culture produced by antiracist Black and white cultural workers.

POETS ON THE LEFT

Different in form, but complementary in content, James Smethurst's *The New Red Negro* is a powerful narrative about the evolution of a single genre. It is also a long-overdue truth-telling that documents central links between African American poetry and the Communist Left. Thus it corrects the work of earlier scholars who have treated the left associations of Black poets in terms of anti-communist conventions and clichés that Smethurst deftly demolishes. The book also rebuts those cultural historians who are intellectual prisoners of diminished narratives of twentieth-century literature that isolate literary radicalism of the 1930s as a decade-limited "moment," rather than understanding it as a crucial stage in a longer-term, mid-century development.

This is a very ambitious book that tries to provide a complex challenge to prevailing views of the evolution of African American poetry, revise conventional notions of literary classification, offer a theory for the various emphases in form and content of a range of Black poets over several decades, counter institutionalized amnesia about the seriousness and subtleties of political engagements, and speculate on the long-term impact of this mid-century experience. Each aspect of the project is carried out with an impressively lucid writing style and a highly polished means of documentation. (Smethurst's footnotes alone require meticulous study.)

The basic thesis of Smethurst's book is that the evolving ideology and institutions of the U.S. communist cultural movement played a substantial role in shaping the form and content of African American poetry in the 1930s and 1940s. The primary poets in the study are Sterling Brown, Langston Hughes, Gwendolyn Brooks, Countee Cullen, Owen Dodson, Robert Hayden, Melvin Tolson, and Margaret Walker; but attention is also paid to Waring Cuney, Frank Marshall Davis, Richard Wright, and several others. While the range of relationships to communist ideology and organizations among this group is diverse, Smethurst finds the influence most evident in the specificities of the gendered folk-street voice of much of this poetry, a result of yoking together "cultural nationalism, integrationism and internationalism within a construct of class struggle" (10). Once the leading poetry of the decade is discussed in this context, one can then gain new insight into complex matters such as the poetry's relation to rural and urban forms of African American popular culture and the interrelations between "high" and "vernacular" art.

Smethurst's introduction incisively reviews the previous scholarship on Black poetry in the 1930s and 1940s, as well as critiques the drawbacks to extant memoirs of and scholarship about the cultural Left. Among Smethurst's most convincing points are his sensible explanation of the ill effects of the tendency to separate the 1930s from the 1940s in regard to periodization, and his emphasis on the crucial mixing of high and low culture. Less convincing is the assertion that the U.S. communist cultural leadership welcomed the 1920s modernist revolution in literary form and sensibility.[6]

Chapter one presents a kind of overview of the origin and evolution of Black writers and communism from the post-World War I era. This is a vivid summary of some familiar episodes that also integrates new information and insights into the narrative. His characterization of the communist approach to the "national question" as providing "a paradigm" with which African American writers felt comfortable is impressive. The chapter additionally contains a fabulous review of communist cultural institutions (mainly journals) in relation to Black writers, as well as provocative considerations of masculinity and gender in recreating the "folk voice" before and during the Popular Front.

Chapter two concentrates on the work of Sterling Brown, beginning with a fine recontextualization of his writing in relation to the communist left as well as a useful explanation of Brown's distinction between a "Harlem" and "New Negro" renaissance. Smethurst's observations about the parallels between Brown's cultural project and the communists' evolving orientation are also exciting. Equally noteworthy, the argument proves its mettle in the consideration of the poetry, starting with Smethurst's astute commentary on the poem "Southern Road" and continuing through a striking comparison of Brown's and Alain Locke's views of the respective contributions of Harlem and rural folk culture to the "New Negro" renaissance.

Chapter three reconsiders Langston Hughes in relation to the communist left. Although the story has been told before, in biographies by Arnold Rampersad and Faith Berry, Smethurst manages to provide an impressively fresh version due perhaps to a more nuanced understanding of the communist project. The consideration of voice in the poetry is informative, and the discussion of Hughes's "Scottsboro Limited" is a fine contribution toward rehabilitating Hughes's 1930s cultural project. Smethurst concludes that Hughes' ability to ultimately establish a genuine base in the African American reading public was intimately connected with his "engagement with the aesthetics of the Popular Front" (115).

In his fourth chapter, Smethurst switches the mode from a focus on individual writers to a thematic survey using categories such as "The Folk Documentary" and three versions of "Narratorial Consciousness." Among the writers treated in this framework are Richard Wright, Lucy Mae Turner, Frank Marshall Davis, Waring Cuney, Countee Cullen, and Ida Gerling Athens. The strategy results in stimulating and compelling readings of many texts.

Chapter five inaugurates the consideration of the late 1930s and first half of the 1940s when poetic styles of the Depression era evolve to what Smethurst calls "neo-modernism" (which comes in "popular" and "high" varieties). Here we have Langston Hughes discussed as an exemplar of the former, with sensitive readings of poems of the 1940s and a suggestive argument about Hughes as a forerunner of the Black Arts movement of the 1960s.

Chapter six treats Gwendolyn Brooks as the paradigmatic figure of "high" neo-modernism. It begins with a much needed challenge to prevailing images of Brooks' alleged distance from the left. Smethurst then shows how Brooks develops a heroic female subject in her poetry.

Chapter seven repeats the effective strategy of the first half of the book by reviewing a range of Black poets (Margaret Walker, Robert Hayden, Melvin Tolson, and Owen Dodson) in light of the paradigms established in the preceding studies of Hughes and Brooks, as well as in relation to topics discussed in the first part of the book. Smethurst frames his interpretations with a brief historical discussion of the transformation of the prevailing folk ethos between the 1930s and 1940s from South to urban North and West. This extraordinary volume concludes with suggestive observations about the implications of this cultural history for Black poets of the 1950s and after, and, more briefly, in relation to the phenomenon of the "New American Poetry" in the 1950s.

THE COMPANION FRONT

Bill Mullen's *Popular Fronts* is distinguished by his intense focus on one particular arena of political and cultural antiracist struggle and Black art—the city of Chicago, from the advent of the Popular Front to the Cold War. For this project he applies Yale professor Michael Denning's appropriation of the concept of "The Cultural Front" as the term of choice for leftists who saw "culture as one arm, or front, of a widening campaign for social, political, and racial equality" (2). Although others besides communists used that term, Mullens believes that the expression became especially important after the call for the People's Front coalition. The call precipitated a shift from a proletarian revolutionary culture to a "people's culture" for the purpose of extending the country's democratic heritage.

The brilliance of Mullen's approach is that he gives a concreteness to this general development. This is the same virtue found in the work of Solomon, Maxwell, and Smethurst, and it is the one that makes all the difference. The concern at this stage in scholarship is not merely exposing the proclamations of official Comintern documents to lay bare the realpolitik motivating political twists and turns (an aspect of the Stalinist legacy in regard to which the four authors represent a range of views). Mullens demonstrates that, whatever the intentions of Kremlin or CP bureaucrats, Chicago as a vibrant city had its own local history of leftist antiracist activism that received a special stamp in early 1936.

At that time the National Negro Congress (NNC) was launched through the presence of nearly a thousand delegates from twenty-eight states, to an audience of an additional four thousand. One of its themes was advancement of culture and cultural workers, alongside political demands. This event introduced to Chicago a style of politics and culture that took root. By the 1940s many of the themes, slogans, demands, and cultural icons of this would-be "Negro People's Front" were virtually hegemonic on the South Side; the *Chicago Defender*, for example, without ever referring to the communists or other leftist organizations, frequently presented the race- and class-based radicalism of the Communist Party. Although the CP as a whole suffered an enormous crisis at the time of the Hitler-Stalin Pact, and even abandoned the Popular Front orientation for a period, Black Party members in Chicago continued to forge an alliance with the *Defender* and with Black liberal forces across the country to launch a famous boycott of the film *Gone With the Wind*.

Simply put, Mullen's book aims to be a corrective to earlier treatments of the Popular Front. It answers not only the negative ones that show a condescending attitude toward the accommodating politics and cultural strategies of the time; it also augments the positive ones that treat Euro-American culture primarily and fail to grasp that there existed a "companion front" for African Americans. The appeal of this companion front was so strong that it lasted far longer than the official Party policy and helped to shape antiracist struggle in the Black community up to the present.

The specificity of Chicago provides a unique testing ground, for Chicago has been the site of a recent revival of cultural scholarship that has hitherto been debilitated by a failure to understand the African American cultural left beyond the canonical figure of Richard Wright. Mullen's view is that what is usually called the 1930s–1940s "Chicago Renaissance" is actually "the fruit of an extraordinary rapprochement between African American and white members of the U.S. left around debate and struggle for a new 'American Negro' culture," a "black and interracial cultural radicalism, best described and understood as a revised if belated realization of the Communist Party's 1936 aspiration for a Negro People's Front" (6). On the one hand, "the 1936 opening of Chicago's black 'cultural front' represented both a culmination and a new beginning for African-American engagement of and revision within the U.S. Left." On the other, "Chicago's cultural 'renaissance' and the CPUSA's Popular Front/Negro People's Front . . . were events that were historically mutually constitutive and in many ways unthinkable in separation" (6).

The roots of revolutionary Marxism in Chicago's South Side (which by the mid-1930s was the largest concentration of Blacks in the U.S. after Harlem) can be traced back to World War I; Mullen cites *The Whip* and the Free Thought Society as the genesis of the local branch of the African Blood Brotherhood. Subsequently, organizations such as League of Struggle for Negro Rights, the American Negro Labor Congress, the United Front Scottsboro Committee, and the National Unemployed Councils were "crucial chapters in black Chicago and the white-dominated Communist Party's reconsideration and reconstitution of each other" (7).

Mullen assesses the radical politics of Chicago as combining two elements: a broad interracial Popular Front on one hand and a "companion" Negro People's Front in Chicago on the other. The latter is understood by Mullen as a "climactic 'Black' moment in the history of U.S. radicalism when African American political culture actively and willingly engaged, revived, reformed and deployed 'Communism' in a manner generally consistent with official party policy, yet primarily derived from and utilized in relation to the 'objective conditions' of life in Black Metropolis" (8). These include a responsiveness to both the proletarian component of the population (men working in stockyards and steel mills; women as domestics) as well as its middle and upper classes aspiring to become players in the democratic capitalist system and its culture. A special emphasis on Black churches was included as well.

Perhaps more emphatically than Smethurst, Mullen argues that the African American cultural left prior to 1936 had been moving autonomously in a manner that would form a symbiotic relationship with the double Popular Front thrust. Writers, artists, and intellectuals such as Margaret Burroughs, Fern Gayden, Alice Browning, Theodore Ward, Gwendolyn Brooks, Horace Cayton, St. Clair Drake, Charles White, Margaret Walker, and Frank Marshall Davis were evolving in that direction; they would make that orientation visible not only through individual writings but also through the "Negro in Illinois" project of the Illinois Federal Writers Project, the South Side Community Center, the Associated Negro Press, the *Chicago Defender,* and *Negro Story.* Moreover, at moments when the Communist Party seemed to diverge from the larger project it had helped to engender—especially during World War II—this trend not only continued but deepened and creatively developed certain aspects.

In particular, Mullen holds that in Chicago the Black cultural Left "constituted among the most aesthetically and politically complex black art of the century, challenging the commonly shared assumption that Popular Front art universally succumbed to an ameliorated populist aesthetics or a mawkish sentimentality" (11). None of this is to deny that there were tensions in the companion front; part of Mullen's story is of the struggles between the members of the "Black bourgeoisie" who ultimately controlled cultural institutions, and the militants who participated in them. Mullen takes note of the fact that very often radical ideas were disguised to appease the Black patronage class as much as to evade FBI surveillance. Ultimately, the Chicago Renaissance was ended in practical terms through a combination of flight—in some cases flight into exile, in other cases into a Black bourgeois intellectual life.

The seven chapters of Mullen's book aspire to map out the political, cultural, and geographical landscape of the companion front from mid-1930s through World War II. He begins with a striking revision of Richard Wright's contribution to the phenomenon; by documenting Wright's atypicality, Mullen both gains a clearer perspective on his achievement and helps bring back into vision the many other cultural workers, institutions, and activities hitherto obscured.

The second, third, and fourth chapters treat key institutions of the Renaissance and Negro People's Front. Foremost is the *Chicago Defender*, which after 1940 not only covered the pro-communist left sympathetically but hired editors and writers from that milieu. In contrast, the South Side Community Arts Center is noted for its interracial alliances among cultural workers. *Negro Story*, published from 1944 to 1946, is reclaimed as helping to "foreground the short story as a genre for black radical voicing" through its blend of the tradition of "proletarian literature" and the racialized wartime experiences of Black women (16).

Shifting gears in the fifth and six chapters, Mullens turns to literary analysis of short fiction and poetry of the 1940s. In the case of the former, the fiction record of *Negro Story* shows the "critical amnesia" which allowed the establishment of a select group of major Black writers to obscure their roots in the companion front and the contributions of lesser-known writers. In regard to Brooks, especially *A Street in Bronzeville*, Mullen offers an extraordinary interpretation of her writing as an "unsystematic feminist skepticism" of leftist culture within a radical framework, even as Brooks herself has denied any past association with the left. Mullen's final chapter and his postscript focus on the combined effects of McCarthyism, postwar political splintering (due to the absence of a common struggle against international fascism), embourgeoisement, and the liberalizing of formerly radical institutions, for the legacy of the companion front experience.

BUILDING A NEW INTERRACIAL LEFT

These four books definitively establish the communist-led antiracist movement in the mid-century as the foundation for any future interracial socialist left. This is not to dismiss the substantial literature documenting the mistakes and delusions of the communist movement—especially its reprehensible policies in World War II (including support of Japanese American internment, opposition to the "Double V" campaign, and collaboration with the Federal government's suppression of the civil liberties of Trotskyists). Rather, it is to conclude that this unconscionable record only problematizes but does not negate the palpable achievements recorded in these remarkable books. Together they embody a series of "lessons" that might be carried over as the starting point of any radical movement in the new millennium. In addition, there are the methodological contributions of this literature to ongoing considerations about the cultural and political history of the left.

Three of the most important lessons might be summarized as follows:

- First, as we have seen from the experiences of the communist movement in the 1920s, militancy, devotion to class struggle, and a fervent belief in equality are inadequate to build an interracial movement. The nature of racism as both material and ideological oppression requires that socialist organizations and projects take special measures in order to transform their membership composition and their relationship to the struggle of people of color. It is not enough to preach the need for unity and promise fair treatment. Black history is replete with examples of betrayals by "white friends," and Communists were correct in understanding why there was the need for Black leadership of autonomous black struggles.

- Second, the communist movement, prodded by the arguments of Black revolutionaries from the left nationalist movement, as well as by the Communist International, developed a basic theory to explain both the historical reasons why "special measures" must be taken, as well as to suggest what these measures should be. That theory is basically the view of "national oppression," as opposed to the stance that the issue to be addressed is simply racism (dislike of people who look different), injustice, and so forth. Understanding African Americans as a nationality helps explain why nationalism of various forms has been an ongoing feature of the struggle, and why revolutionaries should not oppose this nationalist struggle but find ways to relate to it in order to assist its evolution in a radical, anticapitalist, and internationalist direction.

The development of a proletarian-led nationalist movement with an internationalist vision is probably the prerequisite to a unified movement for socialism—a stage over which Marxists may not be able to leap. The communists chose to put this theory into practice by building a working-class movement in two complementary areas: on the one hand, they struggled for an integrated CIO that put the cause of antiracism among its priorities; on the other, they promoted a Black-led labor movement with a broad social agenda, culminating in the National Negro Congress after 1936. (Here it is worth mentioning that the precise decision-making procedures in the NNC are not fully discussed in any of the studies, and Solomon believes that at least one public leader was a secret Party member. So the record of how, exactly, the Party maintained influence in an "independent" Black-led organization remains to be explored.)

From this perspective, it becomes clear why forms of affirmative action (such as taking special measures to insure that all barriers are removed from advancement to leadership of African Americans) are necessary *within* a socialist organization as well as *outside* it; why Black members should be the leaders in areas of Black work, but also in the general political life of the group; why cultural and psychological issues are of crucial importance; why "integration" or "assimilation" into the racist house of capitalism is an inadequate solution; and why an organization's membership must be reeducated to understand the complex and subtle ways in which paternalism and white privilege can exist despite one's best intentions. (Recent scholarship by David Roediger and others has especially emphasized how the choice of European ethnic groups to identify as "white" assisted, and still reinforces, the racist order.)

In regard to this last point, the communists were especially effective in demonstrating to their own membership the truth that the struggle against racism is in everyone's interest, not just that of African Americans. Euro-American members came to see that their own best hope for the future was interconnected with Black liberation, to the point of supporting Black self-defense against other Euro-Americans. In general, antiracism became the duty of every communist, not just Black members.

- A third lesson from the communist experience suggests the manner in which substantial numbers of African Americans will possibly come to join a socialist organization. Some, of course, may join out of individual friendship with members who have won their confidence on the job, in the neighborhood, or in a common struggle. However, if the organization adheres to the kind of attitudes promoted by the communists, broader layers of the most politicized vanguard of the Black struggle will come increasingly to respect the socialist movement; eventually cadres will enter, first by ones and twos, and then these will come to play the key role in the recruitment of thousands more. (However, it is also the duty of Euro-American socialists to themselves actively assist in this effort to change the composition of the organization.) When an organization, like the Communist Party, is willing to defend the Black population from exploitation in general—not just in obvious "political" cases, but also in cases of police brutality and eviction—the culture of the movement will become increasingly hospitable to people of color.

THE DREAM OF CYRIL BRIGGS

Of course, these four books begin but they hardly end the crucial discussions that need to take place in regard to the above lessons, a discussion in which a new generation of activists and Marxist scholars of all colors and both genders will have to participate along with veterans in order to construct a united left

for the new millennium. For example, one of the themes most stresssed by
Solomon is the central role of ideology, vision, and a unified organization. In
fact, even false visions and a relatively undemocratic military-command-type
organization seem to have the ability to empower antiracist activists. Solomon's
own point of reference here is the mistaken view that the Black Belt in the
South was the basis of a potential Black republic.[7]

However, there is also the issue of just how empowering was the false view
that the Soviet Union represented a genuine step forward into the socialist
future, a country in which workers' rights were supposedly defended and racism
virtually expunged. Clearly the belief that the beginning of a new world already
existed gave much self-confidence to a struggling group of Black and Euro-
American communists in an adversarial position. But what about a balance
sheet measuring these benefits against the deficits of having a mostly false dream,
and adjusting national political priorities to the needs of a foreign dictatorship?
Even if one puts aside (for the moment) all the complex debates about whether
communist policies in Germany, Spain, the colonies, and elsewhere, actually
advanced or retarded antifascism and socialist movements, we need to ask ourselves: In the long run, were the gains of a self-comforting illusion worth the
betrayal of idealistic rank-and-file Party members by leaders who banked their
reputations on false information about the Stalin regime? Was it worth the
long-term discrediting of Marxism among millions who, to this day, identify
socialism with the Stalinist horror?

In addition, the ongoing controversy about the politics of the Popular Front
is raised implicitly and explicitly in these writings. By and large, the view of
Solomon (that local practice was the crucial test for the Black movement; that
the Third Period was at best a trial run to learn firsthand the futility of sectarianism) seems to be vindicated by the three other scholars. Still, since Solomon
ends in 1936, and Maxwell and Smethurst are primarily focused on cultural
practice, only Mullen explicitly treats the Popular Front throughout its two
phases (before and after the Hitler-Stalin Pact) as both a high point and something of a model to be emulated. And he does this in a nuanced fashion, emphasizing the semiautonomy of the "companion" front.

Nevertheless, Mullen tends to treat the Popular Front orientation through
euphemisms such as "coalitionist politics" (6). Since no critic of Popular Front
ever objected to coalitions—indeed, the Trotskyist and left socialist critics were
for coalition politics in the days when the CP was perversely for a "United Front
from Below"—this formula is likely to be seen by those skeptical of the Popular Front as sidestepping the hardest and more troubling questions. On what
basis should one build alliances with nonsocialist and nonworking class forces
so as to advance the struggle on all fronts, building for the day when authentic
economic and political reconstruction are truly on the agenda? In my view, it
is impossible to reach a final judgment on the actual degree of autonomy of the

companion front during World War II without a candid, comparative appraisal of the CP's practice on a national and international level.

Finally, there is the issue of the uniqueness of the modern African American liberation movement as a paradigm for "new" twentieth-century social movements requiring a rethinking of classical Marxist projections about the likely course of social advance. Many of the points of analysis about African American "national oppression" seem appropriate not only to other populations of oppressed nationalities in land areas of the U.S. historically linked to these groups (especially Chicanos, Puerto Ricans, and Native Americans), but also to a number of non-European immigrant nationalities (Latinos from Latin America, Asian Americans, Caribbeans) and even to women. To what extent is the declaration of a "national oppression" decisive to the recognition of the legitimacy of autonomous struggles, self-leadership, the need for affirmative action, and the recognition of the importance of psychological and cultural issues? Is it possible that one aspect of communist theoretical work (and corresponding practical intervention) in relation to African Americans is that it simply instigated a rethinking of narrower interpretations of Marxism—a rethinking that socialists of future generations must embrace and extend in order to eventually realize the liberatory dreams of Cyril Briggs and all who came after for a renewed and expanded U.S. left?

NOTES

1. For the sake of consistency, "Black" will be capitalized throughout this essay when referring to the African American nationality, despite spelling variations in original sources.

2. Solomon's narrative runs counter to the version that, on orders from Lenin, the UCP briefly assigned a member named Zack Kornfeder to link up to radical Blacks in Harlem. Solomon could find no evidence of such a command in the Moscow archives and no knowledge of such an episode among Lenin scholars. Thus he makes a compelling case that this is part of the Cold War mythology exaggerating Comintern control of U.S. communists and downplaying the autonomous contribution of U.S. Blacks.

3. Robert Minor, the white Texan (but militant antiracist) in charge of "Negro Work" for the Party, differed with Briggs and argued that defending Garvey against government persecution was the more appropriate strategy.

4. It is unfortunate that Solomon says so little about the fate of Fort-Whiteman in light of his importance to the narrative. If the information contained in John Haynes and Harvey Klehr et al., *The Soviet World of American Communism*, pp. 218–27, is accurate, no assessment of the African-American Left's association with the USSR can be complete without a fuller discussion of the events and their significance.

5. After 1935 the slogan "self-determination" was deemphasized during the Popular Front, and then abandoned in 1943 (by Party leader Earl Browder), revived in 1946 (following the expulsion of Browder), and buried in 1958.

6. In my view, this assessment contradicts the writings of the most authoritative Communist Party critics (V. J. Jerome, John Howard Lawson, Milton Howard, A. B. Magil, Samuel Sillen). It would have been sufficient to observe that perhaps Party critics did not recognize African American or more "populist" versions of modernism for what they were, and that they held a double standard when it came to the treatment of writers who had or had not expressed dismay over the repressive nature of the Soviet regime.

7. It's worth noting that Solomon's opinion is that, even in those periods when the communists' view was clearly that the Black Belt Republic was not a "given" but that the choice was up to the Black population, such a strategy was inappropriate. For me, this calls into question the very meaning of "self-determination." How can one talk of "self-determination" if certain options for self-rule by people of color are ruled out in advance by the white majority? In contrast, after the late 1930s the Trotskyist view was consistently that the issue of a separate state must be settled by the oppressed nationality itself, which could, in fact, opt for a land-based separate state even if socialists thought this was unworkable or undesirable.

WORKS CITED

Haynes, John Earl, Harvey Klehr, Rossiiskli Tsentr Khraneniia Izucheniia Dokumentov Noveishei Istorii, Kyrill M. Anderson. *The Soviet World of American Communism*. New Haven: Yale UP, 1998.

Maxwell, William. *Old Negro, New Left: African-American Writing and Communism between the Wars*. New York: Columbia UP, 1999.

Mullen, Bill V. *Popular Fronts: Chicago and African-American Cultural Politics, 1935–46*. Urbana: U of Illinois P. 1999.

Smethurst, James Edward. *The New Red Negro: The Literary Left and African American Poetry, 1930–1946*. New York: Oxford UP, 1999.

Solomon, Mark. *The Cry Was Unity: Communists and African Americans, 1917–1936*. Jackson: U of Mississippi P, 1998.

CHAPTER TWO

RACE, CLASS, AND COMMUNISM: THE YOUNG
RALPH ELLISON AND THE "WHOLE LEFT"

BARBARA FOLEY

ONE OF THE KEY MOVES INVOLVED IN PRODUCING A "SCHOLARSHIP OF THE 'WHOLE left'"—the worthy goal of the essays gathered in this volume—entails reconstructing our collective understanding of the "Old Left." In the wake of feminism, multiculturalism, and calls for diversity, leftists of today—and not just academic leftists—are challenged as never before to integrate into their critiques of capitalism an understanding of the ways in which race, gender, ethnicity, sexuality, and environmental issues affect, and inflect, the movement to create a world fit for habitation by all. But these concerns are hardly unique to radicals and progressives of our time. Albeit with different premises and emphases—and, admittedly, with relatively little attention to the last two categories—significant numbers of twentieth-century socialists and communists grasped, and organized around, the interconnectedness of class exploitation with other types of oppression. Ignorance of this legacy can only hobble our current attempts to produce an articulation relevant to our moment. Yet another legacy from the past century, the legacy of anticommunism, has made such ignorance—or, more precisely, ignorance parading itself as knowledge—intellectually respectable. For the fallacious notion that "old leftists" forced the multifariousness of oppositional identities into the procrustean bed of class reductionism remains largely uninterrogated to this day, even if a privileging of vernacular authenticity has routinely come to perform the ideological role previously played by plain old attacks on the authoritarian party.

The consequence of many scholars' continuing acceptance of the old canards about the left's insensitivity to anything but economic oppression has been not only to distort history, both political and cultural, but also to sever class analysis from the full range of social experience, both discursive and material. Marxism, in this reading, becomes one more expression of the logocentric Western rationalism responsible for the stifling of heteroglossia; in fact, because of its claim to offer a metatheory of human emancipation, the socialist/communist tradition emerges for some as the most nefarious, because the most "centered," inheritance of the West. The current draining off of energies on the left to which this collection of essays is addressed is thus itself to a significant degree a product of an anticommunist discourse associating class analysis with red domination and positing subversive but of necessity dispersed and fragmented acts of speech and representation as the only possible sites of present and future liberation. In order to get beyond this culturalist paralysis and construct a "whole left" capable of meaningful praxis—and untrammeled by a notion of intersecting oppressions enabling only the most cautious of coalition politics—we must undertake some profoundly revisionary historical investigation.

I offer a contribution to such investigation in this essay by examining the representation of the connection between class and race oppression in the work of the young Ralph Ellison. This choice of authors may come as a surprise to some, since Ellison's hostile portrayal of the Brotherhood—transparently the Communist Party of the United States of America (CPUSA)—in Invisible Man has secured the writer's credentials as a Cold Warrior since the novel's publication in 1952. Is not Ellison part of the problem, then, not the solution? Why not choose another proletarian writer focusing on the relationship between race and class—e.g., William Attaway or Grace Lumpkin—to make this argument? But it is precisely Ellison's status as canon-forming anticommunist that enables this project to proceed on two crucially interrelated levels of inquiry. On the first of these, Ellison's pre-Invisible Man Marxist writings—including his New Masses journalism, proletarian short stories, and early novelistic drafts—render cognition of the ways in which the Communist-led movement, with which Ellison for some time identified, both analyzed the relationship between racism and capitalism as well as featured the fight for racial equality as central to the struggle for communist transformation of society. The work of the young Ralph Ellison thus illuminates important holistic features of the theory and practice of the "Old Left." On another level, however, Ellison's increasingly unsympathetic representation of the CPUSA in successive drafts of Invisible Man hinges upon the countervailing proposition that Marxist class analysis leads to a politics that is at worst antipathetic, and at best irrelevant, to the welfare of African Americans. To track the process by which identity supplants class analysis and culturalism supersedes class struggle in Ellison's Cold War novel is thus to examine in nuce the process by which not communism, but anticommunism, has contributed to the demoralization and fragmentation of the movement for a "better world." Invisible Man's representation of the "Old Left," viewed as not simply a product but a process, helps us understand more fully the ideological forces currently necessitating the resuscitation of the "whole left." (See also Foley, "The Rhetoric of Anticommunism in Ralph Ellison's Invisible Man"; "Ralph Ellison as Proletarian Journalist"; "Reading Redness: Politics and Audience in Ralph Ellison's Early Short Fiction"; "From Communism to Brotherhood: The Drafts of *Invisible Man*"; and "Reading Redness Redux: Ralph Ellison, Intertextuality, and Biographical Criticism)".

When *Invisible Man* appeared in 1952, Ellison's media image was carefully crafted to occlude the author's earlier connection with the left. Random House's dustjacket biography of Ellison featured his previous studies in music and sculpture; his work experience in a factory, for a psychologist, and as a freelance photographer; his World War II service in the merchant marine; and his lectures on American literature at New York University and Bennington College. Nothing was said, however, of the approximately three dozen pieces of left-wing fiction and reportage he had produced in the years before 1946. The biographical sketch appearing in the *Saturday Review* effaced Richard Wright from Ellison's background and claimed that T. S. Eliot was the dominant influence on the young novelist (Hazard 22). The *New York Times* literary profile made no mention of Ellison's many publications in *New Challenge, New Masses, Direction, Tomorrow, Negro Quarterly, Negro Story, Common Ground*, and other left or left-tending organs, noting only his previous appearances in safer venues such as *American Writing* in 1940 and *Cross-Section* in 1944 (Breit 26). Although sardonic reviews of the novel in the left press—by Abner Berry in the *Daily Worker*, and Lloyd L. Brown in *Masses and Mainstream*, for example—remarked upon Ellison's previous left connections, both the original reviews in mainstream publications and the flurry of second-round reviews accompanying Ellison's receiving the National Book Award in 1953 fostered the impression that Ellison had been publishing only in "respectable" organs all along (Berry 7; Brown 62–64).

Ellison's retrospective comments on his relations with the Communist Party were both cagey and contradictory. He routinely declared that "the Brotherhood wasn't the Communist Party" and explained, "I did not want to describe an existing Socialist or Communist or Marxist political group primarily because it would have allowed the reader to escape confronting certain political patterns . . . which still exist and of which our two major political parties are guilty in their relationships to Negro Americans" (Geller 7; Ellison, *Going to the Territory* [henceforth GT] 59). In a 1963 conversation with Wright biographer Michel Fabre, Ellison explained that, while he wrote for the *New Masses* for several years, he "never joined the Communist Party": "I wasn't on the make in that sense. I wrote what I felt and wasn't in awe of functionaries. . . . They never paid me anything. Finally I refused to write without money. . . . I was so surprised [sic] when they paid" (Fabre, "In Ralph Ellison's Precious Words" [henceforth "Precious Words"] 6–7). In the 1965 preface to *Shadow and Act*, Ellison claimed that he "soon rejected . . . Marxist political theory" (Ellison, *Shadow and Act* [henceforth S and A] xxi). In a 1967 interview, he stressed his alienation from left cultural practice, confessing to having written "what might be called propaganda—having to do with the Negro struggle" but maintaining that "my fiction was always trying to be something else. . . . I never accepted the ideology which the *New Masses* attempted to impose on writers" (GT 294). In a 1982 communication with Fabre, Ellison claimed that his outlook had always "emphasized the Negroes' rather than the workers' point of view. . . . [T]here was no way for me to accept the Communist notion that workers and Negroes were unite [sic] without a large dose of salts" (Fabre, "Precious Words" 20).

In the 1967 interview, however, Ellison admitted to having "gone through the political madness that marked the intellectual experience of the thirties" and charged that U.S. Communists

> fostered the myth that communism was twentieth-century Americanism, but to be a twentieth-century American meant, in their thinking, that you had to be more Russian than American and less Negro than either. That's how they lost their Negroes. The communists recognized no plurality of interests and were really responding to the necessities of Soviet foreign policy, and when the war came, Negroes got caught and were made expedient in the shifting of policy. (GT 296).

Reiterated in the published version of *Invisible Man,* this argument suggests that Ellison's frequent claims to political naïveté were disingenuous. Bracketing for the moment whether or not Ellison's judgment about the wartime CPUSA was correct, we note that this critique indicates more than a passing acquaintance with left politics and strategy. With the gradual opening up of the Ellison archive in the past few years, it has become increasingly clear that Ellison's relationship with the Communist left was indeed of substantial duration and seriousness. Lawrence Jackson's recent biography of the young Ellison—based, of necessity, upon limited access to Ellison's letters and journals—further demonstrates that this was the case. The notes accompanying Ellison's drafts of the novel, moreover, contain multiple allusions to Brotherhood members as "communists." As we shall see, the drafts themselves show that Ellison's original representation of the Brotherhood's relationship to Harlem was considerably more sympathetic than the version contained in the 1952 text. In short, Ellison may have furiously backpedaled from his youthful commitments after his novel was published, but there is little doubt that for many years he embraced a politics that envisioned the fight for racial equality as inseparable from the revolutionary struggle against capitalism.

What can Ellison's early work tell us about the "Old Left" in the period preceding the Cold War? To begin with, Ellison's late-1930s interviews with southern migrants living in Harlem for the Federal Writers Project (FWP)—some of which are still accessible only on microfilm in New York's Schomburg Library—reveal not only the pronounced class consciousness of some of the young journalist's interviewees but also his own fascination with Marxist analysis. The richly vernacular speech of one Eli Luster, for example, combines a prediction of Biblical apocalypse with something close to a call for communist revolution. Claiming that God "step[ed] in" to sink the Titanic because it carried "all big rich folks: John Jacob Astor—all the big aristocrats," Luster prophesies that "God's time is coming":

> Money won't be worth no more'n that dust blowing on the ground. Won't be no men down in Washington making fifty thousand dollars a week and folks cain't hardly make eighteen dollars a month. Everybody'll be equal, in God's time. Won't be no old man Rockefeller, no suh!. . . . [T]hem what done took advantage of everything'll be floating down the river. You'll go over to the North River, and over to the East River, and you'll see em all floating along, and the river'll be full and they won't know what struck em. The Lawd's gonna have his day. (257–60)

A musician named Jim Barber recalled a conversation with a white man to whom he had declared, "[White] skin ain't no more good to you than mine is to me. You cain't marry one a Du Pont's daughters, and I know damn well I cain't" (Banks 256). Ellison interviewed other migrants from the South who clung to rural folk identities, such as the woman who, anticipating *Invisible Man*'s Mary Rambo, took as her motto, "I'm in New York, but New York isn't in me" (Banks 250–252). Notably, however, class-conscious voices such as Luster's and Barber's would be absent from the final draft of the novel.

The research that Ellison contributed to the collective project that would result in Roi Ottley and William Weatherby's *The Negro in New York* (1967) shows him exploring the proposition that racism impedes the common class interests of the exploited. A piece about the 1741 New York slave revolt draws explicit parallels between the insurgents' trials and the Scottsboro case and stresses the multiracial character of the rebellion (Ellison, "The Insurrection of 1741"). A summary of Carter Woodson's *The Beginning of Miscegenation of the Whites and Blacks* points out that in early colonial life "the slaves and white indentured servants having a community of interests frequently intermingled, but when class lines were drawn in a locality and laborers were largely of one class or other intermixture was not so prevelent [sic]" (Ellison, "Woodson's *The Beginnings of Miscegenation of Whites and Blacks*"). Although Ellison would later claim that from the outset he accepted the Communist line on the necessity for black-white working-class unity only reluctantly, these FWP writings suggest otherwise.

In various reviews published in the Communist-affiliated *New Masses*, Ellison put African American writers through an exacting proletarian litmus test. Reviewing the 1940 Negro Playwrights' performance of Theodore Ward's *Big White Fog*, Ellison praises the play's "attempt to probe the most vital problems of Negro experience." These include the hardships posed by the Depression and

the experience of Garveyism, embodied in one brother, Victor, and the emergence of communism, embodied in another brother, Lester. But Ellison
chides Ward for placing greater emphasis upon Victor's experience, noting that
"Lester's story . . . should have been in the foreground. The Negro people's consciousness [of the conditions that produced Victor's tragedy] has increased . . .
to the point that they have produced a writer who can objectify those elements
once shrouded in a big white fog." Ward should have created a protagonist as
conscious as himself (Ellison, "Big White Fog" 22–23). Ellison pursues a similar line of critique in his 1941 *New Masses* review of William Attaway's *Blood
on the Forge,* where he faults Attaway for failing to create a "center of consciousness lodged in a character or characters capable of comprehending the sequence
of events." While the novel's portraiture of the Moss brothers' northward migration powerfully portrays "the clash of two modes of economic production," its
dialectic is "incomplete," for it represents "only one pole of the contradictory
experience from which the novel is composed." Neglecting the fact that the
migration produced "the most conscious American Negro type, the black trade
unionist," Attaway "grasped the destruction of the folk, but missed its rebirth
on a higher level" (Ellison, "The Great Migration" 24). Both Ward and Attaway are thus praised for dialectically representing the opposing forces in contemporaneous black experience but faulted for failing to emphasize the primary
(that is, proletarian) aspect of those contradictions. The Brotherhood may be
lampooned for drinking a toast to the historical dialectic in *Invisible Man,* but
the young Ellison clearly took his dialectics seriously.

Although the critique of the Brotherhood in *Invisible Man* is premised upon
the notion of wartime betrayal, it bears noting that Ellison's journalistic writings before he joined the merchant marine in late 1943 conform to the CPUSA
line on war and fascism throughout its various dramatic shifts. In 1939, Ellison
heartily espoused the Popular Front and the view of Communism as "twentieth-century Americanism." In a piece entitled "Anti-Semitism Among Negroes,"
Ellison praises "Negro leaders" such as NAACP Secretary Walter White, Brotherhood of Sleeping Car Porters President A. Philip Randolph, and Abyssinian
Baptist Church pastor Adam Clayton Powell (Sr.) for helping raise funds for
Jewish refugees from Nazism and for "cooperating . . . on the broad front . . . for
Democratic rights" in "this, the greatest of Democracies" (Ellison, "Anti-Semitism Amoung Negroes" 38). Between February and November 1940, by contrast—during the period between the Hitler-Stalin Pact and the Nazi invasion
of the USSR—Ellison made a sharp about-face in evident conformity with the
altered Communist line. Now he vigorously attacked the Roosevelt Administration's pretensions to democracy and moves toward intervention. For
example, in "A Congress Jim Crow Didn't Attend," Ellison places the struggle
against U. S. racism in the context of a struggle against anticommunism, ruling-class liberalism, and imperialist war. Rendering Ellison's response to the
1940 Third National Negro Congress, the piece adheres closely to the altered

CP analysis of the domestic and world situations. Politicians earlier praised for "democratic" leadership are now traitors to the black masses and the New Deal; the "unmistakable notes of Red-baiting" in Randolph's Congress address give Ellison "a feeling of betrayal." Now antipatriotic, Ellison presents himself proudly as a "black Yank" who is "not coming." He praises new leaders in the ranks of the black working class as "the answer to those who wonder why there is such a scramble to raise the Booker T. Washington symbol anew in Negro life" and concludes, "There with the whites in the audience I saw the positive forces of civilization and the best guarantee of America's future." Speech-making, leadership, white people in Negro organizations, Booker T. Washington, betrayal—key themes and motifs in *Invisible Man*—appear here with a very different political spin than they are given in the 1952 novel (Ellison, " A Congress Jim Crow Didn't Attend" 6–8).

Ellison's writings from the years 1942 and 1943 exhibit still another political shift. In accordance with the Communists' swing back toward advocacy of intervention after the Nazi invasion of the USSR in June 1941, Ellison now adopts a "win-the-war" stance characterized by a resuscitated Popular Front rhetoric. In "The Way It Is," an October 1942 *New Masses* account of Harlemites' attitudes toward the war effort as typified by one Mrs. Jackson, Ellison acknowledges the widespread ambivalence toward the war effort among Harlem blacks but maintains that the hardships Mrs. Jackson faces can only be resolved by a steadfast backing of "the President's [price and rent] stabilization program." The cost to be incurred by the nation's loss of Mrs. Jackson's allegiance is otherwise too great: "Only concrete action will be effective—lest irritation and confusion turn into exasperation, and exasperation change to disgust and finally into anti-war sentiment (and there is such a danger)" (Ellison, "The Way It Is" 11). Ellison, in accord with CPUSA policy, clearly fears that African American alienation will impede the war effort.

That a significant shift in Ellison's analysis of African American participation in the war was taking place in the mid-forties is indicated in his 1944 review of Gunnar Myrdal's *An America Dilemma*. Here Ellison remarks that both the left and the New Deal "neglected sharp ideological planning where the Negro was concerned . . . and went about solving the Negro problem without defining the nature of the problem beyond its economic and narrowly political aspects. Which is not unusual for politicians—only here both groups consistently professed and demonstrated far more social vision than the average political party." Ellison's 1944 criticism of the Communist wartime policy is worth reproducing at length:

> The most striking example of this failure is to be seen in the New Deal Administration's perpetuation of a Jim Crow Army, and the shamefaced support of it given by the Communists. It would be easy—on the basis of some of the slogans attributed to Negro people by the Communists, from time to time, and

> the New Deal's frequent retreats on Negro issues—to question the sincerity of these two groups. Or, in the case of the New Deal, attribute its failure to its desire to hold power in a concrete political situation; while the failure of the Communists could be laid to "Red perfidy." But this would be silly. Sincerity is not a quality that one expects of political parties, not even revolutionary ones. To question their sincerity makes room for the old idea of paternalism, and the corny notion that these groups have an obligation to "do something for the Negro." (*S and A* 310)

Here Ellison criticizes for the first time the Communists' acceptance of—or at least refusal publicly to criticize—segregation in the armed forces. Moreover, elsewhere in the review Ellison chastises the CPUSA for its unwillingness to merge Marx with Freud in confronting "the problem of the irrational" which, in American society, "has taken the form of the Negro problem," dubbed by Myrdal the "American dilemma." Yet Ellison still commends the CP for having "far more social vision than the average political party" and in fact refutes the charge of "'Red perfidy'" that would be central to *Invisible Man* and his subsequent comments on the CPUSA. Moreover, Ellison criticizes Myrdal for psychologizing the problem of racism, which leads him to reject the "concept of class struggle and the economic motivation of anti-Negro prejudice which to an increasing number of Negro intellectuals correctly analyses [sic] their situation." Rather than rejecting Marxism, Ellison in 1944 aspires to render it more encompassing and effective. He envisions a "whole left" that is if anything strengthened by a deeper grasp—political, economic, and psychological—of the relationship of race to class.

With the exception of some of his contributions to the FWP, the corpus of Ellison's left-leaning journalistic writings from the late 1930s to the mid-1940s has long been available to scholars taking the trouble to go beyond Ellison's post-1952 disavowals of left affiliations. It was, however, only in 1996—when John Callahan, literary executor to the Ellison estate, brought out *Flying Home and Other Stories*—that the full extent of Ellison's early ambitions as a writer of proletarian fiction would become evident. Callahan's collection does not reproduce Ellison's two unabashedly leftist tales from this period—"Slick's Gonna Learn" and "The Birthmark"—but it contains a number of short stories that, after the novelist's death, Callahan discovered under Ellison's dining room table. While all these early stories have merit, and a few are quite extraordinary, two will serve here to exemplify the young Ellison's efforts to give fictional life to his radical political vision.

"A Party Down at the Square" is a riveting story about a lynching, told from the point of view of an anonymous young white boy from Cincinnati visiting relatives in Alabama. He witnesses the ritual burning alive of an African American man (whom he continually refers to as "that Bacote nigger") one evening on a town square where men and women throng to get a closer look as the sheriff and his deputies stand guard—apparently to safeguard, not stop, what is going on. When the lynching victim calls out in agony, "Will someone please cut my throat like a Christian?" a lyncher calls back, "Sorry but there ain't no Christians around tonight. Ain't no Jew-Boys either. We're just one hundred percent Americans" (Ellison, "A Party Down at the Square" [henceforth "Party"] 8). The "party" is interrupted by the heavy winds and rains of a cyclone, which causes a blackout at a nearby airport and makes the pilot of a plane swoop low over the lit-up town square, which he mistakes for the runway. He zooms upward without crashing, but the plane's wing breaks an electric power line which, whipping like a snake, falls and electrocutes a white woman.

The armed sheriff forces the crowd back to the bonfire, and the lynching is completed. The boy observes that the burning man's back "looks like a barbequed hog" ("Party" 9); he vomits but is reassured by his uncle, who jokes that his nephew, while a "gutless wonder from Cincinnati," will "get used to it in time" ("Party" 10). The story ends with a scene in the town's general store, where two white sharecroppers—who look, the boy says, "hungry as hell," like "most of the croppers"—observe that another "nigger" has been lynched (lynchings are always done in pairs, one says, "'to keep the other niggers in place'"). Another remarks that "'it didn't do no good to kill niggers 'cause things don't get no better'"; he is told by the first that "'he'd better shut his damn mouth.'" The second sharecropper is silenced. "But from the look on his face," the boy surmises, "he won't stay shut long." The story ends with the boy thinking, "It was my first party and my last. God, but that nigger was tough. That Bacote nigger was some nigger!" ("Party" 11).

Besides offering a forceful indictment of the brutality of lynching, the story contains an allegorical commentary on the costs of racist false consciousness to the white working class; its organizing premise is Marxist. The cyclone suggests the cataclysmic coming of fascism, which the whites, orgiastically involved in the ritual murder of the black, do not see approaching. The snake-like whipping power line—which, we are told, leads from the urban industrial center of Birmingham—provocatively signifies the destructive effect of forces of production fettered by capitalist social relations. The electrocution of the white woman—who is even dressed in white—reveals the high price paid by those who, implicated in "100% Americanism" and the lynch violence it entails, align themselves along the same side of the color line as their rulers, embodied here in the armed sheriff and his deputies who compel participation in, or at least acquiescence with, the grotesque public ceremony. But the closing remark by the restive sharecropper, coupled with the boy's statement that this is to be his first lynching and his last (the boy's descendant is perhaps the white youth who repudiates his racist father at the end of John Singleton's movie Rosewood), indicates that the days of the seamlessly unified "white" body politic of 100% Americanism are numbered. The burning—indeed, barbequing—of racial scapegoats will not allay the pangs experienced by whites who are "hungry as hell"; class antagonism, kept under wraps by the rituals of racism, may one day soon erupt.

"The Black Ball" is narrated in the first person by John, a young African American father who, while ambitious to return to college, is working as a janitor in an unnamed town in the Southwest. A single parent, he ponders how to introduce the realities of Jim Crow to his four-year-old son; when the child—who plays regularly with Jackie, the white son of a neighboring gardener—asks whether brown is better than white, he replies, "Some people think so. But American is better than both" (Ellison, "The Black Ball" 111). John is continually anxious that his son's vigorous playing with a white ball will disrupt the resident building manager and imperil John's job. Wary of whites, John is at first put off when a white unionist—whose "lean" face has "a redness [that] comes from a long diet of certain foods" ("The Black Ball" 111)—approaches him with an invitation to join a building-service workers' union: all unions, John declares, exclude black workers from membership. The white worker—who, it emerges, initially organized among "croppers," but now concentrates among urban proletarians—proclaims that his union is different. As proof of his sincerity, he displays his badly burned hands, injured, he says, in a fruitless attempt to prevent a black friend of his from being lynched in Macon County, Alabama.

As John reads Andre Malraux's *Man's Fate* during his lunch break and meditates upon the unionist's message, he sees a nursemaid shepherd her white charges away from Jackie, who disconsolately "drag[s] his toy, some kind of bird that flapped its wings like an eagle." Asked by his son what he is looking at, John replies, "I guess Daddy was just looking out on the world" ("The Black Ball" 118). When an older white boy seizes the white ball from John's son and throws it through the manager's window, the boss angrily warns John that he will find himself "behind the black ball" if the child shows his face again; queried by the child about why the boss thinks the white ball is black, John ruefully thinks, "My, yes, the old ball game," and tells his son that he himself will play with the black ball "in time" ("The Black Ball" 121). The story ends with John putting iodine on his hand, which he has cut cleaning up the broken glass: "[L]ooking down at the iodine stain, I thought of the fellow's fried hands, and felt in my pocket to make sure I still had the card he had given me. Maybe there was a color other than white on the old ball" ("The Black Ball" 122).

"The Black Ball" primarily seeks to address and overcome black workers' skepticism about multiracial unionism. But the tale's implied readership consists of anyone concerned with building black-white workers' unity and, moreover, familiar with the conventions of and debates within proletarian literature. For the white unionist's mention that he has moved from organizing sharecroppers to urban workers—as well as the fact that he now works in New

Mexico—associates him with the CPUSA, which expanded into urban organizing in the Southwest in the late 1930s. The reference to Macon County, Alabama, reinforces the text's allusion to Communist organizing, since it was here, in the heart of the deep South, that the CPUSA conducted its campaign to free the Scottsboro Boys and expose the brutal tyranny of Jim Crow. The white unionist's "fried hands" thus link the possibility for class-based multiracial unity to a specific Communist-led praxis against lynching.

Besides signaling its author's awareness of communist activity, "The Black Ball" refers to well-known works of contemporaneous left-wing literature. The white unionist with the scarred hands is a familiar type of mentor character from the conventions of proletarian fiction; in particular, like the character Hans of Jack Conroy's *The Disinherited* (1933), he is a class struggle veteran bearing the physical marks of the battles he has fought and seeking to raise the consciousness of a naïve younger man. Ellison's allusion to *Man's Fate*, moreover, shows that both John and his creator are conversant with the novel that had prompted heated debate in the letters column of the 1934 *New Masses* about the portrayal of revolutionary choice in works of proletarian literature (Chevalier 27–28; Hicks 28–30; Hirsch 43–44). Ellison's nod to Malraux thus signals not only John's cosmopolitanism and sophistication but also—in this tale about the need for workers to make the class-conscious choice to cross the color line—Ellison's own contribution to the debate occasioned by the book which his fictional character reads, and which he can assume many of his readers will have read as well.

Above all, the attitude toward U.S. nationalism conveyed in "The Black Ball" needs to be understood in the context of late-1930s CPUSA politics. That Ellison construes his protagonist's class-conscious choice as an affirmation of a progressive American nationalism is indicated by John's early remark that "American" is better than either "brown" or "white," as well as by the fact that, when the working-class Jackie is prevented from playing with wealthier children (the family makes enough money to hire a nursemaid), the toy he drags through the dust resembles a crippled eagle. Presumably both racism and elitism violate the principles for which the nation—ideally, at least—stands. Yet "The Black Ball" ends with an affirmation of the necessity for proletarian internationalist leadership in the fight to abolish the distinction between "brown" and "white" in the Jim-Crowed United States. The iodine that John puts upon his cut hand implies that the "old ball game" of racial division will end only when the U.S. working class is healed of its bleeding wounds by the red antibiotic of communism. The ball thus takes on larger meaning, suggesting not merely reform-level unity against the boss but the possibility of unifying the entire globe when it is held by red—or reddened—hands. The U.S. nationalism hesitantly expressed in "The Black Ball" is not the celebratory patriotism that would resonate in the final pages of *Invisible Man*, but the Popular Front patriotism that viewed communism as "twentieth-century Americanism." Ellison may have sneered at this stance in 1967, but some twenty-five to thirty years before he seems to have embraced it seriously.

We come now to the drafts of *Invisible Man*. Ellison began writing his novel in the summer of 1945 at the Vermont home of an interracial fellow-traveling couple who were his and Fanny Ellison's good friends. The novel, which would go through multiple drafts and drastic cutting, took him nearly seven years to complete. While the drafts are quite jumbled, and it will require painstaking textual reconstruction to track Ellison's changing intentions, a trajectory of what we might call "anticommunistization" is unmistakable. I shall trace here certain patterns appearing in the Harlem section of the novel, especially the chapters focusing upon the hero's experiences with the Brotherhood.

Ellison appears only gradually to have reduced his Communist characters, black and white, to the cartoonish exemplars of Stalinist authoritarianism appearing in the 1952 text. Cool and aloof in the published text, Brother Hambro, the invisible man's theoretical mentor, is originally named "Stein," has "three blue stars . . . tattooed on the back of his left hand," and exhibits considerable humility regarding the Brotherhood's attempt to gain a beachhead in Harlem. "We don't know too much about your people," he tells the protagonist. "We thought we did but we don't, even though some of us still think we do. What we have is a theory. . . . So instead of trying to tell you how or what to do I'll tell you to work it out in your own way." Lincolnesque in stature and bearing, the avuncular Stein/Hambro observes that "[t]o be part of a historical period, a people must be organized and able to make themselves felt as a force. To do this a group must find its voice. It must learn to say 'yea' or 'nay' to the crucial decisions of the times." Harlem's Negro population, the Brotherhood theoretician urges, must act rather than react, and prevent lynchings and riots before they happen, "swerv[ing] the developing forces away from the destructive event and transforming it into [a] socially useful one" ("Brotherhood," Folder 1, Box 142, EP). Where the Brotherhood in the 1952 text is shown abandoning Harlem in the hope that a riot will occur, in the earlier drafts its chief ideologist wishes Harlem's inhabitants to become conscious historical agents so that they may stave off disaster. That the sympathetically portrayed Hambro/Stein of the early drafts is demonstrably Jewish further suggests Ellison's intent to defend U.S. Communism from attacks that would portray it as a Jewish conspiracy (see Cruse).

In the drafts, other Brotherhood leaders lack the robotic traits attributed to them in the published version of the novel. As we work backwards, various puns and wordplays disappear. Brother Wrestrum ("restroom"), in one previous version designated as "Brother Thrilkild," is "Brother Elmo" in a still earlier version. That Ellison was quite aware of the political implications of his changing portrayal of Wrestrum/Thrilkild/Elmo is shown in his penciled comment, "a totalitarian type, eager to regiment all aspects of life"—a notation signaling a growing intention to caricature, as well as a Cold War-era awareness that there is indeed such a thing as a "totalitarian type." Brother Jack, demonic in the 1952 text, is considerably less repugnant in earlier incarnations. In the original version of the Cthonian party, there is no scene where Brother Jack asks the hero to become "the new Booker T. Washington" and proposes the mechanistic toast "To History." In the chapter about the arena rally, the statement that "Brother Jack spoke about economics and politics" is crossed out and changed to "Brother Jack spoke coldly." In the early version, too, there occurs no meeting in which the invisible man is chastised by the leadership for political incoherence and opportunism; instead, he and Brother Jack go out for a beer. When the protagonist later realizes that the Brotherhood has been losing its base of support in Harlem, he notes, in an early draft, "When I met Brother Jack he was as bland as ever, but now that I admitted to myself that I no longer liked him I told myself that I was being subjective." This formulation was changed to: "When I met Brother Jack he was as bland as ever, but now I admitted to myself that my old uneasiness had returned." As Ellison worked toward his final draft, apparently it was crucial that his hero should never acknowledge having felt positively at any point toward the Brotherhood leader ("Brotherhood," Folders 3,5,6; "Brotherhood-Arena Speech," Box 143, EP).

Ellison apparently added only late in his writing the climactic scene in which Brother Jack's eye pops out and he starts gabbling in a foreign tongue (presumably Russian), thereby signifying the hero's invisibility to the Russian-ruled reds. Notes accompanying the novel-in-progress further indicate that Ellison considered various options for the events leading up to what he called the "eye scene." Furthermore, although in all the drafts the warning note handed to the hero by Brother Tarp is said to be written in a handwriting that the hero "faintly recognize[s]," all do not contain the culminating episode in which the hero, having crawled down the manhole during the riot, finds in his briefcase the note enabling him to identify Brother Jack as his hidden enemy. Rather than having conceived in advance a narrative structure in which Norton, Bledsoe, Emerson, and Brother Jack possess homologous character structures, Ellison evidently discovered only after extensive rewriting that—as noted to himself in a marginal comment—the novel's "antagonists must all be connected, merged into every other antagonist. White against black" ("Brotherhood," Folders 2, Box 143). The seamless symbolic structure—and political rhetoric—of the 1952 text was the product of years of stitching and re-stitching.

Indeed, if we move from the portrayal of individual members of the Brotherhood to the more general representation of the organization's relation to Harlem's working class, the drafts of *Invisible Man* suggest that, at least when he first conceived the New York sections of the novel, Ellison wished to pay a degree of tribute to the CPUSA's work in bringing a class-conscious politics to Harlem. In an early draft, it is not the recognition that he is in debt to

Mary Rambo and needs money, but instead the impact of seeing a Brotherhood-sponsored march through Harlem after the eviction demonstration, that decides the hero to cast in his lot with the left:

> There were hundreds of them, marching six or eight abreast in a kind of wild discipline beneath a blaze of phosphorescent flares. . . . I now saw the whites, not old and at the head . . . but young, of all ages and mixed indiscriminately throughout the procession . . . .

Their chanted words were now becoming distinct:

> *No more dispossession of the dispossessed*
> *We Say,*
> *No more dispossession of the dispossessed!*

In the wake of the parade, a group of boys do a riff on the marchers' slogan:

> *"I dispossessed your mama 'bout half past nine,*
> *She said, 'Come back, daddy, any ole time.'*
> *I dispossessed your sister at a quarter to two,*
> *Said, 'If you stay 'til six, daddy, you will do.'*
> *I dispossessed your grandma at a quarter to one,*
> *She said, 'Daddy, daddy, daddy, thy will be done."*

> "Jesus Christ," I thought, looking at the strutting, nose thumbing boys. I haven't heard anything like that since I left home. They were playing the *dozens* in the same rhythm as the chant."

The message of the march, moreover, resonates with the invisible man's inherited beliefs and present mood. One of the speakers, a white man, "talked in economic terms . . . describ[ing] scenes of eviction and dispossession and men laid off from jobs, and the work of unions and the activities of strike-breakers and the attempts to set white workers against black workers." The rally concludes with the singing of "John Brown's Body," and the invisible man joins in, remembering that his grandfather "had often sung [the song] in a quavering voice when by himself." Curious and thrilled, the hero ascends the speaker's platform, is congratulated on having sparked the march by his speech earlier that day, and decides to take the job previously offered by Brother Jack ("Brotherhood," Folder 2, Box 143, EP).

Ellison's decision to omit the parade scene from the 1952 novel is critical. Where in the published text the arid theorizing of the Brotherhood is shown to be out of touch with the pulse of Harlem, here black youth take up the rhythms of the left, just as the Communists couple new, radical lyrics with the songs of the black church. The parade testifies to the multiracial mix of people brought together under the banner of Brotherhood, with whites of all ages blending through the crowd. Moreover, the speech underlines the politics of class-conscious multiracial unity. By contrast, the closest Ellison gets to voicing the discourse of the Depression-era CPUSA in *Invisible Man* is in the arena speech, where the hero speaks against "dispossession" and in praise of the "uncommon people" (334–38). The words "white worker" and "black worker," however, never appear. The hero's resistance to the unfamiliar scene dissolves, finally, when he hears whites and blacks join in singing "John Brown's Body," a favorite song, he muses, of his skeptical, subversive grandfather—who, in the epilogue to the 1952 novel, is quoted not as a proponent of the tradition of Brown, but rather as a believer in the message of the Founding Fathers (560–61).

Another omitted episode depicts the hero overhearing a conversation in a tenement called "The Jungle," where the Brotherhood has been attempting to organize a rent strike. One man comments upon his having become friends with a white Brotherhood couple, noting that "these here fays dont act like ofays, they act like people!" While he was first skeptical of the white man's offer of friendship, the Harlemite now concludes, "This is something much bigger than I thought. I'm in it for good now. They invite me to they house, I invite them to mine; they serve me saurkraut and winnies [sic]. I serve em red rice and beans, and we building the movement together" ("Brotherhood-Fired Tenement," Box 143, EP). The red-inspired multiracial unity that the invisible man glimpsed at the parade to Mount Morris Park is apparently being built on the interpersonal level as well.

Indeed, the invisible man's entire experience as a Brotherhood organizer, viewed retrospectively as sheer hoodwinking and manipulation in the 1952 text, is depicted quite nostalgically in the drafts. In the published text, Ellison restricts his account of the hero's Brotherhood organizing to a description of the "Rainbow of America's Future" poster campaign and a brief account of a parade of "fifteen thousand Harlemites . . . down Broadway to City Hall," in which he features the "People's Hot Foot Squad," complete with "the best-looking girls we could find, who pranced and twirled and just plain girled in the enthusiastic interest of Brotherhood" (*Invisible Man* 371). In what appears to be the earliest draft of this material, the protagonist omits the Hot Foot Squad and offers a fuller description of the demonstrations he helped to organize:

> At the time we were stepping up the fight against evictions and unemployment and it was my job to work closely with other community leaders. Oh in those days I worked. Speaking, studying, throwing the old ideology around; marching, picketing. It was nothing to pull five thousand men and women into the streets on short notice; or to lead them to mass with groups from other sections for a march straight down Broadway or Fifth, or even Park, to City Hall. We must have worn an inch or two off the surface of the streets. Just give me the hungry and dispossessed and I could make them forget black and white and rush a squad of police, or throw an iron picket line around City Hall or the Mayor's Mansion. ("Brotherhood," Folder 3, Box 143, EP)

Where the Brotherhood in the 1952 text is shown to engage in only one march upon City Hall, in the earlier draft it does so routinely. Where in the published novel the Brotherhood exploits the nubile bodies of young black women to further its cause, in the draft the Harlem masses respond favorably to the Brotherhood for what seem to be more principled reasons. Even though the retrospective narrator speaks somewhat caustically of "throwing the old ideology around," he looks back on his earlier activism with some fondness.

In this early draft, moreover, the protagonist speaks of the Brotherhood sections outside of Harlem with affection and respect:

> They were like no other people I had ever known. I liked . . . their selfless acceptance of human equality, and their willingness to get their heads beaten to bring it a fraction of a step closer. They were willing to go all the way. Even their wages went into the movement. And most of all I liked their willingness to call things by their true names. Oh, I was trully [sic] carried away. For a while I was putting most of my salary back into the work. I worked days and nights and was seldom tired. It was as though we were all engaged in a mass dance in which the faster we went the less our fatigue. For Brotherhood was vital and we were revitalized.

Ellison later penciled in a number of telling revisions. "Most of my evenings" was changed to "[m]any of my evenings." "They were willing to go all the way" became "[t]hey seemed willing to go all the way." "[T]heir wages went into the movement" became "a good part of their wages went into the movement." The narrator adds to the statement that he contributed "most of my own salary" the comment that "[m]oney was not so necessary, when we found so much in our group" ("Brotherhood," Folder 3, Box 143, EP). Such alterations suggest Ellison's growing desire to ironize the protagonist's naïve faith in his comrades, downplay the extent of their shared commitment, and suggest that the Brotherhood has clandestine ties with the wealthy class it purports to wish to overthrow. It would appear that Ellison came to view even these qualifications as implying too positive a portrayal of the Brotherhood, however, for the entire passage was eventually cut from the novel.

Furthermore, the early drafts do not accuse the Brotherhood of sacrificing Harlem on the altar of Soviet expediency in the period following the collapse of the 1939 Nonaggression Pact and the Nazi invasion of the USSR. In the published novel, the invisible man learns that the Brotherhood has lost its base in Harlem as "a result of a new program which had called for the shelving of our old techniques of agitation" and "a switch in emphasis from local issues to those more national and international in scope," in which "it was felt that for the moment the interests of Harlem were not of first importance" (*Invisible Man* 418). We will recall that Ellison would later make the implied charge here explicit when he observed that "[t]he Communists recognized no plurality of interests and were really responding to the necessities of Soviet foreign policy, and when the war came, Negroes got caught and were made expedient in the shifting of policy."

In the drafts, however, the reasons given for the Brotherhood's diminished influence in Harlem are a good deal more complex. In a handwritten version appearing to be the earliest account, the hero observes that he lost some influence with "the committee" early on by mistakenly carrying out a campaign to free a young Negro writer who had been imprisoned for murder—but who, when freed (largely as a result of the hero's efforts), commits another murder. (This incident would seem to have been based on Richard Wright's experience in securing the freedom of one Clinton Brewer; see Fabre, *The Unfinished Quest of Richard Wright*, 236–37). Thus when the hero tries to caution the Brotherhood of the riot brewing in Harlem, they reject his warnings not because their abstract theory cannot admit the possibility of contingency and chaos, but, in large part, because the invisible man has damaged his own credibility. More strategic reasons are cited as well:

> We found that with the slight rise in the nation's economy our issues were being won too quickly. . . . And it was at this point that the opposition went into action [and] picked Harlem for the showdown and we were given a shock. . . . First membership began falling off, but we were unaware because for some reason the Harlem committee falsified their reports, making it appear that things were going smoothly, or were at least stable. But History forced the truth. I learned that a deal had been made with a congressman back during the time of my first speech and now when with election time drawing near and we would have to throw our support behind him [sic], the people were not responding.

The criticism lodged here focuses primarily on the perils of reformism: the party pays the price for its involvement in electoral politics. But it appears that what precipitates the crisis in the Brotherhood's relation to Harlem is the attack from the "opposition," who "picked Harlem for the showdown," rather than any pattern of manipulation and betrayal on the part of "the committee." Although opportunism is evident in the Harlem leaders' handing in "falsified . . . reports," there is no clear suggestion that the organization has abandoned the fight against racism ("Brotherhood," Folders 2 and 5, Box 143, EP).

Among the most important revisions of the Brotherhood materials in the early drafts of *Invisible Man* is Ellison's decision to efface a young white woman named Louise. In the 1952 text, the hero's interactions with white women in the movement are confined to his flirtation with Emma, mistress to Brother Jack, and his abortive relationship with Sibyl, who lusts to be taken in violence by a black man. In the published text, the woman who was once Louise remains only as the nameless young woman who, in the eviction scene, tells the hero that "you certainly moved them to action." She disappears from the novel, however, after he last glimpses "her white face in the dim light of the darkened doorway" (*Invisible Man* 277–278). In the drafts, however, the young woman plays a significant role. Encountering her at the Cthonian on the evening of the eviction and the parade, the invisible man is taken with her beauty and flirts with her openly, testing the limits of her antiracism. While initially skeptical about her motives for belonging to the Brotherhood, he is attracted by her honesty and openness. Her father is a wealthy businessman, she tells him; she hopes through her Brotherhood activity to undo some of the damage her source of wealth has done. Furthermore, the hero is shown to be fully aware of his own mixed and conflicting motives in wishing to make a romantic conquest of such a markedly "white" woman. The following passage is marginally marked "hubris" in one version and "omit" in another:

> And I knew at that moment that it was not her color, but the voice and if there was anything in the organization to which I could give myself completely, it was she. If I could work with her, be always near her, then I could have all that the Trustees had promised and failed to give and more. And if she was not the meaning of the struggle for the others, for me she would be the supremest prize of all. "Oh you fair warrior," my mind raced on, "You dear, sweet, lovely thing, for you I'd rock the nation with a word. You'll be my Liberty and Democracy, Hope and Truth and Beauty, the justification for manhood, the motive for courage and cunning; for you I'll make myself into this new name they've given me and I'll believe that Brother Jack and the others mean what they say about creating a world in which even men like me can be free . . . ["]
> I took a drink and for an instant I remembered the Vet laughing in the bus as it shot away from the campus. . . . So I would *play* the fool, and if it was my being black that made me desire the white meat of the chicken, then I'd accept my desire along with the chitterlings and sweet potato pie.

Louise's subsequent appearances in the draft text are fragmentary. There is a rather bizarre two-page imitation of the style of *Finnegan's Wake*, in which an unspecified voice riffs on "Sweet Georgia Brown" as he meditates on the whiteness of Louise. There is also is a handwritten paragraph describing the invisible man's forcing Louise to sit under a sunlamp so that she will be less visibly white when they go out. But Louise is referred to several times as the invisible man's love interest: when he follows the parade, he searches for Louise in the crowd, and later it is his pursuit of Louise to the "Jungle" that results in his overhearing the conversation about the hip red "ofays." On the day when he has his grand confrontation with "the committee," the protagonist remarks that he had originally wished to spend the day with Louise; when he cuts his ties with the Brotherhood, his greatest regret is losing her. She was evidently a figure of central importance in Ellison's first conception of the novel's Harlem section ("Brotherhood-Louise," Box 143, EP).

Ellison seems to have removed Louise from the novel only by degrees. In various later drafts she appears as the wife of Tod Clifton. In the 1952 text, Clifton is an exemplar of martyrdom, betrayed by the Brotherhood and then murdered by the Nazi-like New York police; while attractive to all the young women in the Brotherhood, he is single and uninvolved. In at least two of the drafts, however, Clifton's mourning the collapse of his marriage with a young white woman is a crucial facet of his role. In the earlier draft, it is Clifton who reports having put his wife under a sunlamp to minimize her whiteness; moreover, he voices uneasiness at having felt they were in a showcase marriage, "symbolic of this and symbolic of that." Penciled-in editorial changes show Clifton later stating to the invisible man his suspicion that Louise may have married him "under orders" from "the committee"; the hero demurs, thinking, "He hates himself. . . . He doesn't believe that she—any white girl—could love him simply because she is white." In the later draft, Clifton openly charges the Brotherhood with having used Louise as "nigger bait." "I didn't know whether we were together for love or for discipline," he says. "We were like that couple in a sign advertising one of those jungle movies; she was the blonde and I was the gorilla" ("Brotherhood," Folders 1 and 4, Box 143, EP). While Clifton's final bitter comment unambiguously affirms the anti-Communist charge that the CPUSA used white women to attract African American men to the movement, the evolution of Clifton's wife from her earlier incarnation as Louise shows that Ellison originally had in mind a much more nuanced—and sympathetic—depiction of the possible appeal of a white woman to a black man in the radical movement. Ellison's eventual elimination of the Louise character entirely from the text suggests, however, his desire to avoid anything resembling a three-dimensional portrayal of interracial sexuality. Emma and Sibyl, familiar figures from the discourse of anticommunism, were easier to handle.

For all the bitter anticommunism Ellison poured into this last conversation between Clifton and the invisible man, apparently he was not yet ready to accuse the Brotherhood of driving Clifton to his death. For none of the drafts contains a description of Clifton's murder by a policeman in midtown Manhattan. In one version, the hero sees Clifton performing the grotesque dance with his Sambo-doll only in a nightmare, not in reality. In another—apparently earlier—draft, the man whom the hero encounters handling the dancing Sambo dolls is not Clifton but "one of the younger brothers," who chants,

> What makes him happy?
> What makes him wantta dance? heh?
> This Sambo, the joy boy?
> He's more than a toy, he's Sambo the dancing doll.
> He lives in the sun shine [sic] of your smile, thats [sic] his secret [.]
> Ladies and Gentlemen, only 25 cents, because he likes to eat!
> Shake it Sambo, Shake it and take it . . . Thank you.

That a young Negro comrade should engage in such grotesque self-caricature obviously raises important questions about his relationship to the Brotherhood.

But it remains unresolved here whether we are witnessing an allegory of internalized racism or one of leftist oppression. Moreover, the young man is not murdered by a policeman, so the cost of his falling out of history is not so high ("Brotherhood," Folder 4, Box 143, EP). In the 1952 text, by contrast, Clifton's chant contains unambiguous allusions to the Brotherhood as the source of his humiliation. The doll will *"kill your depression / And your dispossession"*; it begs for a *"brotherly two bits of a dollar"* (*Invisible Man*). That the Brotherhood's betrayal of Harlem would propel Clifton into this desperate self-parody, and hence into murder at the hands of New York's finest, was clearly not in Ellison's mind when he first imagined the scene with the dancing dolls.

As is suggested in the parade and tenement episodes, early drafts of *Invisible Man* represent the Brotherhood as both relevant to and welcome in Harlem. The openness of Negro migrants to red politics is further explored in the draft portions of the novel set in Mary Rambo's boardinghouse. In the 1952 text, the Harlem characters who stick most in the mind are those who are the least proletarianized. The street peddler Peter Wheatstraw, master of verbal wizardry, recalls such legendary folk trickster characters as Brer Rabbit and Sweet-the-Monkey. Mary Rambo is perhaps most memorable for owning the grotesquely racist cash-bank that the invisible man cannot get rid of and for stating that she is not a New Yorker. The early drafts of *Invisible Man* reveal, however, that Ellison originally had in mind a more politically and sociologically variegated portrayal of Harlem's working-class population. Mary Rambo is worker at Harlem Hospital who takes the invisible man in after he was injured in a brawl with a white racist. Moreover, hardly a folkish isolate, she runs a boardinghouse where, among other things, the Brotherhood is the topic of everyday dinner conversation. The widowed Mrs. Garfield—whose husband "worked with his hands and believed in unions and strikes and things"—comments that "[our people] are acting really radical," since "every evening or so when its [sic] not too cold you can see a group of both colored and white holding meetings." Mr. Portwood, who admires the Brotherhood because "they got some colored big-shots right along with the whites [sic] ones," opines that perhaps the invisible man "ought to join up with them. Or maybe be a union leader so our folks can get some of the good jobs" ("At Mary's," Box 142, EP).

Above all, it is the hovering shadow of Leroy, the former inhabitant of the invisible man's room, that dramatically shapes Ellison's original representation of the philosophy and politics embraced by Harlem's migrants. A young college student who left the South at the age of fifteen after "escap[ing] from a mob," Leroy lived at Mary's for three years and then, to earn tuition money, went to sea, where he became best friends with a white sailor (also a native of the South) by the name of Treadwell. Visiting the boardinghouse with the news that Leroy has just drowned, Treadwell opines that because Leroy was a union militant, he "might have been pushed off the ship." In early versions of the novel, the invisible man's sense of identification with this touchstone character—he even wears some of Leroy's clothes—was to serve as an index to his expanding consciousness: as Ellison commented in a marginal notation, "IVM must sum up LeRoy in his own mind at different stages of his own development" ("At Mary's," Folders 1 and 2, Box 142, EP).

In several of his meditations on the status of African Americans, Leroy manifests a markedly radical tendency:

> [W]ould it be that we are the true inheritors of the West, the rightful heirs of its humanist tradition—especially since it has flourished through our own dehumanization, debasement, through our being ruled out of bounds; since we have been brutalized and forced to live inhuman lives so that they could become what they consider "more human"? Doesn't the pattern of our experience insist that we seek a way of life more universal, more human and more free than any to be found in the world today? . . . .
>
> To be redeemed my life demands something far larger, broader: A change in the rules by which men live. For now for me to be more human is to be less like those who degrade me. Is to be more appreciative and respectful of those who differ from me in both my thoughts and my actions. I wish to be, in my thinking, neither black nor white, and in my acting, neither exploited [nor] [exploiter]. And yet I'm willing to accept the human responsibility of soiling my hands with the blood of those who spill my blood whether wearing a hood and using a gun or sending out the orders in a telegram. ("Brotherhood," Folder 2, Box 143, EP).

The thoughtful tone of Leroy's journal anticipates the epilogue to the 1952 text; when Ellison eliminated Leroy from his novel, he transferred to his narrator some of his character's concern with what it means for African Americans to be the "true inheritors of the West, the rightful bearers of the humanist tradition." But Leroy's remarks are inflected by a number of Marxist assumptions wholly alien to his successor. African Americans are the group possessing the greatest capacity to understand social reality because they have been most oppressed by and alienated from it: Leroy's thinking closely parallels Engels's formulation of the dialectical relation of knowledge to class in the *Anti-Duhring* (Engels 104). Moreover, in postulating that his "we" are objectively positioned to bring into being a "pattern of life" that will be "more universal, more human, and more free," what Leroy describes in all but words is the classless society of the "Internationale," where the revolutionary proletariat will abolish class and become "the human race." "The change in the rules by which men live" apparently entails the abolition of both race ("I wish to be, in my thinking, neither black nor white") and of class ("and in my acting, neither exploited nor exploiter"). The process by which this "change in the rules" will be achieved will be, of necessity, violent, leading Leroy to "accept the human responsibility of soiling my hands with the blood of those who spill my blood." That he announces his willingness to act violently against both those who are "wearing a hood and using a gun" and those who are "sending out the orders in a telegram" evinces his awareness of the class purposes served by the likes of the KKK, who function as shock troops for elites using racism as a means of social control. Leroy might as well be a card-carrying member not just of the Maritime Workers Union—to which Ellison himself belonged for several years—but of the CPUSA.

Indeed, Leroy's comments on Frederick Douglass show him to the left of contemporaneous Communist doctrine:

> Frederick Douglass, a typical 19th century idealist. Made the mistake of throwing his best energies into speeches. Had he spent his time in organizing a revolt he would have been a far more important man today; he would have fathered a tradition of militant action around which men could rally today. What method? Why guerrilla warfare, the tactic and strategy of John Brown, a man more reasonable in his so-called madness than Douglass dared allow himself to admit. . . . ("Leroy's Journal," Box 145, EP)

Always a CPUSA hero, Douglass occupied an especially important position in the red pantheon during the war years. For during the Civil War Douglass had urged fugitive slaves and freedmen to join the Union Army, even under the prevailing conditions of intense racial discrimination, in order to defeat the greater enemy that was the slave power. Eager to find historical precedent for their call upon African Americans to postpone all-out antiracist struggle until after the defeat of fascism—including acceptance of a Jim Crow army—the CPUSA explicitly analogized Douglass's stance with its own some eighty years later. Leroy, however, expresses skepticism about Douglass and prefers the legacy of John Brown, contrasting the former's reliance upon rhetoric with the latter's "tradition of militant action."

Mary Rambo's departed lodger also serves to draw out the radical potentialities in others. Noting that Leroy disturbed a number of his deep-seated prejudices, Treadwell describes how their friendship gave him insight into the role racism had played in externalizing and deflecting his own antipathy to the different sorts of authority by which he—and, by extension, all Southern white male workers—was being controlled:

> [W]e're trained to hate you, to suppress and repress you. It is our major discipline [sic], our equivalent of a state church, or a recognized military cult, or the entering the service of the king. And so thorough is the dicipline [sic] that everything else that we're trained to suppress becomes mixed up with it—hate for the father, mother, brother; sexual impulses, unclean thoughts—everything becomes mixed up with the idea of suppressing you. So that its [sic] hard to change anything deeply within us without images of you rushing into our minds. ("At Mary's," Folder 2, Box 142, EP)

Thanks to Leroy, Treadwell has come to realize the extent to which white supremacy functions ideologically to bind white workers to their own oppression. Along the lines advocated in Ellison's Myrdal essay, Freud is recruited into an alliance with Marx.

One conversation with Leroy particularly sticks in Treadwell's mind. Describing a group of U.S. white college students disembarking at Le Havre from Treadwell and Leroy's ship, Leroy remarked that the students were "some of the most fortunate and unfortunate people in the world" because, as "unconscious vessels of our whole way of life," they would assume that they were going to visit "an inferior people" and miss the cultural riches before them. By contrast, Leroy opined, there were "only two really and deeply human groups in the whole country," namely "yours and mine. We fight each other and hate each other and fear [one] another. And yet our hope lies in the fact that we do. We're the only two groups that aren't ashamed to admit that we're the most miserable bastards in the world. And that all the money and power in the world is no cure for it" ("Leroy's Journal," Box 145, EP). Here Leroy examines the differential effects of ideology on different sectors of the population. Interpellating the youth of the U.S. elite—"unconscious vessels of our whole way of life"—as superior to the people of all other lands and times, the gospel of American supremacy deprives them—"some of the most fortunate . . . people in the world"—of their full humanity, making them "some of the most . . . unfortunate" as well. Paradoxically, it is the black and white members of the working class—pitted against one another in violence and fear, "the most miserable bastards in the world"—who, by virtue of their having no stake in the survival of the system, have the capacity to "feel love or even real joy." To be "really and deeply human" results from the experience of oppression, which positions its victims to understand that "money and power" are what violate their humanity in the first place. This is a distinctly Marxist formulation of epistemic privilege.

When Ellison decided to banish the inhabitants of Mary Rambo's boardinghouse from the pages of Invisible Man, he was omitting the text's most concrete demonstration of the openness of the black working class to a politics of class-conscious multiracial unity. Especially by effacing all traces of Leroy, he was denying that many key components of those politics were already embraced by Harlem's most advanced denizens. One cannot help wondering what the novel would have looked like if the invisible man of the 1952 text had kept the radical Leroy as a benchmark in "the different stages in his own development."

Until the Ellison archive becomes widely available to scholars, we can only speculate about the full reasons for Ellison's decision to abandon his leftist affiliations and concerns. What a perusal of his early oeuvre reveals, however, is that the young writer was moved to portray revolutionary politics as the route by which working-class people, both white and African American, might become "more fully and deeply human." The dramatic contrast between the radical young Ellison and the canonized Cold Warrior suggests, to me, two conclusions—one negative and one positive—relevant to the project of building a "whole left" capable of meeting the challenges of the present.

First, it is not the heritage of twentieth-century communism, but instead that of *anti*communism, which has delinked the critique of capitalism from an understanding of other modes of oppression (or, to limit this claim to my discussion here, at least from an understanding of U.S. racism). Although since the demise of the USSR the "red menace" no longer holds the same power to terrify, it is crucial that we be aware of the extent to which anticommunism has gone into the cultural groundwater and reemerged as the abiding distrust of totality and master discourses, especially those focusing on class analysis. Understanding that Ellison only by degrees came to the demonization of Brother Jack, correlating the Brotherhood leader's glass eye with the denial of the protagonist's individuality by Bledsoe, Norton, and Emerson, deconstructs the signifying chain that otherwise automatically leads us to assume that communist rationalism is merely one more means to domination. If we grasp the extent to which the reduction of Marxism to cold scientism has persisted into the present-day suspicion of master discourses of all kinds, as well as the consequent valorization of dispersal and heterogeneity as cardinal organizing principles, we may be freer to think beyond the limits imposed by coalition politics and its various rationales.

My second conclusion is a positive extension of the first. If what the young Ellison's writings reveal about U.S. communism in the 1930s and 1940s possesses validity, those committed to the development of a "whole left" in the new century should perhaps not only adopt a cautionary attitude toward anticommunism but also reconsider whether communism might not remain a desirable goal. To propose such an end is not to deny that, during the course of the past century, the left went far off the path toward the construction of societies based upon principles of egalitarianism: I may not share the analysis of Communist perfidy guiding Ellison's final portrait of the Brotherhood, but this does not mean that I do not acknowledge profound errors and tragic losses. Nonetheless I find myself strangely energized, many decades later, by his depiction of the lantern-lit faces of the demonstrators in frosty Mount Morris Park, as well as by the signifying dozens played by Harlem's youth upon the slogan, "No more dispossession of the dispossessed." The critique of exploitation remains indispensable, indeed (dare I say it) central to any program that would aspire to liberate humanity from inequality; the movement that generated those faces and those words is part of a red line in history that we abandon at our peril. Part of our progress toward a better world should therefore entail a thorough-going critique of the strategies and programs that took our predecessors off course. This should not be a critique designed to delegitimate the goal itself—such as appears in Ellison's 1952 text—but instead one committed to analyzing why it has not yet been achieved, so that perhaps in years to come we may bring into existence a world where people can be "more fully and deeply human."

WORKS CITED

Banks, Ann, ed. *First-Person America*. New York: Knopf, 1980.

Berry, Abner. "Ralph Ellison's Novel *Invisible Man* Showa Snobbery, Contempt for Negro People." *Daily Worker* 1 June 1952, sec 2:7.

Breit, Harvey. "A Talk with Ralph Ellison." *New York Times Book Review* 4 May 1952: 26–27.

Brown, Lloyd L. "The Deep Pit." *Masses and Mainstream* June 1952: 62–64.

Chevalier, Haakon. Letter. *New Masses* 4 Sept. 1934: 27–28.

Cruse, Harold. *The Crisis of the Negro Intellectual*. New York: William Morrow, 1967.

Ellison, Ralph. "Anti-Semitism Among Negroes." *Jewish People's Voice* Apr. 1939: 3+.

———. "Big White Fog." *New Masses* 12 Nov. 1940: 22–23.

———. "The Birthmark." *New Masses* 2 July 1940: 16–17.

———. "A Congress Jim Crow Didn't Attend." *New Masses* 14 May 1940: 5–8.

———. *Flying Home and Other Stories*. Ed. John F. Callahan. New York: Random House, 1996.

———. *Going to the Territory*. New York: Random House, 1986.

———. "The Great Migration." *New Masses* 2 December 1941: 23–24.

———. "The Insurrection of 1741." Reel #2. *Federal Writers Project: The Negro in New York*. New York: Schomburg Library.

———. *Invisible Man*. 1952. New York: Random House, 1982.

———. Papers. Library of Congree. Washington, D.C.

———. *Shadow and Act*. New York: Random House, 1964.

———. "Slick Gonna Learn." *Direction* Sept. 1939: 10+.

———. "The Way It Is." *New Masses* 20 Oct. 1942: 9–11.

———. "Woodson's *The Beginning of Miscegenation of the Whites and Blacks*." Reel #3. *Federal Writers Project: The Negro in New York City*. New York: Schomburg Library.

Engels, Frederick. *Herr Duhring's Revolution in Science: Anti-Duhring*. Trans. Emile Burns. New York: International, 1939.

Fabre, Michel. "In Ralph Ellison's Precious Words." Unpublished Manuscript. 1996.

———. *The Unfinished Quest of Richard Wright*. 2nd ed. Trans. Isabel Barzun. Urbana: U of Illinois P, 1993.

Foley, Barbara. "From Communism to Brotherhood: The Drafts of Invisible Man." In *Left of the Color Line: Race, Radicalism, and Twentieth-Century Literature of the United States*. Ed. Bill V. Mullen and James Smethurst. Chapel Hill: U of North Carolina P, 2003. 163–82.

———. "Ralph Ellison as Proletarian Journalist." *Science and Society* 62 (1998–1999): 527–36.

———. "Reading Redness: Politics and Audience in Ralph Ellison's Early Short Fiction." *JNT: Journal of Narrative Theory* 29 (1999): 323–39.

————. "Reading Redness Redux: Ralph Ellison, Intertextuality, and Biographical Criticism." *JNT: Journal of Narrative Theory* (Summer 2004), forthcoming.

————. "The Rhetoric of Anticommunism in Ralph Ellison's Invisible Man." *College English* Sept. 1997: 530–47.

Geller, Andrew. "An Interview with Ralph Ellison." *Tamarack Review* (Summer 1964): 3–24.

Hazard, Eloise Perry. "The Author." *Saturday Review of Literature* 12 April 1952: 22.

Hicks, Granville. Letter. *New Masses* 4 Sept. 1934: 28–30.

Hirsh, Alfred. "The Sympathies of Malraux." *New Masses* 3 July 1934: 43–44.

Jackson, Lawrence. *Ralph Ellison: Emergence of Genius*. New York: John Wiley, 2002.

Ottley, Leroy, and William Weatherby, eds. *The Negro in New York: An Informal Social History*. New York: New York Public Library, 1967.

CHAPTER THREE

TOWARD A POLITICAL ECONOMY OF RHETORIC
(OR A RHETORIC OF POLITICAL ECONOMY)

VICTOR VILLANUEVA

It was the damnedest thing. I was talking with someone from Puerto Rico, the kind of chit chat she and I tend to get into—a kind of heralding back to identity.

In some sense, my identity has always been a question. Not a question unique to me, I understand, since someone sometime came up with Nuyorican to define an identity not Puerto Rican yet Puerto Rican, not Black yet Black, not White yet White. I was talking about how I had gotten to the Pacific Northwest originally— NY ghetto to LA ghetto to the Army, eventually to Ft. Lewis in Tacoma—and the decision to stay in the Northwest (which turned out to be stay, leave, and return).

She says, "Yeah, the life of exile."

And in that moment I had to rethink my whole ideological and economic being, the political economy of this body, this person. I had been constructed as and had accepted the construct of a person of color long ago. I had thought about and recognized the tie between color and colonialism some time ago. But it hadn't occurred to me that part of my estrangement from the Island was the result of a sociocultural and economic banishment—exile.

RHETORIC. POLITICAL ECONOMY. TWO TERMS WITH PRETTY MUCH A SINGLE CLAIM. Rhetoric's claim is to be the art of persuasion, or the finding for any given case the available means of persuasion, to paraphrase Aristotle. With Kenneth Burke, anything that is symbolic (or a sign system, in more European continental terms) and not coercive falls under rhetoric—a symbolic means of inducing cooperation among symbol-using, symbol-misusing creatures (to blend two Burkean definitions). Those symbols are language—the language of the alphabetic sign system, the language of musical and visual arts, the language of mathematics. If we communicate it, it is rhetorical.

Political economy "is concerned with the relationships of the economic system and its institutions to the rest of society and social development. It is sensitive to the influence of non-economic factors such as political and social institutions, morality, and ideology in determining economic events" (Ridell, Schakford, and Stamos, qtd. in Sackrey and Schneider, vi). In other words, it is concerned with the whole configuration of power and the economy. When that power is not coercive, then political economy is concerned with the rhetorical and the economic. Both terms—rhetoric and political economy—are architechtonic, are overdetermined.

Let me put it this way. The role of rhetoric, according to Burke, is the demystification of the ideological. The role of political economy is the demystification of relations tied to the economic. If we're to understand where we are and what is happening to us—and maybe even to affect it—we need the tools provided by both. But we think of "economics" as a numbers game. And we humanities types tend to fear numbers.

But we might fear a little less if we come to regard economics as yet another instance of the rhetorical. At least one economist has made that assertion, and there's a group of economists who believe she's right. That economist is Deirdre McCloskey. She writes that "[most intellectuals] since about 1880—have not read enough economics. They imagine," she goes on to say, "that a smattering of Marx will do. The English professor who has neglected Adam Smith and John Stuart Mill, not to speak of Freidman, Galbraith, Samuelson, Hirschman, Heilbroner, Schelling, Coase, Becker, Fogel, Olson, Buchanan, Kirzner, or the other modern masters is missing a lot. He is missing, for example, the logic of unintended consequences. And he is missing the facts of modern economic growth" (*Knowledge and Persuasion* xi). That's quite a sanction. And it's something of an embarrassment, insofar this economist—Deirdre McCloskey—is writing for an ontology of economics as a rhetoric. The "rhetoric of economics," the title of two of her books and a theme implicit in three others, has been around since the early 1980s. We might argue with her notion of rhetoric or with her ideological leanings, but we would see the connections between the two. Yet those of us who claim rhetoric as our business seem wholly unaware that there is a discussion about our work and economics.

Why is that? I think the answer lies in the history of the resurgence of rhetoric among English professors. Susan Miller and other historians of composition studies (e.g., Berlin) tell us that in the American colleges, composition and rhetoric fell to educational trends established at Harvard and Yale. At Harvard, that influence was particularly wielded by the holders of the Boylston Professorship of Rhetoric, like John Quincy Adams (1805–1809). Francis James Child, during his twenty-five year tenure as the Boylston chair (1851–1876), shifted the focus of his studies from rhetoric to philology, the precursor to modern linguistics, and then to literature. In time, he had his title changed from Professor of Rhetoric to Professor of English. And in time he relinquished his authority over rhetoric. Just prior to his retirement in 1874, Child established Freshman English and designated that it be taught by his teaching assistant (Berlin). Rhetoric became confined to composition, regarded as a lesser function. Rhetoric's scope had been narrowed. Rather than rise to the level of the architectonic, rhetoric had become confined to learning to write about literature. Yale's curriculum on "liberal culture" insisted on the best of belles lettres, literature, for its students, the brightest and the wealthiest. The teaching of writing meant writing about literature (Berlin). Composition in the U.S., then, grew as a subset of literature (Miller).

But with its growth and independence from literature (which resulted from two international conferences in the 1960s) its link to cognitive psychology, and its independent empirical research, composition came to associate itself with rhetoric creating its own history (in much the same way English literature had done a century earlier). There were precedents. Kenneth Burke's brand of literary criticism was tied to rhetoric and had gained popularity at about the same time that composition was becoming a field of study. In 1866, Alexander Bain had written a manual explicitly linking rhetoric to composition, *English Composition and Rhetoric*. And in some sense, the theory of rhetoric had always been tied to writing—from Plato's injunctions against writing in the *Phaedrus*, to Aristotle's discussions on style, to Cicero's claiming never to have passed a day without having written. According to classicist George Kennedy, rhetoric was always tied to *letteraturizazione*—the move from oral discourse to written (xx).

In other words, contemporary composition was an offshoot of literature and so was the U.S. return to rhetoric, by way of composition as well as by way of literary criticism, most notably through Kenneth Burke. The upshot of this has been that rhetoric as discussed in English departments has remained tied to the literary studies rather than to a fuller understanding of rhetorical studies. The rhetoricians we study most are by and large those who literary critics study, with the notable relatively recent exception of the sophists. To the degree that we study political economy at all, it's through those critical theorists who also touch on the economic, critics like Raymond Williams, Terry Eagleton, Lukacs, Benjamin, and others. And there is a political economy to pedagogical theorists we turn to, like Freire or Giroux. But our discussions by and large avoid economy, or at least tend not to confront it.

A case in point: our discussions on racism. We know there's a connection between racism and the relation between power and money. It's in our theory and in the texts we find representative of racism. But being engaged with rhetorical political economists of the past could help us rethink the present. As I've mentioned elsewhere ("Reading Rhetoric"), there's a discussion to be had with W. E. B. DuBois's notions of the birth of U.S. racism against African Americans. In *Black Reconstruction*, DuBois points to an economic cause of nineteenth-century slavery, a matter of liberal economics in that the Southerner had to compete with an industrializing Europe and Northern U.S. DuBois writes, for instance, that

> slavery was the *economic lag* of the 16th century carried over into the 19th century and bringing by contrast and by friction *moral lapses and political difficulties*. It has been estimated that the Southern states had in 1860 three billion dollars invested in slaves, which meant that slaves and land represented the mass of their capital. *Being generally convinced* that Negroes could only labor as slaves, *it was easy for them to become further persuaded* that slaves were better off than white workers and that the South had a better labor system than the North, with extraordinary possibilities in industrial and social development. (37; italics added)

The italics point to how DuBois relates an economy that gives rise to a politic which is represented rhetorically—being convinced, as matters of persuasion. DuBois later goes on to say that as poor white workers became disgruntled, the legislature and the press began a campaign to describe the African American as subhuman (thanks to the new science of naturalism—an offshoot of the also new zoology—and its discussions of evolution). Political exigence arising from economic conditions gave rise to a rhetorical trope—the inferiority of a race, according to DuBois. From 1897, when DuBois spoke on "The Concept of Race" to his 1962 revision of an older essay on Africa, colonialism, and racism, DuBois remained attached to the idea that racism finds its roots in capitalism and imperialism.

The counterarguments that arise from DuBois's theory or history or political economy or rhetoric is that racism is older than trans-Atlantic expansion (though surely American racism begins then). Slavery is ancient. Slavery based on skin color is ancient. And slavery is always economic. The argument goes that since racism can be found to exist long prior to the European trans-Atlantic expansion of the sixteenth century, the causal relation between racism and capitalism mustn't apply. Social theorists like Janet Abu-Lughod write about a time *Before European Hegemony: The World System* A.D. *1250–1350* which gives rise to the work of Andre Gunder Frank—controversial, polemic, and provocative— who, in *ReOrient: Global Economy in the Asian Age*, suggests that capitalism as economic accumulation goes back 5000 years rather than 500.

But these aren't our conversations in rhetoric and composition studies yet. While we English professors of rhetoric and composition studies go around legitimating ourselves to a very young field—English literature—an economic historian like Deirdre McCloskey turns to the ancient study of rhetoric in ways we do not. Yet the history of rhetoric includes figures more recognized by economists than rhetoricians. I think of John Locke, his *Lectures on Rhetoric and Belles Lettres* as well as the *Wealth of Nations*. Thomas Hobbes had written *A Brief of the Art of Rhetoric; Containing in substance all that Aristotle hath written in his three books on that subject*. Hobbes and Locke are the founders of political economy (Vinnicombe and Stevely). Both were rhetoricians as well as economists and philosophers. We tend also to overlook the rhetoric of Adam Smith. Yet an economist like A. M. Andres can write of "Adam Smith's Rhetoric of Economics," in the *Scottish Journal of Political Economy*. The problem, in other words (quoting the economist McCloskey), is that "Rhetoric in the late twentieth century has had to be reinvented in ignorance of its past" (*Knowledge* 38).

Recognize that past, recognize that rhetoric has had but a brief nap in the history of society—maligned for a hundred years and ignored for another in a 2500 year history—and we can begin to recognize that rhetoric has been—and remains—central to all institutionalization. We function as beings rhetorically, using language to convey information, persuading others to accept the truth value of that which we convey, a truth value that has to include the connections between power relations and the systems for meeting material needs. And that defines a political economy—the relations of power to systems for meeting material needs. In Kenneth Burke's terms, *homo sapiens sapiens* can only know that it knows by way of the rhetorical—*homo dialecticus*.

Kenneth Burke's *homo dialecticus* is interesting, not only because it points to our rhetorical natures, but also because it points to our physical natures. There is a dialectic in our being—the rational or rhetorical or cultural and the physical, or material. We are material objects, these bodies of ours. We are a material base to our rhetorical superstructure.

> As a kid, I had to learn all of the "proverbs" of Poor Richard's Almanac. I'd walk around the house saying things like "a rolling stone gathers no moss" or "strike while the iron is hot" or "a penny saved is a penny earned." Dad would chime in with "Money isn't everything," pause for dramatic effect, then say "but it's ninety-nine percent of almost anything."

In considering base and superstructure, Terry Eagleton points out that Hobbes's theory that we are greedy little creatures chasing after wealth and power by nature misses the point. It isn't wealth and power as ends themselves that we seek; what we seek, by and large, is the wealth that will allow us the power to do what we'd rather. "What is most precious in life for merchant bankers," Eagleton writes, "as for us rather less fortunate creatures, is happiness" (233). In so saying, Eagleton is arguing for—as many are beginning to—correcting the corrective. I think, for instance, of Edward Said's assertion in *Culture and Imperialism* that plenty has been said on the political economy of imperialism but not enough on culture. But as it turns out, we now seem to have lost sight of the political economic arguments, those of us who are in the culture industry of text reproduction. Said and folks like Althusser were trying to correct a tendency earlier in the twentieth century toward economic determinism, a causal argument stemming from an often quoted passage from Marx in which "The mode of production of material life conditions the general process of social, political and intellectual life" (qtd. in Milberg and Pietrykowski 87). Eagleton advocates a return to considerations of the classic metaphor of the economic base and the superstructure of state and civil society.

Now, I have distrusted the separation of the cultural from the economic. But, then, I guess that's what's happened in our discussions of culture. For example, a special two-volume issue of *PRE/TEXT* about a decade ago claimed to concern itself with Marxism and Rhetoric. Yet much of the volume ended up focused on the work of Antonio Gramsci, my own contribution as well. The particular appeal of Gramsci, I think, was that he was seen as the theorist of the superstructure. Yet this is more due to how Gramsci has been configured than what he has had to say. A political activist working with auto workers, for instance, Gramsci was deeply tied to the relations between power and the material. Though Gramsci's writings—at least those which have been translated—don't do much with political economy directly, Gramsci did see hegemony as of a piece with economics, a recognition displayed best by Gayatri Spivak's rendering of Gramsci. There is a rhetoric of economics, a rhetoric of political economy. We need only reclaim it.

A poem by Nuyorican poet Sandra María Esteves:

> *We are a multitude of contradictions*
> *reflecting our history*
> *oppressed*
> *controlled*
> *once free folk*
> *remnants of that time interacting in our souls*
>
> *Our kindred was the earth*
> *polarity with the land*
> *respected it*
> *called it mother*
> *were sustained and strengthened by it*
>
> *The european thru power and fear became our master*
> *his greed welcomed by our ignorance*
> *tyranny persisting*
> *our screams passing unfulfilled*
>
> *As slaves we lost identity*
> *assimilating our master's values*
> *overwhelming us to become integrated shadows*
> *unrefined and dependent*

We flee escaping, becoming clowns in an alien circus
performing predictably
mimicking strange values
reflecting what was inflicted

Now the oppressor has an international program
and we sit precariously within the monster's mechanism
internalizing anguish from comrades
planning and preparing a course of action.

The relations between power and the material cannot be ignored. Consider the title from a book by Sharon Beder: *Selling the Work Ethic: From Puritan Pulpit to Corporate PR*. The title presents an economic meta-rhetoric—a rhetoric of the rhetoric of labor. We are caught in unprecedented economic expansion being sold as *globalization*, a term that is as often delivered as much as a panacea as it is a problem. This expansion magnifies many times over the problems we have known in this country. Every year, for example, the Conference on College Composition and Communication awards ten Scholars for the Dream, an award given to a promising young scholar of color in composition studies or rhetoric. Every year I get pulled into a discussion about what constitutes a scholar of color. Although the intention was to address long-term nationalized racism, by defining "of color" in national-historical terms, the global expansion of the American and European economy is such that "color" now envelopes the globe.

We do not have a discourse with which to address the ways in which political economies represent the peoples of the world, particularly those of what we call the Third World, as people of color. When those of the Third World deal with Americans or find themselves among us, identity slips and slides between U.S. terms of identity and nationalistic terms of identity in an increasingly deterritorialized world economy (deterritorialized in part because of the virtual economy brought on by technology). One cannot claim simply to be Bangladeshi, for example. As a Bangladeshi in a U.S. political economy, one is automatically sorted into the "of color" bin, despite having a radically different historical framework from an American of color. We become, in the current world economy, not just a nation of immigrants but a nation of exiles— and the problem magnifies exponentially when the discussion turns to women in a world economy.

Story One:

> We were talking to the visitor from Thailand. Casual. Starbucks. ("So this is Star-
> bucks," she says. There's a Starbucks now in her hometown in Thailand, across
> the street from the 7–11, but she hasn't been able to afford to enter.) We talk about
> tourism in Chiang Mai. I ask about Japanese tourists, curious how the current

economy has affected Japanese tourism, since it has not apparently affected U.S. tourism abroad much. She says, "They only come for sex."

Story Two:

> *A panel, CCCC. On the panel a pioneer for women's voices within composition. She speaks of working conditions for women in the U.S. academy, particularly women who teach composition. Almost as an aside, she says that she is fortunate, since she can afford a live-in caretaker for her children so as to pursue her work. And I think my tongue bled from biting it.*

How do we talk about gender if not tied to political economy? From V. Spike Peterson:

> Characteristics of the sex trade are closely linked to other burgeoning transnational economies of a "domestic" (private, reproductive) nature that are not deemed illicit: the "maid-trade" and mail order bride industry. Domestic work is understood to be unskilled; it attracts women who need paid work, have little training, may require housing accommodation, and/or seek work where citizenship status is not monitored. . . . Moreover, elite women and those who work full time often seek domestic workers to maintain their homes and care for their children. Patterns of migration and the race/ethnic and gender characteristics of who works for whom are shaped by history and contemporary dynamics in the global economy. (14)

Whether it concerns the maid trade or the housewife, the rhetoric of the family is tied to economies that are racialized and gendered and sexed (insofar as family-as-trope suggests heterosexism), thereby deciding on a division of labor. Economies are carried rhetorically. We cannot discuss the ideological and thereby rhetorical reproduction of beliefs about gender, race, class, age, nation, religion, or any other of the axes of difference—without a grasp of how such axes are embroiled in the economic. In short, rhetoric is tied to political economy, if the work of rhetoric is the demystification of the ideological. McCloskey is indeed right: "The English professor who has neglected Adam Smith and John Stuart Mill, not to speak of . . . the other modern masters [of economics] is missing a lot."

WORKS CITED

Abu-Lughod, Janet. *Before European Hegemony: The World System* A.D., *1250–1350.* New York : Oxford UP, 1989.

Andres, A. M. "Adam Smith's Rhetoric of Economics: An Illustration Using 'Smithian' Compositional Rules." *Scottish Journal of Political Economy* 38 (1991): 76–95.

Bain, Alexander. *English Composition and Rhetoric: A Manual.* London: Longman, 1866.

Beder, Sharon. *Selling the Work Ethic: From Puritan Pulpit to Corporate PR*. New York: St. Martin's, 2000.

Berlin, James A. *Rhetoric and Reality: Writing Instruction in American Colleges, 1900–1985*. Carbondale: Southern Illinois UP, 1987.

Burke, Kenneth. *A Rhetoric of Motives*. Berkeley: U of California P, 1969.

DuBois, W. E. B. *Black Reconstruction in America: An Essay toward a History of the Part Which Black Folk Played in the Attempt to Reconstruct Democracy in America, 1860–1880*. New York: Russell and Russell, 1962.

Eagleton, Terry. "Base and Superstructure Revisited." *New Literary History* 31 (2002): 231–40.

Esteves, Sandra María. "From Fanon." *Puerto Rican Writers at Home in the USA: An Anthology*. Ed. Faythe Turner. Seattle: Open Hand, 1991, 186–87.

Frank, Andre Gunder. *ReOrient: Global Economy in the Asian Age*. Berkeley: U of California P, 1998.

Kennedy, George. *Classical Rhetoric and its Christian and Secular Tradition from Ancient to Modern Times*. Chapel Hill: U of North Carolina P, 1980.

McCloskey, Donald N. *Knowledge and Persuasion in Economics*. Cambridge: Cambridge UP, 1994.

———. *The Rhetoric of Economics*. Madison: U of Wisconsin P, 1985.

Milberg, William S., and Bruce A. Pietrykowski. "Objectivism, Relativism, and the Importance of Rhetoric for Marxist Economics." *Review of Radical Political Economics* 26 (1994): 85–109.

Miller, Susan. *Textual Carnivals: The Politics of Composition*. Carbondale: Southern Illinois UP, 1991.

Peterson, V. Spike. "Rewriting (Global) Political Economy as Reproductive, Productive, and Virtual (Foucauldian) Economies." *International Feminist Journal of Politics* 4 (2002): 1–30.

Sacrey, Charles, and Geoffrey Schneider. *Introduction to Political Economy*. Cambridge, MA: Economic Affairs Bureau, 2002.

Said, Edward W. *Culture and Imperialism*. New York: Knopf, 1993.

Spivak, Gayatri Chakravorty. *A Critique of Postcolonial Reason: Toward a History of the Vanishing Present*. Cambridge: Harvard UP, 1999.

Villanueva, Victor. "Reading Rhetoric Outside and In: Theory, Pedagogy, and Politics in *Race, Rhetoric, and Composition*." *JAC* 20 (2000): 195–204.

Vinnicombe, Thea, and Richard Stevely. "John Locke, Thomas Hobbes, and the Development of Political Economy." *International Journal of Social Economics* 29 (2002): 690–705.

II

LEFT COALITIONS BEYOND THE TRIAD

CHAPTER FOUR

THE LEFT SIDE OF THE CIRCLE:
AMERICAN INDIANS AND PROGRESSIVE POLITICS

SCOTT RICHARD LYONS

SEPTEMBER 11, 2001, LEECH LAKE TRIBAL COLLEGE, CASS LAKE, MINNESOTA, LEECH Lake Ojibwe Reservation: When the towers fell, we also gasped in horror. I was with students that morning, our class and some three or four others huddled around our small college's lone television set in the Ojibwe language resource room. When the towers fell, we gasped. A few quietly wept. Most just stared in silence. No one left. Some shook their heads in what appeared to be an inarticulate combination of bewilderment and disgust, and they seemed to seek out eye contact with others, any others, as if asking a silent question, or maybe registering shock, or perhaps simply trying to connect. I remember that many of us were at a loss for words, at least for a single, shocking moment, but it wouldn't be long before we would start talking. Some of us—"leftists," perhaps, but maybe just concerned teachers—would try to begin the discussion in a way that would lead to analysis and understanding, rather than reaction and pathologizing, which is of course where most public discourse on 9/11 eventually went. I remember looking for a way to start those conversations, seeking those important first words that would frame the events in a productive and progressive fashion, yet feeling at a loss, my own bewilderment and disgust colonizing my thoughts in the face of so much televised carnage, so much bloody history. So I simply asked my students what they felt. And I remember John, an Ojibwe student in his late twenties, who said he was glad it was happening.

"It's about high time someone hit those fuckers." The Circle comes around.

It must be stressed that John's statement was not representative of most of my students' opinions on 9/11; it was, in fact, distinctly a minority viewpoint. But it must also be said that John was articulate, and dramatically so; he before anyone else shaped and transformed his feelings into linguistic expression and subsequently framed the 9/11 discussion to follow. Articulate, angry John:

a product of history and violence himself, this young man has lived not *the* Indian life, which does not exist and never has, but certainly *an* Indian life. I know him and his family and history: the alcoholism he was raised around and eventually inherited, the physical and sexual abuse he suffered at the hands of both family and white social service providers, the marginalization he encountered in the public schools, the racism he experienced daily in the reservation border towns where Indians have to do their shopping, the many stints in jail, the self-loathing all of this creates. I also know about his valiant efforts to swim against the powerful currents of his own life: his many attempts to quit drinking, his stubborn refusals to stay in jail, and his efforts to complete his education—that year, 2001, he hitchhiked from his home twenty miles away to campus every day. I know that he was hungry to learn, to understand, to know, and to speak. Yet John was already articulate; his anger had already found words. And even though speaking violence and retribution, expressing satisfaction in the face of human suffering, John's words were not irrational. Far from it: forged and then uttered in contexts of horror, and then of terror, they make sense.

And so it is that any serious attempt to find or create linkages between Native Americans and a "whole left" must contend, at least on some level, with the fact that some Indian people articulate rationally the admittedly startling proposition that "it's about high time someone hit those fuckers." Unpack the statement: "high time" refers to the undeniable fact that the oppressed—the poor, the brown, the indigenous—have long suffered at the hands of what bell hooks consistently calls "patriarchal, white supremacist, capitalist" powers. "High time" says that the chickens have finally come home to roost, positing the suggestion that the "hit" those powers took on 9/11 was actually a counterblow: an act of defense. The hit was done by "someone"—anyone, anywhere, it really didn't matter on that day, not to John, but certainly someone somewhere who, like John, has also suffered. Most importantly, it was not an irrational, random act of violence. No: it made sense, targeting in particular "those fuckers." Those of us who heard the statement knew exactly who "they" were: not just white men or rich capitalists, but even at Leech Lake Tribal College, that little grassroots college with only one television, "those fuckers" were understood to be *Americans*. The Indian wars are not over, indeed.

The Whole Left must start with that reality, even though John's words do not represent a majority Indian viewpoint. Why? Because they are rational. Far from representing a position of blind hatred (or, worse, "evil"), John's angry, articulate statement is actually not that different from the words of Indians past: Tecumseh, who tried to organize a pan-Indian, revolutionary, and, yes, violent resistance to white powers; Little Crow, who for years preached peace until it no longer seemed viable in the face of Indian agents who said that his starving people should eat grass to survive; or even Wovoka, whose millennialist Ghost Dance visions of the Indian dead returning to permanently stop white aggressions, that is, to kill the whites, spread rapidly throughout Indian country, not because Natives were "spiritual" in some simple, primitive manner, but because they were angry and suffering and powerless and rational. Those Indian leaders who promoted violent resistance are now mythologized in the imperialist imagination, in what Gerald Vizenor calls "the literatures of dominance," as tragic Noble Savages: a worthy enemy, now vanquished, whose former eloquence is as sadly beautiful as the sunset image of the Indian slumped over on his horse with the arrow in his back. John, angry and damaged—and young and male—appears irrational only when one accepts the many injustices of his existence as an immutable fact of life, which he himself apparently does not.

Consider the statistics. According to the most recently available U.S. Census Bureau statistics, the median family income for whites in 1990 was $41,922; for Indians, it was $21,619; and for Navajos alone, $13,940. (There is uneven development across Indian country, with some groups faring better than others; the numbers for my reservation more closely resemble the Navajo averages.) The percentage of whites below the poverty line was 9.47; for Indian families, 27.2; for Navajo, 47.3. Sixty-five percent of Indians complete high school, compared to 83.1 percent among whites, and while 22.9 percent of whites receive bachelor's degrees, only 9.4 percent of Indians do (*Statistical Abstract*). According to the Indian Health Service, Native people are fully twice as likely as the American population as a whole to die before age 24, and twice as likely again before age 44; in fact, from ages 5 to 54, American Indians are on average 1.5 times as likely to die as Americans. We have a 430 percent greater chance of dying from alcoholism, a 165 percent greater chance of dying from accident, a 50 percent greater chance of being murdered, and a 43 percent greater chance of committing suicide. The rate of illicit drug use is twice as high among our youth (22.9%) than that of the U.S. population as a whole (9.7%), and those numbers are increasing (*Trends in Indian Health*). Further, as a study by the U.S. Justice Department released in 1999 stated, "Native Americans are far more likely to be the victims of violent crime than members of any other racial group" (SPLC, June 1999: 3). The Report also pointed out that while "70 percent of whites are attacked by whites, and more than 80 percent of blacks are victims of other blacks," when we are attacked, "70 percent of violent crimes against Indians are committed by members of other racial groups, mainly whites" (3). *Those fuckers*.

Startling though they might be, statistics like these don't even begin to address other structural social problems Indians face, like loss of language, culture, or rights to water and land. For instance, the vast majority of Ojibwe speakers in the United States are over 50 years of age, and in some places fluency levels are as low as 1 percent (Treuer 5). Loss of language, and subsequently culture, is directly attributable to U.S. assimilation policies of the nineteenth and twentieth centuries, the boarding schools, and it is nothing less than genocidal in its force: loss of language and culture is loss of identity, of "peoplehood." Losses like those usher in a host of other problems, as well, ranging from low self-esteem to ravaged social networks to the absence of viable

political foundations. Likewise with what's left of our land, another source of
Indian identity and the reproduction of life. According to the Worldwatch
Institute, 317 Indian reservations currently face serious environmental threats,
ranging from clearcutting to toxic waste; as Winona LaDuke points out, "[r]eser-
vations have been targeted as sites for 16 proposed nuclear waste dumps.
Over 100 proposals have been floated in recent years to dump toxic waste in
Indian communities. Seventy-seven sacred sites have been disturbed or dese-
crated through resource extraction and development activities" (2–3). In July
2002, the United States government authorized the use of Yucca Mountain, a
sacred place to the Shoshone, as a national dumping ground for 77,000 tons of
America's most dangerous nuclear waste. Add to that the fact that over the past
45 years "there have been over 1,000 atomic explosions on Western Shoshone
land in Nevada, making the Western Shoshone the most bombed nation on
earth," and John doesn't seem to be quite as violent as do others in our immediate midst (LaDuke, *Relations* 3).

At Leech Lake, people live with things no one should have to get used to:
gang violence, senseless murder, environmental contamination, growing rates
of drug abuse and poverty, and growing fear. According to a recent Minneapolis *Star Tribune* article, "300 Indian gang members live in the sparsely populated
area encompassing the Leech Lake, Red Lake, and White Earth reservations in
northern Minnesota. Some are as young as 8" (Levy). Cass Lake, that little
town in which our tribal college sits, "has become a hub of drug activity . . .
and has a 40 year history of violence. It is home to one of Minnesota's few
all-girl gangs, the Original Tract Girls" (Levy). Authorities at all levels—tribal,
state, federal, community—are searching for explanations and viable solutions,
but too often their discourse reflects the statement by the local sheriff: "our
concern is: will [gangs] infiltrate legitimate businesses? Rather than these little punks beating up on each other, suppose they get more into organized crime?"
(Levy). Those "little punks" are our children; *they are legitimate*. Many of them
are poisoned by industrial contamination, the subject of another recent *Star
Tribune* article which exposed the existence of dangerously high levels of dioxins, furans, and other compounds in the soil, water, and fish of an area long
inhabited by some of the reservation's poorest people (Ruble). White-owned
industry is responsible for that contamination, and they have allegedly shirked
their responsibility for cleanup—if such a thing is even possible at this point.
In the meantime, people are taking stock of their health. As one tribal member puts it, "When you have an entire little community sit down and everybody starts talking about this person who died of cancer and that person who
died of cancer, you really have to wonder" (Ruble). Another resident tells of
losing several relatives to cancer and having a grandson born without thumbs
(Ruble). This is our homeland; these are our people. Meet John.

How will a "whole left" view and address these realities? How will it see the
whole of John's life, the conditions of its making, or John's rational articulations

of his irrational suffering? What kind of politics will a "whole left" profess in the pursuit of justice for Indian people—for people like John, or the Western Shoshone, or the addicted child, or the frightened grandmother? Why should we care? (And who exactly do you think I mean by *we*?) Will John, clearly subaltern, be invited to speak—even though what he speaks is a rational, articulate advocacy of violence? Is the Whole Left willing to sacrifice some of its own comfort and privilege so the Shoshone can keep their holy places holy? Will it bring these problems into the university and legitimize our daily concerns? I think these are questions the "whole left," a worthwhile project to be sure, must discern and answer with the utmost commitment if it truly wishes to realize its relevance to indigenous peoples. Are indigenous people really part of the Whole Left agenda? While we may have more at stake in the debate than many groups, Indian people may also have the strange blessing of having less to lose in the event that a Whole Left is successful at achieving meaningful, radical social change in the twenty-first century. Are you really willing to go there?

For my part, I have been invited to contribute to this discussion because I am an Indian scholar who has advocated leftist positions in my work. I am not like John, with his personal history of suffering and struggle and very dark skin, although we are related and share a common social history as Anishinaabeg. We both have toxic metals, PCBs, dioxins, and furans in our bodies from eating that contaminated fish, but I'm guessing he's still eating fish from those lakes—by economic necessity—while I no longer do (and my daughters never have). *These are positions.* While I used to teach students like John at Leech Lake Tribal College, I now work at a private research university in upstate New York that costs a frankly obscene amount of money to attend, teaching a student body that is predominantly white, economically privileged, and typically sheltered from the sort of everyday violence one finds on my homeland. This is not the grassroots, although I do think it is an important site to do my work, since our students today will very likely occupy positions of power tomorrow. This university was in many ways directly affected by the violence of 9/11, with numerous losses of family and alumni to speak of, and several years ago the community lost the lives of many students on Pan-Am Flight 103, which was attacked and exploded over Lockerbie, Scotland. It is not for these reasons alone that I now say I am generally opposed to political violence, the destruction of human life in whatever form it takes, and do not share John's sentiments in the least. That said, I also recognize that oppressed peoples who physically fight back often fare better in the long run than those who do not. I do think it's too bad Tecumseh wasn't successful—although if he had been, I, a child of mixed-blood, might not exist. People still Ghost Dance. *These are also positions.*

I think a book like this is important. First, it aims to directly influence political struggle, social movements, and by extension policy-making, through the attempted forging and theorizing of a "whole left" in today's postmodern—

which is to say fragmented, rapidly changing, and perhaps disillusioned—world. Second, as an academic book it starts this process by focusing on the generation of new scholarship that will be useful to the politics it professes. This book will reach intelligent thinkers, teachers, students, and scholars and spark conversations and reflections at a time when both are so desperately needed. I want to think—indeed, I truly hope—that it will move Native concerns to the forefront of political academic discourse. As the first people of this land—the first to develop it and the first to suffer its dispossession, the first to love it and the first to be forced to leave it—indigenous people need to be placed at the center of both political and scholarly spheres of action. Not as a marginalized "inclusion," not as an add-on: no, I am saying *first people, first priority*. I am saying it should be our indigenous right to be at the very heart of politics and knowledge-making, a place we used to inhabit naturally on this land but haven't in over five hundred years of occupation and oppression, located as we are now at the bottom of every social indicator, every depressing statistical table, every hierarchy. Progressive scholars in particular should start with this fact by locating their work not on the "frontier" but on *Indian land*, not as "pioneers" but as *settlers*. It has long been the Indian position that there is enough room here for many peoples, so no one's going to be asked to leave. What they will be asked to do is aid in the still unrealized process of decolonization. They will be asked to walk alongside the Indian toward a better future, and perhaps they will, as Gloria Anzaldua put it, "come to see that they are not helping us but following our lead" (85). Must there be another "long walk" between here and there, between now and then, between the status quo and real change? I hope not. But there are some habits of mind that need transformation before we can realize this sort of vision. First, radical thinkers and activists need to understand the somewhat tortured history of Indian-Left interaction in America and think about why so few of us are at your meetings, conferences, and demonstrations. (Hint: it isn't due to "false consciousness.") Second, we all need to change the way we do scholarship and organize our college curricula in significant ways if Indian interests are to become a real priority in academic circles. I'll take each of these in turn.

The story of progressive involvement in Indian affairs is fraught with contradiction and misunderstanding, and to Indian eyes, it is inseparable from the larger history of U.S. colonialism. For starters, take the very word, "progressive." Double-voiced in the extreme, this term was used during the nineteenth and twentieth centuries to signify Indians who were held to be *assimilated*: Christian, individualized, English-speaking, and antitribal. A "progressive" was the opposite of a "traditional," the latter signifying someone who resisted assimilation, who wanted to remain Indian and live as such. A progressive Indian accepted the alleged inevitabilities of history and worked to bring other Indians "into the present"—as did, for instance, the Ojibwe George Copway, who wrote in 1850 that "the most requisite things for the Indians are these three:

a mechanical or agricultural education, a high-toned literature, and a rational moral training. Give him these—you make him exalted. Deprive him of these— you make him degraded" (qtd. in Vizenor, *Chippewa* 64). Indian progressives like Copway actively worked for the assimilation of his or her people, especially during the so-called Era of Assimilation (1879–1934), and they tended to think big. So in 1911, August Breuninger wrote to his colleagues in the Society of American Indians, that

> A University for Indians is the greatest step we educated Indians could take in uniting our people. . . . It would eliminate the general conception—that an Indian only consists of feathers and paint. It would single us out—as REALLY PROGRESSIVE INDIANS. It would give us a better influence with the rising generation, by setting out our character in such a conspicuous manner as to be . . . observed and imitated by them. (qtd. in Crum 20)

Here we see some of the pressures the progressives faced—community disunity, mainstream stereotypes, generation gaps, a question about their own place in both the tribe and society at large—and how they saw assimilation as the only viable answer to such problems. Progressive Indians of those horrifying years in particular—including such notables as Carlos Montezuma, Zitkala-Sa, and Charles Alexander Eastman—wrote and spoke volumes about the need for *more* assimilation programs, *more* American schooling, and *more* Christian missionaries in Indian country, and they lobbied hard for them. Faced with the visible violence of ethnic cleansing, mass murder, attempted genocide, reservations run as prison camps, and unremitting cultural loss, these progressives were a complicated, contradictory, and often sad group of public intellectuals. They were the historical products of a truly terrible time for Indian people, and close readings of their work find plenty of ideological fissures in their otherwise "progressive" discourse (see Warrior; Powell; McClure). But the point is this: the active promotion of assimilation and the decline of the Native is what "progressive" has meant in Indian country for nearly two centuries. And assimilated progressives have never been fully embraced by their own Native people, for reasons that should be obvious. At the turn of the twentieth century, if the opposite of a white progressive was, say, J. P. Morgan, the opposite of an Indian progressive was Crazy Horse.

So much for really progressive Indians. But the historical relationship between Indians and really progressive whites hasn't fared much better; indeed, it has produced some of our greatest nightmares. For instance, by now it should be widely understood that the boarding schools were in many ways traumatic and destructive sites, not only for the children who attended them (who were often physically, emotionally, and sexually abused there) but also for the communities back home who suddenly found themselves childless. What is perhaps less understood is that the assimilationist theory behind the boarding schools came not from right-wingers but rather from the work and thought of nineteenth-century white progressives like Helen Hunt Jackson or the activists of the Lake Mohonk Conference, social agitators who dedicated their lives to raising money and lobbying for what we now think of as very cruel instruments of colony (Adams). Granted, these "kill the Indian; save the man" policies were pursued by Washington bureaucrats who saw them as preferable alternatives to outright Indian extermination through war (the right-wingers' preferred doctrine). But that doesn't mitigate the fact that they nonetheless produced a tremendous amount of intergenerational pain and suffering and were by their nature wholly oppressive. By today's standards, the boarding school system would be understood as a gross violation of international human rights law (Noriega 381).

Another devastating issue white progressives pushed through the policy machine in the latter part of the nineteenth century was allotment, the breaking up of communal tribal lands in an effort to create both private property and individualism (not to mention a great deal of "surplus lands" for white settlement). In 1880, progressive Helen Hunt Jackson saw no other way to save Indians from themselves:

> The study I have given to the Indian question in its various aspects, past and present, has produced in my mind the firm conviction that the only certain way to secure the Indians in their possessions, and to prevent them from becoming forever a race of homeless paupers and vagabonds, is to transform their tribal title into individual title, inalienable for a certain period; in other words, to settle them in severalty, and give them by a patent an individual fee-simple in their lands. Then they will hold their lands by the same title by which white men hold theirs, and they will, as a matter of course, have the same standing in the courts, and the same legal protection of their property. (Jackson 361–62)

This is exactly what was done seven years hence with the passage of the Dawes Act, perhaps the most powerful policy assault on Indian tribes in the modern era. The idea behind allotment was that the creation of private property on formerly tribal land would "naturally" assimilate Natives by turning them into jealous agrarian capitalists, profit-seeking farmers who would develop a sense of entrepreneurship and come to resemble the whites next door. By the time allotment had run its course, around 1930, as Churchill notes, "the residue of native land holding in the United States had been reduced from approximately 150 million acres to fewer than 50 million." Further, "Indians across the country were left in a state of extreme destitution as a result of allotment," dealing with this new destitute state in all the usual ways (Churchill, *Native* 204). Both the boarding schools and allotment policies, the brainchildren of progressive ideology, were designed to assimilate Indians, and both failed miserably.

Other progressive victories to follow were similarly doomed. The 1924 Indian Citizenship Act was hailed by progressives as a major civil rights achievement—Indians suddenly becoming official Americans—but was seen by most tribal people as yet another forced walk toward an unwanted integration into the United States (Deloria and Lytle 11). Shortly thereafter, the 1934 Indian Reorganization Act (IRA), written and cheered by white progressives like BIA chief John Collier who saw the IRA as a new American commitment to indigenous sovereignty, created federally designed "tribal councils" based not on traditional indigenous governance structures but on Western electoral practices (although typically without the important separation of powers clause one finds in most Western governments). Controversial yet today, these councils had the immediate effect of alienating traditional people—who nearly to the number opposed the IRA governments—and created political factions in Indian communities that had never known such ills as political nepotism, "pork," or blacklisting (Deloria and Lytle 15). (We know them all quite well by now, however.) Further, as Ward Churchill argues, even though the IRA tribal councils were and are composed of enrolled tribal members, "their authority stems from—and thus their primary allegiance adheres to—the United States, rather than their ostensible indigenous constituents," which is why Russell Means has so often called them "Vichy Indians" (Churchill, *Native* 28). If not quite the enactment of real sovereignty as claimed by progressives, the IRA tribal governments remain highly contested on reservations today and call into question the ideology that created their existence. Since the thirties, U.S. Indian policy has been handled like an ideological tennis match between right-wingers, who promoted the name-says-it-all policies of "termination" and "relocation" throughout the fifties, and progressives, who continued to promote various versions of "self-determination" in the sixties and seventies, and which remains the official language of Indian policy today.

It might be argued that what I've been calling "progressive" in these pages actually describes "liberal" ideology and not *truly* "progressive" or "radical" or "leftist" theory and practice. *Real* progressives would never blunder in the ways I've been describing, one might reasonably suggest, and it is probably a failing of my own limited historical perception that I just can't see real radical alternatives. But even in the margins of official U.S. political history, the "really radical" progressives operate from the same ideological assumptions everyone else holds: namely, that Indians are essentially backward, caught in time, and need to *progress*, that is, to assimilate. To wit, consider the exchange that took place in 1980 between American Indian Movement (AIM) leader Russell Means and the Revolutionary Communist Party (RCP). The event was the Black Hills Survival Gathering sponsored by AIM, which the RCP was canvassing as a means of recruitment. Noticing this, Means presented a speech (later published as "The Same Old Song") attacking Marxism as ideologically inseparable from "the rest of the European intellectual tradition. It's really just the same old song" (20). For Means, there was nothing "revolutionary" about Marxist thought, based as it was on "industrialization," "abstraction," "despiritualization"—in sum, a whole ideology that Means simply calls "Europe." "All European tradition, Marxism included, has conspired to defy the natural order of things," Means argued. As a result, "Mother Earth has been abused . . . and this cannot go on forever." What's more, "American Indians have been trying to explain this to Europeans for centuries" (29). To explain it once again, Means essentially argued that "Europe" is best defined as a cultural, political ideology that posits humanity as separate from and superior to the natural world, "despiritualizing" the natural world, human beings, and relationships between the two, "abstracting" life and meaning in the process, and pursuing a telos of "gaining" rather than "being" (the Indian way of living). All forms of European ideology—including both capitalism and communism—operate from these basic assumptions, and Marxism in particular seems guilty of these crimes:

> Revolutionary Marxism, as with industrial society in other forms, seeks to 'rationalize' all people in relation to industry, maximum industry, maximum production. It is a materialist doctrine which despises the American Indian spiritual tradition, our cultures, our lifeways. Marx himself called us 'precapitalists' and 'primitive.' . . . So, in order for us to *really* join forces with Marxism, we Indians would have to accept the natural sacrifice of our homeland; we'd have to commit cultural suicide and become industrialized, Europeanized, maybe even sanforized. We would have to totally defeat ourselves. Only the insane could consider this to be desirable to us. (26–27)

In particular, Means noted Marxism's inherent disdain for the spiritual—and by extension its disdain for spiritual (non-European) cultures. "You can't judge the real nature of a European revolutionary doctrine on the basis of the changes it proposes to make within the European power structure and society," Means stated. "You can only judge it by the effects it will have on non-European peoples" (24). Means concluded by calling Marxism "as alien to my culture as capitalism or Christianity," proclaiming, "[w]e don't want power over white institutions; we want white institutions to disappear. *That's* revolution" (33; 29).

Shortly after the Gathering, the RCP responded with an essay of their own, "Searching for a Second Harvest," which basically argued that Means suffered from a bad case of bourgeois ideology. Representing Means's depiction of Native life and culture as an ideological portrait of the "Noble Savage" *par excellence*, the RCP suggested that

> the fact that [Means] would go several centuries backward to fish up aspects of bourgeois myth which has lost whatever feeble justification it may have once had, and which has by now become both hackneyed and reactionary, and that he dredges it up in order to attack revolutionary Marxism—well, all this should be a clue as to what he has to hide and what he is actually up to. (41)

What Means had to hide and what he was actually up to, apparently, was a rampant "idealism" that served "an important function for the rulers of the U.S. at a crucial time in the history of this country" (42). In other words, Means's depiction of his own culture is a pathetic lie that serves ruling class interests, and the RCP *knows* it: "His 'being' is a head-long flight into fantasy over reality, spirit over nature, ideas over matter—all with the end result of keeping man perpetually helpless before forces he would obstinately have us refuse to understand or control" (53). The rest of the essay is basically a treatise on how traditional Indian life—that is, pre-European life—really was a disgusting, savage existence. "The first Native Americans were not really 'native' at all, but came to this continent from Asia," the RCP wrote (invoking the very ideological and controversial, but never proven, Bering Strait theory). Once arrived, the people in the RCP's narrative overkilled the fauna, mistreated and often killed the women and girls of their communities, created "classes" of their own, and even ate their own droppings when food was scarce (this is the "second harvest" of which the title speaks) (44–47). The RCP concludes by proclaiming that a "great historical advance can only come about through the overthrow of the existing social order and the establishment of the dictatorship of the proletariat" (58). As for Indians, "the new proletarian state, *while favoring and encouraging unity and integration*, will ensure these formerly oppressed peoples' right to autonomy as part of a policy of promoting real equality between nations and peoples" (58; my emphasis). In other words, after the Revolution, the "new proletarian state" will continue to try to assimilate Indian people. They simply need to be brought into the present. Especially Russell Means.

I'm not going to beat up on the poor RCP, whose tired and offensive rhetoric here sounds much more trapped in the past than anything Means has ever said (and whose former members today are most likely singing very new songs, indeed). Instead, I simply refer you to Churchill and Larson's lively refutation. But my main point here is simply to show that there are more ideological similarities than differences between progressives and *really* progressive progressives in the history of Indians and the Left. More importantly, I also want to underscore the common assumption—a cultural assumption, but wholly political in its force—that undergirds the entire history of dialogue and interaction between Indians and progressives: namely, the notion of *progress* itself. This, too, is a product of "Europe," and the notion of progress tells a story of its own. First, history is dialectic, moving toward an inevitable telos, from known beginning to predictable end, and entire peoples, cultures, and civilizations can be placed like pushpins upon its illustratable trajectory. Second, indigenous peoples—"savages," "primitives," "precapitalists," etc.—are always located "earlier" on the timeline of history than whites and other peoples. "Earlier": even Little Crow or Wovoka, born after Marx; even the pipe-carrier today, whose name is John; even the Zapatistas, those internet warriors who are currently resisting an allotment disaster of their own; even the author of this essay. Indians are always viewed, and hence are always *used*, as "earlier" beings. And third, as such, real Indian people probably need to be assimilated, which is to say changed in time, brought into the present from the simple past in which they are alleged to exist. Their values and knowledges, after all, quaint though they are, existed before "ours"—so we teach them what we know and ignore what they know: this is assimilation. And this is the ideological assumption the Whole Left must thoroughly discard if it is to ever be meaningful to Native people.

Comparing differences in culture is one thing. Comparing differences in "progress" is another. Knowing the difference is essential if there is to be a new history of Indians and progressives starting in the twenty-first century. But knowing that difference also means recognizing that the Circle has no "left side." The Circle, correctly described by conventional wisdom as philosophically foundational to many if not all indigenous peoples across the globe, represents holism, regeneration, reaping what one sows, and the importance of listening to the past—which is, on this model, also the present, also the future: the Circle always comes around. The Circle symbolizes the Ojibwe concept of *minobimaatisiwin*, usually translated as "Good Life" but equally signifying "continuous rebirth." As Ojibwe scholar Jim Dumont explains:

> Here we are in . . . the twenty-first century, and we say the reality that we live within is totally different from anything we ever knew. It is just a different environment, a different context. Not a very good one, not a very harmonious or balanced one, not a very healthy one, but this is the environment that we live in today. The lifeway that spoke to our people before, and gave our people life in all the generations before us, is still the way of life that will give us life today. How it will manifest itself and find expression in this new time comes as a part of the responsibility of how we go about the revival and renewal. (Thorpe 79)

We've been here before, Dumont seems to suggest, and if not exactly us then a previous us: *still us.* What's more, we should know by now how to proceed. What will we do this time? How will we handle our responsibility?

I'll conclude this essay with two very general recommendations for a "whole left" that wishes to honor the Circle. First, *we should affirm and respect the sovereignty of indigenous nations. Sovereignty,* a contested term in the postmodern world to be sure, means in the Native context nothing more than the right and ability of a people to exist in its own way, on its own terms, on its own land. (Of course, that's saying quite a lot.) One way to support sovereignty would be to renounce altogether American "plenary power" over Indian nations and promote real national self-determination, as Thurman Lee Hester argues. "The clearest link between the problems faced by Native Americans and the actions of the United States is the direct one of dispossession," Hester writes. "As sovereignty has been infringed, Indian people have been harmed; as sovereignty has been reaffirmed, they have recovered" (91). Hester, a non-Indian, argues forcefully for a complete backing away from Indian affairs as the only viable, long-term solution to the social ills I've outlined in this essay, and his bold claim poses a distinct challenge to the left. But powerful interests remain invested in the status quo, in the continuation of our colonized status. Will anyone respond?

Sovereignty means much more than pure politics or land bases, however, as Crystal Echohawk explains:

> Sovereignty is an active, living process within this knot of human, material and spiritual relationships bound together by mutual responsibilities and obligations. From that knot of relationships is born our histories, our identity, the traditional ways in which we govern ourselves, our beliefs, our relationship to the land, and how we feed, clothe, house, and take care of our families, communities, and Nations. Sovereignty is a process which is reaffirmed in basic daily existence through our ability to determine what is best for our communities, by providing basic necessities for our people, and through our ceremonies, songs and stories. Thus, sovereignty is something which does not reside in, rely on, or gain legitimacy through an institution, handful of individuals, a law, or even our treaties. Sovereignty begins with a conscious understanding of our relationship with the Creator, who we are as Indigenous peoples, and our responsibilities to one another and Mother Earth. (21)

As Echohawk describes it, this "process" has to do with the reproduction of a whole way of life, one made in relationships, not only between nations but also between mother and child, not only between peoples but also between humans and the planet. This is not "savagery"; this is a guide for sustainable living that all peoples should learn from.

Of course, one might wish to resist this sort of language for its essentialist rhetoric or foundationalism, or perhaps decide to resist the concept of indigenous sovereignty altogether as yet another separatist form of identity politics. But I agree with Robert Warrior's position that what's really needed is an "expanding . . . definition of the human," one that makes room for Native humans, even while acknowledging that "American Indian people and traditions are necessarily neither more nor less human than any others" (124). As Subcommandante Marcos is oft to remark, "we seek a world in which there is room for many worlds"; above all else, views like these beckon nothing more than a liberal pluralism. However, as Warrior points out, "that humanizing perspective is situated within a context in which the humanity of American Indian people and traditions is rarely recognized or affirmed" (124). Native cultures, like all cultures, are constructed, porous, dialogical, and changing, and Native sovereignty would by definition position Natives as one-among-others; there is nothing essentially essentialist or separatist about either Indians or sovereignty movements. Indigenous status is, if anything, *historical*. But another historical reality is this: Native cultures and people are consistently disrespected. So the first step to taking sovereignty seriously would be to acknowledge the Indian world and show it a little respect.

Finally, *the Whole Left should bring this commitment to sovereignty and respect into the university curriculum*. To acknowledge someone's existence starts with actually seeing that person, but too often Native peoples remain invisible in the academic community. Our histories, philosophies, political struggles, and cultures are often obscured to such an extent that it doesn't even make sense to call them "marginalized." My university, for example, is located in the heart of Iroquois country, itself engaged in ongoing, contentious struggles over land claims (and their backlashes), but our students can and often do graduate without learning about even the very existence of the Nations down the road, much less their histories or pressing issues. It strikes me as very irresponsible for a university to educate students for "the world" while ignoring the world next door, a problem I attribute not only to ignorance (itself a symptom of this very problem) but also to a general lack of respect for Indian peoples. Elsewhere I've already argued for the importance of studying local (but not just local) Indian histories, literatures, philosophies, and the texts of sovereignty struggles, as well as for the crucial importance of affirmative action, so more Native people can be present in the classroom (Lyons). Without rehashing that essay, let me just say that a politicized, situated multiculturalism remains one of academe's unfinished projects in today's violent world, and Native people need to be a significant part of that work. This work would be done out of a desire for justice, yes, but only in part, for it would also be done in order to provide the world with a fuller story of who we all are, and can be, as human beings.

Two books seem noteworthy in the context of these issues and this collection as a whole. The first is Winona LaDuke's *All Our Relations: Native Struggles for Land and Life* (1999), which tells the tale of ten different environmental movements on ten different Indian reservations: the challenges posed to Native life by greedy industrialists and the environmental hazards they create, the ills created by these conditions, and most importantly the grassroots resistance movements that have emerged, most of them led by Native women, to turn the tide against environmental racism and injustice. By and large, these movements were led outside of any university assistance, testifying to the resilience, intelligence, strength, and impressive wherewithal of the local activists. But they also raise the question: where are the universities? The second book, Rick Whaley and Walter Bresette's *Walleye Warriors: An Effective Alliance Against Racism and for the Earth* (1994), shows the workings of an actual multi-race and class coalition successfully united against injustice during the Wisconsin spearfishing troubles of the eighties and early nineties. Cowritten by two men—one white, one Ojibwe—the book is a testament to the power of coalitions when they actually do form, and I think it provides some answers to the well-meaning student's—and the leftist scholar's—common question: what can we do? Self-determination and coalition building are twin strategies for survival in the new world order, and these two books demonstrate how they can be achieved—and why they should be. *Walleye Warriors* ends with the white author Rick

Whaley's question, "Why are Native American subsistence rights and rural culture even important in this information age, in this global marketplace?" His answer: because our destinies are inextricably interwoven (239).

What happens to me will eventually happen to you. What we do now, we also do later. It's this thing that connects us, this natural law, this irrepressible rule of justice and love and mutual respect. It also happens to be the founding principle of terror: the Circle comes around.

The Circle comes around.

WORKS CITED

Anzaldua, Gloria. Borderlands/La Frontera: The New Mestiza. San Francisco: Aunt Lute, 1987.

Churchill, Ward. "Like Sand in the Wind: The Making of an American Indian Diaspora in the United States." Notes from a Native Son: Selected Essays on Indigenism, 1985–1995. Ed. Ward Churchill. Boston: South End, 1996. 191–230.

Churchill, Ward, and Dora-Lee Larson. "Same Old Song in Sad Refrain." Marxism and Native Americans. Ed. Ward Churchill. Boston: South End Press, 1992. 59–76.

Deloria, Vine, Jr. Custer Died for Your Sins: An Indian Manifesto. Norman: U of Oklahoma P, 1988.

Deloria, Vine, Jr., and Clifford Lytle. American Indians, American Justice. Austin: U of Texas P, 1983.

Echohawk, Crystal. "Reflections on Sovereignty: Building Bridges between North and South." Indigenous Woman 3.1 (September 1999): 21–22.

Hester, Thurman Lee. Political Principles and Indian Sovereignty. New York and London: Routledge, 2001.

Jackson, Helen Hunt. A Century of Dishonor. 1881. Norman: U of Oklahoma P, 1995.

LaDuke, Winona. All Our Relations: Native Struggles for Land and Life. Cambridge: South End, 1999.

Levy, Paul. "Gang Activity Growing on Minnesota's Reservations." Minneapolis Star Tribune, 13 October 2002.

Lyons, Scott Richard. "Rhetorical Sovereignty: What Do American Indians Want from Writing?" College Composition and Communication 51.3 (February 2000): 47-68.

McClure, Andrew S. "Sarah Winnemucca: [Post] Indian Princess and Voice of the Paiutes." MELUS 24.2 (Summer 1999): 1–19.

Means, Russell. "The Same Old Song." Marxism and Native Americans. Ed. Ward Churchill. Boston: South End Press, 1992. 19–33.

Noriega, Jorge. "American Indian Education in the United States: Indoctrination for Subordination to Colonialism." The State of Native America: Genocide, Colonization, and Resistance. Ed. M. Annette Jaimes. Boston: South End, 1992. 371–402.

Powell, Malea. "Rhetorics of Survivance: How American Indians Use Writing." College Composition and Communication 53.3 (February 2002): 396–434.

Revolutionary Communist Party. "Searching for a Second Harvest." *Marxism and Native Americans*. Ed. Ward Churchill. Boston: South End Press, 1992. 35–58.

Ruble, Renee. "Leech Lake Band Feels Vindication in EPA Report on Superfund Site." *Minneapolis Star Tribune*, 5 October 2002.

Smith, Linda Tuhiwai. *Decolonizing Methodologies: Indigenous Peoples and Research*. London and New York: Routledge, 1996.

Southern Poverty Law Center. *SPLC Report 29* (June 1990): 3.

Thorpe, Dagmar. *People of the Seventh Fire*. Ithaca: Akwekon Press, 1996.

Treuer, Anton. *Living Our Language: Ojibwe Tales and Oral Histories*. St. Paul: Minnesota Historical Society Press, 2001.

U.S. Bureau of the Census. *Statistical Abstract of the United States 1995*. Washington, D.C.: U.S. Government Printing Office, 1995.

U.S. Indian Health Service. *Trends in Indian Health*. Washington, D.C.: Department of Health and Human Services, 2001.

Vizenor, Gerald. *The People Named the Chippewa: Narrative Histories*. Minneapolis: U of Minnesota P, 1984.

Warrior, Robert Allen. *Tribal Secrets: Recovering American Indian Intellectual Secrets*. Minneapolis: U of Minnesota P, 1996.

Whaley, Rick, and Walter Bresette. *Walleye Warriors: An Effective Alliance Against Racism and for the Earth*. Philadelphia: New Society, 1994.

CHAPTER FIVE

RECONCILING RED AND GREEN

MICHAEL BENNETT

AT A CHRISTMAS PARTY A FEW YEARS BACK, I WAS ADMITTING THAT I'VE ALWAYS been a sucker for the yuletide season when an acquaintance (who we'll call "Big Red," a proudly "vulgar" Marxist) launched into the dialectical equivalent of "Bah Humbug!" Red opined about the manufactured and maldistributed joy of gleeful acquisition as manipulated by the amassed forces of Madison Avenue and capitalism run rampant. Joining the conversation, another friend (aka "the Jolly Green Giant," a dyed-in-the-wool environmentalist) assaulted the holiday's eco-carnage. Green pointed to the hundreds of thousands of trees sacrificed on behalf of Saint Nick, not to mention the wreaths, wrapping paper, and tons of toxic tinsel. I was confronted with a dilemma: Could my belief in Santa survive the combined assault of Red and Green, or were the Christmas colors forever tarnished? I prefer to think that red and green can exist together in a holiday spirit—call it Christmas, Kwanzaa, Hanukkah, Winter Solstice, or, perhaps, ecocriticism. In this litany, ecocriticism—the study of the interaction between culture and the environment[1]—may seem out of place, but I want to explore the possibility that red and green can work together beyond the holiday season to provide a useful theoretical formulation for understanding the challenges that face us year round as the twenty-first century unfolds.

I want to propose a fruitful merger between red (Marxian theory) and green (environmentalism), despite the fact that certain critics make an absolute distinction between them by suggesting that they are hostile or antithetic or that the latter has somehow superseded the former. Jonathan Bate, for instance, traces a literary history of Romanticism in which the red has been deposed by the green: the 1960s and 70s were dominated by criticism that privileged the transcendent imagination (as in the work of Geoffrey Hartmann), the 1980s were the province of a post-Althusserian Marxist critique of Romanticism (as represented by Jerome McGann), and both of these have given way to the kind of literary ecocriticism practiced by Bate himself. In this teleological narrative, "the revolutionary torch now burns in the hand of greens rather than reds" (9). A similar narrative has been provided in the mainstream press. Ecocriticism has been touted as the next wave in academic fashion by *The Chronicle of Higher Education*, the *Voice Literary Supplement*, the *Washington Post*, and *The New York Times Magazine*.[2] That ecocriticism is spoken of in the faddish terms of style, or "what's hot and what's not," is one indication of how its political charge is dispersed in the popular press. This depoliticizing effect is only increased by the focus on ecocriticism as a variety of nature worship, with little to say about contemporary urban life or underlying structures of domination that shape our society's relationship with the environment. However, this movement, if it can be called that, is still young and it seems like an opportune moment for Marxists, socialists, and various kinds of radicals to intervene in the development of the discourse of ecocriticism, productively combining the red and the green in this emergent critical vocabulary. I hope to avoid a simplistic narrative of progress and supersession in discussing the role of red and green in the growth of ecocriticism, while analyzing how and why Marxian and environmental perspectives can and must blend together to shape a "whole left."

This proposition, which has been resisted by many on the left who are wholly invested in a class-based analysis of culture and society, did not at first prove to be popular among my academic and political friends—in other words, almost all the people I know well. They tended to give me a bad time about my transformation into an ecological literary critic. They felt that ecocriticism is essentially a green refuge for supposedly embattled white males fleeing from the analytical rubrics of race, class, gender, and sexuality. They shared, that is, a widely held assumption on the traditional left in the United States that ecological issues distract us from the more important matter of our society's economic inequalities. I admit that I had a similarly dismissive feeling when I first encountered ecological cultural criticism. Though I like to think of myself as an environmentalist, I have long been suspicious of the mainstream environmental movement, which did indeed strike me as worthy of my friends' disapprobation for being remarkably white, privileged, male, and straight. And I suspected that mainstream ecocritics were of a similar demographic as they became one with the wilderness while plumbing the subtleties of their well-thumbed copies of Thoreau's nature essays.

However, I have come to believe that these objections are unfounded, or at least half-truths, and that ecological criticism (the green) is a necessary partner with more traditional left approaches to cultural theory (the red) in the effort to comprehend and respond to the challenges of the twenty-first century. I am starting to convince my doubting friends, and my doubting self, that we have overlooked the variety of ecocritical approaches that are not subject to the limitations of mainstream environmentalism. At its best, ecocriticism incorporates the rubrics of race, class, and gender in studying the underappreciated connections between nature and culture. And understanding these connections is an urgent task for radicals of various stripes at this current historical juncture.

Vandana Shiva has argued that environmental issues of intellectual property will be to the twenty-first century what economic issues of material property were to the nineteenth and twentieth centuries. In other words, the struggles of native peoples to own and control their knowledge of foods, medicines, and technologies are, of necessity, at the forefront of current left movements around the globe. If this is so, and I suspect that it may be, then radicals in the U.S. will have relevant things to say about the most important political struggles of the twenty-first century only if we come to grips with the potential of the environmental movement to reshape our thinking. So it is with a certain sense of urgency that I intend to exorcise the beliefs that have stood in the way of making a fruitful merger between green and red. In what follows, I will address each of the most common radical objections to ecocriticism: 1) Ecocriticism is all about wilderness and wildlife and so is irrelevant for understanding the sociopolitical dimensions of humans and their habitations; 2) Ecocritics only care about the Thoreauvian tradition of nature writing and thus are unable to say anything interesting about most of our culture; 3) The environmental movement is the domain of privileged white males who are uninterested in issues of race, class, and gender.

OBJECTION #1:

ECOCRITICISM IS ALL ABOUT WILDERNESS AND WILDLIFE AND
SO IS IRRELEVANT FOR UNDERSTANDING THE SOCIOPOLITICAL
DIMENSIONS OF HUMANS AND THEIR HABITATIONS.

This objection is to the kind of ecocriticism based in a theoretical stance known as Deep Ecology. The beliefs that have been central for the practitioners of ecocriticism focused exclusively on wilderness and wildlife were laid out in the tremendously influential book *Deep Ecology*, in which Bill Devall and George Sessions describe the movement's "ultimate norms" as "self-realization and biocentric equality" (205). In Michael Tobias's volume of the same name, Arne Naess, the Norwegian philosopher usually credited with founding Deep Ecology, describes the movement through a series of oppositions with "shallow ecology," creating an opposition between the "shallow" focus on Nature as a valuable resource for humans and the "deep" imperative to treat nature as valuable in its own right (257). The primary gospel of Deep Ecology is that we must abandon androcentric planning and develop a biocentric understanding of the environment, an understanding that is to be gained by existing in harmony with unspoiled nature.

In adopting this focus, the Deep Ecology movement has overlooked a variety of environmental concerns that are central to urban life and left politics. At one point, Devall and Sessions acknowledge the range of environmental issues, such as resource extraction and employment policy, that Deep Ecology dismisses by ignoring cities and their inhabitants (158); while admitting that "these are vital issues" (159), Devall and Sessions insist that wild nature alone can provide the experience needed to foster an environmental consciousness (111). They delineate four deep ecological principles that they believe can only be developed through interaction with wide-open spaces: "1) developing a sense of place, 2) redefining the heroic person from conqueror of the land to the person fully experiencing the natural place, 3) cultivating the virtues of modesty and humility and 4) realizing how the mountains and rivers, fish and bears are continuing their own actualizing processes" (110).

I would argue that these four qualities (minus the bears) can just as easily be found in human habitations. The failure to recognize this fact points to one of the major flaws with ecocriticism grounded in deep ecological theory: it tends to engage in a form of wilderness fetishism, analyzed in detail in the work of William Cronon, that disables it from offering a useful analysis of urban environments or of any environments viewed from a sociopolitical perspective. Cronon argues that we need to "see a natural landscape that is also cultural, in which city, suburb, countryside and wilderness each has its own place" ("Trouble" 43). His work is not meant to disparage efforts to preserve the wilderness but to warn against a theoretical orientation that sees only wilderness and wildlife as "natural" and not humans and their habitations. This limited theoretical perspective, traceable to the doctrines of Deep Ecology, is at the root of the type of ecocriticism that has been justly criticized by the traditional left.

There is, however, another alternative. In contrast to the deep-ecological principles critiqued by Cronon and subject to the objection of the left is a branch of ecocriticism that is influenced by Social Ecology. The central tenets of this movement are defined by the Institute for Social Ecology as a set of beliefs that "integrates the study of human and natural ecosystems through understanding the interrelationships of culture and nature" (D. E. Davis 123). The thinker most centrally identified with Social Ecology, Murray Bookchin, has described the movement's "most fundamental message" as the lesson that "our basic ecological problems stem from social problems" (*Philosophy* 35). This focus on how the social, political, and economic decisions made by humans affect our interaction with the environment has been particularly fruitful for analyzing cities—the human decision-making centers that have been the traditional spatial focus of left theory.

Social ecologists have not, however, simply accepted cities as they are; they frequently offer a critique of the ways in which metropolitan culture transforms urban environments. In *Urbanization without Cities*, Murray Bookchin writes about cities as a necessary though flawed step toward human progress, much like the role of the bourgeoisie in Marxist historiography. Social ecologists like Bookchin offer a critique of urbanization at the same time as they note the progressive role played by cities in the ongoing social dialectic that weaves together humans and nonhuman nature. In Bookchin's effort to "redeem the city," he makes a series of connections between the ecology of wide open spaces and that of metropolitan places, noting that this argument "runs counter to the conventional wisdom that city and countryside, like society and nature, are necessarily in conflict with each other, a theme that pervades so much of the writing on urbanity of western society" (x)—including the writings of Devall and Sessions and other Deep Ecologists.

As can be seen from this thumbnail sketch, at the root of the difference between Deep and Social Ecology is a profound philosophical disagreement about the role that humanity and our built environments play in global ecology. Much ecocriticism, following the lead of Deep Ecology, insists that we "must break through our preoccupation with mediating between only human issues" to realize that human domination of the environment, more than human domination of other humans, is "the overriding problem" (Love, "Revaluing" 203). For cultural critics influenced by Social Ecology this position has three theoretical flaws: first, it establishes an absolute dichotomy between domination of humans and domination of the environment, though Social Ecology would argue that they are linked by what Murray Bookchin calls the "epistemologies of rule" (*Ecology* 89); second, humans can only act on human values and make human choices so it makes little sense to speak of moving beyond human issues and adopting a biocentric viewpoint; third, Deep Ecology provides a rationale for sidestepping "androcentric" concerns like race, class, gender, and sexuality.

These theoretical flaws are at the root of ecocriticism based in Deep Ecology. So even as the community of ecocritics has grown from a hamlet into a bustling metropolis, the movement itself has been slow to survey the terrain of human habitations, particularly in the field of literary studies (where ecocriticism has come to be associated with a body of work devoted to nature writing, American pastoralism, and literary ecology).[3] However, a parallel tradition of studying the city in literature was forged by works like Blanche Housman Gelfant's *The American City Novel* and Raymond Williams's *The Country and the City*. And, in recent critical work, literary studies of the city have begun to cross paths with the study of pastoralism and literary ecology to build the foundation for an urban ecological cultural criticism.

My own work in the field of ecocriticism, particularly the volume I coedited with David Teague (*The Nature of Cities: Ecocriticism and Urban Environments*), attempts to sharpen this focus on human habitations and the sociopolitical construction of various environments by exploring the components of an urban ecocriticism. One goal of our volume is to point to the self-limiting conceptualizations of nature, culture, and environment built into many ecocritical projects by their exclusion of urban places and marginalization of sociopolitical perspectives; another objective is to remind city dwellers of our placement within ecosystems and the importance of this fact for understanding urban life and culture. *The Nature of Cities* is especially attuned to the social construction of all environments—"natural" and manmade. The volume begins with my interview with Andrew Ross, whose work I will discuss in more detail in a moment, and his exploration of the potential contribution of Social Ecology-inspired ecocriticism to radical thought.

And, in fact, ecocriticism has developed a subfield focused on social eco-logical/socialist approaches to the study of culture and environment, especially by focusing on urban areas. The closest connections between ecocriticism and urban theory have probably been accomplished on the turf of Marxist environ-mental theory, though this work has largely been peripheral both to ecocrit-ics and to Marxists. Nevertheless, "classic" works in Marxist social geography and ecosocialism have created the groundwork for a recent flourishing of eco-logical Marxism.[4] These works built on the development of urban sociology earlier in the century, in confluence with Georg Simmel's analysis of the ways in which urban living transformed human consciousness and in reaction to the rise of the Chicago School in the 1920s. However, these various sociological and philosophical approaches to urban ecology have tended to lack a thorough-going *cultural* analysis of urban environments. Such an analysis was, however, evident in the work of Lewis Mumford and Paul Goodman. More recently, works by Andrew Ross, Will Wright, and Timothy W. Luke have appeared to fill the cultural gap that exists in much Marxist environmental theory (which has tended to focus on the economic base without sufficient attention to the cul-tural and ideological superstructure). Special issues of *Orion, Terra Nova,* and *American Book Review* have focused on what the latter calls "urban nature."

This growing body of cultural criticism engaged with urban ecology rejects mainstream ecocriticism's deep ecological focus on the genres of nature writing and pastoral, insisting that these genres are not capable of representing the com-plex interactions between political choices, socioeconomic structures, and the densely populated ecosystems that shape urban environments in particular. How-ever, the perspective of Social Ecology/ecosocialism reformulates concerns cen-tral to the project of ecocriticism to make them relevant tools for investigat-ing the social construction of urban and other environments. Among these concerns are: the opposition between natural and manmade ecosystems; the heuristic value of appropriating modes of perception employed in nature writ-ing for comprehending urban realities; and the shaping influence of natural and social environments on culture and identity. This perspective teaches us that all environments are shaped by sociopolitical determinants and that the inhabi-tants of urban places are as much a part of an ecosystem as the denizens of the open spaces explored by some of the most well-known environmental writers from Henry Thoreau to the present. From this perspective, we can contrast some of the founding statements of ecocriticism, which tend to focus on appreciation and defense of pristine natural environments, with more recent perspectives offered by those critics influenced by Social Ecology, who tend to be concerned with the sociopolitical construction of nature in its various manifestations.

OBJECTION #2:

ECOCRITICS ONLY CARE ABOUT THE THOREAUVIAN
TRADITION OF NATURE WRITING AND THUS ARE UNABLE TO SAY
ANYTHING INTERESTING ABOUT MOST OF OUR CULTURE.

Just as there is more than one type of ecocriticism, so there is more than one type of ecocritic. The objection that ecocritics care only about the tradition of nature writing, usually traced in the United States to "founding father" Henry David Thoreau, is generally true of those ecocritics most influenced by Deep Ecology. However, those ecocritics influenced by Social Ecology and ecosocialism are just as likely to analyze cultural texts at a far remove from the nature writing canon. In this section, I will explore the differences between what might be thought of as the relatively more green and relatively more red spectrum of ecocritics, by comparing one seminal work from each perspective: Lawrence Buell's *The Environmental Imagination* and Andrew Ross's *The Chicago Gangster Theory of Life*. Buell's work is firmly within the green branch of eco-criticism, with its deep ecological literary analysis of nature writing, while Ross's work provides a reddish Social Ecology-inspired cultural study of urban life and political structures at work in a wide range of environments.

Buell's book has, in a very real sense, become paradigmatic for literary analyses of the environment. In fact, Jay Parini argues that *The Environmental Imagination: Thoreau, Nature Writing, and the Formation of American Culture* has already become "the standard work on the subject" of ecocriticism (52). The title itself provides a mini history of Deep Ecology-inspired ecocriticism, with its implicit argument that our culture and our understating of the environment is shaped by a nature writing tradition stemming from Henry Thoreau. The book, which Buell describes as a "kind of pastoral project" (31), begins with his statement that despite his intention to write only about Thoreau and nature, he ended up with a "broad study of environmental perception, the place of nature in the history of western thought, and the consequences for literary scholarship and indeed for humanistic thought in general of attempting to imagine a more 'ecocentric' way of being" (1). In clarifying what he means by "eco-centrism," Buell accepts, with slight modifications, Timothy O'Riordan's def-inition: "Ecocentrism preaches the virtues of reverence, humility, responsibility and care; it argues for low impact technology (but is not antitechnological); it decries bigness and impersonality in all forms (but especially in the city); and demands a code of behaviour that seeks permanence and stability based upon ecological principles of diversity and homeostasis" (425). Buell's focus is exclu-sively on the green world; he has little to say about urban ecosystems since "big-ness" is in and of itself the enemy. And he eschews the broadly sociopolitical provenance of social ecocriticism to focus exclusively on literary concerns.

The central chapters of *The Environmental Imagination* reveal Buell to be the kind of ecocritic whose work raises objections when viewed from a radical perspective. Buell focuses on a very narrow canon of U.S. nature writing as the provenance of ecocriticism because he sees it as only proper to focus on "the most searching works of environmental reflection that the world's biggest technological power has produced" (2). He narrows his focus even further by developing a fairly restrictive "checklist" of what counts as an "environmentally oriented work" (7). In the process of outlining his ecocentric literary theory, Buell makes several jabs at the kind of green criticism engaged in by Andrew Ross and others influenced by Social Ecology. In defending "environmental mimesis," Buell argues that it is "far healthier for an individual, and for a society, than the arrogance of cyberspace" (114). Buell characterizes Foucauldian analysis as premised on "the inevitable dominance of constructedness," which he believes is less "productive" than the kind of criticism built on a "theoretical distinction between human constructedness and nonhuman reality" (113). Contrary to social ecologists' insistence that the earth is mute and their warnings against attempts to imbue it with a personal voice that speaks for itself, Buell approvingly points to James Lovelock's Gaia hypothesis as a worthy attempt to "bond ecology to ethics" through "personification of the planet" (201). Buell even suggests that it might be necessary to have a "degree of what passes for misanthropy" in order to obtain some distance from anthropocentrism and make the inward turn needed to transform one's self-consciousness (388).

It is precisely this perspective that worries Andrew Ross and motivates the questions he raises in his also widely influential book *The Chicago Gangster Theory of Life*. Ross would ask Buell, in what way is cyberspace "arrogant" and why should it exist in opposition to (rather than simply in addition to) representations of nature? what does it mean to "extricate art from homocentricism" (161) if art is a human creation? can a human-authored text ever really encounter natural phenomena "as the environment manifests itself" (219)? Such questions problematize the analysis of Deep Ecology-inspired critics like Buell.

Questioning the faith of Deep Ecology in the ability of Nature to speak for itself, the dominant concern expressed in *Chicago Gangster Theory* is that Nature will be used as an authority dictating certain social and cultural policies. This insight underlies much of Ross's analysis of the relationship between the natural and social sciences, technology, and politics. He warns, in particular, that "discourse about scarcity and limitation in the natural world" translates into "calls for a reduction in rights and freedom in our civil society" (12). In other words, Ross is attuned to the ways in which dubious natural science— e.g., much of sociobiology—generates theories of nature that can provide justification for repressive social arrangements on the false premise that such theories are objectively revealed rather than culturally determined. This social-ecological perspective entails a shift from Buell's literary analysis of wide-open spaces to cultural studies of metropolitan places.

Disproving the supposition that all ecocritics limit their purview to nature writing and wilderness appreciation, Ross, critiquing the means by which theories of nature are used to justify what are in fact sociopolitical decisions, analyzes a stunning variety of cultural phenomena, from the movie *Ghostbusters* and the 1993 bombing of the World Trade Center to the Gulf War and the "Chicago Gangster Theory," referred to in the title of his book. The Chicago Gangster Theory is Richard Dawkin's hypothesis that humankind has evolved a "selfish gene" much like a Chicago gangster would, over time, adapt a "ruthless selfishness" to survive in an amoral world. Ross sees this unwarranted transformation of a metaphorical construction loaded with social assumptions into a supposedly disinterested scientific theory as paradigmatic of the misuse of Nature to justify retrograde social theory (Dawkins argued that labor unrest was a sign of the selfish gene). In the process of proving his thesis that images of nature are used to cover over or falsely explain complex social issues, Ross examines the role of urban renewal and its metaphors of the "urban frontier" in creating a new "global city of finance capital and its two-tier post-Fordist service sector/professional economy" (113), while critiquing urban ecosystems theory. Ross also finds support for his thesis while analyzing how the "rhetoric of scarcity" and its accompanying images were used to bestow the mantle of ecological sanctity on the military-media complex during the Gulf War (an important lesson as we struggle with the impacts of Gulf War II).

Underlying these wide-ranging explorations characteristic of socialist/Social Ecology is Ross's insistence that local cultural practices are intimately related with economic and political conditions of global proportions. This insight reveals the potential of Social Ecology-inspired cultural studies at its best. In demonstrating how "ideas that draw upon the authority of nature nearly always have their origins in ideas about society" (15), Ross shows the importance of sociopolitical analysis in getting at the ways we use and abuse nature. This analysis is on display in Ross's brilliant study of Polynesia, "the birthplace of modern ecological romanticism" (28). He contrasts a knee-jerk environmentalism that conceptualizes any disruption of tradition as an assault on the last vestiges of unspoiled nature with a more nuanced analysis of the specific ways in which "tradition" and "nature" are deployed for different purposes. Sometimes, Ross argues, efforts to reclaim "native rights" are strategically useful for combatting the corporate exploitation of native environments and indigenous peoples. In other cases, tradition is manipulated by self-interested elites in order to justify their authority and their own exploitative schemes. Ross points out that "a society bound together by a nature philosophy holds no guarantee of ecological well-being if it is governed by a pyramidal social hierarchy that depends upon selective access to natural resources to maintain its power" (71). Ross deflates the romantic notion that all native islanders live in close harmony with nature, noting that many Polynesian societies degraded and even exhausted their environments. But he also points to indigenous movements, such as Hawaiian groups appealing to *malama 'aina* (reciprocal care for the land), as offering one of the best hopes for socially and environmentally responsible principles of sustainability.

This is a goal on which Ross and Buell could agree. And both critics believe that this goal will only be realized through a fundamental transformation in our relationship to the environment. But there are basic differences in how the two authors, and the critical genealogies that they represent (the green and the red strains of ecocriticism), reconceptualize our role in the natural world. Ross refers to the theories of nature in need of overhauling as ideologies that are manifest in various cultural productions and the global socioeconomic system in which these productions take part; Buell, on the other hand, speaks of philosophies that must be revised through ecocentric literary criticism *before* we can address environmental problems. These divergent perspectives provide two different models of what it means to be an ecocritic. While Ross provides a cultural studies approach to analyze the sociopolitical components of various cultural phenomena, Buell provides a more traditional literary critical approach to interpreting the "metaphysics and ethics" of literary representations of nature.

The problem with taking Buell's version of what an ecocritic should be as paradigmatic is that he fails to reflect a long tradition of radical critical theory that analyzes how a market-driven economy frames and shapes the ways in which we appropriate the environment, a tradition that maintains that individual consciousness cannot directly counteract these larger forces. The critical theorists associated with the Frankfurt School were some of the first radical thinkers to analyze the connection between capitalist modes of instrumental reason, the domination of nature, and the suppression of human nature. A notable attempt to counteract this dynamic has been undertaken by various Green parties, especially in Germany. In *Building the Green Movement*, Rudolph Bahro, a founding member of the former West Germany's Green Party, called for a form of radical ecology and utopian communalism to resist ideologies of control and create a dramatically transformed society. Andrew Ross draws on this tradition when he argues that "an ecologically sane future will not be achieved without some form of revolution in social and economic justice" (16).

For Ross, this future would be lived in a "postscarcity society" where austerity is no longer manufactured by political and socioeconomic systems because these systems have been transformed to provide an equitable distribution of resources rather than to create a state of crisis which justifies a repressive status quo. Based on this vision, the eco-utopian aims that Ross outlines in the conclusion of *Chicago Gangster Theory* have little to do with ideas conventionally associated with environmentalism—preserving endangered species, saving the wilderness, etc.—and more to do with sociopolitical hopes—common prosperity, transnationalism in balance with local self-sufficiency, and hedonism replacing asceticism in green conduct. This last aim must strike some environmentalists as particularly bizarre, but Ross cautions environmentalists who have accepted, and even promulgated, a rhetoric of self-sacrifice and limited freedom on the basis of pseudoscientific theories of scarcity to reexamine their assumptions. Ross argues that Malthusian "laws" of overpopulation have operated as "instruments of social subjugation" and that world scarcity is "induced and manipulated in the interest of maintaining power hierarchies" (263). What offers hope in this bleak scenario is the very fact that, as Ross emphasizes with italics, "*humans alone have the capacity to create societies where such 'laws' are not the primary determinants of survival*" (263). Ross concludes that human societies can eschew the discourse of limits and scarcity in favor of "an anti-Malthusian belief in the power of human need and abilities to reorganize the societal order of the natural and economic world" (272).

However, Buell raises a problem for ecocritics who would fold environmental analysis entirely into a Marxian model. As though providing a cautionary tale for Ross's vision of ecotopia, Buell points out that there is a natural world which, whether or not we can know it in an unmediated form, does have certain features beyond our comprehension and control. In other words, a deep-ecological perspective can act as a check on visions of radical social transformations that, in some versions of Social Ecology, fail to take into account the possible abuse of nature. We must remember that what used to be called the closest thing to "actually existing socialism" was largely an environmental calamity. An example of what happens when androcentric planning reifies Nature, making it just another tool for human decision-making, is provided by the former Soviet Union, where a range of ecological disasters caused a precipitous decline in life expectancy and infant survival, and permanent environmental damage. This experience should provide a warning about what can happen when efforts to actualize the vision of an equitable society are carried out without critical attention to the social and natural ecology of a populace.

And much of this critique has come from within the radical wing of the ecocritical movement. In *Strange Weather*, Andrew Ross argued that

> As the final collapse of plan-oriented state socialism and the spectacle of ecological depletion make clear, our commitments to social growth must everywhere be mediated by limits to technological growth, to human use of the physical world, and to the scientific planning of political and civil life. In short, we must abandon the old idea that the politics of social growth has at its command unbounded resources, both human and natural, that can be marshaled in the service of universal and univocal ideals. (170)

It is for this reason that Ross suggests that an ecologically sound vision of the future should be guided not by Marxist historical teleology, "with its roots in the Enlightenment faith in scientific progress through technical mastery of the natural world's resources," but by utopian socialism, with its visions of a "radically democratic future; a horizon of expectations for *different* people to live by and act upon" (170). Murray Bookchin has also offered a critique of certain forms of Marxism which, he argues, converge with "Enlightenment bourgeois ideology at a point where both seem to share a scientistic conception of reality" (*Toward* 197). Bookchin insists that social and natural environments are linked, and both are under assault by modern institutions of domination and various epistemologies of rule.

For deep ecologists, the dominant androcentric worldview needs to be transformed at the level of individual consciousness in order to develop true ecological awareness. For social ecologists and other radicals, it doesn't make sense to speak as though individual consciousness somehow precedes or escapes from social life. Reading *The Environmental Imagination* and *Chicago Gangster Theory* together, as different voices in the same cultural conversation, might provide a way of reconciling these positions by theorizing how the awakening of an environmental consciousness that Buell argues can happen through literature is a necessary but not sufficient condition for the kind of sociopolitical interventions Ross insists are needed in the realm of ecological praxis. However, both perspectives are united in their vision of a society existing in a non-exploitative relationship with the earth and its inhabitants. Perhaps, on this basis, red and green can be brought into a productive tension within the ecocritical movement.

OBJECTION #3:
THE ENVIRONMENTAL MOVEMENT IS THE DOMAIN
OF PRIVILEGED WHITE MALES WHO ARE UNINTERESTED
IN ISSUES OF RACE, CLASS, AND GENDER.

The challenge that red ecocritics like Ross offers to green ecocritics like Buell is of a parcel with the environmental justice movement's challenge to the mainstream environmental movement to reconceptualize the notions of "habitat preservation" and "endangered species" to include inner-city ghettos and their inhabitants, whose lives are threatened by the results of "environmental racism" (the deliberate targeting of minority neighborhoods for various kinds of environmental hazards). The environmental justice movement has arisen to become one of the most vibrant contemporary social movements because many activists felt that the mainstream environmental agenda was captive to the classist and racist interests of its mostly white and privileged leadership. The focus of mainstream environmentalism on issues like the preservation of wilderness and wildlife for the leisure and recreation of those Americans from the same class as the leadership of the environmental movement, which was almost devoid of people of color, was viewed by many as "another form of 'environmental racism'" (Alston 3). As one Hispanic woman, protesting the effects of a gasoline terminal in her neighborhood, put it, "we are the real endangered species in America, people of color" (Suro A1). Meanwhile, many activists within the civil rights movement felt that their leaders were also slow to see how lead paint and air pollution were indeed a "Black thing" or a concern for Native Americans, Hispanic Americans, and other people of color. In 1987, the publication of the United Church of Christ's report on *Toxic Waste and Race* made it hard to ignore the relevance of environmentalism to the civil rights movement when it revealed that three out of five Black and Hispanic Americans and about half of all Asian/Pacific Islanders and Native Americans live in communities with uncontrolled toxic waste sites (Marks 9).

In the words of Benjamin Chavis, who was then the head of the United Church of Christ Commission for Racial Justice, "the idea of civil rights is expanding to include freedom from pollution, and an emphasis on social justice is being added to the idea of environmental protection" (Suro B7). This reconciliation process resulted in part from a response to the complaints by a variety of civil rights groups that were formalized by a letter campaign in 1990 during which hundreds of organizations sent letters to the "Group of Ten" (the ten largest environmental organizations). These letters charged that the environmental movement had "shown little willingness to recognize the legitimacy of or provide support to the struggle to alleviate the poisoning of communities of color . . . [they] have only token involvement of people of color in their operations and policy-making bodies . . . [and] some national environmental groups have taken steps in local communities which have actually been detrimental to the interests of people of color" (Guerrero and Head 11). Over the last few years, the situation has improved as discussions between mainstream environmentalists and civil rights activists have brought the two movements closer together.

In the past, the environmental movement's emphasis on issues such as wilderness preservation and protecting endangered species often served to deny the relevance of incidents of environmental racism. Now groups exploring the connections between these different forms of ecological destruction can provide a basis for united action. Such connections can also be formed in the theory and pedagogy of ecocriticism if it is not held captive by an exclusively deep-ecological bias. At the same time, the focus of many civil rights groups on urban environments (working in New York and lobbying in D.C.) should not blind us to the insights of movements concerned about "wild nature" or to the fact that environmental racism is not solely an urban phenomena. In fact, many of the case studies in Robert Bullard's classic collection *Confronting Environmental Racism* are devoted to the ecological concerns of rural communities of color. The incident that many credit as the birth of the environmental justice movement occurred in the rural South in 1982 when the mostly black residents of Warren County, North Carolina, staged a protest against a PCB landfill in their community.

Since then, the environmental and civil rights movements have slowly grown closer together, transforming "the pastoral face of green politics" (Ross, *Chicago* 103). As a result, the green movement has extended well beyond its former base among the privileged classes to encompass a much more diverse group of citizens concerned about the spaces in which they live together. And the civil rights movement has found itself expanding to consider the environmental hazards faced by people of color. The environmental justice movement provides fertile ground for bringing the concerns of these two groups together and having an impact on both of the movements from which it was born. And it has done so by building grassroots organizations that function independently of the traditional environmental and civil rights groups at the same time as they apply transformative pressure on these more entrenched bodies. As Dana Alston maintains, the strength of the environmental justice movement has to do with its connection to the grassroots because communities of color have for some time been "integrating 'environmental' concerns into a broader agenda that emphasizes social, racial, and economic justice" (3). Robert Bullard notes that the problem "at the heart" of environmental racism is that "the United States is a racially divided nation" (7). So if the environmental justice movement is to be efficacious, it needs, in fact, to expand to include the public policy and private acts that have functioned to create the hypersegregated areas that become the targets of space-based racism. In the process, the environmental justice movement can incorporate socioeconomic and political concerns beyond questions of clean air and water or the placement of toxic waste sites, taking up such inner-city problems as housing, healthcare, and workplace safety.

As the environmental justice movement has grown to resist various forms of racism, sexism, and classism at the local level, so too has the antiglobalization movement grown to resist these structures of oppression on a transnational level. The antiglobalization movement has productively brought together the red and green ends of the environmental spectrum to challenge the depredations of multinational corporations. And so the crowds at antiglobalization rallies are an interesting mix of labor union members, antiracist activists, radical environmentalists, and many others. As my group of democratic socialists bumped up against an environmental group at a protest against the IMF and World Bank, I found, for instance, that you can learn a lot while marching next to a sea turtle. The greenpeace activist next to me, costumed as the endangered sea turtle she hoped to protect, told me that she had just encountered a teamster holding a placard about the jobs he wanted to save. She had learned that both were protesting against phenomena that are not at all unrelated: the effects of rapacious and unrestrained capital on social and natural environments. The old growth forests that the green elements within the antiglobalization movement would preserve for the sake of biodiversity and aesthetic contemplation are also the focus of union protests against exporting whole trees abroad, where the most labor-intensive work is accomplished at slave wages. Here we encounter another manifestation of how the relatively more green and relatively more red ends of the left can and must work together to confront the full spectrum of the sociopolitical challenges we face.

Thus we can see that two of the most lively and important forms of contemporary left political praxis—the environmental justice and antiglobalization movements—are united in confronting the ecological plight of the poor and of communities of color. It is crucial that radical academics and activists recognize that environmental concerns are often top priorities for these communities and must, of necessity, be ours as well. Despite the objections many of us on the left have had to forms of ecological thinking, we should learn from the recent efforts to bring the civil rights, anticapitalist, and environmental movements together in theory and practice that the red and green are being combined in all sorts of new and dynamic ways. These movements serve as a reminder of the urgency of bringing red and green together in the ecocritical movement as well.

Let us recall that the colors red and green mix to form brown, which is perhaps a more "natural" metaphor for an ecocriticism that is concerned with the soil and bark of forests, whether virgin or clearcut; the rough towering peaks and deep canyons of the American wilderness; as well as the skyscrapers and smog of U. S. cityscapes. Or the color brown might represent the deep roots (which is, after all, the meaning of the word *radical*: "of or relating to roots") that connect these disparate places with global structures of domination. Or the color brown might recall the effort of radicals to get at the root of the problems that confront the red and green elements within ecocriticism and the environmental movement generally, which are so desperately in need of reconciliation.

NOTES

1. For a more extensive effort to define the term ecocriticism and trace the history of the movement, see Glotfelty and Fromm's *The Ecocriticism Reader*. The essays by Glotfelty and Howarth provide particularly useful introductions to the "field."

2. See, for example, Erik Davis's "It Ain't Easy Being Green: Eco Meets Pomo," in the *Voice Literary Supplement*; Jay Parini's "The Greening of the Humanities" in *The New York Times Magazine*, which was attacked by Jonathan Yardley in the *Washington Post*; Jonathan Collett and Stephen Karakashian's "Turning Curricula Green" appeared in *The Chronicle of Higher Education*, which then published Karen J. Winkler's cover story "Inventing a Field: the Study of Literature About the Environment."

3. The "classic" works on American pastoralism are Henry Nash Smith's *Virgin Land* and Leo Marx's *The Machine in the Garden*. The development of "literary ecology" could be traced to Joseph Meeker's *The Comedy of Survival* and Yi-Fu Tuan's *Topophilia*. Building on this foundation, a "new pastoralism" has been constructed by such popular works of ecocriticism as Neil Evernden's *The Social Creation of Nature*, Jonathan Bate's *Romantic Ecology*, and Lawrence Buell's *The Environmental Imagination*.

4. The Marxist influence in social geography is evident in works by Manuel Castells, David Harvey, and Ira Katznelson. Peter Dickens, Joel Kovel, David Pepper, and others have made important contributions to ecosocialism. Other signs of the productivity of Marxist environmental theory include the well-respected journal *Capitalism, Nature, Socialism*, a flurry of articles in various other journals (*Cultural Critique, New Political Science, Telos*), and the popular Guilford Press series on "Democracy and Ecology": *Is Sustainable Capitalism Possible?*; *Green Production: Toward an Environmental Rationality*; *Minding Nature: The Philosophers of Ecology*. Sharply critical of Marxist ecology, but sharing many of its insights, social ecology has also developed a sociopolitical analysis of the ways in which environments are constructed, following the lead of the prolific Murray Bookchin.

WORKS CITED

Alston, Dana, ed. *We Speak for Ourselves: Social Justice, Race, and Environment*. Washington, D.C.: Panos Institute, 1990.

American Book Review 18.2 (December-January 1996–97).

Bahro, Rudolf. *Building a Green Society*. Gabriola Island, British Columbia: New Society Publishers, 1986.

Bate, Jonathan. *Romantic Ecology: Wordsworth and the Environmental Tradition*. New York: Routledge, 1991.

Bennett, Michael. "From Wide Open Spaces to Metropolitan Places: The Urban Challenge to Ecocriticism." *ISLE: Interdisciplinary Studies in Literature and the Environment* 8.1 (Winter 2001): 31–52.

Bennett, Michael, and David W. Teague, eds. *The Nature of Cities: Ecocriticism and Urban Environments*. Tucson: U of Arizona P, 1999.

Bookchin, Murray. *The Ecology of Freedom: The Emergence and Dissolution of Hierarchy*. Palo Alto: Chesire Books, 1982.

———. *The Philosophy of Social Ecology: Essays on Dialectical Naturalism*. Montreal: Black Rose Books, 1995.

———. *Toward an Ecological Society*. Montreal: Black Rose Books, 1980.

———. *Urbanization without Cities: The Rise and Decline of Citizenship*. Montreal: Black Rose Books, 1992.

Buell, Lawrence. *The Environmental Imagination: Thoreau, Nature Writing, and the Formation of American Culture*. Cambridge: Harvard UP, 1995.

Bullard, Robert D., ed. *Confronting Environmental Racism: Voices from the Grassroots*. Boston: South End P, 1993.

Castells, Manuel. *The Castells' Reader on Cities and Social Theory*. Ed. Ida Susser. Oxford: Blackwell, 2001.

Collett, Jonathan, and Stephen Karakashian. "Turning Curricula Green." *Chronicle of Higher Education* 23 February 1996: B1-B2.

Cronon, William. "The Trouble with Wilderness." *New York Times Magazine* 13 August 1995: 42–43.

———, ed. *Uncommon Ground: Toward Reinventing Nature*. New York: Norton, 1995.

Davis, Donald Edward. *Ecophilosophy: A Field Guide to the Literature*. San Pedro, CA: R. and E. Miles, 1989.

Davis, Erik. "It Ain't Easy Being Green: Eco Meets Pomo." *Voice Literary Supplement* February 1995: 16–18.

Devall, Bill, and George Sessions. *Deep Ecology: Living as if Earth Really Mattered*. Layton, Utah: Gibbs M. Smith, 1985.

Dickens, Peter. *Society and Nature*. Philadelphia: Temple UP, 1992.

Evernden, Neil. *The Social Creation of Nature*. Baltimore: Johns Hopkins UP, 1992.

Gelfant, Blanche Housman. *The American City Novel*. Norman: U of Oklahoma P, 1954.

Glotfelty, Cheryll, and Harold Fromm, eds. *The Ecocriticism Reader: Landmarks in Literary Ecology*. Athens and London: U of Georgia P, 1996.

Goodman, Paul, and Percival Goodman. *Communitas*. New York: Columbia UP, 1990.

Guerrero, Michael, and Louis Head. "The Environment—Redefining the Issue." *We Speak for Ourselves: Social Justice, Race, and Environment*. Ed. Dana Alston. Washington, D.C.: Panos Institute, 1990. 11.

Harvey, David. *Spaces of Capital: Towards a Critical Geography*. New York: Routledge, 2001.

Katznelson, Ira. *Marxism and the City*. Oxford: Oxford UP, 1994

Kovel, Joel. *The Enemy of Nature: The End of Capitalism or the End of the World*. London & New York: Zed Books, 2002.

Love, Glen A. "Revaluing Nature: Toward An Ecological Criticism." *Western American Literature* 25.3 (Nov. 1990): 201–15.

Lukes, Timothy W. *Ecocritique: Contesting the Politics of Nature, Economics, and Culture*. Minneapolis: U of Minnesota P, 1997.

Marks, Donovan. "Toxic Wastes and Race in the United States." *We Speak for Ourselves: Social Justice, Race, and Environment*. Ed. Dana Alston. Washington, D.C.: Panos Institute, 1990. 9.

Marx, Leo. *The Machine in the Garden: Technology and the Pastoral Ideal in America*. New York: Oxford UP, 1964.

Meeker, Joseph. *The Comedy of Survival: Studies in Literary Ecology*. New York: Scribner's, 1972.

Mumford, Lewis. *The Culture of Cities*. San Diego: Harcourt Brace, 1996.

———. *The Lewis Mumford Reader*. Athens: U of Georgia P, 1995.

———. *Orion Magazine* 13.4 (Autumn 1994).

Parini, Jay. "The Greening of the Humanities." *The New York Times Magazine* 29 October 1995: 52–53.

Pepper, David. *Eco-Socialism: From Deep Ecology to Social Justice*. New York: Routledge, 1994.

Ross, Andrew. *The Chicago Gangster Theory of Life: Nature's Debt to Society*. London: Verso, 1994.

———. *Strange Weather: Culture, Science, and Technology in the Age of Limits*. London: Verso, 1994.

Shiva, Vandana. *Biopiracy: The Plunder of Nature and Knowledge*. Boston: South End, 1997.

———. *Protect or Plunder? Understanding Intellectual Property Rights*. London: Zed Books, 2001.

Simmel, Georg. *The Sociology of Georg Simmel*. Trans. Kurt H. Wolff. Glencoe, Ill.: Free Press, 1950.

Smith, Henry Nash. *Virgin Land: The American West as Symbol and Myth*. New York: Vintage, 1950.

Suro, Roberto. "Pollution-Weary Minorities Try Civil Rights Tack." *New York Times* 11 January 1993: A1, B7.

Terra Nova: Nature and Culture 1.4 (Fall 1996).

Tobias, Michael, ed. *Deep Ecology.* San Diego: Avant Books, 1985.

Tuan, Yi-Fu. *Topophilia: A Study of Environmental Perception, Attitudes, and Values.* New York: Columbia UP, 1990.

Williams, Raymond. *The Country and the City.* New York: Oxford UP, 1973.

Winkler, Karen J. "Inventing a Field: the Study of Literature About the Environment." *Chronicle of Higher Education* 9 August 1996: A9, A15.

Wright, Will. *Wild Knowledge: Science, Language, and Social Life in a Fragile Environment.* Minneapolis: Minnesota UP, 1992.

Yardley, Jonathan. "'Ecocriticism,' Growing Like a Weed." *Washington Post* 13 November 1995: B2.

CHAPTER SIX

A MONSTROUS EMERGE-AGENCY: CRIPPING THE "WHOLE LEFT"

BRENDA JO BRUEGGEMANN

WENDY L. CHRISMAN

MARIAN E. LUPO

HERE IN THE TWENTY-FIRST CENTURY, WE ARE SURROUNDED, FORMED, MOLDED, impressed by a cripping discourse. We believe disability theory involves both the study of the discourse that crips and the creation of an enabling discourse. It need never wander very far from texts and contexts in our cultural history or contemporary situation. Here, for example, at random (almost) the cover of *Time* magazine, date 19 August 2002: "Inside the Volatile World of the Young and Bipolar," a title that very neatly rhetorically evokes the soap opera, the "Young and the Restless." There is a picture of a (white male) nine-year old on the cover. He is being treated for bipolar disorder. On the same cover, blazoned across the top left-hand corner of the magazine, is the title "The Skinny on the Anti-Fat Hormone." It takes no medical or advertising expertise to know that disease and cure, especially miraculous technologically accomplished cure, sells magazines. Nor does it take any particularly subtle powers of observation to realize that U.S. culture is a drug culture, neatly split into the state-sanctioned drug industry, the pharmaceutical corporations, and the black market of the street drug industry.

The discourse that crips rarely recognizes race, gender, class, sexual preference, or religious affiliation, although it does its work most virulently on the already oppressed. Rather, this discourse, with its center on a presumed healthy body/mind norm, conceptually undergirds discourses that separate the left. It works by defining difference as "aberration" and as "disease": difference needs to be cured for the body to be made whole.

Yet the enabling discourse that disability embodies is built not so much on defining difference as it is on initiating identification (although, as rhetorician Kenneth Burke emphasized, identification is always also about difference). And this initiation is aimed not just at identifying as "disabled"—as proudly claiming an emerging agency in the identity of disability—but also on merging that identity with others that have been radical, and relevant, and leaning toward "the whole left" too: environmentally-invested identities, gendered, racially marked, sexed and out-, over- and underclassed ones as well.

Consider, for example, how this essay itself is wedged neatly between two others (Bennett and Owens) that focus on environmental and ecological landscapes in the frame of the "whole left." How fitting to place disability in the picture here since a considerable thrust of the new disability studies is predicated on the core concept that disability is *in the environment*. The World Health Organization (WHO) definitions and delineations of key concepts around disability with the International Classification of Impairment, Disability, and Handicap (ICIDH) have undergone significant change in the last decade in order to bear this idea out: that while an *impairment* is connected to the specifics of bodily or mental function (things gone wrong) that are in some way medically documented, a *disability* is the social construction of the impairment that manifests itself in the way the impairment actually plays out in relation to the environment the person with *x* impairment finds herself in. Thus, someone who gets around in a wheelchair may have x, y, or z *impairment* but her *disability* appears when she is unable to enter a building or is treated differently in any given situation because of her impairment (Fougeyrollas and Beauregard 2001).

The environment now figures large in disability studies as well as in most discussions around disability (whether legal, medical, social, historical) and it occupies an entire heading area alone these days in the recent revisions of the ICIDH (see <http://www3.who.int/icf/>). Just as the left has consistently "left out" the environment in most of its discourses, disability has also been oddly absent as well—in large part because the significant smoke screen of medicine has cloaked much of our intellectual, political, and public discourse around disability and disabled people.

In *A History of Disability*, recently published by Michigan University Press, Henri-Jacques Stiker quotes at length from the work of Georges Canguilhem, a historian of science who is strategically important for disability studies because he pinpoints, in the nineteenth century, one of the most profound ideological moves made by the medical profession, the decision to study the human body, by nature changeable and always in flux, by relying on a static "norm":

> The existence of monsters calls into question life in its capacity to teach us order. This questioning is immediate, no matter how long our prior confidence may have been, no matter how solid may have been our habit of seeing roses bloom on rose bushes, tadpoles change into frogs, mares suckle colts and,

in general fashion, of seeing like engender like. All that is needed is one loss of this confidence, one morphological lapse, one specific appearance of equivocation, and a radical fear seizes us. Fear? That I understand, you will say, but why radical? Because we are living beings, real effects of the laws of life, and the eventual causes of life in our turn. A failure on the part of life concerns us doubly because a failure could have afflicted us and a failure could come through us. It is only because humans are living creatures that a morphological mistake is, to our living eyes, a monster. Suppose that we were pure reason, pure intellectual machines that observed, calculated and summed up, and thus inert and indifferent to the events that made us think the monster would only be other than the same, of an order other than the most probable order. (Stiker 1999)

Canguilhem's observation is important for demonstrating the effectiveness of the discourse that crips to oppress: it works through not just fear, but a radical fear that places the source of the monster within the individual. This radical fear is not unique to disability studies. The fragmentation of the left can be attributed, in part, to this location of the monster within each of us—monsters of racism, sexism, gender discrimination, sexual preference discrimination, economic discrimination, environmental devastation. Disability studies provides a way of looking at the body[1] and its material conditions and pain, the enduring fabric that connects the whole left.

It does this, most specifically, by articulating the fear produced by the discourse that crips, a fear that places each of us, as individuals, in a constant state of emergency. To create a whole left, we must be proactive, not reactive. We believe that we (all of us, crips and TABs alike)[2] should set the agenda rather than try to absorb and then resolve the constant crisis of postmodernism. September 11th—and the war coverage that has followed—have devolved into a media distraction from the mission of the whole left—a way to involve each of us in a private monster struggle with the constant state of emergency that, as Walter Benjamin reminds us, is fascism:

The tradition of the oppressed teaches us that the "state of emergency" in which we live is not the exception, but the rule. We must attain to a conception of history that is in keeping with this insight. Then we shall clearly recognize that it is our task to bring about a real state of emergency, and this will improve our condition in the struggle against Fascism. One reason why Fascism has a chance is that in the name of progress its opponents treat it as a historical norm. The current amazement that the things we are experiencing are "still" possible in the twentieth century is not philosophical. This amazement is not the beginning of knowledge—unless it is the knowledge that the view of history which gives rise to it is untenable. (Benjamin 1969)

In exploring the tradition of oppression that disability studies explores—that of disabled people—much in the spirit of Benjamin, in the text that follows we propose a slight revision in this state of emergency. We want to suggest a revision that does not erase or fault or cancel out the work Benjamin has done in having us think about the real state of emergency, but that is instead built further upon with "disability as insight" (Brueggemann 2002; Davis 1997), modeled on the emerging field of disability studies, and morphing this state into one of *emergence-y*, a state of developing, of coming out, of monstrous emergence. Further, and perhaps even more monstrously, we want to demonstrate this *emergence-y* carried one step further by focusing here on what happens with disability studies and theory in undergraduate classrooms, offering a state of *emerge-agency* for disabled and able-bodied students (future citizens, scholars, consumers) alike.

In producing an enabling discourse, disability studies traces the history of the "able" body/mind and the creation of a hegemonic "able" body/mind to create a particular real state of *emergenc-y*—emerging as a new body of study that studies the body in not necessarily medicalized emergency (as an impairment) but more in socially constructed space, in a critical geometric configurations with other radical discourses like those surrounding race, class, gender, sexuality, age. In cripping the whole left, disability studies resists the disabling discourse that is as polyvocal as this triply authored essay—an essay that represents, by its very placement in this multivocal volume, the body multiply inscribed by and inscribing the environment—resonating with the reconciliation of Michael Bennett's critical environmentalism and the urgency of Derek Owen's ecocriticism.

Out of disability studies' state of emergenc-y arises the fragile, vulnerable, limited, resource-dependent, multiply-inscribed body/mind that is interdependent on and with others—always in relation to its others—existing in its oppressed and exploited materiality that refuses to go away. Thus, disability theory applies the Butlerian materiality of discourse to the actual, physical human body/mind. Disability is not just in the crippled body that carries it. Rather, as many disability scholars and activists alike insist, disability is in the environment (Fougeyrollas and Beauregard 2001). Political scientist Harlan Hahn makes this point poignantly in the video *Vital Signs: Crip Culture Talks Back:* "Disability activists address a radical agenda that all the identity groups have only taken up in part: we not only want to change attitudes and laws and medical practice, but we want to change the entire physical environment. Yeah, all we want to do is change the world . . ." (Dirs. Sharon Snyder and David Mitchell, A Brace Yourselves Production 1996). It takes the lack of a ramp to disable the wheelchair user; it takes the lack of clean air to disable the breather; and it takes the lack of a recognizable, citable discourse of the unruly, messy, and nonconforming body/mind to disable the actual, physical human body/mind. And from this lack, from this state of emergency, is born the new (disabled) citizen, emerging into agency, existing then in a state of *emerge-agency*.

LEARNING FROM THE LEFT: EMERGE-AGENCY LESSONS

The image of the adult educator that emerges from the combined insights of Gramsci and Freire is that of a person committed to the learners' cause. This entails the educator seeking every means possible to break any barrier that might exist between her/him and the learners in the interest of creating truly democratic and transformative social relations of education.

—Peter Mayo, *Gramsci, Freire and Adult Education:
Possibilities for Transformative Action* (1999)

I take Mayo's emphasis on "barrier breaking" here to mean many things, yet something very specific for me when "teaching from the left." Finding ways to show my commitment, as an educator, to the "cause" of Disability Studies has required breaking barriers of the self, or self-disclosure, in more ways than perhaps any other cause I have committed myself to. I laugh now as I write "committed myself to," not just for the grammatical error and my steadfast resistance to pressures forever put upon me by my language-purist colleagues, but for the heavy (and heady) undertones this statement means in my life as someone professionally and personally invested in disability studies and too, as someone who is disabled, or better said, disordered. In all my other titles, labels, academic identity categories, I do have both personal and professional investments. Yet showing my feminist leanings does not necessarily require an embodied performance of being a feminist 24/7 the same way being disabled does, nor does showing my Marxist leanings or any other theory I subscribe to.[3] Showing true commitment to disability studies however necessitates both voluntary and involuntary self-disclosure and disclosure of self for myriad reasons, for better or for worse. More importantly, disability is not necessarily an identity category of choice the same way feminism or Marxism is; rather it falls into a continuum that is at once bodily, mental, epistemological, phenomenological, and so on, much like gender, race, and sexuality slide along similar continuums.

As a Ph.D. student I had to fulfill a teaching apprenticeship requirement consisting of shadowing a professor in my field in an upper level undergraduate course. I chose working with Brenda Brueggemann because, in addition to being my advisor, her involvement in disability studies is progressive, prolific, and proactive. Having gained much of my own interest in disability studies from being Brenda's student in prior courses, I jumped at the chance of working with her in English 562: Disability and Illness in Drama and Performance Art. What was even more appealing about this course was its location: a computer-based classroom with a heavy accent on participation in web-based discussions via Web CT, Power Point presentations, and web design.[4] My primary roles were to help generate (and, at times, moderate) Web CT and class discussions, help facilitate two student presentation discussions, comment on some student work, and share my knowledge of and enthusiasm for disability studies in general.

Many students in this course were coming in with only basic computer-related experience, and with even more minimal experience with disability. Or so they thought. All of the students, however, came in with opinions, questions, and a dire need for answers. One student in particular was somehow both "in" and "out" of the roles of teacher/student like I was. I met my friend and colleague Marian Lupo on the first day of Disability in Drama and Performance Art. I couldn't sign onto the web-based discussion board because I was already signed on as Brenda, the instructor and designer of the Web CT,[5] so I wouldn't have my own identity in the discussions. I was frustrated, I wanted to share, I wanted to be on board with the class, I wanted my own stake in the way the conversation went, and I felt circumstantially silenced. And, admittedly, a bit of my own brand of narcissism was at work in my thoughts. In a flash, like a cat on a mission for mice Marian slipped over to me and gave me her own password, then introduced herself. Someone here was speaking my language: it is sometimes silent as snowfall, and other times as roaring as thunder. Brenda knew that of me, and now I *knew* Marian did too. I also knew clearly then that we would make this class memorable. If I didn't have an answer, Marian or Brenda would. We had the language, and we'd translate for each other. Perhaps this factor more than any other allowed for Brenda, Marian, and me to take this course as an opportunity to create an educationally transformative environment for these students and for ourselves. Or perhaps the transformations were enabled because of our own personal investments in and experiences of disability as a discourse and state of being. But this is also where our language(s) come from.

In reflecting on my role in this course, I scroll through the web-based discussion board looking for some signs of how I imprinted myself on this experience: how exactly did I present myself, did the others see me the way I saw myself? Not surprising was the first actual post I contributed to the discussion. After a conversation popped up regarding the opening week video *Vital Signs: Crip Culture Talks Back*,[6] I asked the class to consider the ways in which literary genres had been invoked, challenged, revised, resisted, and followed with precision in the performances we had seen. I wrote to them: "How has disability performance added to the discipline of literature and how has the discipline of literature shaped disability performances?" In other words, I was setting up boundaries I thought they would have familiarity with so they could register their own voices into the larger conversation by asking them to define them, defy them, to find how the performers/performances "played" with comedy, satire, parody, drama, hyperbole, and documentary. I saw these disability performances as meriting some thought about how they do or do not "fit" into literary tradition, how they are or are not "literary" at all, how they disrupt it or challenge it or redefine or add to it. No one ever responded to this post; and I still wonder why.

This course presented certain difficulties to the undergraduates, some because of their trepidations of sharing themselves so openly and regularly with a new audience, their dichotomized fear of sharing their views about disability, a fear of being criticized, and their urgent need to be heard. Complicating this was their own perceptions of not having had much, if any, experience or contact with the disabled. My decision about how much of myself to disclose was formed not just in relation to how much Brenda and Marian chose to reveal but also by how open I felt the students were, by considering how much they needed to know to push themselves to shirk their fears and vulnerabilities. I also gauged how much was just too much information for them to process. Certain authority and credibility comes with openly placing oneself on the disability circuit, and devaluement as well as accusations of hornblowing come just as readily, too.

An important question bears asking in regards to private and public disclosure of disability (voluntary and otherwise): is there agency in this performance (and yes, I do think of it here as a performance, a hybrid Butler/Austin/Chrisman performance), and if so, who is transformed and in what way? Two separate instances occurred in our class that not only highlight the intricacies and powerfulness of using webspace in the classroom but that also illuminate performed disclosure in both spheres (classroom and web). Johnson Cheu, our colleague and a graduate student in disability studies, gave a guest lecture alongside a reading assignment our class had about the key idea fueling his dissertation: the prevalence of cure in twentieth-century American literature, film, and autobiography. The students had all been circling around this idea of cure for some time, yet Cheu's work was the impetus for some critical thinking via our web discussion board. One student launched (for better or for worse) right into an analysis of Cheu's use of the term cure. This student began his posting:

> The major problem I have with Cheu's theory of cure as a detractor from a harmonious disabled existence is that everything is a cure, just in differing sizes. The rejection of cure is almost unthinkable and unfeasible for the disabled. If cure is to be retracted, then all wheelchairs should be folded up and discarded. All medical advances in the fields of disabling syndromes and diseases should stop immediately. All medical knowledge whatsoever can be thrown right out the window, never to be used again for any humanitarian aspect. While all this seems preposterous (and it is), it is no more preposterous then the idea of an unwanted cure. . . . Would you allow the child to be born with the disability?

None of the students seemed too certain where to position themselves in relation to this post, almost as if they were silently questioning: "Is it okay to be hopeful? Cynical? Uncertain?" This particular student, however, was straightforward in his thoughts: it was always necessary to remain optimistic for a cure. The catch was, he was defining cure in a rather holistic way. And yet, the catch to this was we could not get him to define the way he was defining it himself. I was first to respond back to him, beginning with my answer to the hypothetical question with which he ended his post: "In a hypothetical world, if you were going to give birth to a disabled child and could take a pill and it would be born without disability, with no moral, religious, or medical implications, would you?"

And here began my own partial disclosure—and with certainty, because I know the timing is right. I post back that "if my mother and father were to answer the question, one would most likely say 'yes, it's for the best' and the other would say 'I'd have to think about it, maybe I should discuss it with my daughter first, she knows more about these things than I do.' I, however, would on my worst day and would never on my best day. And that is a fact." Then I tried to engage him on a more progressive point, that of his idea of cure. From my reading I took him to mean cure could be anything from a wheelchair to a hearing aid to a pill, and this was an interesting take on what the medical model defines in more stable terms: cure/incurable. While I could not open more doors with this student about that assumed stability on the web-based discussion, I did get into some conversations outside the classroom with him. I think this connection was afforded because he was a student of my own in an upper-level composition class a couple of years prior, so we already knew how the other ticked. His postings about cure were provocative and I told him blatantly, as I always have, that I wasn't all the way on board with him, but neither of us anticipated the sorts of responses he received from the other students. In fact, this thread of discussion was the most heated and liveliest during the whole quarter. Multiple positions of what I see as agency, subjectivity, and even dogmatism erupted:

- *I hope I didn't offend anyone when talking about my outlook on cure on Monday. I just don't like to shut out any possibilities for anyone. I believe that if there is technology out there that could better a specific person's quality of life, they should be able to take advantage of it.*

- *I think what Johnson is trying to suggest is that there are so many disabilities that aren't curable today, that to live in expectation of some over-arching cure might be a waste of energy.*

- *Just because the disabled community might want to reject the notion of "cure" does not mean they would reject wheelchair ramps, Braille menus, or anything else that would aid them in their day-to-day activities as a disabled person. After all, a wheelchair ramp is not a cure for a paraplegic. Also, the desire for a "disabled community" (entailing the rejection of "cure," as explained in Cheu's essay) does not center on a "failure of optimism" (my own quotes). It is an attempt to create a culture which rejoices in the disabled identity, countering the normative view (that disability = lesser person, or possible/potential person). It certainly is radically different from the normal viewpoint. . . .*

- *I believe that many people would choose cure over disability, however, society would benefit from changing the overall mindset of acceptance. A cure, or the hope of a cure, does not need to be foisted on a disabled person. Until more is presented to the disabled by the disabled, both pro and con, the discussion can not be complete.*

- *I could not have stated this any better myself . . . I do have a slight hearing loss, and there is a constant ringing in my ears . . . which is something that there is no cure for. The fact is, however, that if there was a cure, I most likely would not want to have it. That would mean that I would lose out on gaining any more experiences such as the ones that I have had since I've had this condition. Sure, there are instances in which I would love to not have this ringing in my ears, such as when I'm trying to sleep, but the fact of the matter is that it has become a part of me, and part of my everyday life. To take that away with a "cure" would be to alter myself as a person. I accept and like who I am, and who is science to tell me I should be someone else?*

Disclosure of disability often as not occurs in the space articulated by this last student—the space between alteration and acceptance. For disability studies, *disclosure* is an *always already* investment, predicament, choice, obligation, and oxymoron. Another way to look at disclosure, though, is as a performance of emerge-agency. In this particular class, the "students" and the "teachers" alike performed disclosure.

In the pedagogical context of this college course, the nuances of how disclosure is performed and theorized, and the consequences of both, certainly fall within that area shaded by circumstance, prediction, and hope that we as teachers are making practical and progressive decisions for ourselves and for our students. Yet there are contexts when disclosure (or access to disclosure) becomes not only a location for agency to emerge but a necessary right or privilege. Disability studies explores the long-standing ways in which the medical models of disability/disorder systematically deny, silence, and erase access to agency not just to those who clearly and specifically identify themselves as disabled, but to the general population as they are experiencing illness, disease, and aging. In *Democracy by Disclosure: The Rise of Techno-Populism*,[7] Mary Graham explores the report that "shocked the nation" published by the Institute of Medicine (IOM) in 1999: more people died each year from faulty equipment, medication mismanagement, and mistakes during hospitalization than from auto accidents. This report launched a paradigmatic change in healthcare management, and now there is a "standardized system of disclosure medical errors" to the public. Prior to this disclosure law we were on our own and at the mercy of our doctors' integrity in figuring out "what went wrong" when "death by hospitalization" occurred. This law ends the stealth and secrecy. Disclosure not only specifically addresses the needs of the disabled community, it is a corrective that leads to social change. While the efficacy of this sort of disclosure is at best ambiguous, the IOM is now required to disclose information to patients about medical errors made during their hospitalizations—so citizens do have *access* to this information. The IOM has made internal changes as well as a call to the nation to understand the disclosure of medical errors is for their benefit but is also to their harm if they do not recognize that the medical errors are not human errors. The Committee on Quality of Health Care in America: Institute of Medicine published the comprehensive report "To Err is Human: Building a Safer Health System," yet maintains, as do all refuting reports after the press exploded upon its publication, that "errors result largely from systems failure, not people failures." So then, why is this not titled "To Err is Systemic," or "To Err is Technological"?

More importantly, who built the systems? Themselves? Or people? And herein lies a parallel to our class. There were countless stories told, some in class, some in private, of the frustrations, secrecy, inadequacies, ineptness, arrogance, and silencing that goes along with all the wonders of dealing with Medicine as an institution and a discourse. While it may not have been easy for these students to think of themselves as disabled (even though in many cases they were, by legal definition), or even ponder too deeply the lives of other people who are disabled, it is next to impossible to imagine a life without having been in a hospital or knowing someone else who has been in a hospital. Disease, aging, and death are inescapable realities of everyone's lives, and there is no disability more disabling than death. I teach sections of the required writing course to the undergraduates at Ohio State and every quarter a point of entry opens up for me to talk about disability studies because students *do* talk about these subjects freely in writing courses, and they want to discuss their experiences of a friend or relative dying, being paralyzed, having cancer, or some other life altering disability.[8] With these conversations always comes the topic of ethics of care, and a composition class takes the shape of writing about social justice, personal tragedy, and identity categories. And while gender, race, class, sexuality, age, and all the frequently theorized markers of identity are always already present, disability has rapidly become one of the most accessible, and in an odd way, most enjoyable, categories for my students to discuss, relate to, and think critically about.

In its own state of emergenc-y, disability studies has often offered my students their own emerging agency as critical thinkers now capable and willing to take on discussions about cure and the err that is human. An important connection I see in the IOM's report, for however much it attempts to deflect attention away from the "real" problems, for all its effort to denounce human culpability in medical errors, is that the IOM is asking for the nation to not only pay attention to the report but to take a part in reforming their health-care standards. In other words, we are (albeit reluctantly, grudgingly) being asked to question authority: the authorities in control of our lives, our health, our deaths.

And, we now "know," are *authorized* to know, what we already knew, that some-times even *they* don't know what will happen when we enter those emer-gency room doors and that we may not walk back out of them. Inclusively, what I want—what I believe Brenda, Marian, and every teacher, or researcher of dis-ability studies or any other discipline wants—is for their students to ask them-selves (and others) those big questions, the epiphanic questions. In this con-text the questions might look like:

- If my family or friend were in the hospital and they died by medical error, what would I do?

- What does the person disabled by medical error do? What do I do? How do I think/feel about this?

- Where does responsibility lie? With whom and why?

- What does disability mean to me now? Has my definition of the term changed? How?

It is not difficult to follow where this line of questioning might lead. These are questions we all might ask ourselves at some point since "disability" is *not* so clearly defined as to say either you are disabled or you aren't, you're born with it or you aren't, you see it or you don't, it's contagious or it isn't. Here again, though, this uncertainty suggests that state of emergenc-y that disability stud-ies engages: finding subject positionings that create agency when one is asking questions with elusive answers, especially when even the medical discourse and the IOM tells us "to error is human."

One of the important elements of the class in Disability in Drama and Per-formance Art, and a primary goal of ours in creating a published web-text about it,[9] was to value and foster the work of students in the newly developing field of Disability Studies. If attitudes and awareness in our culture about disability are ever to change and disability is ever to be understood more broadly as a socially constructed experience in which *all* of us are involved and invested, then it will be many of these students—as the next generation of voters, tax-payers, citizens, and workers—who will foster that change. And if attitudes and awareness in our culture about disability are ever to imagine disability as more than just an impairment—as more than a medicalized condition, a "suf-fering," a site for "cure"—then it is probably these students who will best achieve that imagination.

And finally, because these students could well become the next genera-tion of Disability Studies scholars—or teachers or lawyers or doctors or rehab counselors or journalists or nurses or allied health professionals or social work-ers or psychologists or . . . well you get the picture—the importance of their developing knowledge and attempts to work in and around the "new disability studies" (a discipline distinguished from medicalized and individualized approaches to disability) will help that field grow and grapple especially with intersecting and analogous fields like women's studies, race and ethnicity studies, gender and sexuality studies, gay/lesbian/queer studies, and aging studies. The students' developing knowledge of disability studies will also impact the fields in which they make their careers. In short, we believe that engaging students, all students, in disability studies and disability theory will add to the project of the whole left as we teach (and learn from) them about how to enact a state of *emerge-agency* around the body, crippled or (fictionally) whole, in our current state of real emergency.

CRITICAL GEOMETRY IN THE CLASSROOM:
BETWEEN EMERGENCE-Y AND EMERGE-AGENCY

Disability is not a 'brave struggle' or 'courage in the face of adversity'—disability is an art. It's an ingenious way to live.
> —Neil Marcus, poet/performer/playwright/dancer/storm
> *Storm Reading* (1996)

Standing (or not) in the narrow spaces between authority and accusations (as Wendy was and is), between being one moment all the more credible because you are in fact disabled but then in the very next moment being devalued because of that same label, presents the very paradox of disability and its representations in American history and culture to begin with. Yet this is the space, we argue, where agency around and through the body might emerge. For the state of *emerge-agency* is a powerful operational space, often hyphenated between two seeming oppositions—seamed in. In fact, the real happening in *emerge-agency* erupts in the very hyphen of the concept itself.

Disability theory enables an articulation of that hyphenated state. Disability as both a condition and concept, and people with disabilities then too, are more often than not found between the rocks and hard places of our cultural consciousness: between culture and community; between overdetermined individuality (a positive value in American culture) and an objectified isolation; between medicine and the law; between (unfulfilling) work and (unfulfilling) welfare; between being always the subject of various "services" and yet, too, a tireless (but tiring) self-advocate; between saint and stigma; between being stared at and then ignored, overlooked in both senses of the word; between "special" and "deviant"; between deemed as privileged (those parking spaces!) and yet disenfranchised (nowhere to go); between being too public and/but/too personal; between rights and reasons; and between being the object of pity and the subject of inspiration.

The decisions about disclosure that Wendy faced in this course (and others since then)—like the decisions Brenda has faced in every course she's taught too (whether disability is the subject or not)—are repetitions of disabled reality, the hiccups of having to perpetually perform "passing" while also "coming out" and having to resist the overdetermined normalizing space of a classroom to begin with while continuing to teach the discourse that crips in that space.[10] Balancing this highwire act, managing the supreme stigma associated with the spoiled identity of disability (Goffman 1962), and hauling a subject deemed "too personal" in our culture (*disability*, she whispered and they shuddered) right into the arena of public education, into the classroom, represents an act more radical than anything I've ever put on the syllabus, any text I've ever asked students to talk about, any activity I've ever had them engage in.

Why? Well, first, in large part because even disability plays out and in the hyphenated sliding space between such paradoxes. Second, because they first can't "see" it to begin with, and then they come to see it everywhere and that "blindness to insight" move is a powerful one (and a metaphor I call forth and then myself subvert in my classes), a switch flipped in their own consciousnesses. My students often as not start any class centered around disability with guarded interest frosted lightly with suspended disbelief. They've never encountered this as a subject before; they aren't sure there's really anything here; this seeming absence, however, has somehow beckoned their own presence. And in that beckoning, the strange becomes familiar, while the familiar also becomes strange; the exceptional becomes everyday (and vice versa). Again, as Stiker puts it in discussing Canguilhem's influence in *A History of Disability*, "the existence of monsters calls into question life in its capacity to teach us order."

For example, on only the fourth day of Ohio State's new course "Introduction to Disability Studies" that fronts the new interdisciplinary minor in Disability Studies for undergraduates,[11] students—who mostly said on the first day that they knew "nothing" about disability or disabled people—begin posing questions like popcorn heated to break-point (emerging, as it were, into agency):

- *This weekend I noticed how drive-up ATMs have braille key pads . . . now isn't that strange?*

- *So, what would have to happen for disability to no longer be perceived as negative in our culture?*

- *What's so bad about cure anyway?*

- *The thing I always wonder about cure is, well, when does it stop?*

- *I've had these classes in feminist theory and so now I've been wondering, could there be a disability theory? What would it look like?*

- *When Steve Kuusisto [faculty member, writer, NPR commentator, disability advocate, blind] comes to class next week, are we allowed to pet his dog?*

- *If you choose to identify as disabled, though, couldn't that also leave you trapped in that identity as the major sum of your character? Would you want that?*

- *I was afraid to laugh at anything in that film* [Vital Signs: Crip Culture Talks Back] *because I was afraid of offending anyone here who might have a disability. I was afraid because I wasn't entirely sure if it was funny or not. I was afraid because I knew I didn't have a disability and I wasn't sure I had a right to laugh. I was afraid to laugh because I also kinda felt they might be making fun of me. I was afraid to laugh because even though I could hear people in the audience laughing at her performance, she seemed so angry to me . . . and that didn't seem funny.*

And it often isn't funny. For the third radical act about putting disability in the classroom is the raw and radical fear we begin to recognize that surrounds our relationship to our own (via others') bodies. Again, we go back to Stiker on Canguilhem: "All that is needed is one loss of this confidence, one morphological lapse, one specific appearance of equivocation, and a radical fear seizes us. . . . A failure on the part of life concerns us doubly because a failure could have afflicted us and a failure could come through us." The ideological impetus of this fear is the supposed separateness of the human body from its socioeconomic construction, from its environment, and from other bodies. Experiencing the error of this ideology, an error the disabled recognize and signify, can lead to a sense of loss so profound that one might question reality itself rather than the assumed world of separateness and its corollary, "wholeness." Rather than recognize the betrayal of ideology, the fear coalesces and centers on the body/mind that signifies the error of ideology.

Thus, disability, and disabled people, are feared and in this fear, they are often *overlooked*, in multiple senses of the word: they are looked at too much— stared at on the streets and in stores, gazed at long and hard by medicine and education, to name but a few of our strongest social institutions that interact with and interpret disability every day—and yet they are also ignored, overlooked in that way as well. Understanding this over-looking and the fear behind it makes all the more clear to us, then, how systems of oppression and institutions of othering operate in our culture. Thus, fourthly, disability *emerge-agency* offers a radical interdisciplinarity and interidentity potential.

For example, we've had young college-age women who now consider themselves fairly free and empowered and enlightened and equal ("what's the fuss over this gender pronoun thing?" they query us, "we're past that now, we don't need to fight for our rights in silly ways like that") encounter the still monstrous impact of gender oppression when they've put on disability lenses; their agency emerges in another way with these overlaid frames.

Or too, when reviewing the voluminous and unorganized highlights of Braddock and Parish's "An Institutional History of Disability" that fronts the mammoth *Handbook on Disability Studies*, students offer up the little moments and "facts" that stood out to them and when we step back and look at the board, we notice that what we've recorded there might well look like it came from a Women's Studies or African American Studies or Holocaust Studies classroom:

- That in 1840 when the U.S. census began counting people labeled "idiotic" and "insane," racism was also heavily reflected when all black residents in some southern towns were classified as insane.

- That the Eugenics movement was heavily focused on disabled people, often again, in conjunction with documenting the "inferiority" of these people alongside women and blacks.

- That disabled people have always been, as a group in the entire Western historical record, living in crippling [sic] poverty.

- That once mental institutions arose in America, husbands could (and often did) have their wives committed.

- That the U.S. Supreme Court's 1927 *Buck vs. Bell* decision to affirm the states' right to sterilize people with intellectual disabilities propelled not only the U.S. Eugenics movement (and effectively forced sterilization of between 300,000 and 400,000 people, most of them, of course, women), but it also set in motion a series of acts that "culminated in the murder by euthanasia of between 200,000 and 275,000 individuals with mental and physical disabilities between 1939 and 1945 in Nazi Germany" (40).

That is, the Nazis got it from us first. Who will get it last? That's a question for the whole left—a question disability theory is always already asking—and who has it now?

Bringing this question into the classroom offers each embodied student the potential radical interidentity of the disability emerge-agency. In the discourse that crips, just about everything is an impairment that can be cured. It is a discourse that resonates with a eugenics ideology that pathologizes resistance. In the *Time* article referred to in our introduction, the title asks: "Why are so many kids being diagnosed with the disorder once known as MANIC DEPRES-SION?" a question that the article answers thus: "Some experts believe that kids are being tipped into bipolar disorder by family and school stress, recreational drug use and perhaps even a collection of genes that express themselves more aggressively in each generation. Others argue that the actual number of sick kids hasn't changed at all; instead, we've just got better at diagnosing the illness." For the do-it-yourselfer, the article offers a checklist of behavior to observe in the child, the reader's alter ego. If the reader marks more than twenty of the forty boxes, *Time* magazine recommends that the reader haul herself/her child off to be "evaluated by a professional."

To appreciate the dangerous absurdity of the discourse that crips as well as the complicity of the classroom in pathologizing the personality,[12] here are a few of the "warning signs" of the bipolar child: "is willful and refuses to be subordinated," "argues with adults or bosses others," "defies or refuses to comply with rules." In other words, a resistant personality. Our favorites are warning signs number eight and thirty-nine: "has poor handwriting" and "is fascinated with blood and gore," two warning signs that, in conjunction with the previous three warning signs, would place most doctors we know at some risk for bipolar disorder. The seduction of this article, of course, is the side-bar discussion of "manic genius." As with most elements of the discourse that crips, there is always some trade-off, bonus prize, or badge of honor for being disabled. And so the unwitting parent drugs her child into submission while thinking that she may have a genius on her hands. Interestingly enough, the child featured in the *Time* article was the child of a single mother—the fundamental disorder that is patriarchy (unquestioned obedience, for example) is legitimized by imputing disease to this young child and, by implication, his mother.

Bipolar disorder is just an example of the pathologization of the personality endemic to U.S. culture, a continuation of an (in)visible and (il)legitimate form of violence that outlaws a difference in ontology. The eugenics argument reappears not only as biological determinism, but also as "scientific fact." Medical science will determinedly find a biological basis for the ontology it pathologizes. The *Time* article reports a loss of gray matter and a loss of the branches that connect neurons to explain bipolar disorder: it now becomes a disintegration of the brain, not simply an emotional disorder. Remember, again, some of the personality traits associated with the disorder: "refuses to be subordinated," "argues with adults and bosses others," and "defies or refuses to comply with rules." *Time* and the scientists at the National Institute of Mental Health are working hard to create a hegemonic understanding of resistance as diseased and pathological, a powerful narrative whose fascist implications are clear and yet which also demonstrates the potential of disability as resistance, a place where the painful and the political meet.

RADICAL RHETORICAL RELEVANCE:
EMERGENC-Y CONCLUSION

*It is you, not the astronauts, who are the true pioneers at the frontier of the
human being.*

—Justin Dart Jr., disability advocate,
speaking to group of disabled activists

*No other set of laws [the ADA] so entreats academia to take its own temperature,
examine its traditions, and thoughtfully deliberate about which of its standards are
essential and which are merely unexamined habits. Whether from the insights we
achieve from integration or from self-reflections, the unconventional, nontraditional,
innovative ways in which individuals with disabilities accomplish tasks place us on
new paths that benefit us all.*

—Paul D. Grossman, attorney and law professor

We argue then that introducing disability theory to ourselves and our students
is rhetorically relevant not only for *emerge-agency* in our cure-consumed contemporary culture but in somehow addressing our long-standing state of emergency—in meeting our other-erasing historical past, a past always in hyphenated, contradictory relationship to disability. There is a long (and leftist-leaning)
line moving forward from the Old Testament's mixed messages about disability and disabled persons: on the one hand, protecting them ["*Thou shalt not
curse the deaf nor put a stumbling block before the blind, nor maketh the blind to wander out of the path*" (Leviticus 19:14)] while on the other creating them out of
damnation ["*If you do not carefully follow His commands and decrees . . . all
these curses will come upon you and overtake you: the Lord will afflict you with madness, blindness and confusion of mind. At midday, you will grope around like a blind
man in the dark*" Deuteronomy 28:15, 28–29)]. We move on, the background
changed but the story the same, into the Greco-Roman period where "babies
born with congenital deformities were often regarded as signs that their parents had displeased the gods. However, public support was available to individuals whose impairments precluded them from working" (Braddock and Parish
15) and then to the medieval era where they were equally (and randomly)
demonized and sainted. From there we can skip over millennia of religious persecution and protection, witch-hunting and yet infantalizing, chaining behind
walls and yet setting (too) loose on the streets, benevolence and banishment,
medical inattention and medical surveillance—all with regards to disabled bodies. And all set right beside each other.

   This would bring us right up, lined up, into our present where they (no,
make that *we*) can serve, inspirationally, each week in the "Accent" or "Lifestyle"
sections of our newspapers or for Jerry Lewis' paternalistic passion while we are
also the source of serious public backlash, enacted most often in the recent radical fear against the ADA. We deserve a cure, but we do not deserve, as Lennard

Davis has pointed out in introducing his new collection of essays, *Bending Over Backwards: Disability, Dismodernism, and Other Difficult Positions*, what should probably be the most basic civil right for all—"the right to be ill, to be infirm, to be impaired without suffering discrimination or oppression" (1).

What agency might emerge for all of us then were such a right truly to be enacted? We believe this question to be radical, relevant, and indicative of a critical betweenness—the critical space disability can take the whole left into—in order to achieve an *emerge-agency* that is monstrous—a huge and marvelous morphological hegemonic lapse.

NOTES

1. Here marks a hopeful location of emerge-agency for disability studies itself: finding ways of intersecting body and mind experiences that transcend the traditional duality of mind/body, a binary that leaves little room for understanding the whole (and not so whole) experiences of those within the disabled/disordered community.

2. TAB is a common term in disability studies scholarship and disability activist work that is used to identify a group of people, always in flux, known as "The Temporarily Able-Bodied." Everyone, in fact, is a TAB. PWD is often used to refer to "persons with disabilities" although many who are labeled so actually don't mind—even relish—being called "crips."

3. This is a gross understatement, but for lack of space, let me clarify with an example. I see a vast difference between keeping all my weekly and monthly doctors appointments (physical and mental), having all my blood work completed on time, lab forms filled out, etc. and making sure I have a ride to the Take Back the Night Rally this year. Even if I am on the guest speaker list. I can always be asked back next year or speak at another event that has feminist orientations and is meaningful to my own desire to align praxis with theory. Or maybe one day I may have a huge meltdown, my medications won't work, and I'll wake up (ACK!) a Republican. I'll have to take down all my leftist posters and bumperstickers. But I will never wake up one day and not be disordered.

4. If there is any location where all of my disorders intersect, cyberspace is the place. Because just like the disorders I embody, cyberspace is timeless, it's quicker than the speed of light, it's slower than molasses, it's ordered and chaotic, structured and static, stable and fluid, and I spend most of my waking hours traveling there (and some sleeping ones, too). And yes, cyberspace is as about as left a technological medium as you can find.

5. Because I was Brenda's assistant, I was literally plugged into the Web CT *as* Brenda Brueggemann. When I made posts, I had to remind myself to add "This is from Wendy" or the reader would just assume the post came from Brenda, the instructor, grader, headhoncho of the class. This further shifted notions of identities for all of us, I imagine, because when Brenda and I posted, sometimes even I couldn't remember right away who posted what. As for the students, I imagine further that issues of authority ("who really posted this one, Brenda or Wendy, am I being graded on this part, and how should I respond?") came into play as well.

6. *Vital Signs* is a foundationally important video for disability studies in that it is at once a site of performance, theory, and personal experience—the everyday lived and

embodied experience—of disability. Cheryl Marie Wade, Anne Finger, and Harlan Hahn are among the powerful voices and visions that we see as a location of emerging agency.

7. Graham's *Democracy by Disclosure: The Rise of Techno-Populism* (2002) explores how this micro/macro-management of disclosure is being launched by, among other technological mediums, the Internet—hence *techno*-populism. Because these technological practices are so widespread and pervasive, not to mention easily accessible, citizens will be have access to more information about their medical histories, profiles, and such than previously possible. Again, I see this as pointing towards the leftist inclinations, or at least, possibilities, of the Internet. And cyberspace indeed becomes a location where agency emerges in multivalent ways.

8. Talking about disability in this setting is such a point of entry for me that when my colleague, Nels Highberg, asked me to submit an essay about disclosure in the composition classroom to the Winter 2002 edition of Bedford/St. Martin's *Lore: An E-Journal for Teachers of Writing*, I jumped at the chance. In "The Ways We Disclose: When Life-Writing Becomes Writing Your Life" I explore two narratives of emergent disclosure: my student who tells me she is bipolar and me telling of my own bipolarity. Collectively we do find agency in our telling, and incidentally, we do take a trip to the Ohio State University emergency room, a little visit to the literal "rubber room," an experience from which my student is able to draft a rather insightful essay. I'd say that is leftist teaching, leftist learning, powerful and transformative, a monstrously empowering way to find (or take) agency. <http://www.bedfordstmartins.com/lore/stairwell/index.htm>.

9. See the Spring 2002 issue of *Kairos* <http://english.ttu.edu/kairos/7.1/index.html> for "Performing (Everyday) Exceptionalities: A Web-Text on Disability in Drama and Performance Art" by Brenda Jo Brueggemann, Wendy L. Chrisman, Angeline Kapferer, Marian E. Lupo, and Ben Patton.

10. Notions of "passing" and "coming out" take on strategic importance for disability studies (within the disability community and without) for many of the same reasons as they do for queer theory and gay and lesbian studies. Passing and coming out are performances, theoretical and experiential, that can at once create agency (covertly and overtly) by allowing the subject access to economic and social positions, material things, knowledge, etc. while protecting the timeliness and readiness of the subject's desire for disclosure. *Enforced* passing and coming out, however, are much like enforced medications and pathologizations: they are stringent impositions that restrict access to agency. For further explorations of the ways passing and coming out intersect with notions of sexuality, please see: Brenda Brueggemann and Debra A. Moddelmog's "A Coming Out Pedagogy: Risking Identity in the Language and Literature Classroom," in *For The Teacher's Body: Questions of Embodiment, Identity and Authority in College Classrooms*, ed. Diane P. Freedman and Martha Stoddard Holmes, State U of New York P (2003). For an example of the ways these notions function specifically within disability studies, please see Brueggemann's "On (Almost) Passing," *Lend Me Your Ear: Rhetorical Conjunctions of Deafness*, Washington, D. C.: Gallaudet UP (2002).

11. That URL is: <http://ada.osu.edu/Disability%20Studies%20Webpage/DS%20Draft.htm.>. Please also see the "Introduction to Disability Studies" course website at <http://english.ohio-state.edu/people/Brueggemann.1/intro_to_disability_studies_website/ index.htm>.

12. What actually constitutes "being" bipolar is necessarily contested from multiple angles, including from inside the medical and social construction models of disorder and out. Relying merely on discourses that pathologize disabilities and disorders rather than exploring the myriad ways in which these real, lived (embodied and performed) locations of identity are a part of our lives, is reductive. To erase the possibilities of how disabilities/disorders are diverse in their roots and ways people experience them individually is to erase *agency*. We are denied (and we deny ourselves) access to those places of emerge-agency found in a holistic exploration (and revision) of the socially constructed and medical models of disability unless we intersect these with the everyday realities of *what we actually experience*. As in the *Time* article explored here, authentic voices of the disordered are what has been "left" out of a place where agency may have emerged.

WORKS CITED

Benjamin, Walter. "Theses on the Philosophy of History." Trans. Harry Zohn. *Illuminations*. Ed. Hannah Arendt. New York: Shrocken, 1968. 253–64.

Braddock, David L., and Susan L. Parish. "An Institutional History of Disability." *Handbook of Disability Studies*. Ed. Gary L. Albrecht, Katherine D. Seelman, and Michael Bury. Thousand Oaks: Sage Publications, 2001.

Brueggemann, Brenda Jo. "An Enabling Pedagogy." *Disability Studies: Enabling the Humanities*. Ed. Sharon L. Snyder, Brenda Jo Brueggemann, and Rosemarie Garland-Thomson. New York: MLA, 2002. 317–36.

Brueggemann, Brenda Jo. *Lend Me Your Ears: Rhetorical Constructions of Deafness*. Washington, D.C.: Gallaudet UP 2002.

Brueggemann, Brenda Jo, Wendy L. Chrisman, Angeline Kapferer, Marian E. Lupo, and Ben Patton. "Performing (Everyday) Exceptionalities: A Web-Text on Disability in Drama and Performance Art." *Kairos*. Spring 2002 <http://english.ttu.edu/kairos/7.1/index.html>.

Brueggemann, Brenda Jo, and Debra A. Moddelmog. "A Coming Out Pedagogy: Risking Identity in the Language and Literature Classroom." *For The Teacher's Body: Questions of Embodiment, Identity, and Authority in College Classrooms*. Eds. Diane P. Freeman and Martha Stoddard Holmes. Albany: State U of New York P, 2003.

Cheu, Johnson. *Disabling Cure in Twentieth-Century America: Disability, Identity, Literature, and Culture*. Diss. 2003.

Chrisman, Wendy L. "The Ways We Disclose: When Life-Writing Becomes Writing Your Life." *Lore: An E-Journal for Teachers of Writing*. Winter 2002 <http ://www.bedfordstmartins.corn/lore/stairwell/index.htm>.

Dart, Justin, Jr. *The Freeman Institute*. <http://www.freemaninstitute.com/disabilty.htm>.

Davis, Lennard J. *Enforcing Normalcy: Disability, Deafness, and the Body*. London: Verso, 1995.

Davis, Lennard J. *Bending Over Backwards: Disability, Dismodernism and Other Difficult Positions*. New York: New York UP, 2002.

Fougeyrollas, Patrick, and Line Beauregard. "Disability: An Interactive Person-Environment Social Creation." *Handbook of Disability Studies*. Ed. Gary L. Albrecht, Katherine D. Seelman, and Michael Bury. Thousand Oaks: Sage, 2001. 171–94.

Goffman, Erving. *Stigma: Notes on the Management of Spoiled Identity*. Englewood Cliffs: Prentice-Hall, 1963.

Graham, Mary. *Democracy by Disclosure: The Risk of Techno-Populism*. Washington, D.C.: Governance Institute/Brookings Institute P. 2002.

Grossman, Paul D. *The Freeman Institute*. <http://www.freemaninstimte.com/disabilty.htm>.

———. "Making Accommodations: The Legal World of Students with Disabilities," 87 *Academe: Bulletin of the American Association of University Professors*, 41–46 (November-December 2001).

Kluger, Jeffrey, and Sora Song. "Inside the Volatile World of the Young and Bipolar." *Time* 19 Aug. 2002: 38–51.

Marcus, Neil. *Storm Reading*. Storm Reading Video Production, 1996.

Mayo, Peter. *Gramsci, Freire, and the Adult Education—Possibilities for Transformative Action*. London: Zed, 1999. 141–42.

Mitchell, David T., and Sharon L. Snyder, dirs. *Vital Signs: Crip Culture Talks Back*. Videocassette. Brace Yourselves, 1996.

Stiker, Henri-Jacques. *A History of Disability*. Trans. William Sayers. Ann Arbor: U of Michigan P, 1999.

CHAPTER SEVEN

WHAT THE LEFT LEFT OUT

DEREK OWENS

THE DISCOURSE OF CRITICAL PEDAGOGY, RADICAL TEACHING, PROGRESSIVE PRAXIS, oppositional education, liberatory pedagogy (the terms can begin to blur) has repeatedly invoked a triumvirate of race, gender, and class, "three categories that are so routinely grouped together in the professional literature that they now constitute a kind of stock phrase, like 'reading, writing, and 'rithmetic'" (Yagelski 62). Even the most cursory look at the literature of critical pedagogy over the last dozen years reveals an ongoing consideration of familiar concerns: gender equity; antidiscrimination; homophobia and heterosexism; confrontation of racist workplaces and educational institutions; analyses of dominant discourse; resistance to conservative, centrist, and liberal ideology; attention to class and economic injustices. These concerns have proved to be so influential that radical pedagogy now enjoys a kind of obligatory status within much of English studies and particularly composition. Even if much of the actual teaching done in college classrooms continues to reflect current-traditional and liberal expressionist predilections, a significant number, and perhaps a majority, of publications in composition and rhetoric are now indirectly related if not explicitly rooted in social constructionist objectives. The production of leftist cultural and pedagogical critique is so familiar as to have invited parody, as Stephen North demonstrates in his essay "Rhetoric, Responsibility, and the 'Language of the Left'" (128), a clear sign that leftist discourse has shifted into the mainstream. While some of us can probably relate to North's impatience with the sense of "visionary privilege" that can seem to permeate the literature of radical pedagogy (135)—what Chris Gallagher calls the occasional "lefter-than-thou posturing in our field" (164)—my concern here is not with the "missionary position" exhibited in worst-case versions of social constructionist pedagogy. Nor is it directed at the major tenets of "strong" social constructionism: like many, I have vivid memories of the tremendous impact a book like *Pedagogy of the Oppressed* had on me in graduate school, how profoundly articles like the James Berlin's oft-cited "Rhetoric and Ideology in the Writing Class" wrote themselves into my own pedagogical persona. My concern rather is with what continually gets left out of the left conversation. For in its move towards social change in the name of radical democracy, critical pedagogy has repeatedly failed to undertake a sustained engagement with the environmental and ecological realities of the late twentieth century. "One of the most prominent omissions in the critical pedagogical approach to education . . . is its lack of attention to ecological issues" (O'Sullivan 63). In this essay I want to call attention to this blind spot, examine possible reasons for its existence, and conclude by introducing a connective metaphor that helps me to synthesize traditional social constructivist concerns with environmental realities: the project of "sustainability." For unless the standard arenas of leftist concern (race, gender, class) are demonstrated to be interconnected with ecological systems, leftist pedagogy's anthropocentric humanism will prevent it from understanding and responding to today's environmental crises—crises inextricably woven throughout and impacting upon nearly every other cultural concern.

A DIFFERENT KIND OF NIMBYISM:
NOT INTERESTED IN MY BACK YARD

In the late 1980s ecological economists and scientists started referring to the upcoming 1990s as the "turnaround decade." Their thinking was that developed nations had roughly ten more years to switch over to sustainable economies, thereby halting the rapid depletion of limited resources (Brown et al. 192). If such radical change were not to come about in the 1990s, however, many were of a mind that such change would thereafter be impossible. Some, like David Orr, saw the window of opportunity as slightly larger: "the decisions about how or whether life will be lived in the next century are being made now. We have a decade or two in which we must make unprecedented changes in the way we relate to each other and to nature" (3).

Looking back on the 1990s we see that not only was there no such turnaround, but the final years of the twentieth century were marked by the longest period of global growth in human history. Rather than making the admittedly difficult (some might say impossible) transition to lifestyles based on consuming less, the developed nations of the world, with the United States leading the way, committed themselves to devouring severely depleted and ever finite resources with almost religious zeal. The turnaround decade became the turn-it-up decade in terms of global consumption and runaway growth.

The implications of this consumption are grave. Our short- and long-term futures look startlingly bleak when considered through the lenses of today's environmental and ecological crises. By way of example we need look no further than New York City, where I teach and where many of my colleagues and students live. Recent studies predict increases in coastal flooding, severe droughts, insect-borne diseases and deaths, asthma, and a six- to ten- degree temperature increase over the next eighty years (Newman), along with winter temperatures dropping as much as ten degrees (Joyce A27). All of this is especially bad news for the city's population of homeless families, which increased twenty-three percent over the past year—"the largest one-year increase . . . possibly since the Great Depression" (Egan 34)—along with working- and middle-class people on Long Island, where the gap between rich and poor has increased more than in any other state in the country (Bernstein). New York's Regional Plan Association predicts that unless billions are spent right now on combating sprawl and preserving open space, within twenty years the tri-state metropolitan region will enter a phase of *irreversible* economic, social, and environmental decline (Yaro and Hiss).

But we needn't focus just on just my neck of the woods. Paleobiologists are claiming that "humans may already or will soon have destroyed enough species that it will require a full 10 million years for the planet to recover" (Yoon). At current die-off rates one in three plant species will be extinct in the next fifty years (Stevens), one in four mammals in thirty years (Connor), and one in eight bird species by the end of this century ("One in 8"). Because the oceans absorb the bulk of global warming, scientists now fear that the full, catastrophic effect of climate change will be realized only when the ocean sinks can no longer contain any more excess heat (Stevens "Oceans Absorb"). We now have nerve-racking predictions by petroleum geologists about oil extraction reaching its peak during the current decade, followed by dramatic spikes in oil extraction costs which could result in worldwide economic and political collapses (Deffeyes). In the United States two acres of farmland are lost every minute (Becker). In less than twenty-five years, more than half of the people in less developed countries will be vulnerable to severe flooding and drought due to climate change brought on in large part by carbon dioxide pollution generated in the richest nations (Kirby). In the words of the chief scientist of the Nature Conservancy, "Things are getting worse faster than they're getting better . . . [there is] not much cause for optimism" (Stevens "Conservationists").[1]

But while scholars and practitioners in such fields as architecture, ecology, environmental studies, and planning have frequently focused on matters of sustainability and environmental reform, English studies and most glaringly critical pedagogy have largely insulated themselves from thinking critically about the environment. The appearance in the 1990s of such subfields as ecocriticism and ecocomposition might make this claim seem overstated. We now have studies on the rhetoric of sustainability (Killingsworth and Palmer), environmental rhetoric (Herndl and Brown), environmental discourse and communication (Cantrill and Oravec), ecofeminism (McAndrew), nature writing and composition (Roorda), literacy and postcolonialism (Stephen Brown), and ecocomposition (Dobrin and Weisser). Within the field of ecocriticism, a body of work I have often found troublesome given its frequent fetishization of "literature" and "wilderness" and a marked disinterest in the suburbs and cities most of us live in—a criticism that could be directed at more than a little of the scholarship presented at conferences like the Association for the Study of Literature and Environment—we now have titles like Bennett and Teague's *The Nature of Cities*, Lawrence Buell's *Writing for an Endangered World*, and Jed Rasula's *This Compost: Ecological Imperatives in American Poetry*, all of which broaden the scope of ecocritical studies. And yet, when we compare a dozen or so titles with the wealth of publications in critical pedagogy, we realize the degree to which environmental concerns are marginalized if not invisible within the literature of English studies, composition, and radical pedagogy.

In my office there are two bookcases, one with relatively (starting in the early 1990s) recent titles in composition, rhetoric, discourse, literacy, and pedagogy, the other full of books in ecology, planning, architecture, cybernetics, environmental education, and ecological economics. What concerns me is how the two collections don't speak to each other. Aside from the works listed above in ecocomposition and ecocriticism, the bulk of these titles in composition, critical pedagogy, and English studies can be linked by a prevailing absence of the e-words, "ecology" and "environment." There are edited anthologies of "cutting edge educational theory" and "revolutionary pedagogy" tackling a variety of subjects: institutionalized whiteness, gendered identities, multiple literacies, academic responsibility, classroom heterosexuality, queer praxis, antiracist curricula, material critiques, pedagogy and public accountability, post-Fordist education, alternative discourses, activist teaching, public discourse, service learning, new information technologies, the globalization of the university, working-class student narratives, border pedagogies, liberatory literacies, and so on. Yet despite the theoretical and disciplinary diversity reflected in this rich body of scholarship, references to the basic principles of ecology, an understanding of sustainability, environmental ethics, the limitations of natural systems, and environmental social injustices are nonexistent. Even fat anthologies claiming a more representational, cross-disciplinary array of essays perpetuate a worrisome ecological silence: a recent anthology on literacy fails to include pieces on ecological literacy; a collection on discourse does not include articles on environmental discourse; anthologies of literary theory's greatest hits don't include ecocritical perspectives; collections of feminist theory fail to include any references at all to ecofeminism.

Such a random, idiosyncratic sampling might prove nothing other than that my own private library is woefully inadequate, and I simply haven't been reading the right books. But I don't think so. For another look at just how much the environment has failed to surface on the radar of English, cultural, and pedagogical studies, consider several recent forums addressing the future of English studies. Scholars invited to contribute to a 1999 Symposium on the Future of English Studies published in *College English* presented a mixture of concerns: the effect of new media and information technologies on the discipline, the supposed loss of "close reading" in the classroom, the need to define the role of English studies before a skeptical public, racialized curricular politics, the increased corporatization of the academy, the value of multicultural writing, the role of the working-class student, a defense of community-college teaching, and the need to promote innovative and risk-taking graduate curricula (Symposium). In a collection of papers presented at the 1999 Conference on the Future of Doctoral Education at the University of Wisconsin, a host of different concerns are addressed, among them the need for professionalization of graduate students, perennial concerns over the job market crisis, modes of teacher training, the marketplace's effect on a changing university, teaching assistants and collective bargaining, and various stances on cultural studies, literature, and literary history ("Conference"). And in the ambitiously titled 1996 collection *Composition in the Twenty-First Century: Crisis and Change* (Bloom et al.), the contributing scholars offer various definitions of composition, provide histories of the field, consider changing models of assessment, confront national standards, anticipate the impact of intellectual property rights for composition faculty, look at new modes of research, and consider the evolving role that class, labor, culture, and economics will play in shaping the identity of future students. In one of the summary responses offered in this collection, one author writes:

> In the new century, the economic, social, cultural, and political forces of change will require a presence and responsiveness unlike those of earlier times. This volume is meant to anticipate those hurricane winds of change. It is itself a measure of the profession's awareness and responsiveness. It also represents a call for humility, courage, and dedication. The profession has matured over the past two decades, becoming practiced and self-confident; it can now look toward the unprecedented demands of the approaching century. In a sense, nothing we have done prepares us for what is ahead; at the same time, all of our experience on campus and in the profession has helped prepare us for those challenges. (Herzog 246)

The passage presents a startling combination of truth and oversight. Without a doubt this new century of ours will be utterly unprecedented. But if the papers in these symposia are any gauge, most of the scholars and practitioners working in English studies and composition and rhetoric seem significantly unprepared to consider the impact of current and future environmental changes on their discipline, scholarship, and teaching.

The problem is hardly that the issues, some of them anyway, raised in these forward-looking articles are irrelevant and unworthy of our attention. The danger—the embarrassment—is that nowhere in these position papers by some of the more distinguished scholars in English studies and composition and rhetoric is there any evidence of concern for or even simple awareness of contemporary out-of-control local and global environmental catastrophes. These forums consistently fail to acknowledge in any manner—save for concern with the impact of globalization on higher education—the enormity of present-day environmental catastrophes and their inevitable role in radically altering the quality of life for current and future generations. To read these documents in their larger historical context—attempts at the end of the pivotal turnaround decade at the end of the twentieth century by leading scholars to assess what they consider to be the most pressing issues for their discipline, their students, and themselves—is to see a cocoon engulfing much of the work of our discipline.

How did this happen? What has led so many professionals in English studies to largely ignore the implications of living in a world of radical environmental risk and decline? How, in a discipline as multifaceted and inclusive as English studies—which enjoys a curricula far more motley and cross-disciplinary than perhaps any other in the academy—have scholars consistently looked at the implications of culture (race, class, gender), and increasingly globalization, while turning a blind eye to contemporary environmental realities?

CONFRONTING CRITICAL PEDAGOGY'S BLIND SPOT

One of the most energetic criticisms of critical pedagogy's anthropocentric biases is found in the work of a critic undercited not just in English studies and critical pedagogy but also environmental studies. The writing of C. A. Bowers is an extended, often scathing critique of radical educators like Paulo Freire, Henry Giroux, and Ira Shor who, he argues, have consistently failed to appreciate the degree to which cultures are always inextricably formed by local, environmental realities. "The social justice issues of class, race, and gender," Bowers writes, "need to be framed in terms of a more comprehensive theory of eco-justice" (*Educating* vii):

> Advocates of educational reform fail to recognize that any definition of social justice that does not take account of how human demands on the natural environment are affecting the lives of future generations is fundamentally flawed. Indeed, it seems incomprehensible to write about social justice for women, minorities, and the economic underclass without considering the ways in which the Earth's ecosystems are being rapidly degraded. Nor should any discussion of social justice be framed in a way that ignores how achieving greater access to the material standard of living that is today's measure of personal success depends on market forces that are appropriating the resources of non-Western cultures and displacing their traditional forms of knowledge. (3)

Much of critical pedagogy concerns itself with the cross-examination and ultimately the democratization of cultural belief systems. But because the bulk of such inquiry takes place primarily within the confines of the classroom environment, Bowers criticizes the removal from its local, existing communities: "this transformative process is not to be the responsibility of parents or the community, but of teachers who possess an understanding of the social vision consistent with the practice of a critical pedagogy" (*Educating* 51). Progressive praxis is largely expected to result in the eventual politicization and resultant transformation of discriminatory cultural assumptions—to disabuse students of their heretofore unexamined political beliefs and move them closer to an understanding of social justice. But "categorizing all customs (traditions) as reactionary, mindless habits and oppressive practices cannot be the basis for a pedagogy that contributes to a socially just society. According to [Henry] Giroux's way of thinking, all members of society, regardless of cultural background and degree of participation in their primary and secondary cultures, must be willing to yield to the moral judgments of students and their teachers" (*Educating* 54). What of long-standing cultural practices and traditions that are economically and environmentally more responsible than those fashioned as a result of classroom dialogue in the critical classroom?

This leads to Bowers's frustration with the obligatory demonization of the term *conservative* in the discourse of critical pedagogy, which cannot help risk a rejection of *primitive* communities.[2] Bowers writes:

> The key assumptions underlying modern liberalism—the authority of the individual's subjective judgment, the relentless pursuit of innovative ideas, individual-centered values and forms of expression, disregard for traditions, a proclivity to think in abstractions that lend themselves to being universalized—all lead to an increasingly experimental form of culture. This cultural form, which today finds expression in the use of modern ideologies to design societies and new organisms that further the process of economic globalization, rests on a basic misunderstanding of biological and cultural processes that are inescapable aspects of human existence. The political metaphor that best accounts for these inescapable processes is *conservatism*. (*Educating* 56)

This conservatism—or to use what Bowers admits is his "somewhat awkward phrase" of "cultural/bio-conservatism" (*Culture* 135)—values philosophical and practical knowledge associated with traditional cultures where the interdependencies of humans, communities, and ecological systems are continually emphasized. This is radically different from a Freireian's anthropocentric emphasis on a pedagogy aimed at making students more "fully human," as if one could ever isolate the human from its local natural systems and cultural surroundings.

Bowers goes so far as to compare the logic behind Freireian humanism with that driving contemporary globalism:

> The reference to a universal human nature rather than to the actual patterns of individual-community relationships among the cultural groups of Central America, Africa, India, or Southeast Asia represents the same modern way of thinking that is found in transnational corporations' view of global markets. This abstract way of thinking misrepresents a fundamental reality: namely,

that the everyday life of people is nested in a particular set of cultural traditions, and that these traditions are continually tested by changes taking place
in the environment. Some of the traditions are well attuned to the characteristics of the environment and to the needs of the community, while others
may have a long-term destructive impact. (*Educating* 73–74)

As such, a critical pedagogy that interrogates the political and discursive complexities associated with matters of race, class, and gender while ignoring their
interrelatedness to local natural systems is a pedagogy at risk of perpetuating
such short- and long-term destructive impacts, not to mention misrepresent-
ing concepts of race, class, and gender by rendering their situatedness within
natural systems invisible.

Bowers's critique of critical educators is not without its problems. His criticism sometimes comes across as unnecessarily arch and overstated, his frustration fueled perhaps by the unfortunate ongoing ignorance of his publications
and the omission of Bowers's work within the larger conversation of critical
pedagogy, puzzling given his steady flow of publications. More significantly, his
criticism of the radical educator's failure to move beyond the domain of the
classroom and into the local community reveals Bowers's lack of familiarity
with the wealth of activist pedagogy being done within service learning. While
rarely explicitly envisioned in conjunction with environmental matters, service learning might well be the strongest current example of pedagogies heading in the direction of Bowers's "cultural/bio-conservatism." It's no coincidence
that Christian Weisser, who argues that the logical evolution of social constructionism is the surge in service learning and public discourse (*Moving Beyond*),
is also one of the foremost proponents of ecocriticism (Dobrin and Weisser).
And Bowers's fear of the proliferation of new online technologies (*Let Them
Eat Data*), which he considers a significant threat to the preservation of environmentally responsible cultures, risks promoting the very romanticization of
"the human" elsewhere criticized in his work. He fails to offer a productive
means of engaging with new technologies towards sustainable ends, unlike the
more balanced approach offered by Stephen Doheny-Farina in *The Wired Neighborhood*. Still, Bowers is one of the few voices in educational theory provoking
us to amend cultural pedagogy from a position informed by an awareness of natural systems, sustainability, and ecological limits, and as such he provides a vital
critique of critical pedagogy's most significant failure.

SUSTAINABILITY AND PLACE-BASED PEDAGOGY

Moving beyond Bowers's critiques of cultural studies and critical pedagogy,
Edmund O'Sullivan offers a theory of education where "the fundamental educational task of our times is to make the choice for a sustainable planetary
habitat of interdependent life forms over and against the dysfunctional calling of the global competitive marketplace" (2). In *Transformative Learning:*

Educational Vision for the 21ˢᵗ Century, O'Sullivan demonstrates the degree to which patriarchy, racism, class inequality, and globalization are all integrally "webbed" together beneath a rubric of sustainability, and argues that education for peace, social justice, and diversity are crucial components of an educational vision striving for planetary, human, and cultural survival (133–76). Advocating a holistic approach to introducing "wider biocentric concerns" (64) into the discourse of critical pedagogy, O'Sullivan argues for "a sensitivity to and knowledge of the bio-region in which one is living" (202); "educational institutions at all levels must play a pivotal role in fostering a community's sense of place" (245).

While I don't consider myself a strict bioregionalist, O'Sullivan's emphasis on local communities parallels my own need to conceptualize my courses and curricular concerns around the project of "sustainability." As a holistic metaphor for assembling an array of leftist concerns, the concept of sustainability seems to me a necessary metanarrative at this historical juncture. When we consider the sundry problems in our students' lives and look forward into their troubling futures, we're concerning ourselves with sustainability: matters of intragenerational and intergenerational justice. The most common definition of sustainability can be traced to the 1987 United Nations' World Commission on Environment and Development: "meeting the needs of the present without compromising the ability of future generations to meet their own needs" (World Commission 8). Sustainability is concerned with living our lives in ways that don't obstruct or ignore the needs of current and future generations. As an umbrella concept, sustainability is broad enough that it involves the welfare of our students' immediate cultural, social, and natural communities, the condition and implications of their future careers, the kinds of lives led by their overworked family members, the condition of their local ecologies, and the futures they face.

"At its heart," Gregory Smith writes, "sustainability is about the relationship between human beings and the world; it is about morality" (1). Environmental activist Stephen Wheeler, aware of the complexities surrounding the term, argues that the goal of sustainability should be "the process of continually moving towards healthier human and natural communities" (438). Wheeler summarizes the characteristics of sustainable development for an audience of urban and regional planners. These include maintaining compact, efficient land use; emphasizing fewer automobiles and better pedestrian access; use of efficient resources with less pollution and waste; restoring natural systems; creating and preserving good housing and living environments; promoting healthy social ecologies; supporting sustainable economics; engaging community participation; and preserving local culture (339–443).

Because I've explored the concept of sustainability in greater detail elsewhere (Owens 21–35), I'll not repeat myself here other than to reiterate several of the tenets of what I believe to be fundamental components of a pedagogical ethic constructed in response to local and global environmental crises facing current and future generations. First, conversations about sustainability must permeate most if not all disciplines reflected in the curriculum. Second, our pedagogies must be interventionist, disrupting the unreflective habits of irresponsible consumer culture. Third, our critiques of work must take into consideration not just inequities of class and labor but the degree to which businesses perpetuate or resist sustainable practices. Fourth, our understanding of race and gender needs to acknowledge the ways in which the ecologies of local cultures have always informed such concepts. Finally, a successful catalyst for getting students to investigate the interrelatedness of race, culture, and gender is through an examination of place, a literal as well as an abstract rubric that can lead to a greater understanding of one's local needs and desires within a sustainable context.

As someone living in the heart of Long Island suburban sprawl, and whose daily commute to a campus in Queens involves a two-hour trek by train and bus, I've had little success over the years getting involved with service-learning initiatives in organizations surrounding the campus community. To make service learning work, ideally the professor should have easy access to the local communities and organizations surrounding the campus community. Because I live so far from campus, as do my students—many of whom are commuters and easily spend three hours a day or more commuting to and from Brooklyn, the Bronx, Staten Island, Manhattan, and Long Island—the logistics of becoming involved with community organizations around our campus in Queens, or in helping my students get involved in nonprofit agencies in neighborhoods hours away from mine, can be overwhelming. To complicate matters, the majority of my students work twenty hours a week or more in addition to taking a full course load. Between their complicated work schedules, commuting travails, and family obligations, most of my students are unable to remain engaged with nonprofit agencies and community centers, nor am I able to maintain the necessary ongoing contact between instructor and community site. As a result I've shifted towards a model of service learning I've yet to see represented in the extensive literature on the subject. Instead of bringing students to various community projects, I have my students bring their neighborhoods to me. They research and write about their local neighborhoods, and ultimately my goal is to publish this information on the web, making my students' expert observations available to professionals in community revitalization and suburban and urban planning who might otherwise lack my student's insights.

At first this approach would seem to fit into the second of the three forms of service learning described by Tom Deans: writing to the community, writing about the community, and writing for the community (*Writing Partnerships*). But while my students are writing about off-campus sites, I'm not requiring them to work for nonprofit agencies or community centers. Instead they're expected to investigate a section of their own neighborhoods: a city street corner, a span of several blocks, a tenement house, a suburban cul de sac, a local hang-out behind a neighborhood strip mall. (Because many of my students are commuters, they can examine their neighborhoods any time during the semester; those who live farther away generally conduct site-specific research over breaks during the semester.) Whether they love, hate, or are bored by their chosen place doesn't matter; it just needs to have a certain degree of importance to them, for better or worse.[3]

After spending a month of my writing course getting my students to research the past, current, and possible future histories of their chosen site, students revise their drafts, which often take the shape of photo-essays, with the intention of eventually publishing them on the World Wide Web. Ultimately my goal is to publish this material on a website, funding for which I am currently seeking through several grants leading to the creation of a national consortium of writing faculty interested in creating opportunities where their students might articulate concerns associated with their local communities. My goal is that within several years thousands of student testimonies will be published on a dedicated website, creating a virtual map where students, who are certainly authorities in terms of the strengths and weaknesses of their local communities, can enlighten students, teachers, and policy makers on the status of contemporary neighborhoods. This web-based "map" of student communities (many of them at risk) is my attempt to bring the insights of students out of the classroom and into a larger public conversation.[4]

The kind of locally-based project I'm envisioning, along with other assignments revolving around the articulation, preservation, and revitalization of specific sites and places, seems to me one modest yet worthwhile way of making sustainability relevant to students' immediate lives and concerns. Whatever one's approach, however—whether through place-based pedagogies, the incorporation of principles of ecology into cultural studies, or a more sophisticated understanding of the "webbed" nature of race, class, and gender within larger environmental contexts—it seems clear that the liberatory objectives of critical pedagogy must, if they are to remain relevant in an age of catastrophic local and global environmental crises, embrace orchestrating metaphors like "sustainability," "conservation," "preservation," and "survival" as viable catalysts for furthering the objectives of progressive teaching and learning. I see this approach as a tremendous opportunity for those engaged in progressive praxis to make more precise, local connections between their teaching and their students' communities.

NOTES

1. Readers interested in keeping abreast of current environmental news should consult <www.envirolink.org>, <www.worldwatch.org>, and <www.dieoff.org>. Those interested in reviewing news stories that have shaped my own growing sense of concern can find a summary of new stories in Owens, *Composition and Sustainability* (165–72).

2. Jerome and Diane Rothenberg's work in ethnopoetics provides an essential rein-
terpretation of the word *primitive* as signifying cultural sophistication—see *Symposium
of the Whole*.

3. For a detailed look at how I use "place" as a theme in my writing courses, see
Owens (36–76, 184–89).

4. I am currently writing grant proposals that would create funding for graduate
teaching assistants, part-time faculty, and tenure-track faculty to participate in a national
consortium for writing faculty interested in designing place-based pedagogies and publishing student "neighborhood testimonies" on the web. Interested readers are encouraged to contact me for more information at owensd@stjohns.edu.

WORKS CITED

Becker, Elizabeth. "Two Acres of Farm Lost to Sprawl Each Minute, New Study Says."
New York Times. 4 Oct. 2002: A22.

Bennett, Michael, and David W. Teague. *The Nature of Cities: Ecocriticism and Urban
Environments*. Tucson: U of Arizona P, 1999.

Bernstein, Nina. "Widest Income Gap Is Found in New York." *New York Times*. 19 Jan.
2000: B5.

Bloom, Lynn Z., Donald A. Daiker, and Edward M. White. *Composition in the Twenty-
First Century: Crisis and Change*. Carbondale and Edwardsville: Southern Illinois
UP, 1996.

Bowers, C. A. *The Culture of Denial: Why the Environmental Movement Needs a Strategy
for Reforming Universities and Public Schools*. Albany: State U of New York P, 1997.

———. *Educating for Eco-Justice and Community*. Athens: U of Georgia P, 2001.

———. *Let Them Eat Data: How Computers Affect Education, Cultural Diversity, and the
Prospects of Ecological Sustainability*. Athens: U of Georgia P, 2000.

Brown, Lester, et al. *State of the World 1989*. New York: Norton, 1989.

Brown, Stephen Gilbert. *Words in the Wilderness: Critical Literacy in the Borderlands*.
Albany: State U of New York P, 2000.

Buell, Lawrence. *Writing for an Endangered World: Literature, Culture, and Environment
in the U.S. and Beyond*. Cambridge: Harvard UP, 2001.

Cantrill, James G., and Christine L. Oravec, eds. *The Symbolic Earth: Discourse and Our
Creation of the Environment*. Lexington: UP of Kentucky, 1996.

"Conference on the Future of Doctoral Education." *PMLA 115* (October 2000):
1137–1276.

Deffeyes, Kenneth S. *Hubbert's Peak: The Impending World Oil Shortage*. Princeton: Princeton UP, 2001.

Dobrin, Sidney I., and Christian Weisser, eds. *Ecocomposition: Theoretical and Pedagogical Approaches*. Albany: State U of New York P, 2001.

———. *Natural Discourse: Toward Ecocomposition*. Albany: State U of New York P, 2002.

Doheny-Farina, Stephen. *The Wired Neighborhood*. New Haven: Yale UP, 1996.

Egan, Jennifer. "To Be Young and Homeless." *New York Times Magazine*. 24 March 2002: 32–37, 58–59.

Gallagher, Chris W. *Radical Departures: Composition and Progressive Pedagogy*. Urbana, Ill.: NCTE P, 2002.

Hardin, Joe Marshall. *Opening Spaces: Critical Pedagogy and Resistance Theory in Composition*. Albany: State U of New York P, 2001.

Herndl, Carl G., and Stuart C. Brown. *Green Culture: Environmental Rhetoric in Contemporary America*. Madison: U of Wisconsin P, 1996.

Herzog, Carol Petersen. "Imagining the Future: Composition in a New Economic and Social Context." *Composition in the Twenty-First Century: Crisis and Change*. Ed. Lynn Z. Bloom, Donald A. Daiker, and Edward M.White. Carbondale: Southern Illinois UP, 1996. 243–46.

Joyce, Terrence. "The Heat Before the Cold." *New York Times*. 18 April 2002: A27.

Killingsworth, M. Jimmie, and Jacqueline S. Palmer. *Ecospeak: Rhetoric and Environmental Politics in America*. Carbondale and Edwardsville: Southern Illinois UP, 1992.

Kirby, Alex. "Red CrossWarns on Climate." *BBC News Online* 28 June 2000. 17 June 2002 http://news.bbc.co.uk/hi/english/sci/tech/newsid_808000/808537.stm>.

Kunstler, James Howard. *The Geography of Nowhere: The Rise and Fall of America's Man-Made Landscape*. New York: Simon and Schuster, 1993.

McAndrew, Donald A. "Ecofeminism and the Teaching of Literacy." *College Composition and Communication* 47 (1996): 367–82.

Newman, Andy. "Study Sees Hard Future if Climate Keeps Heating." *New York Times*. 20 June 2000: B5.

North, Stephen. "Rhetoric, Responsibility, and the 'Language of the Left.'" *Composition and Resistance*. Eds. C. Mark Hurlbert and Michael Blitz. Portsmouth, N.H.: Boynton/Cook Heinemann, 1991: 127–36.

"One in 8 Birds Faces Extinction in Next 100 Years." Yahoo! News, Science Headlines. 14 October 1999. 14 June 2001 <http://forests.org/archive/general/envibird.htm>.

Orr, David. *Ecological Literacy: Education and the Transition to a Postmodern World*. Albany: State U of New York P, 1992.

O'Sullivan, Edmund. *Transformative Learning: Educational Vision for the Twenty-First Century*. London: Zed Books, 1999.

Owens, Derek. *Composition and Sustainability: Teaching for a Threatened Generation*. Urbana, Ill.: NCTE P, 2001.

Popkewitz, Thomas S., and Lynn Fendler, eds. *Critical Theories in Education: Changing Terrains of Knowledge and Politics*. New York: Routledge, 1999.

Rasula, Jed. *This Compost: Ecological Imperatives in American Poetry*. Athens: U of Georgia P, 2002.

Roorda, Randall. *Dramas of Solitude: Narratives of Retreat in American Nature Writing*. Albany: State U of New York P, 1998.

"Symposium: English 1999." *College English* 61, (July 1999): 659–751.

Rothenberg, Jerome, and Diane Rothenberg. *Symposium of the Whole: A Range of Discourse toward an Ethnopoetics*. Berkeley: U of California P, 1984.

Smith, Gregory A., and Dilafruz R. Williams. *Ecological Education in Action: On Weaving Education, Culture, and the Environment*. Albany: State U of New York P, 1999.

Stevens, William K. "Conservationists Win Battles But Fear War Is Lost." *New York Times*. 11 Jan. 2000: F5.

———. "The Oceans Absorb Much of Global Warming, Study Confirms." *New York Times*. 24 March 2000: A14.

Weisser, Christian R. *Moving beyond Academic Discourse: Composition Studies and the Public Sphere*. Carbondale: Southern Illinois UP, 2002.

Wheeler, Stephen. "Planning Sustainable and Livable Cities." *The City Reader*. 2nd ed. Ed. Richard T. LeGates and Frederic Stout. New York: Routledge, 2000: 434–45.

World Commission on Environment and Development. *Our Common Future*. Oxford: Oxford UP, 1987.

Yagelski, Robert. *Literacy Matters: Writing and Reading the Social Self*. New York: Teachers College P, 2000.

Yaro, Robert D., and Tony Hiss (Regional Plan Association). *A Region at Risk: The Third Regional Plan for the New York-New Jersey-Connecticut Metropolitan Area*. Washington. D.C.: Island P, 1996.

Yoon, Carol Kaesuk. "Study Jolts Views on Recovery from Extinctions." *New York Times*. 9 March 2000: A20.

III

THE ACADEMIC LEFT, CRITICAL THEORY, AND THE GLOBAL CONTEXT

CHAPTER EIGHT

GLOBALIZING DISSENT AND RADICALIZING DEMOCRACY: POLITICS, PEDAGOGY, AND THE RESPONSIBILITY OF CRITICAL INTELLECTUALS

HENRY A. GIROUX

THE DANGER OF NEOLIBERALIST RHETORIC

NEOLIBERALISM ON BOTH THE DOMESTIC AND INTERNATIONAL FRONTS HAS BECOME the most dangerous ideology of the current historical moment. Not only does it assault all things public and sabotage the basic contradiction between democratic values and market fundamentalism. It also weakens any viable notion of political agency by offering no language capable of connecting private considerations to public issues. As democratic values give way to commercial values, intellectual ambitions are often reduced to an instrument of the entrepreneurial self, and social visions are dismissed as hopelessly out of date. Public space is portrayed exclusively as an investment opportunity, and the public good increasingly becomes a metaphor for public disorder. As corporate culture extends even deeper into the basic institutions of civil and political society, there is a simultaneous diminishing of noncommodified public spheres—those institutions engaged in dialogue, education, and learning—that address the relationship of the self to public life, of social responsibility to the broader demands of citizenship, and provide a robust vehicle for public participation and democratic citizenship.

Without these critical public spheres, corporate power goes unchecked and politics becomes dull, cynical, and oppressive, radicalism rendered merely irrelevant.[1] But more importantly, in the absence of such public spheres it becomes more difficult for citizens to challenge the neoliberal myth that citizens are merely consumers and that "wholly unregulated markets are the sole means by which we can produce and distribute everything we care about, from durable goods to spiritual values, from capital development to social justice, from profitability to sustainable environments, from private wealth to essential commonweal" (Barber 59). Divested of its political possibilities and social underpinnings, freedom finds few opportunities for translating private worries into public concerns or individual discontent into collective struggle. Moreover, as market forces become more deregulated and deterritorialized, the political state increasingly is transformed into the business state and, as Noreena Hertz observes, "Economics has become the new politics, and business is in the driving seat" (66). Within this discourse, anyone who does not believe that rapacious capitalism is the only road to freedom and the good life is dismissed as at least a crank, if not worse.

All over the world, the forces of neoliberalism are on the march, dismantling the historically guaranteed social provisions provided by the welfare state, defining profit-making and market freedoms as the essence of democracy, while diminishing civil liberties as part of the alleged "war" against terrorism. Secure in its dystopian vision, as Margaret Thatcher once put it, that there are no alternatives, neoliberalism eliminates issues of contingency, struggle, and social agency by celebrating the inevitability of economic laws in which the ethical ideal of intervening in the world to promote social justice and inclusive democracy gives way to the idea that we "have no choice but to adapt both our hopes and our abilities to the new global market" (Aronowitz 7). Coupled with a new culture of fear, market freedoms seem securely grounded in a defense of national security and a defense of property.

Educators and other cultural workers need a new political and pedagogical language for addressing the changing contexts and issues facing a world in which capital draws upon an unprecedented convergence of resources—financial, cultural, political, economic, scientific, military, and technological—to exercise powerful and diverse forms of hegemony. If educators are to counter neoliberalism's increased power to both depoliticize and disempower, it is crucial to develop educational approaches that reject a collapse of the distinction between market liberties and civil liberties, a market economy and a market society. This entails developing forms of critical pedagogy capable of appropriating from a variety of radical theories—feminism, postmodernism, critical theory, post-structuralism, neo-Marxism, etc.—those progressive elements that might be useful in both challenging neoliberalism on many fronts while resurrecting a militant democratic socialism that provides the basis for imagining a life beyond the "dream world" of capitalism. More specifically, this suggests, on the one hand, resurrecting the living, though blemished traditions, of Enlightenment thought that affirmed issues of freedom, equality, liberty, self-determination, and civic agency. On the other hand, critical theory's engagement with Enlightenment thought must be expanded through those postmodern discourses that problematize modernity's universal project of citizenship, its narrow understanding of domination, its obsession with order, and its refusal to expand both the meaning of the political and the sites in which political struggles and possibilities might occur.

CULTURAL POLITICS MATTERS

Against the growing separation between a postmodern cultural politics and modernist material politics—defined primarily over the issue of what constitutes "real" politics—educators need to avoid the modern/postmodern divide that proffers that we can do either culture or economics but that we cannot do both.[2] Cultural politics matters because it is the pedagogical site upon which identities are formed, subject positions are made available, social agency enacted, and cultural forms both reflect as well as deploy power through their modes of ownership and mode of public pedagogy. Critical theorists from Marcuse to Adorno have always recognized that the most important forms of domination are not simply economic but also cultural—that the pedagogical force of the culture with its emphasis on belief and persuasion is a crucial element of how to both think about politics and enact forms of resistance and social transformation. If radical cultural politics in its various postmodern and poststructuralist forms deepened our understanding of the political value of ambivalence and how culture works within a wider variety of spaces and sites, critical theory politicized its meaning and refused to collapse such an understanding into either the exclusive study of texts or the narrow engagement with the polysemic nature of language. Drawing on the insights of each tradition, the issue that becomes primary is not how culture cancels out material relations of power, or texts override politics. Instead, we must examine how each works through and on the other within as well as across specific historical contexts and social formations in ways that both enhance and close down democratic relations and practices.

AFFIRMING MODERNITY'S DEMOCRATIC LEGACY

Modernity's ongoing project of democracy is not something that can be dismissed against the postmodern infatuation with irony, simulacra, or the alleged death of the subject. Critical theory's engagement with modernity and democracy must be rethought and reformulated in light of the postmodern assertion that democracy is never finished and must be viewed primarily as a process of democratization. Postcolonial theorist Samir Amin echoes this call by arguing that educators should consider addressing the project of a more realized democracy as part of an ongoing process of democratization. According to Amin, democratization "stresses the dynamic aspect of a still-unfinished process" while rejecting notions of democracy that are given a definitive formula (12).

Central to any attempt to address the project of a more realized democracy is the necessity to challenge the current neoliberal assumption that democracy is a metaphor for the alleged "free" market. Of course, this is not to suggest that a genuine democratic public space once existed in some ideal form and has now been corrupted by the values of the market. Rather it acknowledges that these democratic public spheres, even in limited forms, seem no longer to be animating concepts for making visible the contradiction and tension between the reality of existing democracy and the promise of a more fully realized democracy. While liberal democracy offers an important discourse around issues of "rights, freedoms, participation, self-rule, and citizenship," it has been mediated historically, as John Brenkman observes, through the "damaged and burdened tradition" of racial and gender exclusions, economic injustice and a formalistic, ritualized democracy which substituted the swindle for the promise of democratic participation (123). Part of the challenge of creating a radical democracy necessitates constructing new locations of struggle, vocabularies, and subject positions that allow people in a wide variety of public spheres to become more than they are now as well as to question what it is they have become within existing institutional and social formations. As Chantal Mouffe points out, this will require people "give some thought to their experiences so that they can transform their relations of subordination and oppression" (Olson and Worsham 178).

In spite of the urgency of the current historical moment, educators should avoid crude antitheoretical calls to action. More than ever, they need to appropriate scholarly as well as popular sources and use theory as a critical resource to name particular problems and make connections between the political and the cultural, to break what Homi Bhabha has called "the continuity and the consensus of common sense" (Olson and Worsham 11).

As a resource, theory becomes important as a way of critically engaging and mapping the crucial relations among language, texts, everyday life, and structures of power. However, this can only be a part of a broader effort to understand the conditions, contexts, and strategies of struggle that will lead to social transformation. I am suggesting that the tools of theory emerge out of the intersection of the past and present, and respond to and are shaped by the conditions at hand. Theory, in this instance, addresses the challenge of connecting the world of the symbolic, discursive, and representational to the social gravity and force of everyday issues rooted in material relations of power.

The overriding political project at issue here recommends that educators and others produce new theoretical tools (a new vocabulary as well as set of conceptual resources) for linking theory, critique, education, and the discourse of possibility to creating the social conditions for the collective production of what Pierre Bourdieu terms realist utopias (43).

Such a project points to constructing both a new vocabulary for connecting what we read to how we engage in movements for social change, while recognizing that simply invoking the relationship between theory and practice, critique and social action is not enough. As John Brenkman points out, "theory becomes a closed circuit when it supposes it can understand social problems without contesting their manifestation in public life" (130). Theory's avoidance of the material is also symptomatic of a kind of retreat from the uneven battles over values and beliefs characteristic of some versions of postmodern conceptions of the political. Any attempt to give new life to a substantive democratic politics must consider producing alternative narratives to those employed by the producers of official memory, and address what it means to make the pedagogical more political. Such a task requires engaging the issue of what kind of educational work is necessary within different types of public spaces. It must enable people to use their full intellectual resources and skills both to provide a profound critique of existing institutions as well as to enter into the public sphere in order to interrupt the operations of dominant power. To do so will enable educators to more fully address what Bauman calls the "hard currency of human suffering" (5).

If emancipatory politics is to be equal to the challenge of neoliberal capitalism, educators need to theorize politics not as a science or set of objective conditions. Instead, such politics need to provide a point of departure in specific and concrete situations. We need to rethink the very meaning of the political so that it can provide a sense of direction but no longer be used to supply complete answers. Instead we should ask why and how particular social formations have a specific shape, come into being, and what it might mean to rethink such formations in terms of opening up new sites of struggles and movements within a global public sphere. Politics in this sense offers a notion of the social that is open and contingent, providing a conception of democracy that is never complete and determinate but constantly receptive to different understandings of the contingency of its decisions, mechanisms of exclusions, and operations of power (Critchley 1).

In the absence of such languages and the social formations as well as public spheres that make them operative, politics becomes narcissistic and reductionist, catering to the mood of widespread pessimism and the cathartic allure of spectacle (or, should I say, the seductions of being clever). Emptied of its political content, public space increasingly becomes either a site of self-display—a favorite space for the public relations intellectual, speaking ever so softly on National Public Radio—or it functions as a site for reclaiming a form of social Darwinism represented most explicitly in reality-based television shows such as "Survivor" and "Big Brother" with their endless instinct for the weaknesses of others and masochistic affirmation of ruthlessness and steroidal power. Escape, avoidance, and narcissism are now coupled with the public display, if not celebration, of those individuals who define agency in terms of their survival skills rather than their commitment to dialogue, critical reflection, solidarity, and relations that open up the promise of public engagement with important social issues. Reality TV embraces the arrogance of neoliberal power as it smiles back at us, legitimating downsizing and the ubiquitousness of the political economy of fear.

Cynicism coupled with an ongoing depoliticization of public life represents a primary challenge to any notion of radical relevance and politics. The pervasiveness of such cynicism calls for a massive pedagogical attempt on the part of critical intellectuals globally to reinvigorate politics. We must resurrect the hope of alternative visions, dreams, politics, and struggles. Such hope is not rooted in the airy dream world of new-age politics. Rather it is rooted in the concerted political and pedagogical struggles that push against the physics of dominant power while linking such power to the struggles in which people live out their everyday lives. It is this issue that I want to address before taking up the further challenge of making the pedagogical more political.

THE VALUE OF EDUCATED HOPE

Against an increasingly oppressive corporate-based globalism, progressives need to resurrect a language of resistance and possibility. This will be a language that embraces a militant utopianism while constantly being attentive to those forces that seek to turn such hope into a new slogan or punish and dismiss those who dare look beyond the horizon of the given. Hope, in this instance, is one of the preconditions for individual and social struggle, the ongoing practice of critical education in a wide variety of sites, and the mark of courage on the part of intellectuals in and out of the academy who use the resources of theory to address pressing social problems. But hope is also a referent for civic courage, offering the ability to mediate the memory of loss and the experience of injustice. Hope can act as part of a broader attempt to open up new locations of struggle, contest the workings of oppressive power, and undermine various forms of domination.

The philosopher, Ernst Bloch, is instructive here. He argues that hope must be concrete, a spark that not only reaches out beyond the surrounding emptiness of privatization, but anticipates a better world in the future, a world that speaks to us by presenting tasks based on the challenges of the present time. For Bloch, utopianism becomes concrete when it links the possibility of the "*not yet*" with forms of political agency animated by a determined effort to engage critically the past and present in order to address pressing social problems and realizable tasks.[3] Bloch believed that utopianism could not be removed from the world and was not "something like nonsense or absolute fancy; rather it is *not yet* in the sense of a possibility; that it could be there if we could only do something for it." As a discourse of critique and social transformation, utopianism in Bloch's view is characterized by a "militant optimism," one that foregrounds the crucial relationship between critical education and political agency, on the one hand, and the concrete struggles needed, on the other hand. Hope, then, gives substance to the recognition that every present is incomplete. For theorists such as Bloch, utopian thinking was anticipatory not messianic, mobilizing rather than therapeutic. At best, utopian thinking, as Anson Rabinach contends "points beyond the given while remaining within it (11). The longing for a more human society in this instance does not collapse into a retreat from the world but emerges out of critical and practical engagements with present behaviors, institutional formations, and everyday practices. Hope in this context does not ignore the worst dimensions of human suffering, exploitation, and social relations; on the contrary, hope acknowledges the need to sus-

tain the "capacity to see the worst and offer more than that for our consideration" (Dunn 160). The great challenge to militant utopianism, with its commitment to keeping critical thought alive, rests in an emerging consensus among
a wide range of political factions that neoliberal democracy is the best we can
do. The impoverishment of intellectuals, coupled with their increasing irrelevance and growing refusal to adequately address human suffering, is now matched
by the poverty of a social order that cannot conceive of any alternative to itself.

Feeding into the increasingly dominant view that society cannot be fundamentally improved outside of market forces, neoliberalism strips utopianism
of its possibilities for social critique and democratic engagement. By doing so
neoliberalist politics undermines the need to reclaim utopian thinking as both
a discourse of human rights and a moral referent for dismantling and transforming dominant structures of wealth and power.[4] Moreover, an anti-utopianism
of both the right and left can be found in those views that reduce utopian thinking to state terrorism and progressive visionaries to unrealistic, if not dangerous, ideologues. The alternative offered here is what Russell Jacoby calls, a "convenient cynicism," a belief that human suffering, hardship, and massive
inequalities in all areas of life are simply inherent in human nature and an irreversible part of the social condition (80). In its liberal version, this amounts to
the belief that "America's best defense against utopianism as terrorism" will
entail "preserving democracy as it currently exist[s] in the world"—a view largely
shared by the likes of Lynne Cheney, John Ashcroft, and Norman Podhoretz
(Willis 110). Within this discourse, hope is foreclosed, politics becomes militarized, and resistance is privatized, aestheticized, or degenerates into all forms
of hypercommercialized escapism. Against a militant and radically democratic
utopianism, the equation of terrorism and utopianism appears deeply cynical.
However, the rhetoric of neoliberalism not only appears flat. Importantly, it
also offers up an artificially conditioned optimism—operating at full capacity
in the pages of *Fast Company*, *Wired Magazine*, *The Wall Street Journal*, and
Forbes. In addition, it is at work in the relentless entrepreneurial hype of figures such as George Gilder and Tom Peters, as well as the Nike and Microsoft
revolutionaries. The constraints of neoliberalist rhetoric make it increasingly
difficult to imagine a life beyond the existing parameters of market pleasures,
mail-order catalogues, shopping malls, and Disneyland.[5] Profound anti-utopianism is spurred on by neoliberalism as well as its myths of the citizen as consumer and the markets as sovereign entities. It is aided by the collapse of the
distinction between both market liberties and civic liberties, between a market economy and a market society. As a result, the rhetoric of neoliberalism not
only commodifies a critical notion of political agency. It also undermines the
importance of multiple democratic public spheres.

Against the dystopian hope of neoliberalism, I want to argue for the necessity of educated hope as a crucial component of a radically charged politics
"grounded in broad-based civic participation and popular decision making"

(Boggs 7). Educated hope as a form of oppositional utopianism makes visible the necessity for progressives and other critical intellectuals to be attentive to the ways in which institutional and symbolic power are tangled up with everyday experience. Any politics of hope must tap into individual experiences and at the same time link individual responsibility with a progressive sense of social agency. Politics and pedagogy alike spring "from real situations and from what we can say and do in these situations" (Badiou 96). At its best, hope translates into civic courage as a political and pedagogical practice that begins when one's life can no longer be taken for granted. In doing so, it makes concrete the possibility for transforming hope and politics into an ethical space as well as a public act. Such a view of hope and politics confronts the flow of everyday experience and the weight of social suffering with the force of individual and collective resistance as well as the unending project of democratic social transformation. Emphasizing politics as a pedagogical practice and performative act, educated hope accentuates the notion that politics is played out not only on the terrain of imagination and desire. Educated hope is also grounded in relations of power mediated through the outcome of situated struggles, struggles dedicated to creating the conditions and capacities for people to become critically engaged political agents.

Combining the discourse of critique and hope is crucial to affirm that critical activity offers the possibility for social change. Intersecting discourses of critique and hope view democracy as a project and task, as an ideal type that is never finalized and has a powerful adversary in the social realities it is meant to change. Utopianism is not flight into fantasy. It is a necessity made desirable by the bleakness of the current historical moment. Utopianism as educated hope does not only provide the mental space to discuss alternative visions of society or to imagine otherwise, to act otherwise. Utopianism as educated hope also does the important political and pedagogical work of relativizing the present, evoking future possibilities, and creating room for a range of positions (Beilharz 59). But educated hope is not merely theoretical. Educated hope is also linked to the need to create those institutional and public spaces in which critical dialogue can take place, ideas can be produced, and policy enacted. Simultaneously, any viable cultural politics must address the necessity to develop collective movements that can challenge the subordination of social needs to the dictates of commercialism and capital. I will return once again to this issue later in this chapter.

MAKING THE PEDAGOGICAL MORE POLITICAL

The search for a new politics and a new critical language that crosses the critical theory/postmodernism divide must reinvigorate the relationship between democracy, ethics, and political agency. This can only occur by expanding both the meaning of the pedagogical as a political practice while simultaneously

making the political more pedagogical. In the first instance, it is crucial to recognize that pedagogy has less to do with the language of technique and method-
ology than it does with issues of politics and power. Pedagogy is a moral and
political practice that is always implicated in power relations. Pedagogy must
be understood as a cultural politics that offers a particular version as well as a
particular vision of civic life, of the future, and of how we might construct representations of ourselves, others, as well as our physical and social environment.
As Roger Simon observes,

> As an introduction to, preparation for, and legitimation of particular forms of
> social life, education always presupposes a vision of the future. In this respect
> a curriculum and its supporting pedagogy are a version of our own dreams for
> ourselves, our children, and our communities. But such dreams are never neu-
> tral; they are always someone's dreams and to the degree that they are impli-
> cated in organizing the future for others they always have a moral and politi-
> cal dimension. It is in this respect that any discussion of pedagogy must begin
> with a discussion of educational practice as a form of cultural politics, as a par-
> ticular way in which a sense of identity, place, worth, and above all value is
> informed by practices which organize knowledge and meaning. (372)

An oppositional cultural politics can take many forms. However, given the current assault by neoliberalism on all aspects of democratic public life, it seems
imperative that educators revitalize the struggles to create conditions in which
learning would be linked to social change in a wide variety of social sites. As
such, pedagogy would take on the task of regenerating both a renewed sense of
social and political agency as well as a critical subversion of dominant power
itself. Under such circumstances, agency becomes the site through which power
is not transcended but reworked, replayed, and restaged in productive ways.
Central to my argument is the assumption that politics is not only about power.
In addition, as Cornelius Castoriadis points out, politics fundamentally "has to
do with political judgements and value choices," indicating that questions of
civic education as well as critical pedagogy (learning how to become a skilled
citizen) are central to the struggle over political agency and democracy (8). In
this instance, critical pedagogy emphasizes critical reflexivity, bridging the gap
between learning and everyday life, understanding the connection between
power and knowledge, and extending democratic rights and identities by using
the resources of history. However, among many educators and social theorists, there is still widespread refusal to recognize that this form of education
is not only the foundation for expanding and enabling political agency. It
also takes place across a wide variety of public spheres mediated through the
very force of culture itself, ones we cannot afford to ignore.

   Pluralizing the spaces of pedagogical engagement can make the pedagogy
more political by raising fundamental questions such as the following: What is
the relationship between social justice and the distribution of public resources

and goods? What are the conditions, knowledge, and skills that are a prerequisite for political agency and social change? Making the political more pedagogical in this instance suggests producing modes of knowledge and social practices that not only affirm oppositional cultural work but offer opportunities to mobilize instances of collective outrage, if not collective action. Such mobilization opposes glaring material inequities and the growing cynical belief that today's culture of investment and finance makes it *impossible* to address many of the major social problems facing both the U.S. and the larger world. Most importantly, such work points to the link between civic education, critical pedagogy, and modes of oppositional political agency that are pivotal to elucidating a politics that promotes autonomy and social change.

At the very least, critical pedagogy proposes that education is a form of political intervention in the world and is capable of creating the possibilities for social transformation. Rather than viewing teaching as technical practice, radical pedagogy in the broadest terms is a moral and political practice premised on the assumption that learning is not about processing received knowledge but actually transforming it as part of a more expansive struggle for individual rights and social justice. This implies that any viable notion of pedagogy and resistance should illustrate how knowledge, values, desire, and social relations are always implicated in relations of power. It must also involve examining how such an understanding can be used pedagogically and politically by students to further expand and deepen the imperatives of economic and political democracy. The fundamental challenge facing educators within the current age of neoliberalism is to provide the conditions for students to address how knowledge is related to the power of both self-definition and social agency. Central to such a challenge is providing students with the skills, knowledge, and authority they need to inquire and act upon what it means to live in a substantive democracy, to recognize antidemocratic forms of power, and to fight deeply rooted injustices in a society and world founded on systemic economic, racial, and gendered inequalities.

At the very least, such a project involves understanding and critically engaging dominant public transcripts and values within a broader set of historical and institutional contexts. Unfortunately, many educators have failed to take seriously Antonio Gramsci's insight that "[e]very relationship of 'hegemony' is necessarily an educational relationship." Gramsci's implication is that education as a cultural pedagogical practice takes place across multiple sites and diverse contexts. And we must understand the degree to which these moments of education constantly make us both subjects of and subject to relations of power (350).

In the age of neoliberal global plunder characterized by an unchecked market authoritarianism and the expansion of empire abroad, it is crucial that intellectuals and social movements move away from the narrow confines of a particularized politics. We must join in efforts to engage in a plurality of forms of political and pedagogical interventions. These include challenging the historical inevitability of global capitalism, defending the historical advances associated with nation states by pushing for "more education, more health, more guaranteed lifetime income," mobilizing marginalized groups on all fronts to address capitalism's relationship to labor and the environment, and making antiracist and class struggles paramount to any struggle for democratization (Wallerstein 17). Economic restructuring on a global level makes class a more central category than ever before. We witness increasing divisions between the rich and the poor, accelerated by the massive transformation of power from nations to transnational corporations, on the one hand. On the other hand, we are faced with the equally massive transfer of wealth from the poor and middle class to the upper classes. But any attempt to abolish forms of class, racial, gender, and other types of oppression requires that we construct an altogether different kind of politics than what has been traditionally associated with the politics of class struggles. A new politics must be steeped in an attempt to publicly confront oppressive relations, explain them, situate them historically, engage how they take place through the intersection between the local and the global, and refuse to accept their inevitability. A radical pedagogy of persuasion and transformation in this instance becomes crucial to any viable politics of democratization. Any feasible movement that challenges neoliberalist rhetoric on both a domestic and international level will need, once again, to develop pedagogical strategies that debunk the cherished myths of capitalism, offer knowledge, skills, and tools that "will be immediately useful in people's lives" and, at the same time, "point to longer-run, more fundamental changes" (Wallerstein[19]). For critical intellectuals, this suggests engaging in pedagogical practices that address the new strategies and politics being fashioned within the global justice movement. While there have been numerous analyses of globalization, what has been undertheorized is what Imre Szeman has called "the pedagogy of globalization." What Szeman means by this is

> both the conditions of social and cultural learning and reproduction in the context of globalization and the way in which globalization itself constitutes a problem of and for pedagogy. The triumphalist rhetoric of politicians and business leaders, the lessons proffered by newspaper columnists and TV news anchors, as well as the fast-cutting globe-hopping ads of dot.coms, financial services companies, and hardware giants—all of this constitutes a form of public education in the contours and realities of the new global situation. (4–5)

Szeman argues that any viable understanding of globalization must address the pedagogical conditions for its reproduction. But if educators are to move beyond simply making visible the connection between globalization and new modes of social, cultural, and economic reproduction, they will have to learn both how to engage this newly constituted pedagogical force and how to resist it through new political discourses and pedagogical strategies. Such strategies will have to open up new global spaces of pedagogy—employing a vast array of old and new media including digital video, magazines, the Internet, computers, and newspapers.

Fortunately, nascent examples of such interventions already exist in the vast array of student antiglobalization protests that have taken place both on campuses across the United States as well as in Seattle, Washington, D.C., London, Prague, Genoa, and other cities in the last few years. Connecting a wide variety of communicative approaches from street theater to People's Summits to inventive uses of the Internet, global justice advocates are rejecting "the official pedagogy of globalization circulated through press releases and the culture industry [by attempting] to construct new modes and sites of learning that might enable a broad, collective response to the powers that be" (Szeman 4).

I think Szeman is right in claiming that these protests constitute a new space of pedagogy. Employing relatively fresh modes of communication such as the Internet and digital video, student protesters offer the global public new ways of understanding, contextualizing, and engaging issues that are both readily attainable in the dominant media as well as information that is entirely different and critical—made available to the larger public through new pedagogical interventions (i.e., documentaries, digital photography placed on the Internet, publicly distributed hand outs). Ordinary citizens, educators, and students need more than rapid-fire sound bytes, disinformation, and outright corporate propaganda. They also need entry to alternative sources of information, new pedagogical sites to access it, and new tools to historicize and critically engage what they confront. The emerging campus student activist and global justice movements offer pedagogical tools and modes of analysis that might prove invaluable in rethinking both the meaning of a pedagogy of globalization and its implications for working with students and adults within as well as outside of schools.

In addition to the global justice movements such as those that took place in Seattle, youth movements have also occurred on many campuses across the United States and are spreading to other countries as well. Campus activism can be seen in the fight against the growing corporate influence on higher education, attacks on affirmative action, the exploitation of sweatshop workers, the ruination of nature, the prison-industrial complex, low wages for university workers, and university licensing policies, among others. Organizations such as the Student Labor Action Coalition (SLAC) have made great strides in educating students about the importance of unions in preventing corporations from taking over higher education; United Students Against Sweatshops has mobilized thousands of students in support of fair labor policies and economic justice. The Democratic Socialist of American Youth Section tries to bring youth together around a variety of pressing economic, racial, and social issues. Hip-hop mogul Russell Simmons has mobilized a number of artists, executives, politicians, and civil rights leaders to form The Hip-Hop Summit Action Network which focuses on issues crucial to African American youth such as voter education and encouraging political activism in the hip-hop community. In Boston, Project

Hip-Hop consists of students who use the resources of antiracist struggles to educate youth "to recognize themselves as agents of social change" (1). Through the development of their own curricula, employing the concept of the "rolling classroom," Project Hip-Hop takes students to the South to learn the lessons of civil rights struggles. The group has also enabled young people to visit South Africa to study its ongoing fight against racism as well as its struggle to create a multiracial democracy.

In all of these instances, students are providing an important political and pedagogical service by connecting corporate power to its social consequences, demonstrating the importance of both collective resistance to the corporations and the need to struggle for global justice through a widely related set of issues. Garment industry abuses are now part of the public lexicon. Sweatshops are no longer removed from public consciousness in the advanced countries of the West. The assault by corporations on public and higher education has become more visible in recent years because of student protests all across the country. Militant, global anticorporate activism has made debt relief for poor countries a matter of public interests, especially in light of U2 rock star Bono's willingness to take up the issue.

The rise in militant student activism not only puts pressure on university administrators, corporate executives, and the leaders of International Monetary Fund and the World Trade Organization. Student activists also teach "themselves and their fellow students to question facts of social and economic life that they had long been taught to take for granted" (Featherstone 113). And as such activism gets more media attention, it also serves to offer valuable lessons in global pedagogy, economic injustice, and the politics of globalization to a much larger set of diverse audiences. Moreover, it offers a challenge to the prevailing cynicism that seems to work against any viable notion of a future that does not simply reinvent the present.

At the same time, student activists involved in the campus as well as the global justice movements face some serious challenges. The biggest challenge these diverse activists need to confront centers around developing a theoretical language that connects their various struggles to a broader project such as radical democracy while at the same time being able to increase alliances that provide the collective force of a major international political movement. Inequality and injustice take many forms, and some of the most ruthless include forms of racism, poverty, and class inequities that are not adequately addressed in the anticorporate rhetoric. If radical ideas and social practices are to become popular, more is needed than creative anarchism, revolutionary theater, and a faith in disparate actions. As Jonathan Rutherford observes,

> Politics requires analysis, the connection of disparate issues, and the creation of a coherent argument with which people can understand and sympathize. . . . The antiglobalization movement has recaptured a sense of idealism and

hope in a cynical age. But if it is to consolidate itself as something enduring
and politically effective, it needs to be matched by critical analysis and an
elaboration of political economy. The politics of spectacle without any accountable forms of leadership or ideology is easily hijacked.(14)

While I think Rutherford overstates the shortcomings of the student activists,
he is certainly on target with his call for a more careful analysis of how global
neoliberalist discourse works and what it would take politically and strategically for these diverse movements to challenge it.

   While it is crucial for educators to learn from young people, labor and
green party activists, and others in order to fight against the effects of neoliberalism and finance capital, academics and other public intellectuals can also
offer their own expertise by working collectively with such groups in order
to develop global institutions "of effective and political action as could match
the size and power of the already global economic forces and bring them under
political scrutiny and ethical supervision" (Bauman 12). Such projects and
interventions, while not offering a politics with guarantees, can create a new
discourse of politics and hope while simultaneously unleashing the pedagogical and political energies necessary to combine a strong hostility to the
existence of human suffering and exploitation—especially among children
throughout the world—with "a vision of a global society, informed by civil liberties and human rights, that carries with it the shared obligations and responsibilities of common, collaborative citizenship"(Bhabha B12). Instances of
such movements can be glimpsed in the antiglobalization protests that have
taken place all over the globe. But the move from protest to building astute
analyses and international alliances is of particular concern, and can be seen
in meetings such as the World Social Forum that took place recently in Porto
Alegre, Brazil.

THE URGENCY OF NOW

In this chapter I have argued that in the early years of this new millennium,
educators, parents, and others should reevaluate what it means for adults
and young people to grow up in a world that has been radically altered by a
hyperneoliberal capitalism that monopolizes the educational force of culture
as it ruthlessly eliminates those public spheres not governed by the logic of the
market. Such a task demands new theoretical and political tools for addressing how pedagogy, knowledge, resistance, and power can be analyzed within
and across a variety of cultural spheres, including but not limited to the schools.
Eduardo Galeano has stated that "By saying no to the devastating empire of
greed, whose center lies in North America, we are saying yes to another possible America. . . . In saying no to a peace without dignity, we are saying yes
to the sacred right of rebellion against injustice" (29). Galeano speaks clearly

to the urgent task of elevating the politics and possibility of resistance so that we may address all those issues, spaces, and public spheres in which the intersection of language and bodies becomes "part of the process of forming and disrupting power relations" (Patton 183).

Too many intellectuals and educators are disconnected from social movements and have trouble connecting their work both to pressing public issues as well as wider constituencies outside of the university. More often, intellectuals cut off from the wider society often fall prey to forms of professional legitimation that not only deny the political nature of their own labor and theoretical work. These forms of political legitimation also reinforce a deep-rooted cynicism about the ability of ordinary people to take risks, fight for what they believe in, and become a force for social change. This suggests that educators should work to form alliances with parents, community organizers, labor organizations, and civil rights groups at the local, national, and international levels to better understand how to translate private troubles into pubic actions, arouse public interests over pressing social problems, and use collective means to work toward a "whole left" so as to more fully democratize the commanding institutional economic, cultural, and social structures that dominate our societies.

George Lipsitz rightly argues that progressives need to challenge a key goal of conservative political work since the 1980s. He is referring to attempts on the part of conservatives to

> hide public concerns while foregrounding private interests—to encourage people to think of themselves as taxpayers and homeowners rather than as citizens and workers, to depict private property interests and the accumulated advantages accorded to white men as universal while condemning demands for redistributive justice by women, racial and sexual minorities, and by other aggrieved social groups as the 'whining of special interests.' (84)

At the risk of overemphasis, educators and others require a politics of resistance that extends beyond the classroom as part of a broader struggle to challenge those forces of neoliberalism that currently wage war against all collective structures capable of defending vital social institutions as a public good. In times of increased domination of public and higher education it becomes important, as George Lipsitz reminds us, that academics—as well as artists and other cultural workers—not become isolated "in their own abstract desires for social change and actual social movements. Taking a position is not the same as waging a war of position; changing your mind is not he same as changing society" (81).

Resistance must become part of a public pedagogy that works to position rigorous theoretical work and public bodies against corporate power, connect classrooms to the challenges faced by social movements in the streets, and provide spaces within classrooms for personal injury and private terrors to be translated into public considerations and struggles. For some educators this represents a violation of academic neutrality, a politicizing of the educational process, or a contamination of the virtues of academic civility and the principles of high culture. But the issue is not whether public or higher education has become contaminated with politics. The issue is more importantly about recognizing that education is already a space of politics, power, and authority. The crucial matter at stake, then, is how to appropriate, invent, direct, and control the multiple layers of power and politics that constitute both the institutional formation of education and the pedagogies that are often an outcome of deliberate struggles to put into place particular notions of knowledge, values, and identity. As committed educators, we cannot eliminate politics, but we can work against a politics of certainty, a pedagogy of terrorism, and an institutional formation that closes down rather than opens up democratic relations. This requires, in part, that we work diligently to construct a politics without guarantees—one that perpetually questions itself as well as all those forms of knowledge, values, and practices that appear beyond the process of interrogation, debate, and deliberation.

There is a lot of talk among social theorists in the United States about the death of politics and the inability of human beings to imagine a more equitable and just world in order to make it better. But rather than make despair convincing, I think it is all the more crucial to take seriously Meghan Morris's argument that "Things are too urgent now to be giving up on our imagination" (Grossberg 114).

I would hope that of all groups, educators would be the most vocal and militant in challenging this assumption, thus reclaiming the university's subversive role by combining critiques of dominant discourses and the institutional formations that support and reproduce them with the goal of limiting human suffering while at the same time attempting to deepen and expand the meaning, if not the reality, of a radical democracy.

Combining theoretical rigor with social relevance may be risky politically and pedagogically. However, the promise of a substantive democracy far outweighs the security and benefits that accompany a retreat into academic irrelevance and the safe haven of a no-risk professionalism. This no-risk professionalism requires, as Paul Sabin observes, "an isolation from society and vows of political chastity" (B24). Critical scholarship is crucial to such a task, but it will not be enough. Individual and social agency only becomes meaningful as part of the willingness to imagine otherwise in order to act otherwise. Knowledge, then, should be used for amplifying human freedom and promoting social justice, and not for simply creating profits or future careers. Intellectuals need to take a position, and as Edward Said argues, they have an obligation to "remind audiences of the moral questions that may be hidden in the clamour and din of public debates. . . . and deflate the claims of [neoliberal] triumphalism" (504).

NOTES

1. I address this issue in Henry A. Giroux, *Public Spaces, Private Lives: Beyond the Culture of Cynicism* (Lanham: Rowman and Littlefield, 2001). See also Michael Peters, *Poststructuralism, Marxism, and Neoliberalism: Between Theory and Politics* (Lanham: Rowman and Littlefield, 2001).

2. I take this issue up in great detail in Henry A. Giroux, *Impure Acts: The Practical Politics of Cultural Studies* (New York: Routledge: 1999) and Henry A. Giroux, *Public Spaces, Private Lives: Beyond the Culture of Cynicism* (Rowman and Littlefield, 2001).

3. Bloch's great contribution in English on the subject of utopianism can be found in his three volume work, Ernst Bloch, *The Principle of Hope*, Volume I. II.& III [originally published in 1959] trans. Neville Plaice, Stephen Plaice and Paul Knight (Cambridge: MIT, 1986).

4. See Jacoby, "A Brave Old World," in Frank and Tambornino, eds., pp. 72–80; Geras, "Minimum Utopia: Ten Theses," in Frank and Tambornino, eds., pp. 41–42; Leo Panitch and Sam Gindin, "Transcending Pessimism: Rekindling Socialist Imagination," in Leo Panitch and Sam Gindin, eds. *Necessary and Unnecessary Utopias* (New York: Monthly Review Press, 1999), pp.1–29; David Harvey, *Spaces of Hope* (Berkeley: U of California P, 2000); Russell Jacoby, *The End of Utopia: Politics and Culture in an Age of Apathy* (New York: Basic Books, 1999).

5. For a critique of entrepreneurial populism of this diverse group, see Thomas Frank, *One Market Under God: Extreme Capitalism, Market Populism, and the End of Economic Democracy* (New York: Doubleday, 2000).

WORKS CITED

Amin, Samir. "Imperialization and Globalization." *Monthly Review* (June 2001): 6–24.

Aronwitz, Stanley. "Introduction." Paulo Friere. *Pedagogy of Freedom*. Lanham: Rowman and Littlefield, 1998.

Badiou, Alain. *Ethics: An Essay on the Understanding of Evil*. London: Verso, 2001.

Barber, Benjamin R. "Blood Brothers, Consumers, or Citizens? Three Models of Identity—Ethnic, Commercial, and Civic." *Cultural Identity and the Nation State*. Eds. Carol Gould and Pasquale Pasquino. Lanham: Rowman and Littlefield, 2001.

Bauman, Zygmunt. "Global Solidarity." *Tikkun*. 17:1(2002): 12–14, 62.

Bauman, Zygmunt. *Globalization*. New York: Columbia University Press, 1998.

Beilharz, Peter. *Zygmunt Bauman: Dialectic of Modernity*.London: Sage, 2000.

Bhabha, Homi. "A Narrative of Divided Civilizations." *The Chronicle of Higher Education*. (September 28, 2001): B12.

Bloch, Ernst. "Something's Missing: A Discussion Between Ernst Bloch and Theodor W. Adorno on the Contradictions of Utopia Longing." *The Utopian Function of Art and Literature: Selected Essays*. Cambridge MIT Press, 1988. 1–17.

Bloch, Ernst. *The Principle of Hope*. Volume I, II,& III [originally published in 1959] trans. Neville Plaice, Stephen Plaice, and Paul Knight. Cambridge: MIT Press, 1986.

Boggs, Carl. *The End of Politics: Corporate Power the Decline of the Public Sphere*. New York: Guilford Press, 2000.

Bourdieu, Pierre. "For a Scholarship with Commitment." *Profession*. (2000): 40–45.

Brenkman, John. "Race Publics; Civic Illiberalism or Race After Reagan." *Transition*. 66 (Summer 1995). 4–36.

———. "Extreme Criticism." *What's Left of Theory*. Eds. J. Butler, J. Guillary, and K. Thomas. New York: Routledge, 2000. 114–136.

Castoriadis, Cornelius. "Institutions and Autonomy." *A Critical Sense*. Ed. Peter Osborne. New York: Routledge, 1996. 1–21.

Critchley, Simon. "Ethics, Politics, and Radical Democracy—The History of a Disagreement." *Culture Machine*. Available on-line at:www.culturemachine. tees.ac.uk/frm_f1.htm.

Dunn, Thomas L. "Political Theory for Losers." *Vocations of Political Theory*. Eds. Jason A. Frank and John Tambornino. Minneapolis: University of Minnesota Press, 2000, 145–165.

Espada, Martin. "Viva Vieques!," *The Progressive*. (July 28, 2000): 27–29.

Featherstone, Liza. "Sweatshops, Students and the Corporate University." *Croonenbergh's Fly*. 2 (Spring/Summer 2002): 107–117

Frank, Thomas. *One Market Under God: Extreme Capitalism, Market Populism and the End of Economic Democracy*. New York: Doubleday, 2000.

Geras, Norman. "Minimum Utopia: Ten Theses." *Necessary and unnecessary Utopias*. Eds. Leo Panitch and Colin Leys. New York: Monthly Review Press, 2000. 41–52.

Giroux, Henry A. *Public Spaces, Private Lives: Beyond the Culture of Cynicism*. Lanham: Rowman and Littlefield, 2001.

Giroux, Henry A. *Impure Acts: The Practical Politics of Cultural Studies*. New York: Routledge, 1999.

Giroux, Henry A. *Public Spaces, Private Lives: Beyond the Culture of Cynicism*. Lanham: Rowman and Littlefield, 2001.

Gramsci, Antonio. *Selections from the Prison Notebooks*. New York: International Press, 1971.

Grossberg, Lawrence. "Why Does Neo-Liberalism Hate Kids? The War on Youth and the Culture of Politics." *The Review of Education/Pedagogy/Cultural Studies*. 23:2 (2001): 111–136.

Harvey, David. *Spaces of Hope*. Berkeley: University of California Press, 2000.

Hertz, Noreena. *The Silent Takeover: Global Capitalism and the Death of Democracy*. New York: Free Press, 2001.

Jacoby, Russell. *The End of Utopia: Politics and Culture in an Age of Apathy*. New York: Basic Books, 1999.

Jacoby, Russell. "A Brave Old World: Looking Forward to a Nineteenth-Century Utopia." *Harper's Magazine*. 301(Dec. 2000): 72–77.

Lipsitz, George. "Academic Politics and Social Change." *Cultural Studies and Political Theory*. Ed. Jodi Dean. Ithaca: Cornell University Press, 2000. 80–92.

Olson, Gary and Lynn Worsham. "Rethinking Political Community: Chantal Mouffe's Liberal Socialism." *JAC*. 18.3 (1999): 163–199.

Olson, Gary and Lynn Worsham. "Staging the Politics of Difference: Homi Bhabha's Critical Literacy." *JAC*. 18.3 (1998): 361–391.

Panitch, Leo, and Sam Gindin. "Transcending Pessimism: Rekindling Socialist Imagination." Eds. Leo Panitch and Sam Gindin. *Necessary and Unnecessary Utopias*. New York: Monthly Review Press, 1999.

Patton, Cindy. "Performativity and Spatial Distinction: The End of AIDS Epidemiology." *Performativity and Performance*. Eds. Eve Kosofsky Sedgwick and Andrew Parker. New York: Routledge, 1993. pp. 182–190.

Peters, Michael. *Poststructuralism, Marxism, and Neoliberalism: Between Theory and Politics*. Lanham: Rowman and Littlefield, 2001.

"Project Hip-Hop." Available on-line at: http://www.aclu-mass.org/youth /hiphop.html.

Rabinach, Anson. "Ernst Bloch's *Heritage of Our Times* and the Theory of Fascism." *New German Critique*. 11 (Spring 1977): 5–21.

Rutherford, Jonathan. "After Seattle." *The Review of Education/Pedagogy/Cultural Studies*. 24.1–2 (January-June, 2002): 13–28.

Sabin, Paul. "Academe Subverts Young Scholars' Civic Orientation." *The Chronicle of Higher Education* (February 8, 2002): B24.

Said, Edward W. *Reflections on Exile and Other Essays*. Cambridge: Harvard University Press, 2001.

Simon, Roger. "Empowerment as a Pedagogy of Possibility." *Language Arts*. 64:4 (April 1987): 370–382.

Szeman, Imre. "Introduction: Learning to Learn from Seattle." *The Review of Education/Pedagogy/Cultural Studies*. 24.1–2 (2002): 4–5.

Wallerstein, Immanuel. "A Left Politics for An Age of Transition." *Monthly Review*. 53:8 (January 2002): 17–23.

Willis, Ellen. "Buy American." *Dissent* (Fall 2000): 108–111.

CHAPTER NINE

TOWARD A CONTEMPORARY
PHILOSOPHY OF PRAXIS

NOAH DE LISSOVOY

PETER MCLAREN

INTRODUCTION

IN A WORLD IN WHICH THE OPPRESSORS OFTEN APPEAR TO BE ASSURED OF VICTORY, and in which they hold a near monopoly on the means of representation, it can sometimes be difficult to believe the left has a fighting chance, or even that it can be capable of the hope and ambition that have motivated radical and revolutionary movements historically. We suggest, however, that a creative and committed oppositional vision is needed now more than ever. It is our view that faithfulness to a fundamental and radically imaginative theoretical practice, which does not so much rethink as think newly (which *produces* rather than *reproduces*), as well as attention to new organic and popular forms of resistance, can suggest original and fruitful directions for continued revolutionary reflection and action. The puzzle remains that of envisioning, with the forms and materials of one world, the possibility of another; but if we can begin to read, in the unexpected rhymes and unremarked faultlines of the former, the partial intrusion of the latter, we can start to find a concrete basis for hope.

We believe that the fashioning of a coherent and viable left politics necessitates an urgent creativity in our vision and method as scholars and activists. It means thinking together, in principled fashion, issues posed by different struggles and discourses. To this end, we will begin by considering the importance of the *imagination* in revolutionary praxis and by outlining some of the important aspects of such a praxis. We will argue that this project depends upon an attention to and development of popular modes of understanding social contradictions, as well as on the formation of an enlarged conception of the revolutionary subject. Marxist analysis constitutes an indispensable framework for this effort. In particular, the notion of social *relations of production* should focus theoretical attention on the systematic logic of oppression and help to move "common sense" analyses toward a more developed account of the political economies of different forms of oppression. We will also suggest that in order to discover a meaningful view of this entire panorama, we will need to bring disparate perspectives and locations in dialogue toward a vision of a provisional whole politics, rather than merely juxtaposing incommensurable views, or on the other hand arbitrarily assimilating them into an artificial unity. We believe that this project of refiguration follows firmly in the tradition of revolutionary thinkers like Gramsci, Fanon, and Freire who have always responded imaginatively and synthetically to the transformed situations of their own moments.

The foregoing analysis of praxis will provide some approaches for the project of our second section: a reconsideration of *imperialism*, and how it can be understood as the nexus of different forms of oppression both in North America and globally. This theoretical framework represents a tentative application of the methods we propose in the first section. We will make the case for the usefulness of a conception of imperialism for analyzing domestic conditions within the imperialist countries, as well as for reorienting current discussions of globalization. Rather than representing a fully determined problematic, imperialism as a conceptual framework can serve as a useful space in which to work towards a negotiation of left discourses; its development depends on bringing to bear traditional definitions alongside analyses developed from the perspective of the periphery. Finally, in our third section, we will look at how contemporary imperialist processes reconfigure political *struggle*, and how we can detect and build radical opposition, particularly in the field of education. Education, we believe, is a crucial site of social and political contest, and thus also an important arena in which to develop anti-imperialist strategies. Our analysis in this essay is preliminary and does not pretend to offer any detailed prescriptions; nevertheless, we believe that the ideas it proposes can be important starting points in the working out of more developed projects on the left.

REVOLUTION AND IMAGINATION

A Philosophy of Praxis

We believe that in order to conceive and organize an effective and meaningful "whole left" it is necessary to specify not merely a narrowly theoretical basis for its possibility, but a philosophical one as well. Following Antonio Gramsci, a possible "philosophy of praxis" must be historically adequate—i.e., it must not merely solve a problem from a remove, but must also be popularly viable. Such a philosophy is not merely an abstract analysis of objectivities; it is the motivated representation of our organic experiences, impulses, and intuitions—as human beings engaged in struggle. This philosophical attention to experience is too often avoided in radical theory and politics, which is usually organized around a split between the practical and the theoretical, the activist and the intellectual. This split, however, is damaging to the prospects of the left since it reduces action to the merely technical sphere and consigns intellectual work to the abstract or scholarly. We believe that a viable "whole left" will only emerge from a fundamentally imaginative engagement with contemporary struggles. Such an engagement must attempt to think disparate struggles together, rather than only in their own terms, without thereby forcing them into artificial unities.

According to Gramsci, the job of the (socialist) philosopher is to develop the intuitions already present in the consciousness of the people, to extend and modify them into an efficient coherence:

> A philosophy of praxis . . . must be a criticism of "common sense," basing itself initially, however, on common sense in order to demonstrate that "everyone" is a philosopher and that it is not a question of introducing from scratch a scientific form of thought into everyone's individual life, but of renovating and making "critical" an already existing activity. (331)

The philosopher seizes upon emerging oppositional currents to forge them into a systematic hegemony. Critique is essential, but it must begin from the popular "common sense." In the terminology of radical educator Paulo Freire, the productive ground for the operation of liberatory praxis will be found in the "generative themes" that are truly lived in the "limit-situations" of the people.

The measure of success of such a philosophy, according to Gramsci, is its capacity to act upon the context in which it is produced:

> One could say that the historical value of a philosophy can be calculated from the "practical" efficacity it has acquired for itself, understanding "practical" in the widest sense. If it is true that every philosophy is the expression of a society, it should react back on that society and produce certain effects, both positive and negative. The extent to which precisely it reacts back is the measure of its historical importance, of its not being individual "elucubration" but "historical fact." (346)

Revolutionary philosophy attains to a historical status in taking effect within the social, and discovering/fashioning a set of contradictions that mobilize popular resources. The sides of these social contradictions must be traced, developed, and made possible as points of reference for those who join the struggle. They must permit the potential development of what Gramsci calls a "historical bloc." This *taking* of sides, which is first of all a discovering and *making* of sides, is equally important for Frantz Fanon, who points out, in other terms, that "There is no other fight for culture which can develop apart from the popular struggle" (233).

To illustrate what we mean, let's take as an example the analysis of racism in North America. Even the simple liberal call for everyone to "just get along" represents a theory of oppression, although it is clearly a weak one. According to this theory, racism is simply the antisocial pathology of an individual. Such an analysis demands that racists be enlightened, but can offer no organized collective response. This view is held by many white people; it ignores the pervasive experiences of racism of people of color. A theory of racism advances when it bases itself on these experiences and recognizes an organizing contradiction between whiteness as dominative power in society and people of color as systematically oppressed: "While a psychological analysis of racism focuses on what is in people's heads and asks how to change it, a structural analysis focuses on distribution of power and wealth across groups and on how those of European ancestry attempt to retain supremacy while groups of color try to challenge it" (Sleeter 158). Antiracism at this point becomes a philosophy capable of organizing collective intellectual and practical political work against oppression at the individual and institutional levels. Nevertheless, such a philosophy must itself run up against its own limits if it cannot appreciate the larger logics of capitalism and neocolonialism that organize systems of white supremacy. At this point, the theory needs to further expand to accommodate these realities and to make possible a consciously revolutionary antiracist praxis. Our point here is that it is precisely in this dialectic between analysis and new experience/insight that philosophy becomes robust and new practical possibilities emerge; it is impossible to decide a priori and apart from actual struggle upon a correct understanding.

The correctness of a theory must always be tested in its political efficacy, in its ability to "react back" on society; it cannot be true in a merely abstract sense. Thus, while it is important to understand racism as an expression of class oppression (which works to divide the working class and reduce its power to win demands against capital), to build a praxis on this analysis alone is to ignore the knowledge that has been built in years of struggle by people of color and whites against white supremacy per se. In the Civil Rights Movement, in struggles against police brutality, and elsewhere, a race-based analysis of oppression has realized important gains. Such struggle has grappled not only with abstract sociological determinants, but with a cultural and discursive context in which race as an independent category takes on tremendous meaning and force. This is not to deny the necessity of contextualizing these movements within a larger mode of production (i.e., capitalism) but rather to point to the relative autonomy of particular moments in this system, and the need to confront them in their own terms.

Furthermore, the fractures and confusions of the left cannot simply be patched up through skillful juggling and splicing. If revolution is a process, and if Gramsci is correct that ideologies, at the level of the masses rather than of individuals are organic and hence adequate, in a limited sense, to their historical environments, then this confusion itself represents an essential moment in the movement toward transformation. This does not mean of course that these aporias should be celebrated (as in, for example, the unfortunate valorization by post-Marxists of political fracture on the left—see especially Laclau and Mouffe), or that the need to think our way through them is not urgent. The point is rather that it represents an underestimation of the left to assume that it is merely reactive to the ideological assaults of the rulers, and thus has simply been disoriented by them. Following Gramsci and Freire, we should recognize that the inadequacy of received ideologies to mobilize is to be expected, that in the *learning* of revolution there must be a searching for new forms, meanings, and incorporations which cannot be decided ahead of the organic and popular experience of their discovery. It is essential to reaffirm, however, that the horizon of political praxis must be a socialist and revolutionary one. We strongly oppose a pseudo-Gramscian position popular in the academy. As noted by educationalist John Holst, many cultural studies scholars—i.e., radical pluralists, postmodernists, and post-Marxists—offer a perniciously narrow reading of Gramsci that situates his work within the limited precinct of reform-oriented practice. These scholars insist on the centrality of civil society as the arena of struggle; however, as Holst points out, Gramsci viewed civil society as only *part* of the hegemonic aspect of the state that essentially works to balance its coercive aspect.

What, then, would this revolutionary philosophy be in the current era? We will propose here an *anti-imperialist* philosophy of praxis (described later in more detail). We believe that this framework can best organize disparate instances of oppression at the present time, and that it can best retain the provisionality that we have so far been arguing for while simultaneously opening up possibilities for action. Such a philosophy would be able to analyze global domination and exploitation in the political, economic, and cultural spheres without immediately prioritizing one particular dimension in any simple fashion. It would bring together different resistance movements without flattening them into mere examples of a unifying principle. And it would pose, in *imperialism*, a system and subject of oppression with a global reach which would still retain a coherence (as opponent) for local movements.

THE BACK OF THE SUBJECT

> It is her reluctance to cross over, to make a hole in the fence and walk across, to cross the river, to take that flying leap into the dark, that drives her to escape, that forces her into the fecund cave of her imagination where she is cradled in the arms of Coatlicue, who will never let her go. If she doesn't change her ways, she will remain a stone forever. No hay más que cambia.
>
> —Anzaldúa 71

Conceiving of a viable and radically oppositional politics means considering the question of subjectivity. There has been an important emphasis on this question in recent feminist theory, cultural theory, post-structuralism, and post-colonial thought. These discourses have demonstrated the shortcomings of the Eurocentric positivism that have inflected Euro-American philosophy, including even radical theory and practice. However, we have now reached the point of exhaustion with regard to the moment of critiquing subjectivity. In order to imagine a viable left, we have to trace the possibility of new productions as well as dissolutions, and point to potential openings toward a new dialectic between radical subjectivity and the world.

Revolution, fully realized, leaves no social figure intact. This struggle is not merely for a different distribution of resources within established relationships, nor even only for different forms of relationship. In transforming social relationships we transform the participants themselves in these relationships. Such a horizon, therefore, encompasses not just the reorganization of social forms, but the reimagination of subjects. In embarking on such a project, we undertake a fundamental translation of ourselves, and it is only this translated subject who will be able to carry forth the project and for whom it will have meaning. In constituting the revolutionary subject, revolutionary praxis thus undertakes a process that directs itself toward openings or cracks in the contemporary logic of subject production in order to step forth from them into the unknown light that waits on their outside. It is simultaneously the production of a different meaning for the self and the social, perhaps at first even an anti-meaning, but one which will then claim a coherence in the context of a reinvented sociality.

It has often been observed that the building of a social movement is also the building of a new historical subject. The Marxist narrative of the historical constitution of the proletariat is at the same time the story of the emergence of revolutionary possibility; the figure of the organized worker is the prefiguration of transformed society. The problem of consciousness in the Marxist tradition (the organization of a proletarian "class-for-itself") is a crucial opening into the problematic of the radical subject. The question of subjectivity, however, is larger than the question of political consciousness. Revolutionary praxis requires a reconstitution not only of modes of thought, but of solidarities, affinities, and contexts. In this process, fundamental senses of individual and agency are interrogated and recast. Frederic Jameson suggests that "one cannot too often emphasize the logical possibility, alongside both the old closed, centered subject of inner-directed individualism and the new non-subject of the fragmented or schizophrenic self, of a third term which would be very precisely the non-centered subject that is a part of an organic group or collective" (344). Such a decentering and reconstitution of the subject takes place among activists who participate in oppositional social movements: they discover that their notions of agency and identity unravel and are rearticulated in a new collaborative context (Montaño et al.). This reconstitution makes possible an identification with larger social and historical forces and an expanded sense of possibility. In the Los Angeles Uprising of 1992, the partial and imperfect realization of a moment of mass insurgency challenged dominant modes of understanding social agency, and so was misunderstood as a mere "riot." This was a moment of crisis, not only in strictly political terms, but also in social terms: the hegemonic atomization of social subjectivity into *individuals* was temporarily threatened as the subject of insurgency was collectivized into the mass.

The point of departure for the revolutionary reimagining of subjectivity, the place where it first exceeds the determinations of contemporary sociality, is not the whole, centered subject itself, but rather the *back* of the subject, or its edge—the place of the very boundary that divides it from the outside. It is only from this original moment, from the place where it forks from a radical indeterminacy into its determinate being, that we can find the point of possibility for a new imagination. Gayatri Spivak writes that "the 'self' is always production rather than ground" (22); we would modify the emphasis somewhat and argue (following Marx) that production, within the materiality of the given, *is* the ground of the subject. Thus, in struggling to reorganize social reality, we are really conceiving of its production, of the production of a new reality, whose terms will be different from those that we know. This does not mean that a transformed reality is therefore unimaginable by us, sealed off in some absolutely inaccessible alterity, but rather that we can only *begin* to imagine it, that we can only see the first stretch of the pathway that leads toward and into it. In beginning to free ourselves from the reality that holds us, we will start to make possible the process of creating a new one.

These reflections suggest that political transformation needs to be understood according to more than a narrow struggle over external objective results. Such changes are crucial, but struggle around them should not obscure the importance of subjectivity itself as a vital material arena of political contest. Paulo Freire emphasized the importance of reflection in addition to action in revolutionary movement. We are suggesting further that reflection as dialogue, self-interrogation, and imagination is itself a kind of action within the political field of the subject. One concrete example of such a praxis within education is represented in critical study groups for teachers, networks of which exist in California and elsewhere. These groups make possible a "collaborative, supportive environment for critical educators to study, reflect, dialogue and form alliances to resist oppressive educational practices" (California Consortium for Critical Educators). Such spaces of solidarity give teachers the support they need to speak out at their school sites and in progressive actions. But in addition, and this is our emphasis here, they become workshops in which ideological, emotional, and ontological structures of oppression within the field of the subject itself can be made visible and resisted. The splitting apart of the narrow professional identification of the teacher as technician into a horizon in which teachers can reimagine themselves as fundamentally social beings, in solidarity for resistance, and decisively vulnerable to the risks of a loving commitment to struggle is itself a deeply political process. This subjective process is itself part of the social labor that must be accomplished toward the revolutionary reconstruction of society.

Just as labor-power, according to Marxist analysis, reproduces the relations of capitalist production, so does the imagination, in its own work, create the real for us. In other words, in capitalism, work produces the value that is itself the sense and substance of this system (i.e., capital) and by which alone the system is reproduced. Similarly, the imagination is a social faculty in its organization of our sense of the relation between self and world. This is true not only in the negative sense described by Althusser (2001), in which ideology represents our imaginary relationship to our real conditions of existence. The imagination is the limit of the subject, in that it operates both the undoing and the production of specific social forms of subjectivity. Capitalist exploitation alienates this imaginative potentiality from the subject and shuts the latter down into a finished and singular positivity; i.e., it turns "*man's* [sic] *species being*, both nature and his spiritual species property, into a being *alien* to him, into a *means* to his *individual existence*" (Marx 114). We are emphasizing here that the *empowerment* of the counterhegemonic subject is simultaneously a process of *undoing* of the dominant forms of subjectivity. Transformative social potential inheres in this limit of subjects and sociality. This is analogous to Przeworski's observation that "Political class struggle is a struggle about class before it is a struggle among classes" (71). Rather than calling for the end of the consolidated subject altogether (as some postmodernists do), we argue that the revolutionary subject is always a *subject-in-formation*.

READING HEGEMONY AND RESISTANCE

An effective "whole left" will need to proceed in its reading of the organization of oppression globally with the same flexibility we have discussed in relation to subjectivity. At this point, the process of the philosophy of praxis we have described will be multiplied: it will be necessary to bring together numerous and disparate "common senses" to discover a meaning for imperialism internationally and to imagine routes of resistance. A tentative subject of resistance, or a side to take toward the realization of a revolutionary hegemony, must at this point be articulated in a global idiom. However, the grammar of this idiom is not given in advance. It must be worked out, discovered, cooperatively produced. For example, Cornel West argues that the struggle against white supremacy must be at or near the center of any progressive/revolutionary politics. His analysis of the subjugation of African Americans points to the relative autonomy of this oppression vis-à-vis the overall exploitation of the working class. How can we think these two moments of race- and class-based oppression together, without reducing one to the other, but also without artificially compartmentalizing them? We believe that the Marxist notion of the *relations of production* crucially sets the scene for such an effort, though it does not completely determine it. This concept, most familiarly, specifies class as a positioning within the process of production. But it is important to understand race, as well, as a differential social process, rather than an essence of any kind, and thus itself as a positioning within systems of social production. In this context it should be possible to bring a variety of positionalities-in-struggle together into a new coherence and to generate a, new, if provisional, reading of the political terrain. On the other hand, it is also essential to point out that culturalist theories of difference have often failed to acknowledge the importance of struggles based on class, which are "ontologically distinct" (Harvey 7) from struggles against other forms of oppression in that the former direct themselves against the founding processes of the capitalist mode of production.

An anti-imperialist hermeneutic, beginning from this position of creativity, can be conceived of as the loose sketching out of a composite portrait of the oppressor from many oppositional locations or moments. This portrait will not be the mere summation of the superimposed images produced from the various perspectives. It will come instead from the *rhymes* between the principle features of each of these images. These correspondences will provisionally suggest a set of characteristic processes, themselves subject to rearticulation with the addition of information from other vantage points. Naturally, this effort cannot escape the necessary contention involved in any revolutionary intellectual production: "Critical understanding of self takes place therefore through a struggle of political 'hegemonies' and of opposing directions, first in the ethical field and then in that of politics proper, in order to arrive at the working out at a higher level of one's own conception of reality" (Gramsci 333).

An example of an important occasion for this reflective process is the antiglobalization movement. In North America at least, this movement has been very much influenced by a "fair trade" orientation which points to injustices in working conditions internationally, often without questioning the underlying processes of capitalist exploitation which produce them. Socialists, on the other hand, point to the necessity of a critique in terms of global political economy: "The ideological fog that pervades all aspects of the globalization debate is bound to dissipate eventually, as it becomes clear that the contradictions of capitalism, which have never been surmounted, are present in more universal and more destructive form than ever before" (Foster 3). In our view, this is an indispensable advance in the terms of analysis; still, it must be proven in the course of the movement rather than merely announced.

Furthermore, in the course of the developing movement, from the Battle of Seattle in 1999 to the demonstrations in Genoa in 2001, activists of color have critiqued the white left for ignoring issues of racism, Eurocentrism, and the international division of labor: "the gatherings in Seattle, DC and elsewhere have been riddled with bitter racial politics stemming from the marginalization of people of color from every aspect of these actions. Many activists of color look askance at . . . a contemporary protest movement which risks life and limb to fight corporate globalization, only to ignore the third world people most brutally oppressed by these forces" (Daniel 1). Indigenous activists and scholars have pointed out that the universalistic idiom of the left excludes their concerns with regard to autonomy and sovereignty (Grande). A proper appraisal of globalization, and the building of an oppositional movement, must acknowledge and incorporate these perspectives. A useful reading and response to oppression must come from the conversation of all of the voices involved. This does not mean, however, advocating a simple relativism in which all views are equal; we are suggesting, rather, that an effective revolutionary movement must be forged from the collision between them, from negotiation, and from a constant testing of the effects and senses of different understandings in the context of actual struggle.

In this process of movement-building, a clearer vision of the oppressor will also begin to emerge—not as a complete and decided subject (though popular images of it have their own efficacy), nor as a transparent structure or system (though we should not surrender our useful senses of its functioning in this regard), but more like a *visage*, that is to say, a composite that we are able to grasp as a whole and make sense of, without being able to give any ultimate accounting of the relationships between its parts or predicates. In other words, the logic of global capitalist oppression is not totally determined; instead it is partly produced in the moment of its activity. We need to be able to trace the entire movement in its characteristic narrative, the narrative of imperialist desire that reaches past any fixed structure or meaning to produce itself as expansive, transformative violence. In beginning to see the provisional paths and arcs of the violence of the oppressor, we can start to gather our forces together to contest them in the moments toward which they are tending.

IMPERIALISM: A REARTICULATION

We have so far traced the outlines of a contemporary revolutionary praxis, as well as the forms of resistance and subjectivity that this praxis would involve. Having outlined some of the methodological parameters of this project, we will propose here a positive formulation and interpretation of processes of exploitation and domination which this project would contest. In this regard, we believe that *imperialism* is a crucial concept for making sense of oppression both globally and within the U.S. We intend this term to indicate more than the political, military, and economic expansionism of the most powerful capitalist nations in the nineteenth and twentieth centuries. Rather, it should refer to ongoing worldwide processes of capitalist exploitation and domination that are also cultural, racialized, and gendered: the consolidation of social power, value, and material wealth at one pole within each of these moments of contradiction within the social field. Thus, while we propose a definition of imperialism that is more expansive than the primarily economic one he suggests, we agree with Lenin that rather than representing a mere historical event, imperialism is constituted by a systematic social *logic* (in his account driven by the forma-tion of monopolies, the need to export excess capital, and inter-imperialist rivalry) of annexation and exploitation on a global scale.

Edward Said has shown that the cultural productions of Europe and the U.S. cannot be understood without reading them alongside ("contrapuntally," in Said's terminology) the history of these countries' political-military adven-tures in other parts of the world. In addition to responding to the imperative of economic exploitation, this imperialist project involves an investment of political, ideological, and cultural imagination in the imperialist countries which systematically occludes and justifies the violence of empire. Said's account allows us to see the posture of the rulers against the full backdrop of their dominative enterprises; what he does not emphasize, however, is the operation of imperi-alism in the metropolitan society itself. Our sense of the term refers equally to global processes as well as to oppression within the metropole (core capital-ist countries). That is to say that we refer through the use of this term *imperi-alism* to systems of economic, cultural and imaginative investments that organ-ize dominative violence and exploitation everywhere, including within the imperialist centers of Europe and North America.[1]

IMPERIALISM "AT HOME"

bell hooks has described how class, race, and gender oppression cannot be hier-archized or separately combated:

> Privileged feminists have largely been unable to speak to, with, and for diverse groups of women because they either do not understand fully the interre-latedness of sex, race, and class oppression or refuse to take this interrelated-ness seriously. Feminist analyses of woman's lot tend to focus exclusively on gender and do not provide a solid foundation on which to construct feminist theory. They reflect the dominant tendency in Western patriarchal minds to mystify women's reality by insisting that gender is the sole determinant of woman's fate. (15)

This analysis potentially suggests that the racism of white women against women of color is also sexist, since the subjectivity of the latter cannot be separated into different compartments each of which is separately subject to its own oppres-sion. Not only is this view different from an orthodox prioritization of class, it also differs from a parallelist view in which each distinct form of oppression operates individually along different axes. hooks suggests that it is an under-lying philosophical or cultural tendency in the West to create systems of sub-ordination that give rise to these interlocking oppressions. But doesn't a philo-sophical tendency ultimately have to do with a material social and political situation? How can we make sense of the intertwining and interlocking dimen-sions of race, class, and gender at this level?

Within the metropolitan capitalist societies, violence and coercion are increasingly essential in maintaining a social order based on racial, class, and gender oppression. A sensitivity to the importance of this violence in the operation of this "domestic imperialism" should suggest the ways in which these oppressions are conjoined in a unified process of structuration. It will help in this effort to get away from the common objectification of these as fully hardened categories and instead to highlight their processual and provisional aspect. Instead of looking at these phenomena as artifacts of an achieved sociality, it makes more sense to pay attention to the way they act themselves as principles of production of the social. In this connection, it is useful to recall Althusser's notion of the *conjuncture*, i.e., "the essential articulations, the interconnections, the strategic nodes on which the possibility and the fate of any revolutionary practice [depend]" (178). Revolutionary practice consists in a correct appraisal of these factors in the current situation and not on a mechanical application of theory.

In his careful analyses of the nature of imperialist domination in colonial India, Ranajit Guha suggests that inherent in the notion of imperialism is the idea that explicit force predominates over the bourgeois-democratic power of persuasion that pacifies the proletariat in the Western hegemonic bourgeois state. He argues that historiographers have overlooked the importance of coercion in the Indian colonial period in their tendency to assimilate its political forms to European models. We believe that his insights are useful in analyzing the metropolitan society as well. Force and persuasion are at work in both colonialism and bourgeois democracy. The question is at what point, even within the metropole, a mature capitalist regime, in ceasing to depend on strictly *hegemonic* strategies and in turning increasingly to explicit violence to maintain order, devolves into an *imperialist* formation, even internally. Thus, the police state, prison industrial complex, and militarized borders of the U.S. are often described as "fascist." However, their participation in a *geopolitical* colonialism that is continuous from the "sphere of influence" to the metropolitan society (death squads in El Salvador, police chokeholds in L.A.) is in fact more consistent with the conceptual framework of imperialism that we are proposing here.

There is also the possibility of looking at the metropolitan society as a variegated structure, shading from bourgeois-democratic conditions to neocolonial ones and back again, in pockets and parcels across its surface (Blauner). We could then read the superracism and patriarchal violence of the U.S. as signaling an imperialism mediated not by distance but by race and gender. The argument for the nomenclature of "imperialism" versus that of "racism" (for example) in the North American context would be that the former highlights the political, geographic, historical, and cultural dimensions of this oppression, whereas the latter is depoliticized, deterritorialized, and individual in its connotations. In addition, a close attention to the way in which race, class, and gender oppressions interact should show not just how they are braided together, but also how they interpenetrate, merge, and refract each other. For example, as an organizing principle, class, in becoming identified with race, does not merely make use of this category to express itself but is partly twisted out of its initial reference to a location in the economic system to *potentially* encompass all members of a status group (i.e., people of color). Conversely, this points to the need to analyze racism not just as a collection of individual experiences, but as the effect of a system (white supremacy) that in its systematicity exceeds the category of a prejudicial effect based on status group membership. Racism, then, needs to be analyzed as a necessary organizing principle (not just stratifying principle) of the social relations that form the basis of U.S. capitalist society, and thus as constituting a deep principal of structuration.

IMPERIALISM AND GLOBALIZATION

The work of the Subaltern Studies Collective of historiographers (see Guha and Spivak) suggests new possibilities for thinking about domination and exploitation globally. Their refusal to read colonial history as a function merely of European history, and colonial insurgency as a function merely of European post-Enlightenment problematics, suggests rather urgently a rereading of Europe itself as well as of oppression and revolution generally. In particular, their emphasis on the impossibility of understanding the "periphery" as a mere effect of the center calls into question the validity of this entire political geometry. This analysis implicitly points the way forward beyond easy sociological divisions such as racism, class oppression, and colonialism. We need to begin to see global imperialist capitalism as a whole system, no less complete (although different) at the periphery than at the center—as constituting rather a transmutable exploitative drive that communicates variously between all global points of its insertion in an accelerating accumulative frenzy.

It is crucial to analyze the political economy of imperialist processes currently demanding so-called development. Much has been said in recent debates over globalization about the new cooperation among producers on a global scale, an achievement of world-historical status that supposedly sets the stage for developing countries finally to cross the threshold of despair. But emerging from the sewer of international debt and broken dreams into the new radiant light of the capitalist future places one squarely beneath the Augustan arch of imperialism, where one soon realizes that production has private owners and controllers and the conditions of "free trade" are set by Western carpetbaggers and the global overlords of the transnational ruling class. William Robinson and Jerry Harris have underscored the fact that such a ruling class has emerged on the global stage, a ruling class that "controls the levers of an emergent transnational state apparatus and of global decision making" (12). The emergence of a new global capitalist historic bloc has been conditioned by the new global structure of accumulation and production. Many accumulation processes are no longer coextensive with specific national territories; we are witnessing the transnational integration of social classes and production systems within a globally stratified population.

The calculus of exploitation that shaped the development of the so-called Third World during the years of Keynesian-style economics is surprisingly the same under neoliberalism: the greater the number of workers subsumed under exploitative social production, the greater the concentration of wealth in the hands of the global capitalist elite. There exists now more than at any other time in history a group of nonelected officials that possess tremendous power over the world's populations: these are the officials of the central banks and economic and financial ministries of Europe and the U.S. and their appointees in the International Monetary Fund, the World Bank, the Asian Bank, the Inter-American Development Bank, and other international financial systems. However, as James Petras and Henry Veltmeyer point out, these objective conditions within the social universe of capital also create "opportunities for revolutionary forces to challenge the claim that capitalism and democracy are coterminous" (158) and bolster the case for socialism as the path to real democracy.

Fashioning a socialist anti-imperialist philosophy of praxis globally will require grappling with these economic and political challenges. It will require moving from a globalized export strategy to an integrated domestic economy which entails reorienting the economy away from the subsidizing of financial elites and replacing privatization with a socialization of the means of production.[2] In addition, challenging the sacred truths of imperialist economic development means challenging the global white supremacy with which it is associated. It means confronting the construction of the global North as the norm and telos of social production. As Che Guevara wrote, as imperialism exploits, it also pathologizes:

> All this [colonialism] resulted in a monstrously distorted economy which has been described by the shamefaced economists of the imperialist regime in an innocuous term which reveals the deep compassion they feel for us inferior beings (they call our miserably exploited Indians, persecuted and reduced to utter wretchedness, "little Indians"; all Negroes and mulattos, disinherited and discriminated against, are called "colored"; individually they are used as instruments, collectively as a means of dividing the working masses in their struggle for a better economic future). For us, the peoples of America, they have another polite and refined term: "underdeveloped." (31).

Struggling against imperialist exploitation means dismantling a Eurocentric system of cultural valuations that rationalizes globalization as "development" and "progress," and portrays those who suffer its violence as the beneficiaries of the favors of the magnanimous and "advanced." In this discourse, the *effects* of imperialism worldwide (poverty and misery) are recycled and represented as *proof* of the need for intervention by elites (i.e., further exploitation). Dismantling imperialism means destroying this unholy marriage of capitalist accumulation and neocolonial violence, and creating the possibility of anticolonial reconfigurations of political and cultural space at the same time as systems of socialist production are initiated.

SEEING THE STRUGGLE:
EDUCATIONAL TRENDS AND PEDAGOGICAL IMPLICATIONS

We have so far discussed some tentative directions for the method of a revolutionary praxis that could crystallize a "whole left," as well as the outlines of the imperialist enemy that confronts it. We will now discuss in more substantive terms how we can begin to see and intervene in struggles that are actually taking place. Rather than examining this question in general terms, we will consider the field of education as a case study, both because this field is our particular concern and because as a social process it represents a crucial site in which imperialist processes can be seen and contested. Our discussion of education will be limited to the U.S. since we are most familiar with developments in this country. Hegemonic processes in this arena share the characteristics of imperialist formations as we have described them in the previous section, so hopefully our thoughts here suggest useful lines of exploration in other fields and locations.

Education is politically important not only to the extent that it acts as a mechanism for reproduction of class structure (Bowles and Gintis), nor simply because it is often the battleground on which contests for symbolic legitimation are fought between opposing ideological forces in society at large (Kliebard). In addition, as pedagogical process, education represents perhaps the most important site of social construction of dominant forms of public intersubjectivity. The regulation of the textures of school and classroom relationships begins the process of the official structuring of the meaning of human sociality. In addition, the aggressive movement of the state to intensify control in public education through accountability measures has had the effect of making education an even more critical theater for anti-imperialist struggle. The ratcheting up of repression in this arena has prepared a fertile ground for the development of oppositional movements that directly confront, through campaigns against these hegemonic trends, processes of exploitation and subordination at work beyond the field of education as well. Across the U.S., student, teacher, and community organizations have challenged the proliferation of standardized tests, high school exit exams, and merit pay schemes. While in some cases those concerned hope merely to ease excessive assessment, in other cases struggle around these educational issues is the occasion for the elaboration of popular antiracist and potentially anticapitalist, socialist forms of praxis.

In short, the present imperialist moment operates in the field of education a hyperdisciplinary and neocolonial staging of instruction as surveillance and control (De Lissovoy and McLaren). Accountability initiatives such as standardized tests, scripted curricula, and zero-tolerance disciplinary policies organize an assault on the very possibility of critique. These trends are part of a general social process of intensification of coercion and structural violence, against which educators must imagine a revolutionary pedagogy (McLaren).

In 1970, George Jackson described the U.S. political system as "a police state wherein the political ascendancy is tied into and protects the interests of the upper class—characterized by militarism, *racism,* and imperialism" (18). The fact that "the system" is less often described in these terms at the present time should suggest to us neither that this analysis was mistaken, nor that a decisive victory has been achieved by U.S. imperialism. Rather, we should pay attention to the ways in which the violence of this confrontation has been recoded, transposed, and relayed in new ways under twenty-first-century capitalism. With increasing frequency, the logic of imperialism reconfigures this assault within strategies of erasure, deferral, and supplantation. For example, in the writings and speeches of political prisoner Mumia Abu-Jamal (1995; 1997) and the movement to free him, an organized challenge to white supremacy in the U.S. is thriving. This struggle, however, has encountered an almost incredibly aggressive strategy of marginalization. The state/media apparatus has fashioned a wall of "learned ignorance" around the case, a strategy of hypererasure that attempts to render it invisible in the face of international attention.[3] These same strategies are at work in the educational trends we have described.

On the other hand, just as strategies of repression have been reconfigured, so too we should learn to read struggle and resistance in new ways. We are used to looking for a visible and singular protagonist (heroic individual or movement) etched against the background of the limit-situation that encompasses it. But the contemporary economy of imperialism, in its tendencies toward deferral and erasure, should suggest to us also a different set of figures and tactics that the life of resistance of the people discovers. Thus, we should learn to read the movement of resistance also in the moments of refusal, disengagement, and countersilence that have always been important tools in the repertoire of the oppressed. For example, in education, the figure of the alienated working-class antihero, who is usually imagined as posed against the operation of a mature, functioning hegemony, ought to be rethought. Paul Willis's a famous portrait of a group of working-class students in Britain casts their oppositional practices against a larger scene of student conformity. But in the contemporary urban public school universe, in which the vast majority of students already occupy this alienated status (as members of working-class communities of color) in relation to official school culture, and in which they are subject to an active and continuous coercion, resistance itself is transposed from the isolated gesture of defiance to the *general* experience and activity of being in school.

It might be better to say, then, that in the context of this generalized alienation, student culture does not so much resist as *secede* from official school space.

This secession calls forth ever more energetic measures of discipline and control from the system. Educational accountability in the form of standardized testing and scripted curricula, along with intensified classroom and school-wide management of behavior, attempts with more and more frenzy to name and constrain the working-class students of color who make up the majority in schools where these practices are most common. The balance is difficult, and the tendencies inherently contradictory, since the instrument of a more pervasive control (e.g., the proliferation of standardized testing) also externalizes the student in relation to the system and creates the conditions for the development of a radical separation of student subjectivity from official school structures and meanings. Likewise, student silence acquires a definite ambivalence, since it appears both as the effect of an apparently successful mechanism of silencing and also as the sign of resistance to the extent that the system seeks to produce and enforce a legitimate vocality.

These moments of refusal, secession, and silence should not be overestimated as oppositional strategies. Revolutionary movement will need to involve moments of dissolution *and* production; it will include the deterritorialization of regulated identities (e.g., students refusing to participate) *and* the expressivity of the representative subject (e.g., students involved in critical dialogue). Changes in the terrain—i.e., the deepening of repressive and disciplinary trends—do not obviate the necessity for organization and collective political struggle. If there is indeed a movement from the incorporative end of the spectrum of the operation of class rule (e.g., the curriculum as tool of dominant ideologies) toward the coercive end (e.g., zero-tolerance disciplinary policies), the corresponding alterations in the "common sense" of the people still call for an organized theoretical and practical labor of dialogue in order to enrich and sharpen this analysis, as Gramsci outlined. Once again, however, our emphasis here is on the importance of a more careful listening, a return to Gramsci's emphasis on the sense in which "everyone is a philosopher." If radical praxis is constantly learning and changing, so too is the work being done by this popular philosophy, and the former should never decide that it has learned all there is to learn from the latter.

What do these considerations suggest in terms of pedagogy itself? How should we respond, as educators, to this hypercontrol, surveillance, and coercion? To begin with, the foregoing suggests the importance in teaching of turning the focus of attention in the classroom explicitly *on the school itself* within imperialist society—its culture and procedures—not in order for teachers to illuminate them, but for students to present and analyze their experiences, and for teachers to help in making sense of them. For example, while many educators have discussed the importance of a critical multiculturalism in the curriculum in general, beyond this we suggest a collective investigation by students and teachers of racism as organizing the school itself—their own schools and education as a whole. Similarly, patriarchy might be confronted, not by *demanding* the participation of female students (itself a paternalistic gesture), but through a collective investigation of the ways in which male and masculinist discourse is privileged, and also of the ways in which girls and women contest these processes through an array of strategies, including but not limited to speaking out. Furthermore, research could be undertaken into school disciplinary procedures, with students as participant-observers, and into the connections between these procedures and ultrapunitive trends in the judicial system; these phenomena could together be explored as representing an important turn in mechanisms of exploitation within contemporary capitalism. Strategies could be formulated for resistance that would call on teachers to collaborate on the side of students against forms of disciplinary violence.

In addition to these (perhaps) teacher-initiated projects, space ought to be made for the autonomous intervention of students in the process of education. This does not mean creating an atmosphere of permissiveness in which the teacher abdicates her responsibility to organize an effective learning environment. Rather, it means a careful attention to students' own interpretations and activities as themselves productive. We are suggesting here more than simply taking account of prior knowledge; instead, we are proposing that the teacher's proprietary vigilance over the classroom space, itself a deep cultural fact rather than an individual style, needs to be struggled against by the teacher herself, so that it becomes possible for this space to be invaded by the imagination of students, with all the risks this entails. In conceiving the crucial dialogue between teacher and students, we are here returning some of the priority to student self-determination. The "critical educator" must be on guard against her own mediation of processes of student learning and becoming, her own tendency to reprocess student discourse and meanings into a predetermined idea of voice, participation, and subjectivity.

Too often, student agency is imagined as no more than a function of the situation of the classroom, as a reaction to this situation, and not as well in its own legitimate autonomy. Allowing this autonomy to impinge on the school does not mean ceding the authority of the teacher, though it does mean refusing the teacher's ownership of the educational situation; it means that the direction that learning and knowing will take cannot be completely specified before the intervention of students. For example, the offering of apparently tangential ideas and projects, and in some cases even interruptions of the curriculum by students, must become possible (though this does not mean that all student speech or action should be unthinkingly valorized). The corollary here is that student subjectivity is never fully decided or continuous. Rather than aiming to discover what is imagined as a complete, if subjugated, positivity, the teacher should be attentive to the ways this subjectivity both proposes and flees its own determinations, and will never settle into the teacher's finally transparent interlocutor.

In other words, pedagogical praxis must itself respond creatively to contemporary educational trends. The overdetermined disciplinary space of the classroom calls for a pedagogy that is more than critical. An insurgent pedagogy must be imagined (De Lissovoy) which betrays the implicit solidarities between the professional teacher and schooling regimes. The anti-imperialist educator must develop the capacity to actively negate the architecture of violence that seeks not merely to constrain the possibility of conscientization, but even to erase it by eliminating all (ideological, pedagogical, cultural) mobility in the classroom. In this context, the traditional Freirean encounter which engages the oppressed, in a space of dialogue, in the critical analysis of social life, must address itself first *against* the (officially) pedagogical, against the immediate and intimate context of the school itself. The Freirean praxis of "humanization" must first of all envision a line of flight from an educational situation that has become more carceral than domesticating.

These observations with regard to pedagogy have some implications for the larger context of struggle. Movements in official politics and civil society that aim to improve equity and increase opportunity usually do so without being substantively informed and shaped by the desires and understandings of the communities on behalf of whom they ostensibly work. In this sense, these movements are false to their explicit missions in that they do not represent, but ignore, those whom they serve. But in addition, the positivistic, Newtonian space imagined by most public policy discourse tends to reduce political reality to inert data and attenuated horizons. This discursive space very often shuts out other crucial ways of understanding the struggle and imagining interventions in it: cultural, theoretical, and spiritual traditions and expressions that interpret and animate differently. In short, to the extent that a technicist, Eurocentric, bourgeois discourse dominates left politics, it repeats symbolically the violence perpetrated against the oppressed by the rulers and eliminates important opportunities for furthering the struggle. Countering this tendency will mean measuring possibilities, successes, and failures in the context of the pervasive imperialist violence that structures the social, psychological, and symbolic experiences of oppressed people so that the daily triumphs of those who survive the systematic injury of their persons in every dimension will not be discounted or made invisible. In this context, the possibilities for strategic intervention and success will multiply, since the face of imperialism will become recognizable not merely in the distance of the sociologist's charts and graphs, but in the proximity of the words we use from moment to moment, the feelings we feel, and the orientations we choose toward the universe.

CONCLUSION

As Leo Panitch points out, "Contemporary socialists cannot claim to have a foolproof blueprint for a new type of political and economic democracy. It often occasions impatience that this is so" (43). Rather, the forging of a coherent international anti-imperialist movement requires the collective production of a revolutionary imagination that starts from a diversity of constituencies but which does not end there—an imagination which is synthetic and philo-sophical, responsible to the particularity of its immediate surroundings yet intent on elaborating a vision of a common project beyond those particularities. Gram-sci's conception of a philosophy of praxis returns us to a sense of the organic and processual nature of political struggle and its necessary communication with popular modes of understanding.

As we have described, fashioning a meaningful "whole left" will involve more than merely adding together a variety of different views. Rather, it will mean reading through the perspectives of different locations toward the pro-duction/discovery of a subject of oppression and a countersubject of revolution. Rather than the rapid shifting between different radical nomenclatures that we are accustomed to on the left, we propose the simultaneous application of these discourses to the building of an image (in full color, in full concept) of the elu-sive order of imperialism. This image-concept would arise from our tracing of the systematic exploitation, appropriation, and accumulation of power, the sys-tematic organization and distribution of violence, along every social and polit-ical axis, following the lines of force backwards in each case toward the bound-ary beyond which lies, in obscure potentiality, the face of the oppressor. Our task is to name that face and bring it forth into the concrete. This naming is at once the becoming concrete of coherent revolutionary process.

Only such a politics, both absolutely creative and uncompromisingly com-mitted, can confront a global capitalist imperialism that represses and exploits through both a constructive/incorporative mode and a violently dominative one. In the field of education and elsewhere, only an equally flexible and imag-inative praxis, encompassing moments both of consolidation and evasion within the process of producing a new sociality, can adequately confront the hyper-control and repression of the present moment. With such flexibility and imag-ination, revolutionary pedagogy and praxis will be capable of hope, as struggles at every level will produce for it a better vision of itself and of the pathway into and among the emerging moments of a different world.

NOTES

1. In attempting to capture the relationships between the global and metropolitan moments of social violence, Michael Hardt and Antonio Negri have suggested that *imperialism* is obsolete, and that we are now faced with a network of Empire that is pervasive, total, centerless, and identical at every point. However, we believe that this characterization greatly errs in ignoring the ongoing importance of national capitals and the state in organizing exploitation worldwide. Furthermore, it tends to erase the con-nection of contemporary imperialist processes to historical ones, the partiality of exploita-tive processes (which are never fully successful), and their processual nature. Finally, Hardt and Negri ignore the differing meanings that imperialism takes on in different

instances and locations, and the importance of these differences, taken together, for suggesting an overall picture.

2. Petras and Veltmeyer suggest a "structural adjustment program from below" which would involve redistributing land, income, and credits; breaking up private monopolies; reforming the tax system; protecting emerging industries; opening the trade of commodities that don't compete with local producers; eliminating speculative activity by means of financial controls; redirecting investments towards human capital formation and employment; decentralizing the administration of state allocations and redistributing them to local recipients in civil society able to vote on their own priorities; generating public works and interregional production; imposing a tight monetary policy by refusing state bail-outs of corrupt companies; eliminating cheap credit to exporters and tax abatements for multinational corporations in "free" trade zones; and creating local and regional assemblies to debate and resolve budget allocations.

3. In addition, the endless deferral of decisions in the judicial system seeks to project the case into the limbo of "undecidability." Although Abu-Jamal recently won a victory in a judgment that struck down the sentencing phase of his trial, he remains in prison, serving a life sentence pending the decision of prosecutors on whether to seek a new sentencing hearing. The movement to free him must combat both a vicious countermobilization on the part of the police (which in Philadelphia actively targets Mumia supporters) as well as the systematic silencing of discussion around the case.

WORKS CITED

Abu-Jamal, M. *Live from Death Row*. New York: Avon Books, 1995.

———. *Death Blossoms: Reflections from a Prisoner of Conscience*. Farmington, Penn: The Plough Publishing House, 1997.

Althusser, L. *For Marx*. (Trans. B. Brewster). New York: Verso, 1965.

———. *Lenin and Philosophy and Other Essays*. (Trans. B. Brewster). New York: Monthly Review Press, 2001.

Anzaldúa, G. *Borderlands/La Frontera: The New Mestiza*. San Francisco: Aunt Lute, 1987.

Blauner, R. *Racial Oppression in America*. New York: Harper and Row, 1972.

Bowles, S., and H. Gintis. *Schooling in Capitalist America: Educational Reform and the Contradictions of Economic Life*. New York: Basic, 1976.

California Consortium for Critical Educators. Study Groups. 2000.

Daniel, V. "Ralph Nader's Racial Blindspot." *Colorlines*. 2000. <http://www.arc.org/C_Lines/CLArchive/story_web00_01.html>.

De Lissovoy, N. "Insurgent Pedagogy." Unpublished Manuscript, 2002.

De Lissovoy, N., and P. McLaren. "Educational 'Accountability' and the Violence of Capital: A Marxian Reading." *Journal of Education Policy*, 18.2 (2003): 131–143.

Fanon, F. *The Wretched of the Earth*. (Trans. C. Farrington). New York: Grove Press, 1963.

Foster, J. B. "Monopoly Capital and the New Globalization." *Monthly Review* 53.8 (2002): 1–16.

Freire, P. *Pedagogy of the Oppressed*. (Trans. M. B. Ramos). New York: Continuum, 1996.

Gramsci, A. *Selections from the Prison Notebook*. (Trans. Q. Hoare and G. N. Smith). New York: International Publishers, 1971.

Grande, S. "American Indian Identity and Intellectualism: The Quest for a New Red Pedagogy." *Qualitative Studies in Education*, 13.4 (2000), 343–59.

Guevara, C. *Che Guevara Speaks: Selected Speeches and Writings*. New York: Pathfinder, 1967.

Guha, R. *Dominance Without Hegemony: History and Power in Colonial India*. Cambridge: Harvard UP, 1997.

Guha, R., and G. C. Spivak eds. *Selected Subaltern Studies*. Oxford: Oxford UP, 1988.

Hardt, M., and A. Negri. *Empire*. Cambridge, Mass: Harvard UP, 2000.

Harvey, D. "The Practical Contradictions of Marxism." *Critical Sociology* 24.1—2),1 (1998): 1–36.

Holst, J. D. *Social Movements, Civil Society, and Radical Adult Education*. Westport, Conn: Bergin and Garvey, 2002.

hooks, b. *Feminist Theory: From Margin to Center*. Cambridge, Mass: South End, 2000.

Jackson, G. *Soledad Brother*. New York: Coward-McCann, 1970.

Jameson, F. *Postmodernism, or, The Cultural Logic of Late Capitalism*. Durham: Duke UP, 1991.

Kliebard, H. M. *The Struggle for the American Curriculum*. New York: Routledge, 1995.

Laclau, E., and C. Mouffe. *Hegemony and Socialist Strategy: Towards a Radical Democratic Politics*. London: Verso, 1985.

Lenin, V. I. *Imperialism, The Highest Stage of Capitalism*. Moscow: Progress, 1975.

Marx, K. *The Economic and Philosophic Manuscripts of 1844*. (Trans. M. Milligan). New York: International, 1964.

McLaren, P. *Che Guevara, Paulo Freire, and the Pedagogy of Revolution*. New York: Rowman and Littlefield, 2000.

Montaño, T., L. López-Torres, N. De Lissovoy, M. Pacheco, and J. Stillman. (In Press). "Teachers as Activists: Teacher Development and Alternate Sites of Learning." *Educational Excellence and Equity*. 35 (3), 265–275.

Panitch, L. " Renewing Socialism." *Monthly Review*, 53.9 (2002): 37–47.

Petras, J., and H. Veltmeyer. *Globalization Unmasked: Imperialism in the 21st Century*. London: Zed, 2002.

Przeworski, A. *Capitalism and Social Democracy*. Cambridge: Cambridge UP, 1986.

Robinson, W. I., and J. Harris. "Towards a Global Ruling Class: Globalization and the Transnational Capitalist Class." *Science and Society*, 64.1 (2000): 11–53.

Said, E. W. *Culture and Imperialism*. New York: Vintage, 1993.

Sleeter, C. E. "How White Teachers Construct Race." In C. McCarthy and W. Crichlow, eds., *Race, Identity, and Representation in Education*. New York: Routledge, (1993): 157–71.

Spivak, G. C. "Subaltern Studies: Deconstructing Historiography." In R. Guha and G. C. Spivak, eds., *Selected Subaltern Studies*. Oxford: Oxford UP, 1988. 3–32.

West, C. "Marxist Theory and the Specificity of Afro-American Oppression." In C. Nelson and L. Grossberg, eds., *Marxism and the Interpretation of Culture*. Chicago: U of Illinois P, 1988. 17–29.

Willis, P. *Learning to Labor: How Working Class Kids Get Working Class Jobs*. New York: Columbia UP, 1977.

CHAPTER TEN

GLOBAL/LOCAL LABOR POLITICS AND THE PROMISE OF SERVICE LEARNING

WENDY S. HESFORD

THE ECONOMIC CULTURE OF EDUCATION

BILL READINGS ARGUES IN *THE UNIVERSITY IN RUINS* THAT ECONOMIC globalization and the subsequent decline of the status of the nation-state as a reproducer of national culture has led to a shift in the University's sense of itself and its mission. The University no longer envisions itself as a producer of cultural capital—the legacy of the Enlightenment—but rather functions as an autonomous bureaucratic consumer-oriented corporation whose mission is defined by the needs of the global market. As Readings puts it,

> The University no longer has to safeguard and propagate national culture, because the nation-state is no longer the major site at which capital reproduces itself.... The idea of national culture no longer provides an overarching ideological meaning for what goes on in the University ... The economics of globalization mean that the University is no longer called upon to train citizen subjects. (13–14)

Readings does not document in any detail the extent to which this shift has occurred; however, there is ample evidence that this shift has begun.

The flight of capital from urban areas has left poor communities across the United States with limited opportunities. As large corporations relocate factories to "developing" countries and suburban areas, more and more universities and colleges have become the largest employment base in their communities. Increasingly universities are playing a role in public housing, buying up properties in poor urban areas that surround their campuses. But as David Maurrasse rightly notes, such acquisitions do not always benefit residents; "[g]entrification fueled by universities has tended to displace neighborhood residents and make it increasingly clear to these communities that they are unwanted in their own backyards" (21).

More and more universities function as marketing agencies for corporate franchises, such as Barnes and Noble (who has bought out a number of university bookstores), and fast-food services (McDonald's, Burger King, etc.) housed in student dorms and student union buildings. Market forces have fostered the downsizing of tenure-track faculty positions and an increase in flexible part-time and adjunct labor, the commercialization of instruction (such as distance learning), and the corporate underwriting of university funding-in-exchange for technological and brand rights (Smith 105). Furthermore, some universities continue to service transnational capitalist exploitation through contracts with corporations that rely on sweatshop labor to produce university apparel and sports equipment—a three billion-dollar industry. The success of campaigns such as United Students Against Sweatshops, which have established educational internships, discussed in more detail later, have forced universities to adopt stricter codes of conduct for manufacturers of apparel that bear their logos.

More and more university administrators embrace corporate management schemes, evidenced by the decentralization of budgets and responsibility-centered management, where departments function as separate units and compete for funds and resources. Responsibility-centered management ties resource allocations to enrollments, so that large departments and disciplines fare much better than smaller interdisciplinary programs. Public schools and universities face demands by government funding agencies to make themselves accountable to market forces. In addition, social services once provided by the government are now taken on by private, nonprofit organizations and institutions of higher education (Maurrasse 5). The rhetoric of market outcomes and performance management propelled by the shift from the state funding of public education to the state's increased regulation of public education ties economic policy to curriculum (Blackmore 134). The curriculum is modified to meet perceptions of the new global economy and notions of flexible citizenship. Modifications include an increased focus on entrepreneurial practices,[1] cross-cultural skills, consumer relations, and corporate multiculturalism. Corporate multiculturalism refers to watered-down diversity initiatives that ignore asymmetrical social relations of production. Corporate multiculturalism and right-wing conservative attacks on mainstream multiculturalism appear contradictory; for example, conservative talk show host Rush Limbaugh criticizes multiculturalism on the grounds that it glorifies "anti-American victimology." Yet corporate multiculturalism and neoconservative positions share an underlying assimilation ideology that promotes uniformity among diversity and identities (whether corporate or national) permeated by capitalist modes of production (McLaren 32–33).[2] Within this context, students are construed as mobile and autonomous consumers (Blackmore 135), "as human capital" (Apple 60).[3] Michael Apple puts it succinctly, "[E]ducation is seen as simply one more product . . . democracy is turned into consumption practices . . . [and] the ideal citizen is that of the purchaser" (60).

How are we to understand the role of service learning in the context of global capitalism and the corporate university, namely the trend toward client-oriented education? Is the current interest in service learning within English departments simply nostalgia for a university (or disciplinary identity) that claims a national cultural mission? Does the push to institutionalize service learning as a general education requirement represent a resurgent nationalism? And if so, how is this resurgent nationalism shaped by the feminization and privatization of service? If participation in the global economy can no longer be posed in terms of a national subject, as Readings suggests, how are we to understand the citizen subject in service learning? Is service learning functioning as a mere alibi for the corporate university? My call to examine the economic implications of service learning emerges from my admiration for the progressive intent of such initiatives as demonstrated by the educational internships established by labor organizations such as AFL-CIO's Union Summer program,[4] and my own participation in the development of a community literacy initiative at a local shelter for women victims of domestic and sexual violence in Bloomington, Indiana, discussed in more detail below. The community literacy program was funded by Indiana Campus Compact[5] and provided service learning opportunities for graduate students at Indiana University. As a critical insider, I urge administrators, faculty, and students to intervene in the discussions about service learning to ascertain how and whether particular programs counter and/or comply with the exploitation of local/global labor practices.

The true crisis for education, as David Geoffrey Smith rightly notes, lies in the clash of "corporate economic fundamentalism with the dreams of liberal democratic culture" (100–101). Economic fundamentalism is a term that refers to the "radical, zealous turn to free market principles and a systematic appropriation of the reins of secular power by the forces of transnational capital" (94). The religious connotations in the term are appropriate, as Smith and others argue, because the "Market is becoming the first truly world religion," with economics as "a theology pretending to be a science" (David Loy quoted in Smith 94).[6] For example, Michael Novak from the American Enterprise Institute defines corporations as "natural extension[s] of God's natural law" (quoted in Kintz 217). Grassroots social groups such as some Christian communities can inform radical politics. The intersection between the Catholic left, liberation theology, and community service has yet to be explored in terms of the implications for service learning in the academy. For instance, the Catholic working movement, which doesn't focus on rehabilitation or conversion of individuals (classic missionary rhetoric) but on the rehabilitation of society through mutually dignifying relationships, might have implications for how we understand and counter the symbiosis between economic and religious fundamentalism. But as Linda Kintz importantly notes, neoconservatives have redefined the emphasis on human rights within Catholic social teaching and liberation theology and reclaimed it as economic fundamentalism.[7] As Novak writes, "the personal economic initiative is a fundamental human right [and] to exercise that right is to fulfill the image of God inherent in every man and woman" (quoted in Kintz 226). The entrepreneur is cast as the "Logos of God" (223) in a narrative where commercial interests equal civic interests in much the same way as the corporation comes to stand for the common man in populist American rhetoric "oppressed by government and burdened by taxes" (224).[8]

The clash between economic fundamentalism and the dream of liberal democratic culture is played out on the terrain of the academy through the jostling over territories and funds and debates over disciplinary specialization and professionalization[9] facilitated by limited resources and corporate management paradigms. The pressures of globalization have transformed the practices of nation-states, and national economies have lost control to transnational finance. But claims that we live in an age of postnationalism, as Readings implies, obfuscate the fact that nationalism has not come to an end but rather that the source of its force has shifted (Sassen). For instance, in the early 1970s, more than half of the five hundred multinational corporations were American-based, but by the early 1990s, only half of those were American-based, with Japan and Europe responsible for most of the others (Smith 96–97). The economic power and global reach of multinational corporations might be considered a "'new kind of corporate colonialism" built on the exploitation of poor countries and of the poor in rich countries (97). Nations are not powerless; rather nations work in conjunction with multinational corporations, who are dependent upon international commercial laws and trade regulations legitimized by national and international systems of arbitration (Appiah xiii).[10]

The critical fiction that sustains market liberalism is the illusion that markets are neutral. But, of course, markets are anything but value-free. "Markets are abstractions premised upon normative models of how people should behave" (Blackmore 144). In an economic climate where the "nation is nothing but a conduit for business globalization" (94), we need to consider the role of education, and how the radical promise of service learning fares in larger economic and pedagogical schemes. One could argue, as has Blackmore, that "the concept of globalization has been loosely, if not promiscuously, used in educational policy . . . to justify the radical restructuring of state education systems since the mid-1980s in most Western, liberal capitalist, and increasingly many developing nation-states" (134).[11] Flexibility has been a seductive discourse; it has lead to flexible workplace arrangements, family-leave plans, part-time employment, which have benefited some teachers. Flexibility characterized by the deregulation of labor markets and decentralization of wage bargaining, however, has led to greater inequity between men and women and to a decrease in a teacher's control over her own work through educational management and efficiency discourses (141–143). Of course, at the same time that globalization focuses on fluid identities and flexible workforces, we are witnessing the reinvigoration of traditionalism and fundamentalism, including economic fundamentalism, of which the economic orthodoxy of market liberalism is an example. Markets are influenced by anxieties about differences and "social prejudices and fears about race, gender, and class identities" As Blackmore puts it:

> Globalization, despite the rhetoric of flexible markets and generic "gender-neutral" skills has not reduced market segmentation premised upon class and race. Skilled and mobile educated women may experience more opportunities, but working-class black or migrant women are more likely to experience more exploitation, while at the same time the normative model of the white skilled, mobile educated male worker limits all women's possibilities. (145)

Thus in the "arena of transnational masculinities,"[12] women bear the responsibility as the competitive state withdraws from its social welfare obligations while reprivatizing women's productive labor (135). What are the gender, racial, and class dynamics of service learning in the academy? Are certain identities expected to become global citizen subjects?

THE PROMISE OF SERVICE LEARNING

Service learning has been uncritically positioned in recent national educational reform as a herald for democracy, diversity, and civic responsibility. The concept of community outreach is not new. For example, it is resonant with the concept of "land grant" in the late eighteenth century, which was based on the need to provide practical education to enhance skills of farmers as colonizers moved west. With the Morrill Act of 1862, which established the higher education land-grant system, higher education adapted to the demands of enhancing local agriculture economies. Beyond the land grants, late nineteenth- and early twentieth-century scholars such as John Dewey encouraged community partnerships through the concepts of "participatory democracy" and "participatory action research." Historically black colleges have a history of responsibility to the concerns of local communities (Maurrasse 16–20). The concept of community outreach may not be new, but, as David Maurrasse wisely notes, "recent socioeconomic circumstances have spawned a new angle—and interest—in approaches to partnerships" (21). As those of us who have been engaged in service learning can attest, pedagogical initiatives that attempt to create partnerships across social, economic, and disciplinary boundaries do not automatically undo socioeconomic divisions and structures.[13] Therefore, we need to consider the value of service learning for community agencies and organizations and how this value is configured in relation to its value to the university.

For example, as I contemplate the value attributed to the community literacy project which I developed in consultation with a team of graduate students and community workers for women residents at a shelter for victims of domestic violence (Middle Way House) and a low-income housing project (The Rise) in Bloomington, Indiana, I confront the economic hardships that these two nonprofit organizations continually face and their reliance on student labor. More particularly, the relationship of Indiana University (my former place of employment) to Middle Way House and The Rise is based on volunteerism. Over two hundred IU students and many faculty volunteer each year on the crisis lines, at the childcare center, in the courts, and at the shelter itself. Such volunteerism ensures the survival of the shelter and its programs, which otherwise depend solely on ever decreasing state funds and individual and business contributions. Although money may not pass from the university to the agency, student labor is exchanged as a form of cultural capital and amounts to over $200,000 a year in matching funds. In addition to the numerous students and faculty who donate time year after year from a personal commitment, many students volunteer through service-learning classes. Such students receive course credit for volunteering at Middle Way House or The Rise as part of course requirements if they are enrolled in a designated community service-learning course. Unfortunately, educational programs at Middle Way House and The Rise are in jeopardy because of financial cuts in the state budget for education and social services. For example, Middle Way House did not receive a summer grant this past year from the state to make up for all the university help they lose during the summer months. Whether it would be more effective for graduate students and faculty to picket at the state house to demand an increase of funds to support social and educational services for victims of domestic violence or to continue the labor of community literacy at such sites is not the definitive question. Efforts are needed on all fronts. Indeed, one of our long-term goals is to apply for a federal seed grant to fund a liaison position to be filled by a resident at The Rise in order to work with the University in setting up service learning and educational internships and to create economic opportunities for women in the community (see Hesford, 1999, and Barker, Hesford, and Locklin).

Service learning thus is implicated in the commerce of higher education. In order to garner financial support from the private sector (in a climate of decreased state funds for education and other social programs), some administrators have appropriated the discourse of service learning in ways that have far diluted its progressive potential. Some university programs have mobilized the discourse of service learning to generate more university/corporate partnerships. Consider, for instance, a promotional brochure for a technological initiative at a large public university to promote technology-based business partnerships between the college and community. The project is described as the university's "response to the challenges of a rapidly evolving economy . . . [and as] the framework for building and leveraging the University's intellectual capacity to create value—and to drive economic growth—[at the state level]." These partnerships are configured through the neoliberal rhetoric of globalization and flexible accommodation. For example, the articulated goals are to connect "knowledge with a global market place," "accelerate technology transfer," "strengthen . . . research universities' ability to educate knowledge workers and develop and commercialize technology," and "link university and faculty resources to corporate research needs." What's new about that? Business as Usual. *The University in Ruins*. Universities are businesses—"economic engines" (Maurrasse 38). But is the corporate takeover of education good for the business of education? Isn't there an inherent conflict between profits and education? "No way," declares the chairman of Whittle Communications, a company that gives computer technology to schools in exchange for rights to project Channel One into classrooms. Yet, we do need to look at the inherent conflict between profits and education.

Internships have long been a staple of education, namely business education. While we should not conflate internships, whether at profitable corporations or nonprofit organizations, with service-learning initiatives (though internship programs often do contain a service-learning component), we do need to recognize that educational internships at nonprofit organizations such as the AFL-CIO's Union Summer program, in fact, have fostered labor consciousness among college students. But the outsourcing of faculty and student labor to the corporate and private sector, designated as service learning, without attending to the effects of such gestures on local communities and economies, not to mention the integrity of academic freedom, is unacceptable. We need to consider how community service learning factors into the mission of corporate universities and how particular projects may challenge, alter, or be complicit with inequitable labor relations within and outside the university. Additionally, universities sell out faculty who engage in service learning. Many faculty at universities and colleges throughout the United States confront a tenure and promotion system that does not recognize service learning or know how to "measure" its institutional worth, unless it has led to publication. Research universities value work defined by expertise and autonomy and external fellowships and grants, which, of course, support and fund the university.

In "Transforming the Public(s) of our Service," Anita Plath Helle importantly points out the links between pedagogical models of civic rhetoric (such as service learning) and its association with women's social work in the community (16). Helle asks us to consider the gendered terrain of service (e.g., "women . . . are disproportionately the ones engaged in service learning"), and how the labor of service has been naturalized and feminized. As she puts it:

> The fact that the gendered position of women's participation in service learning, community literacy projects, and community-school research is not yet mapped onto this picture of rethinking the public(s) of our service should lead us to inform the ongoing analysis of service constructions in English, at

minimum, with some of the ironies that work in "service learning" or community literacy entails. (18)

If we are to employ the rhetoric of accountability, and I'm not convinced that we should, we need to become more accountable for the ways in which service learning may inadvertently serve the interests of capitalist exploitation, particularly in institutions driven by corporate management paradigms such as responsibility-centered management. Responsibility-centered management pits departments and programs against each other in an academic cockfight over resources, credit hours, and enrollments. If service learning becomes housed, for example, in English departments and creates more labor (wanted or unwanted) for composition teachers, most of whom are graduate students and part-timers, English departments may reap the benefits of enrollments and student "service" and therefore profit under RCM. But at whose expense?

Consider, for example, what might appear to be a strategic move on the part of English departments to hold onto their economic capital (much of which has been accumulated through required writing courses and the labor of graduate students) by integrating service learning into the undergraduate writing curriculum. Service learning has been integrated into composition programs as a conduit for "real" writing, thereby employing false divisions between "real" (public writing) and "unreal" academic writing. Such divisions do not take into account working students' daily movements between these spheres or competing identifications of "work" in composition. Nor do they acknowledge writing as a materialist practice. The materiality of writing, as Bruce Horner importantly argues, includes writing technologies, socioeconomic conditions that shape writing production within the academy, networks for its distribution, physicality of teaching, relations between students and teachers, and global relations of power articulated through these controls, networks, and conditions (xviii). In what ways, we might ask, could the integration of service learning in English departments and composition programs inadvertently facilitate the exploitation of undergraduate and graduate student labor and already marginalized teachers? How might service learning exploit members of the community and community agencies? What, for example, is the value of having students interview individuals living in a homeless shelter and then reflecting on these interviews in a writing class, and how is this value determined? How might, for example, the pedagogy of having students translate and reflect upon the stories of homeless people be co-opted by the very forces—capitalist hierarchies—that it proposes to expose (Mahala and Swilky 376)?

As English departments grapple with questions over curricular content, disciplinary status, and whether culture is something the university produces or studies—a facile binary but one which has nonetheless divided departments—service learning enters the scene with promises to revitalize the humanities through links to the community. When considering the integration of community service learning in English departments and writing programs across the country, particularly at large public universities, we would be wise to take into account its institutional resonance with and structural relation to composition programs and university-wide writing requirements.

Most public universities across the nation have a one or two semester writing requirement. At large state research universities English departments offer hundreds of sections of first-year writing courses per year, including Basic Writing. Graduate students and part-time lecturers teach the majority of these courses. Given the existing structures of compensation, low wages for graduate student teachers, and the rising costs of student tuition, the university gets more than a fair deal out of graduate student labor.[14] Across the country, graduate students have formed unions to address the inadequacy of viewing graduate student labor as "service" or apprenticeship and the institutionalization of unfair working conditions and wages. These unions have had some success. Graduate student organizations and unions have made important inroads in getting the profession to pay greater attention to labor practices. The relevance of radicalism and the growing unionization of graduate students and contingent faculty can be seen by the efforts of professional associations to collect data on labor practices. For instance, the Modern Language Association, pressured by graduate students and faculty in the MLA Delegate Assembly, conducted a survey of part-time and nontenure track faculty's working conditions and published the salaries and working conditions on its website (Schell). Similarly, the CCCC Committee on Part-time/Adjunct Issues has conducted a study of labor practices and, at the time of this writing, released recommendations. In addition, critiques of the institutionalization of writing requirements and their staffing patterns might provide a window into the labor issues raised by the institutionalization of service learning and thus help us develop a more informed and critical response (Crowley, Schell, Schell, and Stock).

THE PUBLIC INTELLECTUAL, CRITICAL ETHNOGRAPHER, AND/OR ACADEMIC ACTIVIST?

What relevance can leftist discourse have in exposing the paradoxes of service learning in the academy and for reimagining its potential pursuit of social justice? Economic and social critique within composition studies and critical pedagogy has been filtered, for the most part, through the figures of the public intellectual and critical ethnographer. For instance, in *Bootstraps*, Victor Villanueva characterizes academics as traditional intellectuals (bourgeoisie) in service of hegemony in our focus on technical minutia (i.e., publish-or-perish mode, specialization of knowledge, etc.) (130). Yet he also characterizes the professoriate as the new proletariat, as "no less [than] the new working class." Villanueva puts it this way:

> We too wear collars, even if looser than many. American academics can enjoy the social prestige granted to the elite but suffer the economic status of the rest. Academics enjoy a great deal of latitude in going about their work, but are nevertheless wage earners, subject to bureaucratic controls; no punch clocks or requirements to stay at the office, but long work days and nights nevertheless. (137–138)

Well, which is it? Are we traditional intellectuals (bourgeoisie) or the new proletariat? Can we occupy both social and economic classes simultaneously? Are these categories really all that useful in characterizing the positions of academics in the corporate university? If there is a "new proletariat" in the university, it might be more accurate to characterize graduate students as such, in that their labor supports faculty privileges. But even that equation is problematic if we consider the cultural capital that affiliation with graduate school affords. Villanueva recognizes the symbolic capital that professors carry (though he gives this little attention in his work). He calls for teachers to help the disenfranchised recognize themselves as organic intellectuals and to fuse with them in order to recreate ourselves as new intellectuals (138). To earn the label of organic intellectual, Villanueva notes, one must undertake political economic initiatives that serve the group or class from which s/he came.

But how does this configuration, in effect, account for the privileges of the majority of academics, namely white middle-class privilege? Is this the model "public intellectual" that community service learning promises to reclaim? Villanueva's image of the fusion of organic and new intellectuals advocates that we "play out our contradictions as deputies of hegemony and as subversives, agents of traditions, and with our students, potential agents of change" (138). On this latter point, I concur. However, his (and others) reliance on the binary categories of proletariat and bourgeoisie is not conducive to an analysis of the contradictions faced by writing program administrators (such as ourselves) and administrators in service learning centers or the multilayered dynamics of capital in the corporate university. Although many writing program administrators "feel overworked and implicated by their perpetuation of the non-tenure track system," as Eileen Schell importantly reminds us, activist writing program administrators have emerged (4). In addition to unionized and activist graduate students and contingent faculty, as administrators of writing programs we need to lead the way to address the labor practices of service learning within our own programs and colleges. Therefore, I am not suggesting that we eliminate the concept of the public intellectual, as much as I want to argue, as does Bruce Horner, for recognition of the materiality of intellectual practices. As Horner notes, in the Gramscian sense, intellectuals are those paid to do work perceived to be "intellectual" (9). In Gramsci's words, the intellectual is a "permanent persuader"

(*Notebooks* 10), or as Villanueva himself puts it, "the intellectual actively seeking substantive social change is a rhetor" (128–129).

Similarly, Ellen Cushman's formation of the rhetorician as an agent of social change calls for greater civic participation and activism through the figure of public intellectual as rhetorician and critical, reflexive ethnographer (1996). In her discussion of community literacy work in Troy, New York, Cushman highlights distinctions between "missionary activism, which introduces certain literacies to promote an ideology, and scholarly activism, which facilitates the literate activities that already take place in their community" (13). Her attention to rhetorical context appears most vividly in her call to take into account how "people use language and literacy to challenge and alter the circumstances of daily life" (12). Self-reflexivity about the politics of our location and our roles as participant-observers may push us to think through the ethics of service-learning pedagogy. Self-reflexive rhetoric and methodologies do not necessarily lead, however, as Cushman seems to suggest, to the empowerment of people in the community or the breakdown of "sociological barriers between universities and communities" (12).

In a later essay (2002), Cushman notes the increase in outreach initiatives and the rising popularity of community literacy projects as part of a "social turn" in English studies (204). She views service learning as an alternative to cultural studies' answer to the tradition and alleged elitism of literary studies, and claims that service-learning can increase English studies "real-world relevance in new markets" (212). Cushman employs a rhetoric of accountability. She does not advocate, however, vocational training, utilitarian knowledge, and pragmatism. But she claims that "the most self-defeating stance that English studies scholars can adopt is the one that ignores considerations of the economic and social worth of cultural capital that universities produce" (213). She argues that service learning can bridge class-based schisms between universities and communities, but she never articulates fully the complex relationship between university, local community, and global economies. Cushman and others in composition and rhetoric (Adler-Kassner, Crooks, and Watters; Deans; Flower and Health; Minter and Schweingruber, among others), as well as organizations such as Campus Compact (http://www.compact.org) tend to focus on the pedagogical and institutional challenges of the day-to-day work of service learning. Self-reflexivity about our methods and curricula will not automatically facilitate an analysis of the symbolic, cultural, and economic capital set in motion through service learning and community outreach initiatives within an increasing corporate university.[15] Moreover, we need to be careful not to romanticize service learning as the radically local. My concern is that service learning creates a localism held up as a pedagogical and political ideal, a utopian fiction, which is viewed as an automatic site of resistance. Rather, I am interested in how service learning defined at one scale (that of its civic mission as part of the university and national culture) intersects with laboring bodies and global economies that function at the local scale.

In pursuit of exemplary activist pedagogy, Bill Readings harks back to campus radicals of France in 1968, at which time, he argues, "questions of value arose alongside the recognition of the University [as] a bureaucratic system" (135). Educators do not have to nostalgically hark back to discontent among French students in 1968 to see resistance to the conflation of the production of commodities and knowledge or for a materialist analysis of university culture and labor practices that take into consideration ethical obligations. In addition to the radical relevance of the scholarship and actions taken on behalf of exposing exploitative labor practices in the academy in terms of the increase of part-time, adjunct, and graduate student labor (Nelson, Schell), we might turn to United Students Against Sweatshops, an activist organization that has brought an analysis of global labor politics and university culture to the forefront, and embraced participation by university and college faculty, students, staff, and community members.

United Students Against Sweatshops [USAS] is a national campaign formed in 1998, which has organizations on over two hundred campuses, though students began collectively questioning labor conditions under which products in their campus stores were made as early as 1996. USAS has taken on individual companies such as Nike and pressured the United States Department of Labor to enforce standards, criticized ineffective monitoring proposals, and demanded workers a living wage (Global Exchange). For instance, No Sweat at Indiana University (my former place of employment) first started as part of a campaign sponsored by the local chapter of Jobs with Justice in the spring of 1999. Throughout the 1999–2000 academic year, No Sweat gave educational presentations to classrooms, churches, students, and community groups. They initiated negotiations with the university administration, asked for and were successful in getting full public disclosure of factory locations, campaigned to get IU to join the Workers' Rights Consortium (WRC), and negotiated with the administration on the Code of Conduct, to which IU now must hold its licensees accountable. IU joined the WRC in March of 2000 along with the University of Wisconsin-Madison and the University of Michigan. As of January 21, 2003, there are 112 colleges and universities that are currently members of the WRC <www.workersrights.org>.

At Indiana University, I designed a special topics course on the literature of work and contemporary rhetoric of globalization and labor politics. Students were urged to attend a presentation organized by No Sweat as part of their work for one unit. In February of 2000, No Sweat brought Jim Keady and Leslie Kretzu from the Living Wage Project to speak about their Nike Corporate Accountability Campaign, which exposed Nike's unjust labor practices. The Living Wage Project, like many service learning projects, is based on pedagogical principles of immersion, critical reflection, and action. Members attempted to identify with the factory workers by living with Nike's factory workers on $1.25 a day for one month in an Indonesian village, home to many of Nike's workers. In 1992, the entire annual payroll for the Indonesian factories that make Nikes was less than Michael Jordan's reported twenty-million-dollar fee for promoting them (Brecher and Costello 16–17). Upon their return, their goal, as stated in their mission statement online, has been to "educate the public about the human stories of Nike's factory workers and to educate the workers about their rights and worth in the global marketplace." Keady and Kretzu reached a primarily white midwestern middle-class audience at IU by putting a human face to the problem through the use of documentary footage and the translation of workers' testimonies. Students, who were brought up to the front of lecture hall, were likewise asked to imagine themselves in the position of a sweatshop worker as the facilitators described the workers' daily experiences.

The 2000–2001 Living Wage tour brought the stories of Nike's Indonesian workers to over ten thousand people at universities and high schools throughout the country. In fact, this was the largest student audience I have ever seen at a public lecture on IU campus, aside from the Bobby Knight rally after he, IU's renowned basketball coach, was fired by the administration. Part of the proceeds generated by the Living Wage Campaign reportedly helped fund the establishment of an Education and Resource Center in Tangerang, Indonesia. The presentation inspired many of my students to get more involved with No Sweat, though some found troubling the Living Wage Project faith-based narrative that framed Keady and Kretzu's personal journey, in the sense that it seemed to filter economic justice and activism through missionary rhetoric. I considered students' engagement with the No Sweat campus organization and their exploration of the university as a corporate entity as a form of service-learning. In doing so, however, it was not my goal to construe the antisweatshop movement in utopic terms. For example, today's student movement (USAS) and the predominately white anticorporate movement are marred by racial tensions (Featherstone, esp. 62–67).

Moreover, I do not intend to caricaturize service-learning practitioners as docile servants in the house of the devil of capitalism or as corporate vampires feeding off the laboring bodies of the community. It is also not my goal to romanticize student activism or to turn political activism into an academic exercise. Rather my intention is to urge us to consider how service learning, community outreach, and activism are configured, valued, and marked by material bodies and labor relations within and outside university culture. The goals of campaigns like No Sweat to unite community workers and university students, staff, and faculty through shared political critiques of economic justice and human rights might provide a better model for service-learning and its interventionist potential than charity models or the figure of the public intellectual or critical ethnographer. There are certainly service-learning initiatives and college-community partnerships designed to respond to social and economic injustices, and I do not want to minimize their importance. However, we must ask: If community service becomes institutionalized, will service learning lose its radical relevance?

SERVICE-LEARNING PARADIGMS AND
NOTIONS OF THE PUBLIC SPHERE

Leaders in service learning have drawn important distinctions among various types of service education, including internships, service learning, volunteer community service, participation-action research, experiential education, and career training. These distinctions highlight differing pedagogical relations between students and community agencies as well as reflect different assumptions about citizenship. Keith Morton has described four models of service and civic education: liberal democracy, participatory democracy, social justice, and service as citizenship. These models differ in their configuration of the relations between individuals, communities, and the state. According to Morton, the subject of liberal democracy is "freedom"; therefore, the tensions between individual rights and state authority are foregrounded in service-learning projects that draw on this paradigm. Participatory democracy emphasizes a bottom-up approach to understanding power and focuses on projects that attempt to give voice to those served and thus underrepresented. Social justice paradigms view service as an opportunity for students to witness injustice and envision distributive justice, and to recognize the role of the political economy in shaping individual lives. Finally, the service-as-citizenship paradigm places service as the sole defining act of citizenship and therefore privileges relations between individuals and the community (Morton 1).

Despite crucial differences, all of these models rely upon certain notions of the "public sphere," which, I would argue, are out of sync with the material realities of the global economy and the multiple layers of capital that characterize universities and colleges. How does the flow of global capital within the university and our communities alter our notion of the communities that service learning imagines? In the social-justice paradigms, which I myself have used as models for service learning projects, the configuration of a "counterpublic" remains dependent upon the notion of a stable "public" as its counter.

One might say that Readings actually does provide a framework for the examination of disjunctures among cultural and economic capital and the shifting publics that define our universities (though he himself doesn't provide any systematic analysis or evidence in particular institutional contexts). Readings urges us to think of the university in terms of a "dissensual community," rather than seeing its mission (as the etymology of the word "university" suggests) in terms of universality or unity. Readings calls for a pedagogy that refuses to rationalize the university through a metanarrative of emancipation, redemption, or consensus (128). Instead, Readings insists that "pedagogy is a relation, a network of obligation" (158), and suggests that we think of the "teacher as rhetor rather than magister, one who speaks in a rhetorical context rather than one whose discourse is self-authorizing" (158). I find this ethical formulation of pedagogical and rhetorical obligations the most radically optimistic aspect of his book. However, to situate these relations in a larger narrative of ruin, or to see these networks as only arising out of the ruins, locks us in an institutional rhetoric of belatedness, which responds only after casualties are known.

RETURN OR RERUN OF THE REPRESSED?
THE RHETORIC OF RUIN AND REDEMPTION

The critique of the changing university and its complicity with corporate culture may indeed be belated, and community outreach as well as service learning may indeed be functioning as alibis for or parasites of the corporate university (189). The contradictory nature of service learning in the corporate university has its media parallels in the post-September 11, 2001 "war on terrorism," in the United States where we see the dropping of humanitarian aid to refugees in Afghanistan along with the dropping of bombs in target areas.[16] What, we might ask, is lost or forgotten in this simultaneity? What are the consequences of these contrary gestures and for whom?

On the one hand, we have the self-proclaimed radicals who view service learning (like composition) as a complete sell-out to corporate culture and the logic of consumer capital. On the other hand, we have those who idealize service learning as a site of salvation and redemption for the university. But both positions sell out in their categorical sweep of service learning as the Evil Demon or as savior. Is service learning the result of what is now in ruins—the ghost that haunts yet promises redemption—or are the contradictions of service learning the result of what Readings calls for—a reconfiguration of community as dissensus? Rather than frame the question this way, I concur with Dominick LaCapra, who in his critique of Readings, argues that "the very idea of a university in ruins is itself phantasmic" (39). LaCapra claims that Readings "is himself so marked by the idea of the university of culture that he is unable to inquire into the extent to which it was always a phantasm" (39). His point is that both the "university of culture" and the "university in ruins" are "critical fictions" that ignore the "uncontrollable, adverse effects" of the academy. "What, for example," LaCapra asks, "was the relevance of the university culture for women, workers, colonial subjects, and various minorities?" Even if one were to view the university of ruins as a critical fiction, one must still ask, as LaCapra does, whether "the nature of the fiction has some uncontrolled, adverse effects" (39).[17]

Like LaCapra, Patrick Brantlinger is critical of the dystopic visions of posthistory theorists, such as Readings. Instead, Brantlinger calls for a return to "historical understanding" (180) and the "critical-emancipatory thought (above all, of Marxism) that have, in both the past and the present opposed capitalism and its liberal ideological underwriting" (196). Brantlinger argues that "Marx needs to be rescued from the mounting ruins *both* of 'official' Marxism *and* of transnational capitalism" (200).

What is needed is a more discerning but no less radical critique of service learning and the critical fictions and economic realities that make the push toward its institutionalization and glorification relevant. We need to find effective and thoughtful tactics to intervene, shape, and interrupt this momentum and to redefine the terms and material bodies upon which and through which the market economy and the economy of service learning operate. We might fare well to consider the promise of service learning in the terms that Rey Chow ascribes to "para-sites of contention" in the academy, as "borders . . . that never take over a field in its entirety but erode it slowly and tactically" (16). How might we reform service learning so that it can tactically function as a parasitical intervention in the corporate university—in a world that can no longer be clearly divided "into the state and civil society in Gramsci's terms, nor be clearly demarcated into national and transnational spaces" (16)? The penetration of globalization into the essential infrastructures of education, cannot, as Smith puts it, "simply be wished away by nostalgic sentiment" for an unimplicated public university (115). For public universities, colleges, and schools, this means more than curricular reform and oversight, which characterizes most service learning and outreach centers across the country. We need to return to the historical emphasis of Marxist thinking, but not in a nostalgic way; rather we need to broaden Marxist definitions of class and class relations to account for the "internal contradictions of multiple positionalities within which human beings operate" (Harvey 102). Given the economic realities faced by universities, including decreased funding from state and federal governments, we must create opportunities for a fuller discussion and analysis of the radical promise and role of service learning in the academy. For inspiration, we might turn to grassroots social movements, such as the antisweatshop organizations on our own campuses, that operate outside of organized parties but are nevertheless devoted to constructing a unified labor politics and generating alliances across boundaries of university and community cultures, and between local and global workers.

NOTES

1. See Slaughter and Leslie for more detailed description of entrepreneurial rhetoric and the ways universities have changed as a result of global economic pressures.

2. Both corporate multiculturalism and right-wing attacks on multiculturalism contrast "critical multiculturalism," as defined by McLaren and Farahmandpur, which includes critical self-reflexivity, the "collective experiences of marginalized groups in the context of their political activism" and a systematic critique of differential and asymmetrical construction of social groups in the United States and their links to global relations of development and underdevelopment (38–39).

3. As Blackmore notes, "Human capital theory is premised upon the self-maximizing, autonomous, individual chooser and upon national productivity measures . . . [that] ignore child-rearing responsibilities, domestic labor, and the contribution of voluntary labor to national productivity. Likewise, structural adjustment policies simplistically position the public sector as bad and the private sector as good, quite the contrary to many women's experiences" (144).

4. AFL president John Sweeney launched the Union Summer program in 1996. The program placed college students in summer internships with unions. Within this context, some students began to research and challenge their universities' contracts with apparel companies producing university sports gear. A number of antisweatshop organizations, such as UNITE, have established educational internships that offer new models for faculty and students to rethink and develop service-learning partnerships with nonprofit agencies in their own communities based on labor consciousness. Information about educational internships that focus on antisweatshop campaigns and unionization can be found on the websites of various organizations, including UNITE and the AFL-CIO.

5. Campus Compact is one of the leading external funding sources that support community service learning initiatives. The leading source for higher education and community partnerships is the federal government Community Outreach Partnership Program (COPC) through the department of Housing and Urban Development (HUD). Many outreach programs and centers within large public universities rely on external funding for their existence. Campus Compact's Declaration on the Civic Responsibility of Higher Education calls for a "recommitment of higher education to its civic purpose." The declaration also states, "If students are to use their knowledge and skills to make their nation and its communities better places to live and work, we must ask whether the colleges and universities that educate them are, in fact, using their store of knowledge and skills for democratic engagement" (quoted in Maurrasse 27).

6. Also see the final chapter of Fukuyama's *Trust: The Social Virtues and the Creation of Prosperity*, "The Spiritualization of Economic Life," for yet another recent contribution to capitalist theodicy.

7. I would like to thank Rebecca Dingo for introducing me to Linda Kintz's *Between Jesus and the Market*.

8. While the Christian fundamentalism/free market symbiosis is evident in neoconservative and right-wing discourse, we must recognize that the rise of non-Western religious fundamentalisms rage against new forms of Western imperialism (Smith 95).

9. See Zebroski's discussion of the professionalizing of composition and rhetoric at Syracuse University and its links to the "logic of knowledge creation in capitalist society" (165).

10. Smith notes that the origins of this "new corporate colonialism" lie in the 1930s and 1940s with the United States Council on Foreign Relations, which called for the U.S. to "dominate economically and militarily to ensure materials for its industries" (Korten, quoted in Smith 97), and for the creation of global financial institutions that would stabilize currencies and facilitate capital investment in underdeveloped regions (97). These early actions set the stage for the Bretton Woods Agreement of 1944, where Western international economic leaders came together after the war to discuss how to manage the world economy. Keynes was at the helm as chief advocate for structures that would ensure social and economic security for average citizens while also giving free

reign to corporations and industries to grow. Two other developments took place at this time that were significant to "new corporate colonialism," including the formation of the new World Bank and establishment of the International Monetary Fund (IMF), which laid the basis for GATT (General Agreement on Tariffs and Trade), a set of international trade rules.

11. Blackmore is referring specifically here to the U.S., U.K., New Zealand, Australia, Canada, and South Africa.

12. Blackmore defines "transnational masculinities" as the remasculinization of the professional middle-class and high-wage positions.

13. Student involvement, appreciated on the whole, can be marred, however, by those who are inconsistent in fulfilling their pledges. Two organizations aid in the exchange between university and community. Indiana University's recently formed Office of Community Outreach and Partnerships in Service-Learning (created 1998) functions as a liaison between community and university, helping to ensure that teachers develop partnerships which avoid exploiting community agencies or using them as labs. Indiana Campus Compact offered assistance through Scholarship of Engagement Grants, and continues to fund The Women on the Rise literacy project, now under the directorship of Professor Laura Yow. Scholarship of Engagement Grants are provided by the Learn and Serve America: Higher Education Program of the Corporation for National Service.

14. See Nelson's *Will Teach for Food.*

15. Some faculty, such as myself, have opted to focus on labor politics and labor education, integrating working-class studies, literature about work, and analysis of civic rhetoric and university labor practices into the English curriculum. See Bose, "A Three Point Plan for a Big Ten University: Pedagogy, Politics, and Activism," Lazare's "Teaching the Conflicts about Wealth and Poverty," Atwill's "Toward a Streetwise Civic Rhetoric," hooks's "Confronting Class in the Classroom," and Zandy's *What We Hold in Common.* Other useful resources include the anthology *No Sweat,* edited by Andrew Ross (a book accessible to undergraduate students), "Teachers for a Democratic Culture," and a weekly on-line newsletter, "Labor Matters." For information on Teachers for a Democratic Culture, go to their website: </www.temple.edu/tdc>. Also see Scholars, Artists, Writers for Social Justice website: sage.edu/html/sawsj, which emphasizes links between academics and labor. Sweat Free IU Campaign has a popular education workshop on their website: <usasnet.org/resources/iuworkshop/workshop.html>. Another interesting phenomenon is the emergent focus in composition textbooks on labor practices and student antisweatshop movement—a topic of analysis for another time.

16. See the Art Spiegelman image on the 26 November 2001, cover of *The New Yorker.*

17. John Guillory makes a similar argument in *Cultural Capital,* where he notes the erosion of humanistic culture as an educational goal with the rise of the technical-managerial class. Also see Aronowitz.

WORKS CITED

Adler-Kassner, Linda, Robert Crooks, and Ann Watters, eds. *Writing the Community.* Urbana, Ill.: NCTE, 1997.

Apple, Michael. "Between Neoliberalism and Neoconservatism: Education and Conservatism in a Global Context." *Globalization and Education: Critical Perspectives*. Ed. Nicholas Burbules and Carlos Alberto Torres. New York: Routledge, 2000.

Aronowitz, Stanley. *The Knowledge Factory*. Boston: Beacon, 2000.

Atwill, Janet. "Toward a Streetwise Civic Rhetoric." *College Composition and Communication Conference*. 2002. Unpublished paper.

Barker, Jennifer, Wendy Hesford, and Amy Locklin. "Women on the Rise: Literacy Partnerships, Trauma, and Violence Against Women." In progress.

Blackmore, Jill. "Globalization: A Useful Concept for Feminists." *Globalization and Education*. Ed. Nicholas Burbules and Carlos Alberto Torres. New York: Routledge, 2000. 133–56.

Bose, Purnima. "A Three Point Plan for a Big Ten University: Pedagogy, Politics, and Activism." *Concerns* 27.2 (2000): 74–89.

Brantlinger, Patrick. *Who Killed Shakespeare: What's Happened to English Since the Radical Sixties*. New York: Routledge, 2001.

Brecher, Jeremy, and Tim Costello. *Global Village or Global Pillage: Economic Reconstruction from the Bottom Up*. Boston: South End, 1994.

Chow, Rey. *Writing Diaspora: Tactics of Intervention in Contemporary Cultural Studies*. Bloomington: Indiana UP, 1993.

Cushman, Ellen. "Rhetorician as an Agent of Social Change." *College Compostion and Communication* 47.1 (1996): 7–27.

———. "Service Learning as the New English Studies." *Beyond English Inc.: Curricular Reform in a Global Economy*. Ed. David Downing, Claude Mark Hurlbert, and Paula Mathieu. Portsmouth, N.H.: Boynton/Cook, Publishers. 2002. 204–18.

Deans, Tom. *Writing Partnerships: Service-Learning in Rhetoric and Composition*. Urbana, Ill.: NCTE, 2000.

Downing, David B., Claude Mark Hurlbert, and Paula Mathieu. *Beyond English Inc.: Curricular Reform in a Global Economy*. Portsmouth, N.H.: Boynton/Cook, 2002.

Featherstone, Liza, and United Students Against Sweatshops. *Students against Sweatshops*. London: Verso, 2002.

Flower, Linda, and Shirley Brice-Heath. "Drawing on the Local: Collaboration and Community Expertise." *Language and Learning Across the Disciplines* 4.3 (October 2000): 43–56.

Fukuyama, Francis. *Trust: The Social Virtues and the Creation of Prosperity*. New York: Free Press, 1995.

Guillory, John. *Cultural Capital: The Problem of Literacy Canon Formation*. Chicago: U of Chicago P, 1993.

Harvey, David. *Spaces of Hope*. Berkeley: U of California, 2000.

Helle, Anita Plath. "Transforming the Public(s) of Our Service." *Concerns* 27.1 (2000): 16–24.

Hesford, Wendy. "(In)Visible Literacies: Women and Domestic Violence." *College Composition and Communication Conference*. 1999 Unpublished paper.

hooks, bell. "Confronting Class in the Classroom." *Teaching to Transgress: Education as the Practice of Freedom*. New York: Routledge, 1994. 177–90.

Horner, Bruce. *Terms of Work for Composition: A Materialist Critique*. Albany: State of New York, 2000.

Kintz, Linda. *Between Jesus and the Market: The Emotions that Matter in Right-Wing America*. Durham and London: Duke UP, 1997.

LaCapra, Dominick. "The University in Ruins?" *Critical Inquiry* 25 (1998): 32–55.

Lazare, Donald. "Teaching the Conflicts about Wealth and Poverty." *Left Margins: Cultural Studies and Composition Pedagogy*. Ed. Karen Fitts and Alan W. France. Albany: State U of New York P, 1995.

Maurrasse, David. J. *Beyond the Campus: How Colleges and Universities Form Partnerships with their Communities*. New York: Routledge, 2001.

McLaren, Peter, and Ramin Farahmandpur. "Critical Multiculturalism and the Globalization of Capital: Some Implications for a Politics of Resistance." *Journal of Curriculum Theorizing* (1999): 27–46.

Minter, Deborah Williams, and Heidi Schweingruber. "The Instructional Challenge of Community Service Learning." *Michigan Journal of Community Service Learning* (Fall 1996): 92–102.

Morton, Keith. "Models of Service and Civic Education: An Occasional Paper of the Project of Integrating Service and Academic Study." *Campus Compact* (1993): 1–11.

Nelson, Cary, ed. *Will Teach for Food: Academic Labor in Crisis*. Minneapolis and London: U of Minnesota P, 1997.

Readings, Bill. *The University in Ruins*. Cambridge: Harvard UP, 1996.

Ross, Andrew, ed. *No Sweat: Fashion, Free Trade, and the Rights of Garment Workers*. New York: Verso, 1997.

Sassen, Saskia. *Globalization and its Discontents*. New York: New Press, 1998.

Schell, Eileen. "Toward a New Labor Movement in Higher Education: Contingent Labor and Organizing for Change." *Workplace*. 4.1 June 2001. <http://www.louisville.edu/journal/workplace/issue//schell/html>.

Schell, Eileen E., and Patricia Lambert Stock. *Moving a Mountain: Transforming the Role of Contingent Faculty in Composition Studies and Higher Education*. Urbana, Ill.: NCTE, 2001.

Slaughter, Sheila, and Larry L. Leslie. *Academic Capitalism: Politics, Policies, and the Entreprenuerial University*. Baltimore: Johns Hopkins UP, 1997.

Smith, David Geoffrey. "Economic Fundamentalism, Globalization, and the Public Remains of Education." *Interchange* 30.1 (1999): 93–117.

Villanueva, Victor, Jr. *Bootstraps: From an American Academic of Color*. Urbana, Ill.: NCTE, 1993.

Zebroski, James Thomas. "Composition and Rhetoric, Inc.: Life after the English Department at Syracuse University." *Beyond English Inc.: Curricular Reform in a Global Economy*. Ed. David Downing, Claude Mark Hurlbert, and Paula Mathieu. Portsmouth, N.H.: Boynton/Cook. 2002. 164–80.

CHAPTER ELEVEN

BETWEEN SCHOOL AND WORK:
CLASSROOM AND CLASS

EVAN WATKINS

IT'S NOT ENTIRELY A CONSERVATIVE CLICHÉ THAT CAMPUS CULTURE IN THE U.S. is permeated with leftist radicals completely out of step with the broad majority of U.S. citizenry. After all, it has been a concern for some time among left academics that "we" seem to have so little influence beyond campuses. In their different ways, university-based intellectuals like Edward Said, Cornel West, bell hooks, Stanley Aronowitz, Henry Louis Gates, and others who have some visibility in public forums beyond the university have also spoken out about the general absence of left academics in such forums, as well as the absence of politically organized connections between left-themed university-centered research, publication, teaching, and conferences on the one hand, and activist movements centered "elsewhere" on the other. My introductory phrase, however, "in their different ways," of course registers one of the primary concerns of this volume. While it may appear to a number of conservatives that the academic world is governed by a threatening vision of radical politics, from the inside that not only looks almost amusingly exaggerated, but also ignores how even self-designated academic leftists rarely seem in agreement about much of anything among ourselves, let alone programmatically united toward some common end. Thus, perhaps needless to say, there's little agreement either about the reasons for the absences noted above.

A growing chorus of self-critique throughout the last decade and a half has targeted "theory" as a primary cause. In film studies, for example, Stephen Prince has recently echoed a now lengthy series of claims that an investment in the always more convoluted, extreme, and jargon-laden theorizing of cinematic representations has rendered academics virtually silent about the issues that exercise a great deal of public concern and controversy, such as film violence and its effects. And roughly parallel claims are available in an extraordinary range of academic fields of study that purport to connect in some way with major issues of the day. Theory, the arguments run, imposes a terminology of conceptual abstraction so remote from everyday perceptions and languages as to be at best impenetrable and at worst merely a sign of elitist distance and privilege. Theory also continues to have its defenders, of course, who often point to the necessarily difficult intellectual effort of working through the layers of ideological mystification that ground "common sense" perceptions, as well as to the inherently conservative tendencies of established university disciplines to contain and manage more radical theoretical insights.

Critics like Stanley Aronowitz and Henry Giroux, however, who in the past have themselves argued powerfully for academic theorists to learn the art of translation in effect toward the end of making their influence felt in more public forums beyond the university, now point instead toward what they see as a more considerable ensemble of dangers. They (and in fact a number of others who haven't necessarily been identified with left politics at all) see higher education generally in the U.S. as increasingly oriented away from educational ideals of preparation for democratic citizenship and toward a kind of "vocationalizing" that would put educational institutions completely at the service of the corporate world and of public policies driven by the economic imperatives of the marketplace. In these circumstances students can no longer risk taking courses that can't promise an immediately visible career payoff, even should they want to. Faculty are constrained by the pressures of accountability and administrative mandates to channel their efforts into offering "productive" research connected to curricula that can "efficiently" deliver educational programming to larger and larger numbers of students. In this view the specific dilemmas of academic left politics pale in comparison to a direction that threatens to undermine the very institutional matrix of an educational system that has functioned as one important condition of possibility for the development of *any* politics of an informed, democratic citizenry.

I'm beginning with this admittedly very quick and overgeneralized schematic of what I hope are familiar debates, arguments, and counterarguments because I want to address the concerns that motivated this collection from a slightly different angle of entry than the question of how to forge the alliances that might lead to a more "united" left politics. I don't at all mean to dismiss issues of fragmentation on the left, the by now considerable history of debate over the disconnections between academic- and activist-based politics, or the often cited failures of academics to function as public intellectuals. But I do think it especially important in this general context to consider more directly the specificities of how academic work is organized and carried out. The arguments I referenced briefly above about the languages of theory can serve as a useful introductory example of what I have in mind.

On the one hand, it seems to me true enough to say that any roughly defined and organized field of work develops a terminology specific to its practices. If one lays stucco for a living, for example, terms like "scratch" or "wiring" have meanings that simply can't be immediately understood by an outsider until one becomes at least vaguely familiar with the actual work practices involved. There is a sense in which theories in an academic discipline or program like film studies or cultural studies seem to function in terminologically similar ways. And like any number of other teachers I'm sure, I often find myself explaining theory terms to students in ways not unlike how "the stucco person" on a construction crew might explain "laying scratch" to someone who knows the term only from drag racing. A great many arguments about how academics might learn to address nonacademic publics in newspaper or magazine writing often expand on this basic pedagogical operation. Crudely, you've already learned to do this kind of translation in class with your students; you can learn to do it in other kinds of public forums as well. It doesn't necessarily have to involve some gross simplification of otherwise complex issues. It's a necessary part of pedagogy, and entails a reciprocal obligation to learn from those you would teach toward the end of forming potential alliances and common causes.

On the other hand, however, there's also a sense in which theory terminologies in academic fields of study don't behave quite like the terminologies of laying stucco or metal lathe operation or respiratory therapy or other types of work. The difference isn't a matter of theory vs. practice; it would be a mistake to imagine that working with the oxygen regulators used in respiratory therapy or with the tools used in laying scratch don't involve any theoretical understanding of what you're doing. The immediately significant difference I want to emphasize has to do with the relation between terminologies and work operations. In a university poetry class, for example, when one introduces discussion by announcing that today we're going to *deconstruct* the metaphorical equation of light imagery with intellectual enlightenment in the text, that italicized theory term references only a relatively small part of the work operations and relationships of labor about to be engaged. It may well be that students hear "deconstruct" as an instance of an as yet unfathomable jargon, or as a name for a now roughly recognizable direction discussion will follow out. But it's not at all unreasonable for students to hear the announcement as "today the instructor is going to demonstrate the trick that must be repeated on A papers."

In other words, to assume that "deconstruct" names only a specific kind of intellectual work operation on a poem, even with all that might imply, simultaneously ignores a whole set of evaluative grading practices that is not only every bit as much a part of the work of the day as the operation on a poem, but also in a direct sense recognized by such student response as *exactly the same work operation*. It's as if, comparably, "laying scratch" had to mean simultaneously performing this action with a trowel and paste *and* making sure the job invoice was filled out in triplicate. The difference, again, isn't that "deconstruct" is a theory term and "laying scratch" simply a name for performing a specific type of work. It's that "deconstruct," understood to mean "this type of work with a poem," references only a small part of the work practices engaged in the classroom situation when one is busy "deconstructing."

At the same time, however, there is another sense in which a jargon-of-the-trade term like "deconstruct" used in a poetry class is charged with carrying considerably more weight and range than a "jargon-of-the-trade" term like "laying scratch" in stucco construction. For the pedagogical *value* of learning to deconstruct metaphorical equations in a poem is assumed to lie in a putative portability extending well beyond doing it for poem after poem in class after class in conference presentation after published paper, and so on. To some extent, of course, this applies as well to a skill like laying scratch. One doesn't simply stucco house after house after house with no carryover value at all in relation to a whole set of issues involving both needs and aesthetics. The difference here is a matter of a certain generalizing power attributed to the portability of deconstruction. Whether we like it or not, or are willing to admit it or not, there is some sense in which in teaching our classes we assume it's generally a good thing that all our students not only can but *should* learn to do the work and a great many more similar work operations.

That is part of the bite of that other and so often unreferenced element of what deconstructing the poem names. Students who don't do it so well on their papers typically don't do so well in our classes either, *even though the putatively general value attributed to the work of deconstructing an element of a poem doesn't really admit to being parsed into relatively finer and finer discriminations among levels of doing the work well or badly.* That is, one aspect of the work practices named by the term "deconstruct" in this context depends upon an assumption of some general and uniformly significant value for everyone in learning to do the work, while another aspect in contrast involves a finely tuned mechanism of discriminating how well each worker performs. All of which can help focus an altogether familiar point of classroom conflict that typically finds expression in instructor complaints about students who seem interested in nothing but a grade, and student complaints about instructors who fail to recognize that no student can really afford the luxury of imagining that grades are irrelevant. For students after all, most of whom don't intend to deconstruct poems for a living, the grade can't be ignored. But before thereby returning my argument by this already circuitous route to the point where I left it earlier with the concerns about the process of "vocationalizing" university education, I want to take one more turn through the landscape of work sketched out by my small example.

As I suggested, there does seem a powerful discontinuity between, on the one hand, the generalized portability and value attributed to specific work practices like deconstructing poems, and the discrimination among levels of performance of the work on the other. At the same time, however, for anyone who *does* intend to pursue academic work in a discipline like English where this work practice is (still) valued, the disconnect doesn't carry a lot of weight. For both aspects continue to mind their force across a long itinerary, from competitive admissions into differentially ranked graduate departments right on through the difficulties of getting an academic position in a crowded field of applicants, securing publications in privileged venues, prestigious conference presentations, the rigors of tenure, the determination of merit raises, etc. Whatever the disconnect within the current conditions of academic labor, neither aspect ever recedes very far from view. In addition, as one proceeds further and further along such a career itinerary of academic labor, all too often it also becomes easier to objectify a certain generalizing power about, precisely, the *process* of making finely tuned discriminations among levels of performance. I mean more by the word "objectify" here than that all too familiar academic passive voice—"nothing to do with me, standards simply haven't been met." I mean a sense in which work practices arguably very specific to the conditions of academic labor are first generalized as if they occurred virtually everywhere in one form or another, and then reimagined to be an alien force impinging from the outside to contaminate an educational process that ideally should be serving other and higher ends altogether.

Taking the two halves of this proposition in order, I think the first and generalizing move occurs something like this. In the example I elaborated earlier, it's certainly true enough that stucco workers laying scratch do often discriminate better and worse work; to some extent at least it's often the case that better workers are rewarded with more pay and more responsible positions. Obviously things don't always turn out this way, any more than the grading determinations in any given classroom only register and reward specific levels of achievement. The generalization lies in the assumption that competitively graded work performances are typically a feature of the working world of stucco construction every bit as much as they are in the academic world of the classroom. Yet if competitively graded performances are thus a general and objectified condition, that sentence is of course reversible. That is, it may be read as above, or it may be read as "competitively graded performances are typically a feature of the academic work of the classroom every bit as much as they are in the working world of stucco construction." In this second form, however, it permits an assumption that even if competitively graded performances are a typical feature of the working world, they *shouldn't* necessarily have anything like the same priority and force in a process of education dedicated not only to training specific work skills like laying scratch, but also and far more importantly to the preparation of informed and empowered citizens of a democracy. Indeed, if allowed to intrude too powerfully and pervasively, the entire educational process is in danger of being reduced to a "vocational" experience determined through and throughout by the competitive exigencies of an economic free enterprise marketplace.

The much larger argument I've been elaborating indirectly out of my initial and rather simpleminded terminological example of "deconstruct" and "scratch," however, is that the competitively graded performances that contribute to the structuring of academic labor are never directly generalizable into a process like laying scratch in stucco construction. Or vice versa. Academic grading is as specific to the conditions of academic labor as the multiple naming powers of "deconstruct," and it is as different from whatever competitively graded performances of stucco construction as the naming powers of "scratch" from the naming powers of "deconstruct." I don't at all mean to imply that the whole idea of a "vocationalizing" of the educational system in the U.S. is thereby merely an illusion created by some massive lack of awareness of the specificities of academic labor. But I do want to suggest that if indeed there are any number of reasons to worry about the effects of such a vocationalizing process, there are also good reasons to recognize and understand the potential effects of what, by analogy, might be called a kind of "academicizing" of both worker-training programs and the organization of labor processes elsewhere in the social formation, such as construction work.

Here, for example, is part of a recent (16 May 2002) letter to the editor appearing in *The Sacramento Bee* from Curt Augustine, the Executive Vice-President for the California Coalition for Construction in the Classroom, who echoes an increasingly familiar complaint from a number of different trade representatives. "I read with dismay, but not surprise, of the closure of Sacramento City College's welding program," announced in a *Bee* story dated 3 May 2002. "This is one more unfortunate example," his letter continues, "of how many of today's educators disregard the needs of students and businesses. At a time when contractors cannot find qualified welders and are forced to bring in out-of-state and foreign welders to finish projects, our schools should be opening more programs. These closings are not solely in community colleges. Since 1982, 60 percent of high school technical education programs in California have closed. . . . According to the state Employment Development Department, the construction industry has the need for 16,000 new workers a year, yet contractors cannot find enough trained workers today." And this situation obtains, he concludes, despite the fact that "industry education programs lead students to high-paying jobs and unlimited opportunities."

Augustine's complaint echoes a great many similar arguments, and while he states that the closure can be attributed to the "disregard" of educators "for the needs of students and businesses," the letter suggests signs of deeper troubles. After all, Augustine isn't arguing that the immediate effect of the closure will be to curtail future construction work. Rather, the construction trades continue to be in high demand to the point that contractors "are forced to bring in out-of-state and foreign welders to finish projects." The thinly veiled racism of "foreign welders" emphasizes Augustine's angry recognition that hiring a construction workforce now seems to require a decidedly second-order operation. He and others like him must reactivate what in his eyes appears as an inert and undifferentiated labor pool whose qualifications are at best unknown, and at worst suspect, instead of drawing directly from a pool of already available skilled labor whose individual qualifications are a matter of record, vouched for by a familiar educational process. That is, it's not at all far-fetched to imagine Augustine's picture of himself in this new situation as forced to engage in a kind of retroactive process of picking and choosing as best he can from a discard pile of wasted labor those individuals necessary to fill out the required workforce for any upcoming construction project. Thus the larger complaint against educators isn't really a matter of their disregard. It's that current educational processes privilege forms of purely academic work whose esoteric grading criteria for competitive success produce only a waste of untrained and undifferentiated failures for the actual, necessary tasks of production.

Behind Augustine's letter, however, there exists a considerably more complicated and far-reaching social process. The history of closures he alludes to had its sources in a complex shift of vocational training occurring throughout the eighties and nineties. Very briefly and schematically, the dominant narrative explaining the shift goes like this. As we leave behind the familiar economic landscape of standardized mass production, this story goes, we must learn to rethink entirely our assumptions about work itself and what it involves. The emergent new world of globalized markets and financial circuits, decentralized small-scale flexible production and burgeoning service industries, always more rapid technological innovation, and the growing demand for high-skilled high-tech workers—all this may indeed seem frightening at times. But these developments also provide an occasion to recognize that whatever benefits industrialization brought, it also meant for a great many people that work was reduced to the routinized, repetitive, deskilled labor of industrial production. Correspondingly, leisure time then had to bear almost the whole burden of possibility for realizing not only some measure of personal satisfaction, but also the exercise of civic responsibility and the rights of democratic citizenship.

Among other things, these criticisms the story directs at the recent past are intended to imply that worries about a reduction of education to the task of job preparation simply continue to reflect the conditions imposed by an industrial production. That is, according to this narrative, the fear of "vocationalizing" should rightly be seen as a classic kind of retrospective misrecognition. Having realized to the full all those social costs of industrial organization, skeptics now misread the signs of fundamental workplace change and reorganization as instead a fatal attempt to extend a coercively economic mandate for public education. Even sectors that heretofore had managed to preserve at least a relative autonomy would be swallowed up into a routinized world of work and jobs. Given the fundamental facts of large-scale economic change, however, the opposition between ideal educational goals and the practical necessity of vocational training becomes illusory. At best it's a dismal reminder of a receding past, and at worst the source of conflictual rearguard prejudices that function to prevent a clear understanding of the very real problems we must learn to face and resolve. Together.

In other words, according to this narrative, what might seem the bad news that in fact we must undergo a complete overhaul of the educational system in the U.S. toward the end of training a postindustrial workforce is indeed only apparently bad news. The real news is that we have a unique opportunity to shape collectively a future for ourselves where work and leisure no longer mean utterly different things. Where necessity and personal satisfaction are no longer contradictory imperatives. And perhaps most significantly, where rather than enforcing highly stratified and hierarchical social relations, the workplace itself might contribute to the actual realization of a democratizing equality everyone ostensibly shares as citizens. The "factory town" of the past, as a kind of symbolic image for a social unity that never really existed, must then give way to something like the "university town" as a metonymic stand-in for a process of forging new and more powerful democratic relationships.

Recent events such as the rapid decline of the stock market and the collapse of the IPO world of dot.coms have of course undermined the rosy optimism of a brave new postindustrial future that had sustained this narrative in its origins. Nevertheless, the effects of the directions of educational change emphasized by this dominant narrative have been considerable. The cultural pressures on students (and their parents) to go to college, get a degree, secure a good job, and so on that were already considerable have accelerated dramatically. In a book symptomatically entitled *Other Ways to Win: Creating Alternatives for High School Graduates*, Gray and Herr supply statistical data to support the perception of a great many educators that they are caught in an impossible bind. From the mid-seventies to the mid-nineties, they report, the percentage of high school graduates planning to attend a four-year college or university increased from 63% to 84%. By far the most common reasons cited for university plans were getting a better job and making more money. Meanwhile, well into the nineties the percentage of high school graduates who actually completed a four-year degree remained remarkably stable at around 25%. Although 57% of male high school graduates and 74% of females indicated a desire for professional employment, such professional-level jobs made up only about 20% of existing jobs. Parental pressures on children to aim for a college degree have increased as well, and Gray and Herr's data indicate that the increase is most dramatic among parents with "low-achieving" children. Fully 60% of students in the lowest quartile of their high school class reported significant parental pressure to get into college (4–10).

The cultural imperatives Gray and Herr document, and the enrollment issues so much a part of college and university education in the U.S., suggest that there are good reasons to pay particular attention to those fields of education located at critical pressure points of intersection. Composition seems to me a striking example of such a field. For composition occupies two crucial boundary zones. Even when part of an English department, it occurs nevertheless between English and other university disciplines. It bears the burden of enormously conflicted intellectual expectations among the disciplines it inter-sects, at the same time that it faces directly into the educational and career expectations of nearly every college and university student. Typically, however, composition is also located between two labor forces: tenure-track/tenured instructors on the one hand, and graduate student, lecturer, and temporary instructors on the other. Composition, that is, occurs at the larger intersection of the disciplinary demands of university education and the labor issues every-where increasingly a part of university education. The location of the field thus makes it an especially useful angle of entry for understanding the larger stakes involved in the current process of educational change.

I've been sketching only the barest outlines of a number of what I hope are familiar issues, toward the end of emphasizing in conclusion something of the difficulties involved in trying to create conditions for left political alliances against the fragmentation and disconnections that indeed lead to such consid-erable concern. One powerful temptation, I think, is to imagine that it's possi-ble to identify the dimensions of a "cause" whose scale is so large that it can provide an occasion for the will to submerge differences in the necessity of com-mon struggle—whether galvanized by protests over globalization, a war with a foreign country such as Iraq, or, as some critics have suggested, an ongoing transformation of the university into voc-tech. As someone who has benefited immeasurably from a study of Gramsci, I'm not about to undercut such opti-mism of the will, but not without also remembering that the other half of his injunction urges a necessary pessimism of the intellect, perhaps especially with regards to common identifications around a cause.

As I suggested at the beginning, there has been a great deal of debate about the potential for left academics to become more publicly visible intellectuals, about the disconnects between academic and activist leftists, about the role of theory and the putatively elitist languages of academic leftists, and about the multiple pressures of academic life that often seem to lead to little more than endless internal squabbling. But without at all dismissing the value of such debates, I've wanted to point my argument in a rather different direction, toward what seem to be the problems that are generated within the rapidly shifting intersections between, broadly, "school" and "work." The recent criticisms directed at the vocationalizing of higher education address some of those prob-lems, but as I've tried to suggest there are a great many other elements at stake, not the least of which involve the complex ensemble of conditions that organ-ize and structure the multiple forms of academic labor.

"Class," the cliché runs, never did receive quite the same new energy and attention as "race" and "gender" within that famous triple mantra of the eight-ies, and by some accounts class has become an anachronism in the current social formation. Yet to the extent vocational education in the U.S. was initiated early in the twentieth century toward the end of creating a working class for an industrial economy, it has always been a part of class politics. The virtual disappearance of vocational education in that original sense through the long process of educational history doesn't at all mean the disappearance of class politics from education. But it does point to significant shifts in the ongoing social process of class formation in the U.S., shifts that bear at every point on the potential for left political alliances. Optimism of the will is a good thing altogether, but it can never substitute for a kind of intellectual pessimism that keeps a focus on what we need to know in order to do anything at all.

WORKS CITED

Gray, Kenneth and Edwin L. Herr. *Other Ways to Win: Creating Alternatives for High School Graduates*. Thousand Oaks, CA: Corwin Press, 1995.

CHAPTER TWELVE

ANOTHER WORLD IS POSSIBLE

Mark Wood

The emancipation of the working class must be the work of the working class itself.
—Karl Marx

Since the containment of 1960s radical political movements and especially since the collapse of the Soviet Union, the capitalist class has significantly extended its control over the world's natural resources, productive property, financial assets, and state apparatuses. Without noncapitalist nations and working class organizations limiting capitalism's expansionary proclivities, capitalism has dramatically advanced the project of creating "a world after its own image" (Marx, M-E Reader 477).[1] Its forces have integrated the great portion of humanity, including tens of millions of children, into the free-trade workhouses of commodity production, extended the culture of thoughtless consumption to every corner of the globe, worsened already horrifying inequalities between and within nation-states, and further plundered an already depleted natural world.[2]

In *One World, Ready or Not* (1997), William Greider writes, "the economics of globalization relies upon a barbaric transaction—the denial of individual rights—as a vital element of profitability" (388).[3] The accumulated result of capital's barbaric transactions is a world in which, on the one hand, one out of five persons lives on less than a dollar a day and, on the other, "the assets of the world's three richest people . . . are more than the combined GNP of all least developed countries on the planet" (Shalom; see Yates). One of these persons, Bill Gates, is well aware of these inequalities. Though it may be true that his personal fortune and position as owner of one of the most powerful corporations in the world make it difficult, if not impossible, for him to consider noncapitalist solutions to the problems created by capitalist organized development, Gates has nevertheless been remarkably open and insistent regarding the nature of these problems. Speaking in Seattle at a conference on investment opportunities and the digital divide, Gates challenged his Starbucks-saturated audience members to imagine why investing in poor nations remains an absurd proposition.[4]

> Mr. Gates: I mean, do people have a clear view of what it means to live on $1 a day? . . . There's no electricity in that house, none. So is somebody creating computers that don't require electricity?

> Question [sic]: No, but there are solar powered systems.

> Mr. Gates: No, there are no solar power systems for less than a dollar a day, honest. You can't afford a solar power system for less than $1 a day. You're just buying food, you're just trying to stay alive.

> Question: There are government and World Bank initiatives to place these systems in these villages. There's money coming to do this work, and buy this technology.

> Mr. Gates: You don't understand. When people say $1 a day, that includes every government thing that's given to them, everything they have shared across that entire village. It includes everything. And there's no solar power system in there for $1 a day. There's just not.

> Question: Okay. I mean—

> Mr. Gates: You live in a different world.

Of course the person to whom Gates was speaking, like Gates, like all of us, lives in the same world as do persons living on a dollar a day, a world divided into hundreds of millions who wake hoping to find a morsel to eat and millions who wake wishing they could stop themselves from eating so much. That the world is divided into starving and supersized, homeless and multihomed, penniless and prosperous, is not coincidentally related to the capitalist mode of production but rather an intrinsic consequence of this mode.[5] The goal of the capitalist mode of production is the production of more capital. Nothing else. In his pursuit of profits, Mr. Moneybags, as Marx personified capital, blithely sells weapons to dictators, dumps toxic wastes into drinking water supplies, outlaws the production of generic drugs for persons dying of AIDS, and condemns children to industrial slavery without losing a wink of sleep. As long as profits are up, all is well in the kingdom of capital. Or, as former currency trader Ted C. Fishman writes, "in the logic of free markets, allowing investors to underwrite mass murder is the system at work" (37).[6]

At the same time, however, as capitalist forces globalize socioeconomic inequality and ecological devastation, millions of individuals and thousands of grassroots organizations are resisting "globalization from above" with greater energy, enthusiasm, and militancy.[7] In fact, resistance to capitalist domination has been spectacularly on the rise in recent years as persons of all faiths, ethnicities, and nationalities work to gain control over the conditions of their own existence.[8] While academics in the United States have struggled over the past twenty-five years to support the development of anticapitalist politics, citizens from around the world have been vigorously forging a multinational movement that seeks to reform or replace capitalist forms of social organization.

Though often initially focused on a particular issue (e.g., debt relief, militarism, poverty, AIDS), individuals and organizations are increasingly discovering structural connections between their respective issues and as a result increasingly working together. "An incredible range of movements and concerns that once seemed unrelated or even antagonistic have learned," as Jeremy Brecher and Tim Costello note, "to cooperate in the face of corporate-led globalization from above. Activists around the world have forged a new internationalism with a global vision. They have developed organizational forms—ranging from global advocacy networks and temporary affinity groups to global forums—to share ideas and coordinate actions over vast areas with a minimum of hierarchy." (2002).[9] The 200,000 individuals who gathered on 18 January 2003 in Washington, D.C., to protest against Bush's war on the world carried signs that read: "Stop U.S. Intervention in Colombia," "Consume—> Consume—> Bomb—> Bomb—> Consume—> Consume," "Let Exxon Send their own Troops," "Down with U.S. Imperialism," "Our World Is Not for Sale," "Drop the Debt, Not Bombs," "End the Sanctions," and on a scarf worn by a black Lab, "Dogs for Peace in the Middle East." Punks, hippies, retirees, workers, students, teachers, Buddhists, Muslims, Jews, Hindus, Protestants, Catholics, pagans, atheists, environmentalists, feminists, gay liberationists, animal rights advocates, gray panthers, liberals, anarchists, socialists, and communists marched together in recognition of the interdependent nature of human existence. As a brightly colored banner carried by energetically chanting college students declared, quoting Martin Luther King, Jr., "injustice anywhere is a threat to justice everywhere" (290).[10]

Demonstrations against capitalist institutions, organizations, governments, and forums are protests *and* simultaneously educational events. Protestors learn from leaflets, pamphlets, and banners on the street, by attending teach-ins held before and after major demonstrations, and through conversations with each other. Citizens around the world are using the Internet to teach each other about and organize opposition to capitalist-controlled globalization. The Internet made it possible for millions of human beings around the world to coordinate the largest demonstration in human history, in this case against Bush waging war on Iraq, on 15 February 2003.[11] In this and many other ways, capital not only produces its own gravediggers in the form of wage-laborers, it produces many of the tools required for workers to dig capital's grave. While students may not learn much, if anything, to borrow from Marvin Gaye, about "what's going on" and especially about how to change what's going on from their college courses, they are learning much in this regard from such independent news, information, and educational sources as 50 Years is Enough, Corporate Watch, Democracy Now, Global Exchange, Indymedia, Rainforest Action Network, and Z Magazine. The movement for global justice not only educates citizens about capitalist-controlled globalization, it brings people together to discuss how to construct institutions that promote the well-being of all persons.

One cannot ignore, moreover, the highly optimistic tone of this movement. A joyous sense of possibility, so drearily absent from academia, pervades demonstrations and inspires demonstrators to keep their eyes on the prize of global justice. Few among the millions of individuals who *are* the movement for democratic globalization need to read Ernst Bloch on the utopian imagination or any other treatise on utopian thinking. They are committed to building a society that is guided by the principles and supports the practices of human solidarity, social justice, and ecological sustainability. Demonstrators use puppets, street theater, art, dancing, singing, music, as well as rallies, speeches, boycotts, bike parades, sit-ins, and shut-downs to protest capitalist domination and to partially represent a global society that affords every person the opportunity to participate in the making of culture. The tens of thousands who protested in Seattle on the eve of the new millennium and millions who since have gathered in Prague, Madrid, Sao Paolo, Genoa, Santiago, Dakar, Berlin, Manila, London, Paris, Johannesburg, and Washington, D.C., are drawn together by the conviction that all hope is not lost, that the socially-generated terror of poverty, hunger, militarism, and environmental degradation are not inevitable facts of existence, that the poor need *not* always be with us, that to quote placards carried by demonstrators who gathered with tens of thousands to protest against the G-8 meeting in Genoa, Italy, in July of 2001, "*un altro mondo è possibile.*"

Capitalist globalization has not only integrated human beings from around the world into interdependent relations of production and consumption, it has also fostered, quite unintentionally, a growing appreciation for the value and necessity of building a society organized by, of, and for the people. Indeed, I would suggest that we are very much in the midst of what historians may one day refer to as the Global Justice Era, an era that will not end until we build institutions that ensure all human beings may develop themselves in a socially and environmentally responsible manner.

As professors we can recover our relevance to real-world politics by linking our scholarship, teaching, students, and ourselves to the international movement for global justice. We may accomplish this goal in various ways. Among these are the following. First, we can help individuals and organizations refine their analyses of society and clarify the conflicting perspectives that comprise the movement for global justice. We have access to educational resources (e.g., libraries, the Internet, communication systems) that we can use to support this movement. Our research on race, ethnicity, nationality, gender, sexual orientation, the environment, and class can provide useful insights to citizens working to improve their conditions of life. Second, we can help forge a counterhegemonic culture of international solidarity by teaching our students about other cultures and by linking our students to students, organizations, and movements around the world that are working to build a just mode of socioeconomic organization. We can, quite significantly, foster the development of international solidarity against the siren call of nationalism. Third, we can regain our relevance to real-world politics by helping students develop their abilities to analyze capitalist social relations, including the cultural, educational, religious, and political ideologies and institutions that support and are supported by these relations. Demonstrating the linkages between, for example, militarism, ecology, low wages, health care, education, and capitalist development is key in this regard. Fourth, we can help students develop the pedagogical skills they need to teach others what they know and the organizational skills they need to mobilize friends, co-workers, and community members in the fight for global justice.[12]

Getting our students involved with the movement for global justice is crucial to its success inasmuch as this movement has failed to inspire the imagination and inform the practices of the majority of U.S. citizens. While some union organizations, including the United Steel Workers and the AFL-CIO, have endorsed protests against the IMF, World Bank, and WTO, by and large most citizens do not understand how these institutions and capitalist property relations are related to their own problems, let alone understand what they can and ought to do to challenge and transform these institutions and relations.[13] Moreover, the movement for global justice must not only contest global regulatory institutions such as the World Bank and IMF, it must also contest capitalism at the point of production. The establishment of economic democracy requires democratizing control over productive resources and social planning and democratizing the goals of production so that workers can effectively promote the general welfare of the entire community.

The failure of U.S. workers to join the movement for global justice weighs heavily against its progressive development. As pedagogically and politically productive as protests against the IMF, World Bank, WTO and other capitalist institutions have been, the task of building a postcapitalist society is not likely to succeed without a significant portion of U.S. workers "shaking things up." Given their relatively privileged position in the global economy and the U.S. state's pivotal role in protecting, promoting, and propping up capitalist rule, U.S. workers have the potential to make a fundamental contribution to building a just world community.

Whether U.S. workers realize this potential in no small measure depends on the development of revolutionary theory and practice among broad sectors of the working class. Capital's domination of the means of consciousness production, including print and electronic media and public and private educational institutions, has never been more thorough. In addition, more citizens are working longer hours and have less time and energy to learn about how capitalism works and what they can do to challenge the powers that be. For these reasons, the development of revolutionary theory and practice more than ever depends on educators working to radicalize environmental, social justice, faith, citizen, and labor organizations and teaching students the theoretical, pedagogical, and organizational skills required to contribute to this radicalization. Through our scholarship and pedagogy we cannot only help students learn how to interpret the world in different ways but also give them the tools with which to change it.

THEORY AND POLITICS

I want to say to you as I move to my conclusion, as we talk about "Where do we go from here?" that we honestly face the fact that the movement must address itself to the question of restructuring the whole of American society. There are forty million poor people here. And one day we must ask the question, "Why are there forty million poor people in America?" And when you begin to ask that question, you are raising questions about the economic system, about a broader distribution of wealth. When you ask that question, you begin to question the capitalistic economy.

—Martin Luther King, Jr., 1968

During the 1980s and 1990s, self-identified progressive academics became increasingly disconnected from struggles for social justice, human rights, and ecological sustainability. This was also a period in which many academics, informed by poststructuralist discourses, contended that racial, ethnic, gender, and sexual discrimination and oppression (a category whose ubiquity was matched only by its operational ambiguity) are as significant as capitalist exploitation and state repression. Many theorized social relations as being constituted primarily if not exclusively by discourse, culture, and subjectivity. Eventually, as Terry Eagleton notes in *The Illusions of Postmodernism*, in "speaking materially about culture, [many] began to speak culturally about the material, not least about that most obvious material bit of us, the body" (48).[14] Oppression could therefore be challenged, if not overcome, by writing transgressively, constructing countercultures, and forging subversive identities. While some theorists included class in their list of ills afflicting humanity, in practice the analysis of class received scant attention. Once the "the empirical" was placed "under erasure" as one among a plethora of Western metaphysical ruses used to dominate the "Other," many academics abandoned research on capitalist-imperialist exploitation and repression of real (other) men, women, and children. Questions of power became metaphysical, which is to say, onto-theological problems that could be addressed by subverting the Western metaphysics of presence, a project that, after all, required little more than writing differently, which is to say, incomprehensibly, and, in any case, was no more realizable than is, for example, ridding the world of evil. One must search far and wide to find anything but a smattering of references to empirical realities in the so-called subversive books written by self-identified leftists and progressives during the 1980s and 1990s. While much was written about *jouissance* and the subversive play of libidinous bodies, much less was said about the individuals whose labor made possible this writing. Cyborgs, transsexuality, and *différance* received far more attention than did janitors, the working day, and justice. As John Rosenthal indicates, "with its fetishization of 'identities' and infatuation with 'discourse,' with its vague celebration of 'democracy' (whether 'radical' or 'deliberative' but not, of course, *economic*), and . . . equally vague and thereby non-threatening demands for 'recognition,' . . . 'social theory' is," or, I would suggest, social theory was and in large measure remains, "mostly asocial. It rarely engages those fundamental social relations which make a society a society, much less those specific social relations which make a capitalist society a capitalist society" (111–112).[15]

As scholars on the left devoted less time to class matters and more time to race, ethnicity, gender, and sexual orientation, and, as noted, theorized these identities as being primarily if not solely the product of discourse, culture, and subjectivity, the ruling class wasted no time intensifying its ongoing war against workers of all races, ethnicities, nationalities, genders, and sexual orientations, making no distinction regarding who it would and would not submit to the grinding wheels of capitalist production. And so, as progressives waved farewell to the working class, Marxist theory, and socialist politics, capital expanded its domination of planetary life. Preoccupied with more "sophisticated" problems, problems largely irrelevant to all but a handful of tenured and wanting-to-be-tenured scholars, academics offered little, if any, direct resistance to capital's extension of cultural, political, economic, and military power.[16]

The failure to challenge capital's assault on labor and life came home to roost, however, at the end of the 1990s when the corporate vultures, always hungry for more, sunk their talons deeper into the heart and soul of public education. Academics could no longer easily ignore class matters as business-trained administrators and presidents cut deals with corporations, downsized departments and programs, reduced tenure-track lines, increased adjunct employment, and reorganized curricula to better serve corporate interests.

Fortunately, capital's invasion has not occurred without resistance, resistance that is currently growing on campuses nationwide. Graduate students and adjunct instructors, sometimes with faculty support, too often without, are now fighting for better wages, health insurance, and the right to collective bargaining. Students are demanding their schools stop purchasing apparel made by workers in sweatshops and protesting against the corporate takeover of research and curricula. Students and faculty are joining campus union and living wage movements and faculty are once again devoting increased time and energy to researching and teaching about state power, imperialism, and class struggle.

CLASS MATTERS

The resurgence of concern for researching and teaching about class was and remains a politically salubrious turn away from postmodernism's political dead ends. Further developing this research and teaching is key to recovering our relevance to real-world politics. This is so because class relations, the relations that organize the production and appropriation of wealth, are not determining in the last instance or one in a series of oppressive conditions but rather constitute the material framework within which racial, ethnic, gender, sexual, and national identities are produced over time.[17] The ontological status of class is qualitatively different from that of racial, ethnic, national, gender, and sexual identity. *Class* refers to the objective organization of individuals in relationship to each other and productive resources. *Identity* refers to the subjective characteristics of the individuals who comprise these relationships. In a society marked by racial, ethnic, national, gender, as well as sexual discrimination and prejudice, racial, ethnic, national, gender, and sexual identity are determinants in the overall distribution of power and privilege. Nevertheless, the condition that fundamentally determines an individual's capacity to satisfy his or her needs and achieve his or her goals, whether that person is black or white, gay or straight, female or male, is the quality and quantity of productive property that person owns and controls. Prejudice and discrimination remain barriers to mobility within the existing system of social relations. The primary factor, however, that prevents the vast majority of individuals from enjoying generous and generative conditions of existence is the concentration of wealth in too few hands and the continuing organization of human beings, socially created resources, and the earth itself for the purpose of making profits and the private accumulation of wealth.

According to economist Edward N. Wolff, as of 1998, the top 20% of American citizens owned a little more than 83% of the nation's wealth, while the next 80% split a little less than the remaining 17%. Similar maldistributions obtain in other nations and between nations. Thus, while overcoming prejudice and discrimination would improve everyday relations among working people, failure to link this goal with the goal of redistributing wealth and transforming the property relations that organize the production of wealth can at best result in a demographically proportionate distribution of different socially categorized persons (assuming, that is, there can be agreement about who is what, e.g., "black," and assuming, wrongly in my view, that individuals should be so identified) throughout the existing division of labor, property, and power (e.g., a demographically proportionate number of black and white, gay and straight, male and female CEOs, professors, and janitors). Without redistributing wealth and

reorganizing control of its production and distribution, the majority of working people would still lack access to quality education, health care, employment, and safe environments as well as control over the production and distribution of these goods.[18] What is needed above all else is working class affirmative
action: in effect, the abolition of class divisions and the oppressive human relations that derive from and reproduce these divisions.

Attending a session on race, class, and gender at the Socialist Scholars
Conference several years ago, I heard a young man who waited tables at a restau-
rant in New York City make essentially this argument. After several presentations on the need to take race, gender, and sexual orientation seriously, he
stood up and said, in effect, "So I'm gay, but really the main thing is that I'm
poor as shit trying to live in this city waiting tables. And the people I work with,
whatever their color or sexual preference, are mostly in the same boat. What I
need, what we need, is not gay rights but better pay, health care, shit like that."
He added that he was, in any case, tired of people talking about his sex life, and
that he wished they would start talking about how to make a revolution in this
country, how to redistribute wealth more equally, how to make life a little more
fair for working people.

We are rightly concerned to combat prejudice and discrimination. There
is a danger, however, that linking politics to racial, ethnic, national, gender,
sexual, as well as class *identities* makes it difficult, perhaps impossible, to forge
and fight for the redistribution of wealth and the establishment of workers'
management of social planning. For this reason, our politics ought to emphasize issues (e.g., access to health care, decent wages and benefits, environmental protection) and not identities (e.g., gay rights, women's rights, black
rights). A gay man infected with HIV needs access to health care. But then
so do fifty million other Americans. Inner city kids need better quality education. But then so do a majority of rural kids. Focusing on issues does not
mean abandoning the fight against discrimination. It does mean resisting the
temptation to formulate the fight against discrimination in terms that institutionalize racial, ethnic, national, gender, and sexual identities as factors that
ought to play any role in the organization of labor, property, and power.[19]
The problem with identity politics, even when articulated as a strategic essen-
tialism, is not just that it runs the risk of essentializing and, when it's made policy, institutionalizing categories of discrimination, though this is problematic
enough. It is also that identity politics divides citizens and thereby weakens
their capacity to act on the basis of shared interests.[20]

The practical implication of this argument is that constructing a movement for the revolutionary transformation of society is most productively
advanced not by forging coalitions between, for example, black and white communities (i.e., identity-based coalitions), but rather by inviting, educating, and
organizing individuals, whatever their racial, ethnic, national, gender, or sexual identity, to work individually and together to improve, for example, health

care, education, environmental protection, wages, and benefits. The common denominator that runs through this agenda is, I would add, control of social and natural resources, the resources without which none of these goals can be achieved. It is for this reason that the struggle to establish worker control over productive property and societal planning is key to unifying individuals across both issues and identities.[21] Movements against racism, ethnocentrism, nationalism, sexism, and heterosexism assume their deepest political value when they are linked to the movement to establish economic democracy.

REVOLUTIONARY SOLIDARITY

As national capitals extend their productive operations around the world and in so doing become less solely dependent on domestic labor, the state has become less responsive to the needs of the people it claims to represent. At the same time, capital turns increasingly to supra-state institutions like the World Bank, International Monetary Fund, and World Trade Organization to coordinate global economic planning in the interests of the ruling class. Nevertheless, the ruling class has not in the least abandoned using the state as an instrument for maintaining and expanding its control. Capital uses the state to market its exploitation of humanity as being good for everyone, to negotiate trade agreements that extend capital's hegemony, to pass legislation that weakens labor and protects the rights of the owning class, and to pay for the development and maintenance of transportation and communication systems, scientific research, technological inventions, agricultural production, and most importantly, the armed forces required to render human beings defenseless against corporate plunder and pillage.[22] Though politicians gain much ground by condemning "government spending," the ruling class, whom these same politicians aggressively represent, would not be able to maintain its rule for long without massive state financial, political, legislative, and military support.[23]

In these and others respects the state manages the common affairs of the capitalist class or, more often, the common affairs of the most powerful sectors within the capitalist class. NAFTA and GATT represent means for solidifying U.S. corporate control over resources and labor throughout the Americas and simultaneously means for fighting against Asia and European Union capitalists (the European Union represents, it perhaps deserves repeating, less a humanistic defense against American imperialism than it does the organization of European capital to assert its own, primarily German-led, brand of imperialism). The age of interimperialist rivalries is in no way behind us. Meanwhile the World Bank and International Monetary Fund, under the direction of the most powerful banks in the world, manage the flow of finance capital by directing state leaders around the world to implement structural adjustment programs (SAPs) under threat of debt discipline, divestment, embargo, political manipulation, and military occupation.[24] As is well known, SAPs involve cutting the value of currency, reducing spending on social programs that do not directly facilitate the production of capital, that is, that benefit people (e.g., education, health care, food subsidies), selling off state-owned enterprises to corporate looters (e.g., water, power, and communication systems), offering land and other resources to corporate exploitation, and constructing free-trade zones that are liberated from such "unfair" social requisites as taxation and legislation protecting workers and the environment. World Bank-directed SAPs have devastated hundreds of millions of people around the world. As ex-chief economist for the World Bank Joseph Stiglitz said of his former employer, "it has condemned people to death" (Globalizer).[25]

Though politicians advance their programs in the name of what is "good for America," in fact their programs are frequently good for the ruling-class minority and not so good for the working-class majority (the latter pays for what the former accumulates). Identification with one's own nation generally suppresses awareness of class divisions within nations as well as awareness of the interests citizens share between nations. As long as workers remain segregated into, restricted by, and encouraged to identify their interests with those articulated by representatives of capital as their own, capital enjoys a decisive political advantage in its war against the working class. The ruling-class directed war on terrorism not only makes the world more terrifying, but it also discourages workers from identifying this class as responsible for their difficulties.

As teachers we can do much to encourage students to identify less with national interests and more with the project of building a just and democratic global society. We can help build an international culture of solidarity. Teaching world literature, music, architecture, art, history, philosophy, and religion within the context of global capitalist realities, for example, helps deepen student awareness of and concern for human beings in other nations. We can also link our students with students from other nations through international study abroad programs, the kind of educational "reality tours" sponsored by organizations such as Global Exchange, and through Internet courses that put students from different nations in conversation with each other. By strengthening solidarity with students from around the world, our students will be better positioned to resist the nationalist trap and to fight for change that benefits all persons. Building a culture of international solidarity, a culture that inspires us to fight against injustice everywhere, does not mean abandoning the goal of improving conditions in one's own nation. Rather it means defining national interests in terms of building a just world community.

RECENTERING THE SUBJECT

The post-structuralist displacement of the subject was politically salubrious to the extent that it shifted politics away from thinking in terms of changing individuals toward changing structures (even if Marxists, and not just Marxists, have been arguing as much all along). To the extent, however, that this displacement weakened the concept of agency, it also displaced concern for empowering individuals to act against the ruling elite as well as the social, political, economic, and military institutions that protect this elite. By arguing that every individual is subject to complex systems of power relations, that no individual or even group of individuals can be said precisely to possess or lack power, and that individuals are sometimes oppressed, sometimes oppressors, and often both at once, it became increasingly difficult to identify clearly who exploits, represses, and dehumanizes whom. The phrase "It's more complicated than that," in which "that" referred to claims that named who does what to whom and claims that asserted that class is more fundamental than, for example, skin color in determining individual freedom resounded with great frequency in the hallways of academia. What causes people to suffer and what must be done to address this suffering became such exceedingly complicated things that few scholars could say much of anything with sufficient clarity to enable anyone to act decisively. The trope of "dissemination" as much described the dominant mode of academic production during this period, a mode in which something more always needed to be written and published before anyone could act, as it did the endless play of signifiers.

To the extent that post-structuralism emphasized that we are products (subjects) of existing systems of power, it presented an incomplete understanding of human beings. We are, after all, subjects *and* agents, products *and* producers of our individual and collective circumstances. Though, as Marx wrote in 1977, "the laws of capitalist production confront the individual capitalist as a coercive force external to him," individual capitalists nevertheless decide, for example, to invest capital here or there, to bomb this or that nation, to send money to this or that dictatorship (381).[26] Though the laws of capitalist production also confront the individual worker as a coercive force external to him or her, individual workers nevertheless decide, for example, to be dutiful, slow down production, form a union, or go on strike. Individuals make choices and pursue different courses of action within the range of possibilities presented to them by their objective and subjective circumstances. Encouraging our students to become involved in struggles for social justice means foregrounding the power of individuals to challenge and change their circumstances. To speak philosophically, it means recentering the subject as agent who oppresses and exploits as well as the subject as agent who resists oppression and exploitation. We can teach our students how to investigate and identify the individuals who exploit and oppress other human beings as well as how to transform the institutions that divide society into exploiters and exploited. What is key is to combine classroom study with extra classroom practice. In this way students learn, as a student returning from a protest against the World Bank put it, that "we can totally make a better world if we just get off our butts and start doing it."

DOING IT

In the film "Good Will Hunting," there is a scene in which Will, the character played by Matt Damon, is interviewed for a job at the National Security Agency. When asked why he might *not* want to work for the NSA, he proceeds to make a series of connections between the work of code breaking, the U.S. military's bombing of civilians in poor nations, his buddy from Southie being wounded while helping to install a procorporate government and returning home to find that his job has been exported to that nation, oil companies raising prices at home, "a cute, little ancillary benefit for them but it ain't helping my buddy at two-fifty a gallon," and corporate destruction of the natural environment. "So what'd I think?" says Will regarding the offer. "I'm holdin' out for somethin' better. I figure I'll eliminate the middleman. Why not just shoot my buddy, take his job and give it to his sworn enemy, hike up gas prices, bomb a village, club a baby seal, hit the hash pipe and join the National Guard? Christ, I could be elected President" (Damon and Affleck).[27]

This is one of those rare moments in a Hollywood film in which important truths are told regarding the nature of global capitalism. That Will/Damon makes these connections is no accident. Damon, who wrote the script with his friend and co-star Ben Affleck, has read Howard Zinn's classic *A People's History of the United States* and supports working-class politics.[28] I show this scene to students as a model of what it means to make connections between what might otherwise seem to be unrelated aspects of global life and as a model of what it means to take a stand against the status quo—indeed, after 9/11, with the war on terrorism raging and media glamorizing the forces of repression carrying out this war, Will's refusal to "be all he can be" assumes added significance. Thanks to an education system that has little concern for teaching students about how capitalism works or developing other-concerned thought and action, most students would take the job. Our goal is to help students hold "out for somethin' better" and commit to building a global society that does not require organizations like the NSA to exist.

Since the protests in Seattle in November of 1999, more and more students are learning about how capitalism works and forming their own organizations to contest capitalist rule. Nevertheless, the majority of students lack even a basic understanding of how corporate institutions and policies are responsible for creating human suffering and environmental destruction. Many, if not most, students assume that people living in poor nations are poor for reasons that have little, if anything, to do with capitalist relations of exploitation. They accept, moreover, the socially generated division of the planet into the relatively impoverished and privileged as being more or less natural and, in any case, as unrelated to their own lives.

We can help students liberate their minds from capitalist ideologies and develop the "Good Will capacity" by teaching them theoretical skills to investigate how capitalism works, pedagogical skills to teach others, and organizational skills to affect practical change.

THEORETICAL SKILLS

It is vital to provide tools to investigate the connections between education, culture, work, the media, militarism, and corporate power and, most importantly, to grasp the relationship between these realities and the social relations that make capitalist society capitalist. Grasping these relationships is especially important because it highlights the need to establish democratic control over productive property. Students may learn about the exploitation of labor in Colombia, Haiti, Indonesia, and Nigeria and yet think that we can build a better world primarily by boycotting those companies that are most brutally exploiting people in these nations (e.g., Coca-Cola for their support of paramilitary death-squads in Colombia; Shell Oil for their support of the same in Nigeria) and by consuming conscientiously, that is, by buying from companies that are committed to fair trade, not free trade. While boycotts and conscientious consumption represent important dimensions of the struggle to build a just society and especially to creating a culture of international solidarity, we are not likely to shop our way to another world. These practices are not likely to accomplish this goal precisely because the problems facing human beings in these and other nations around the world derive from relations of production governed by the principles of profit-making and capital accumulation.

I teach courses on contemporary religion, ethics, and society. These subjects lend themselves to incorporating material on the IMF, World Bank, WTO, debt, hunger, labor, militarism, and the environment. In addition to researching these subjects, I also have students do research on and teach other students about secular and religious organizations that are working to build a postcapitalist society. So, for example, students do research and present information on the affect of IMF structural adjustment programs on such things as health care, the environment, the spread of diseases, labor rights, poverty, hunger, homelessness, and unemployment. They read about and report on the work of organizations such as the American Friends Service Committee, Buddhist Peace Fellowship, Bread for the World, Catholic Worker, the Mennonites, Pax Christi, and United Methodist Women. I ask students to identify the weaknesses of their approaches. Have they gone beyond addressing symptoms to consider the institutional causes of debt? Do they make connections between debt and the dominant mode of socioeconomic organization? Students sometimes interview local religious leaders and members of these organizations to learn more about their positions on debt and other social, political, and economic matters. Because some of these religious organizations advance highly critical perspectives on global capitalism, having students read their material provides a productive way to introduce perspectives that exceed the boundaries of bourgeois politics.

I always teach a section on military spending and the role of military forces around the world. Doing so provides a fruitful way to discuss much of current politics in the United States. Students are shocked to discover that half of discretionary spending goes to the military and that only one tenth goes to education. In general most students believe that most tax money goes to people who refuse to work and are looking for handouts, in short, to an indolent poor. Unfortunately, they do not include, as they should, the real vultures, the capitalist class. Michael Moore's chapter in *Downsize This!* on corporate welfare, "Big Welfare Mamas," information on corporate subsidies, stories about people trying to survive low-wage jobs, such as those Barbara Ehrenreich describes in *Nickel and Dimed*, provide productive resources for combating this misconception. We ought always, in my estimation, to be educating students regarding the nature of military production, the environmental nightmare it leaves in its wake, and the military's role in keeping the world safe for corporate investment. Two videos in particular that I have found especially helpful in this regard are *Arms for the Poor*, on the U.S. arms trade, and *SOA: Guns and Greed*, on efforts to close the School of the Americas.[29] These videos provide a basis for thinking about the war on terrorism, how terror is defined, the role capitalist institutions play in creating terror, and about perspectives on what can be done to build a world without terror. There is no way to overestimate the importance of teaching students about the history and function of the armed forces: from its perpetuation of patriarchal ideas to its transformation of youthful energy into lethal force, from its continuous drain of thousands of billions of public dollars that might otherwise be used for social betterment to the military's brutal devastation of our lovely planet.[30]

There are many creative ways to connect humanities and science courses to the movement for global justice. Following a section on the international division of labor in which we focused on the displacement of rural workers, the creation of free-trade zones, and the role of military and paramilitary forces in maintaining worker subordination, students investigated what United Students Against Sweatshops <www.usasnet.org>, the Maquila Solidarity Network <www.maquila-solidarity.org>, and the Campaign for Labor Rights are doing—and what they as students might do on campus and in their communities—to support workers here and around the world. The key to making pedagogy relevant is to situate course material in the context of capitalist realities, to formulate assignments that help students become knowledgeable about these realities and, as importantly, to teach others what they know and to form organizations that can translate this knowledge into practice.[31]

PEDAGOGICAL AND ORGANIZATIONAL SKILLS

It is not enough to teach about how capitalism works or about the student, environmental, labor, and human rights organizations that are committed to building another kind of world society. We ought also to help students develop the skills necessary to teach and publicize what they have learned. These skills include how to use the Internet to do research and establish alliances, organize film series and hold public forums, do street theater and performance art, write editorials and short stories for publication in local newspapers, do radio and television interviews, give public addresses, stage public discussions, and organize marches and demonstrations.

Most students, like most citizens, are de-politicized and in large measure democratically disabled. Their participation in the work of shaping the development of society rarely goes beyond signing a petition, attending a benefit concert, voting every once and a while, if at all, and watching political races and results on television. A good portion of students, even students who are graduating, do not know the names of their state, county, and city representatives, let alone how to contact and express their views to them. Many students are not registered to vote, let alone aware of how to become critically informed citizens.[32] We should, of course, have no illusions regarding what can be changed through electoral politics. It remains crucial, nevertheless, to teach students how to intervene effectively at every level of power and to develop an understanding of democracy as something that people must actively do or risk having aggressively done to them.

We can also link students to campaigns for social justice, environmental protection, and human rights around the world. In my courses this has involved such things as establishing a campus branch of the national organization, Students United Against Sweatshops, participating with a local organization concerned with passing a living wage amendment in the city of Richmond, promoting awareness regarding the costs exacted by global militarism and linking these costs to what's happening to higher education.

These projects require students to engage theoretically *and* practically with the real problems of society and in so doing learn invaluable skills and develop invaluable capacities that cannot be learned or developed in the classroom alone. Students learn how to respond to the complex problems that arise as they seek to accomplish their goals. They learn to think on their feet and to act in response to changing circumstances. They learn how to work with others, a capacity that is, in our highly individualizing education system, no small accomplishment. They learn the importance of being responsible to those with whom they are working, to the communities in which they live, and to the larger human community to which they belong.

Over the past three years my students have studied indigenous perspectives on the environment, spirituality, human rights, and economic justice. We have focused on several contemporary issues through which these concerns intersect: displacement of indigenous populations, radioactive mining and waste disposal, and efforts on the part of the Mattaponi Indians, environmental activists, and concerned citizens to prevent the construction of a reservoir that would flood the Mattaponi river, one of the last unspoiled rivers in Virginia, home to rare and endangered animal species and setting of important archeological sites. Students not only studied this problem. They also produced literature and held information tables in the student center, arranged for speakers to address this issue on campus, circulated petitions, started a letter-writing campaign, and produced a twenty-minute video documentary on the reservoir controversy. By doing these things students not only helped to raise awareness about the Mattaponi and environmental issues generally, they also deepened their knowledge about the intimate relationships between politics, economics, and the environment.

Similarly, students studying Southwestern history and culture might connect with the Indigenous Environmental Network at <www.ienearth.org> to learn more about what the Hopi and Navajo are doing—and what they can do—to protect the lands in and around Black Mesa/Big Mountain in northern Arizona from being destroyed by mining companies. Research on nuclear power might be combined with research regarding what the Western Shoshone are doing—and what they can do—to protect the planet from both nuclear weapons development and capitalist colonization (see <www.shundahai.org>. Their contributions might include some of the things presented above in my discussion of the Mattaponi, as well as writing letters to congresspersons, forming solidarity organizations, and arranging a film series that addresses environmental, human rights, and social justice issues.

Students might combine their study of Latin American literature, art, music, and religion with projects that enable them to act in solidarity with citizens seeking to improve their conditions of life. So, for example, students might explore such web sites as Colombia Watch <www.colombiamobilization.org>, the Campaign for Labor Rights <http://www.summersault.com/~agj/clr/>, the American Friends Service Committee <http://afsc.org/>, and Global Exchange <www.globalexchange.org> to find campaigns to support. Global Exchange in particular offers a number of campaigns that students can quite easily and immediately support; among these are the Colombia campaign, which seeks to counter current U.S. policy of supplying the Colombian government with billions of dollars in primarily military aid and the Cuba campaign, which seeks to end the U.S. embargo, normalize U.S.-Cuban relations, and learn more about Cuba's development of alternative environmental, economic, and social policies.

For the past three years many of my students have attended meetings and organized events in support of the Richmond Coalition for a Living Wage. This coalition seeks to pass a living wage ordinance that would require the city to join over one hundred cities and municipalities nationwide that pay a living wage to all contracted and subcontracted employees. Raising awareness about the living wage movement is, of course, key to its passage. To this end my students have organized campus rallies, voter registration campaigns, and benefit concerts. There are many ways that humanities, social science, and life science professors can support this and other campaigns for social justice. Quite often organization members do not have the time, energy, or resources to research, organize, and present the information that is required to achieve their goals. With regard to a living wage campaign, professors who teach courses in sociology and statistics might require students to do research about the distribution of wealth, poverty, and unemployment rates. Students from an advertising course might develop slogans that can be used by living wage activists to educate the public about the living wage and to enlist support for its passage. Students in a journalism class might read and write about low-wage workers in the city. In these and many other creative ways, faculty and students can support campaigns for social justice, environmental protection, and human rights.

GETTING ENGAGED, GETTING INSPIRED

The key to making our work as scholars and teachers relevant to real-world politics is to expand the educational project beyond the classroom and to help our students become theoretically sophisticated and organizationally skillful activists in the movement for global justice. Engaged pedagogy, as outlined above, concretizes the study of the humanities and sciences in a way that brings that study to life, makes it relevant to the world in which we live, and offers students opportunities to participate in the work of transforming their world. What otherwise are presented as statistical abstractions, theoretical positions, and ethical perspectives (e.g., one out of five children are born into and live in poverty in this country; poverty is a consequence of uneven development; the U.S. Catholic Bishops condemn this reality as unjust) are grasped in their concrete nature, for example, in the stories told by workers that students interview for a video documentary. As students become more involved in the work of social change, their apathy begins to dissipate. They feel angry that the world is the way that it is, as well as inspired to make a difference. Student interest in course material also increases as their appreciation for its relevance to their own lives and to the real problems of society deepens. In addition, as more faculty and students become involved in social justice education, they sow the seeds for the creation of a genuinely counterhegemonic education, that is, education for the kind of transformation required to build a better world.

Though students are educated to support the status quo, I find that when they learn about what's going on and if—and this is the key to making pedagogy relevant—they are presented with concrete possibilities for how they can make a difference, many express a desire to "do the social justice thing." For the past three years I have given a talk at the end of the semester on the ethics of globalization to international business management students. Not surprisingly most students know little, if anything, about the human consequences of management decisions. What does surprise me, however, and happily so, are the number of students who express an interest in learning more about what they can do to act with concern for our shared future. This experience always reminds me that we ought not assume that any of our students—even business students!—are beyond hearing and responding to our words.

When the study of capitalism as both a general system and in its concrete manifestations is combined with stories that describe people and especially students working to build a better world, students often feel hopeful. As one young man expressed to me after watching the video *Showdown in Seattle,* "for the first time in my life," he believed that individuals matter, that we can accomplish great things if we put our heads, hearts, and hands together. Students who enter the classroom outraged that corporations are burning down forests, displacing indigenous people, exploiting children, and building weapons of mass destruction, almost always lack the research skills required to explain the structural causes of these outrages, to go from "it is a shame the world is in such a horrible state" to understanding how these phenomena are related to capitalist development and what they can do to address them. By teaching students how to investigate, analyze, and publicize global capitalist realities as well as by providing students with possibilities for taking action, we help our students develop the capacity to make the decision good Will Hunting makes and fight the powers he rejects.

Along these lines, we should also bear in mind that among the most important sources of inspiration for our students is our own example. Teaching about past and present individuals, organizations, and movements concerned with constructing a more just world inspires many students to commit themselves to this work. Perhaps nothing, however, is more inspiring to students than seeing that their professors don't just talk the talk. By participating in organizations and campaigns for social justice, showing up and speaking at demonstrations and marches, meeting with students to organize forums and rallies, in short, doing what we educate and encourage our students to do, we demonstrate by our actions that our interest in building a better world is not just academic. By marching side-by-side with students protesting against the School of the Americas at Ft. Benning, Georgia, working with students on a living wage campaign, and speaking at a student organized rally against militarism and for education, we teach by example the value of being involved in the work of improving our shared world.

ANOTHER WORLD IS POSSIBLE

There is much work to be done. We occupy a pivotal institutional position from which to contribute to the revolutionary transformation of global society. Every semester hundreds of new students enter our classrooms brimming with energy and ready, if not always eager, to learn. We should not forget that many revolutions were led by students who plotted overthrowing the powers that be on university campuses—and in cafés and pubs—around the world. Most of our students work and/or will be working in the future. The difference between a student who completes his or her degree, finds work, and supports the existing system and a student who commits himself or herself to building a humane alternative is often only a matter of the influence of a single professor whose ideas about, commitment to, and passion for social change inspire that student to participate in the struggle for human betterment.

We do ourselves and our students a service, moreover, by acknowledging, for lack of a better word, the spiritual dimension involved in taking up the fight for social justice. The fire for justice is lit not solely by learning about how capitalism works or about human suffering, though this knowledge is necessary to refine one's sensitivity to suffering and develop the capacities required to fight the forces that cause people to suffer. To light the fire for justice also requires that we attend to the profound human need to find a sense of purpose and meaning in life, purpose and meaning that may be, as we know and should let our students know, richly forged through the work of overcoming our alienation from each other, other living creatures, and the natural world. Students are especially hungry today to find purpose and meaning beyond that provided by professional ladder climbing and the rituals of mass consumption. We ought not shy away from making it known that a life devoted to working with others to build a humane society, a society guided by and supportive of the values of equality, beauty, affection, peace, and justice, is certainly a life worth living. We have, after all, everything to lose if we fail in this regard and a beautiful world community to gain if we succeed.[33]

NOTES

1. Marx and Engels, 1978: 477.

2. In *Global Village or Global Pillage* (1998), Jeremy Brecher and Tim Costello describe capitalist development thusly: "All over the world, people are finding themselves reduced from human beings with the right to speak, vote, organize, and act collectively—and entitled to food, housing, healthcare, and job security—to mere flotsam and jetsam of the labor market, surviving only by selling their labor on a short-term, contingent basis. Meanwhile their environment is being destroyed by an unrestrained global economy that poisons the air and water, turns plains into deserts, chops down forests, and disturbs the most basic balance on which all life depends through the uncontrollable emission of greenhouse gasses" (xx).

3. Greider, 388.

4. Speech available at <http://www.microsoft.com/billgates/speeches/2000/10–18digitaldividends.asp>. This transcript reads awkwardly because statements are designated as "questions." The conference provides a useful reminder that from the point of view of capitalist development poverty is primarily a problem because it limits the accumulation of capital.

5. One only need consider what Marx referred to as the "rosy dawn" of capitalist development, that is, the period of so-called primitive accumulation, to appreciate

capital's lengthy and still growing rap sheet of crimes against humanity, beginning with the destruction of indigenous populations around the world, the destruction of millions of Africans through slavery and the slave trade, the entire, as yet unfinished, history of interimperialist wars, as well as its systemic failure to satisfy the most basic of human needs for billions of human beings around the world. In the time it takes to read this essay, for example, assuming one hour, almost 1,500 children will die from lack of food while rice is burned to sustain "acceptable" profit rates.

6. Fishman, 37. Also see Jeffery Udin, "The Profits of Genocide," available at <www.zmag.org>.

7. The phrase "globalization from above" refers to capitalist-controlled development, that is, fundamentally antidemocratic control. For more on this and growing opposition to globalization from above, see Jeremy Brecher and Tim Costello, *Globalization from Below: The Power of Solidarity* (2000); Kevin Danaher, *Globalize This! The Battle against the World Trade Organization and Corporate Rule* (2000); Janet Thomas, *The Battle in Seattle: The Story Behind and Beyond the WTO Demonstrations* (2000); William K. Tabb, *The Amoral Elephant: Globalization and the Struggle for Social Justice in the Twenty-First Century* (2001).

8. Among some of the organizations working to construct a humane mode of global life are: ACERCA Action for Community and Ecology in the Rainforest of Central America, Art and Revolution, Campaign for Labor Rights, Center for Economic Justice, Earth First! San Francisco Bay Area, Ecumenical Program on Central America and the Caribbean (EPICA), Indigenous People's Alliance, Native Student's Association at the University of Toronto, Justice Action Coalition (Takoma Park, MD), Stop MAI Coalition, Western Australia (Australia), Gray Panthers (Washington, D.C.), jubilee2000, Burundi, AFL-CIO, 50 Years Is Enough Network, Jobs with Justice, Nicaragua Network, Global Exchange, Jubilee South Africa, Native Forest Network—Gulf of Maine, STITCH, Freedom from Debt Coalition (Philippines), INSAAF International (India), CIRPED (Senegal), LALIT (Mauritius), Global Justice Center (Brazil), Queers for Racial and Economic Justice, Youth Counsel (Macedonia), Development VISIONS (Pakistan), Alliance for Global Justice, Campaign for Labor Rights Mexico Solidarity Network, Alabama Artisans for Social Justice (Leesburg, AL), Alliance for Democracy (Washington, D.C.), Animal Rights New Jersey (Ewing, NJ), BankBusters (Boston/Cambridge, MA), Cal Poly Progressive Student Alliance (SLO CA), Center for Education and Social Action, New College of California (San Francisco, CA), college voice (Staten Island, NY), Committee for Global Justice (New York City, NY), Dominican Sisters of San Rafael, San Rafael, final outpost, bed and breakfast collective (Seattle, WA), Free Range Graphics (Washington, D.C.), FUNDACION SOLON (La Paz, Bolivia), Harm Reduction Institute (The AIDS Brigade), (Indianapolis, IN), the Ithaca Coalition for Global Justice (aka the SHARKS) (Ithaca, NY), Madison Fair Trade Action Alliance (Madison, WI), Maryland Food Collective (College Park, MD), Missouri Campus Greens (St. Joseph, MO), QueersAgainstCorporateGlobalization, Revolutionary Beats (Rockville, MD), Sisters of the Holy Name, St. John's Mobilization for Global Justice, and the Women's Environment and Development Organization.

9. Jeremy Brecher and Tim Costello, "Globalization from Below," available at <www.zmag.org>.

10. King, 1986: 290.

11. In "Of Gods and Mortals and Empire," William Rivers Pitt writes, "The numbers, and the locations were staggering. More than 100,000 people took to the streets of Sydney, Australia, a nation that has been solidly in Bush's corner on this matter. In Spain, another member of Bush's 'Coalition of the Willing,' several million protesters took over Madrid, Barcelona and 55 other cities. Italy, another Bush ally, saw over a million citizens take to the streets of Rome. Britain, Bush's go/no go ally of allies, saw over a million people protesting in London. Police there said it was the largest demonstration in that nation's long history. The Netherlands saw one hundred thousand protesters, as did Belgium and Ireland. There were protesters by the tens of thousands in Sweden, Switzerland, Scotland, Denmark, Austria, Canada, South Africa, Mexico, Greece, Russia and Japan. 500,000 protesters demonstrated in Germany, joined by three members of Gerhard Schroder's cabinet who defied their Chancellor by being there. It was the largest demonstration ever in post-war Germany. Another 500,000 people marched in Paris and 60 other French cities. The United States of America saw protests from coast to coast in over 100 cities nationwide. New York City was paralyzed by over a million marchers. San Francisco was taken over by well over 200,000 protesters, and Los Angeles saw over 100,000 people take to the streets. Thousands upon thousands joined them in Chicago, Philadelphia, Miami and Seattle. This was a gathering of ordinary citizens who came together in the streets of the world in an organized event that has no precedent in all of human history. They were brought together by a global word-of-mouth activism rooted entirely in the Internet. Were it not for this planetary connection, no such coordination could have ever taken place. Once upon a time, the world wide web was a realm dominated by dreams of profit and marketing. Those dreams have soured, leaving behind a marvelous network now utilized by very average people who can, with the click of a button, bring forth from all points on the compass a roaring deluge of humanity to stand against craven injustice and ruinous war" (12 February 2003). We can expect this trend of using the net for democracy to continue.

12. After learning about children stitching baseballs in Nicaragua, one of my students wrote the following: "Prof. Wood, I was wondering if you could find information on baseballs made in sweat shops? My father is on the board of a little league team in Chesterfield, Co. We're very close to the president and all involved. I don't want the children overseas to slave in a shop for our children of Chesterfield to have fun playing baseball! I don't know how much I can do, but if there are baseballs made in the USA, I can hopefully persuade them to switch to that brand. Let me know what you find" (email correspondence).

13. While the AFL-CIO demanded the Chinese government accept higher labor standards as a prerequisite to being admitted to the World Trade Organization, it did not and has not contributed financially to the formation of Chinese labor unions. Members of the largest U.S. labor union are in no small measure divided between internationalist, anticapitalist politics and protectionist, procapitalist politics.

14. Eagleton, 48.

15. Rosenthal, 111–112.

16. As a graduate student at Syracuse University I was a member of an organization called the Student Marxist Collective. While we published a critical journal with the aim of provoking the development of revolutionary theory and practice, we were in large measure working under the politically sterilizing influence of postmodernist dis-

courses and as a result had little if anything relevant to say regarding the actual conditions of labor and life among workers. We were, in the truest sense, "academic Marxists."

17. In the preface to A *Contribution to the Critique of Political Economy*, Marx writes, "In the social production of their existence, men inevitably enter into definite relations, which are independent of their will, namely relations of production appropriate to a given stage in the development of their material forces of production. The totality of these relations of production constitutes the economic structure of society, the real foundation, on which arises a legal and political superstructure and to which correspond definite forms of social consciousness. The mode of production of material life conditions the general process of social, political and intellectual life" (20–21).

18. See <http://www.inequality.org/factsfr.html> for more information.

19. The 1997 United Postal Service strike provides one of the most successful recent examples of workers fighting together without significant concern for personal identities. Gloria Harris, a thirty-nine-year-old single mother, related that "'We now feel more like brothers and sisters than co-workers,' she said, noting the diversity of the strikers, who, until the walkout, had often kept to their own racial or ethnic group. 'We all learned something about color. It comes down to green'" (cited in Brecher 1998: 361).

20. I am indebted to John Rosenthal for insights regarding the limits of identity politics.

21. The Richmond Coalition for a Living Wage does not formulate its goals in racial terms but rather in terms of providing a living wage for all working persons, even as the majority of workers in the city are black. Formulating this goal either as a matter of combating "racist" policies or extending "black rights" would be problematic both because three of the five city council members opposed to a living wage are black, including the mayor, and because the goal is to achieve this wage for all working people. The black city council members do not oppose a living wage because they are black, of course, but rather because they represent the interests of the business-owning class, a class that is composed, like the workforce, of individuals across the color spectrum. What is key, in this and other social justice movements, is to grasp the class dynamics that inform the articulation of racial, ethnic, national, gender, and sexual relations.

22. This force, it should be noted, has cost U.S. taxpayers more than 5 trillion dollars since 1980 and now that the ruling-class-led war on everything that terrifies them is in full swing, it will cost this much, it appears, every twelve years. For more on military spending see <www.warresisters.org>.

23. Michael Parenti puts it this way: the "important goal of U.S. policy is to make the world safe for the *Fortune 500* and its global system of capital accumulation. Governments that strive for any kind of economic independence or any sort of populist redistributive politics, that attempt to take some of their economic surplus and apply it to not-for-profit services that benefit the people—such governments are the ones most likely to feel the wrath of U.S. intervention or invasion"; for example, Guatemala under Arbenz; Chile under Allende; and Nicaragua under the Sandinistas (1995: 39).

24. For an excellent discussion of the changes that are taking place in regulation of global capital, see Behzad Yaghmaian.

25. Joseph E. Stiglitz (2002). Also see Joseph E. Stiglitz, *Globalization and Its Discontents* (2002).

26. Marx, 381.

27. Matt Damon and Ben Affleck.

28. Damon and Affleck were active in the living-wage movement at Harvard University.

29. Both videos are produced by Maryknoll World Productions, Maryknoll, N.Y. Bullfrog Films at <www.bullfrogfilms,com> and Labor Video Project at <www.igc.apc.org/lvpsf> are also useful sources for alternative videos.

30. End the Arms Race at <www.peacewire.org>, International Network on Disarmament and Globalization at <www.indg.org>, Nonviolence Web at <www.nonviolence.org>, and the War Resisters League at <www.warresisters.org> provide helpful information on militarism and how to end militarism. The War Resisters League provides an excellent guide to resisting the militarization of our planet entitled "Tools for Anti-Nuclear Organizing in an Age of Terror." Go to <www.warresisters.org/Reviving_Resistance.pdf>.

31. There are a number of Internet resources that can greatly aid in the work of learning about how capitalism operates and how to investigate problems related to capitalist development. These include Znet at <www.zmag.org>, 50 Years is Enough at <www.50years.org>, Corporate Watch at <www.corpwatch.org>, the Economic Policy Institute at <www.epinet.org>, and Global Exchange at <www.globalexchange.org>.

32. Congress.org at, that's right, <www.congress.org> provides an easy way for students to raise an electronic ruckus with their elected officials and to learn about electoral politics.

33. I want to thank Maria Christina Ramos for her suggestions regarding the style, organization, and content of this chapter.

WORKS CITED

Brecher, Jeremy, and Tim Costello. "Global Self-Organization from Below." <www.zmag.org>. 10 May 2002.

———. Globalization from Below: The Power of Solidarity. Boston: South End, 2000.

———. Global Village or Global Pillage. Boston: South End, 1998.

Brecher, Jeremy. Strike. Boston: South End, 1998.

Damon, Matt, and Ben Affleck. Good Will Script. <http:www.dailyscript.com/scripts/goodwillhunting.html>. 1997.

Danaher, Kevin, and Roger Burbach, eds. Globalize This! The Battle against the World Trade Organization and Corporate Rule. Monroe, Maine: Common Courage, 2000.

Eagleton, Terry. The Illusions of Postmodernism. Cambridge, Mass.: Blackwell, 1996.

Fishman, Ted C. "Making a Killing: The Myth of Capital's Good Intentions." Harper's (August 2002): 33–41.

Gates, Bill. Speech. <http://www.microsoft.com/billgates/speeches/2000/10–18digital-dividends.asp>. 18 October 2000.

Greider, William. One World, Ready or Not. New York: Touchstone, 1997.

King, Martin Luther, Jr. *A Testament of Hope*. Ed. James M. Washington. San Francisco: HarperSanFrancisco, 1986.

Marx, Karl. *A Contribution to the Critique of Political Economy*. Trans. Dietz Verlag. Moscow: Progress Publishers, 1970.

———. *Capital: A Critique of Political Economy*. Vol. 1. Trans. Ben Fowkes. New York: Vintage: 1977.

———. *The Marx-Engels Reader*. Trans. Robert C. Tucker. New York: Norton, 1978.

Parenti, Michael. *Against Empire*. San Francisco: City Lights Books, 1995.

Pitt, William Rivers. "Of Gods and Mortal and Empire." 22 February, 2003. <www.truthout.org>.

Rosenthal, John. "Hegel's Decoder: A Reply to Smith's 'Reply.'" *Historical Materialism: Research in Critical Marxist Theory* 9 (Winter 2001): 111–151.

Shalom, Stephen R. "The State of the World." <http://www.zmag.org/ZSustainers/ZDaily/1999-09/14shalom.htm>. 14 September 1999.

Stiglitz, Joseph E. "The Globalizer Who Came in from the Cold: Interview with Greg Palast." *Alternet*. 19 March 2002. <www.alternet.org>.

———. *Globalization and its Discontents*. New York: Norton, 2002.

Tabb, William K. *The Amoral Elephant: Globalization and the Struggle for Social Justice in the Twenty-First Century*. New York: Monthly Review, 2001.

Thomas, Janet. *The Battle in Seattle: The Story Behind and Beyond the WTO Demonstrations*. Golden, Col.: Fulcrum, 2000.

Udin, Jeffrey. "The Profits of Genocide." 1996. <www.zmag.org>.

Yaghmaian, Behzad. "Globalization and the State: The Political Economy of Global Accumulation and its Emerging Mode of Regulation." *Science and Society* 62.2 (Summer 1998): 241–265.

Yates, Michael. "Poverty and Inequality in the Global Economy." *Monthly Review* 55.9 (February 2004) <http://www/monthlyreview.org/0204yates.htm>.

Zinn, Howard. *A People's History of the United States*. San Francisco: Harper Perennial, 2001.

CHAPTER THIRTEEN

FEMINISM(S) AND THE LEFT:
A DISCUSSION WITH LINDA MARTÍN ALCOFF

LAURA GRAY-ROSENDALE

IN THIS BOOK MANY OF THE AUTHORS HAVE FRUITFULLY INCORPORATED GENDER issues—alongside concerns about racism, colonialism, discrimination, and troubling constructions of disability as well as the problems of environmental degradation that now face us—into their visions for leftist coalition-building. However, many of us who engage in feminist theory and political activist work on behalf of women may be more than somewhat concerned that issues of gender could be eclipsed by other leftist political agendas. Michele Barrett's *Women's Oppression Today: Problems in Marxist Feminist Analysis* and Lise Vogel's *Woman Questions: Essays for a Materialist Feminism* among other books have offered clear overviews of the rhetorical and philosophical problems that have historically kept feminists and leftists apart. As we have witnessed, too frequently gender becomes an afterthought, an add-on to the central political issues, something that can be trotted out when it is especially convenient or suits other, seemingly more immediate political aims.

This has happened for a wide variety of reasons. In order to get at such critical concerns, I thought it important to close the book by including a discussion with a well-known scholar and friend who has worked hard throughout her career to articulate relationships between theory and practice, Linda Martín Alcoff. In her activist work Alcoff has repeatedly attempted to build coalitions that include gender as a key term while also recognizing the important intersections between gender and other forms of oppression. In point of fact, as Alcoff's work advocates, gender may be the most significant of such terms since it readily impacts all of us doing work on the left.

In the 1990s I had the pleasure of watching Alcoff's scholarly and activist work in action as we fought together to challenge violence against women occurring on the Syracuse University campus. At that time I was like some of the leftist students we meet in our classes today—an outspoken undergraduate English major with an interest in feminist philosophy, one committed to political change and rights for all women. Alcoff was an untenured Assistant Professor of Philosophy, one unwilling to forego her political aims in the face of university bureaucracy. Instead Alcoff was always working hard to make her activism inform her research, committing herself to political work on campus in ways that few other faculty members were willing to do. We were both vocal on campus about being survivors of sexual assault and about the importance of fighting for the rights of all survivors.

Besides acting as an intellectual mentor to me during those early years and the many years since then, our paths crossed at many political events throughout my undergraduate and graduate studies. Each year we would meet at Take Back the Night marches, each of us speaking publicly and loudly about our own experiences, about various incidents of sexual assault, about the silencing of survivor discourses, about forcing university administrators to take action. When we first met, there were no support groups available for survivors on most college campuses. This troubled us both greatly. I was a student who saw other young politically motivated survivors in pain, struggling alone. Alcoff knew other faculty members, staff, and employees across the university who had nowhere to turn. As a result, we worked together with several other survivors to create Women For Women, a campus-based support group run by survivors for survivors. Eventually support groups for male survivors were formed as well. Our sense was that some of the most efficacious political strides for survivors would not be made through conventional therapeutic models but rather through collective action, through the communal theorization of our own experiences. This was critical leftist work, collective struggle by women on our own behalves to challenge our own oppression.

During this time the number of reported assaults on our campus seemed to be rising to astronomical proportions. We knew that the incidences of sexual assault were not necessarily growing—but that women were finally beginning to speak about them, sometimes in fits and starts. We witnessed survivors starting to talk loudly at public meetings, utilizing guerilla tactics such as plastering posters on bus kiosks that named perpetrators, engaging in informal, politically-oriented conversations in small groups, and using graffiti as a form of public protest in hallways and women's bathrooms. Harried administrators attempted to do damage control while network television news program producers, in an effort to boost ratings, hovered like vultures, trying to entice shell-shocked survivors to come onto their shows and tell their stories.

In *The Color of Rape: Gender and Race in Television's Public Spheres* Sujata Moorti rightly suggests that the representations of sexual violence that dominate the mainstream American media often reproduce as well as depend upon carefully constructed sexist and racist narratives about rape. Therefore it was not surprising to us that in our work with survivors we too often found young women were afraid to speak about their experiences. Such survivors knew only too well how their identities would be framed and taken up by the mainstream media. In addition, they were scared to press charges within a legal system that seemed to favor the perpetrator at every level. Further, they feared the uphill fight against the university's desire to keep violence against women on the campus quiet so as not to draw media attention and ultimately affect enrollments.

We believed then as we do now that the voices of survivors of sexual assault are critical voices on the left, voices that have the power to challenge dominant, oppressive discourses. In "Survivor Discourse: Transgression or Recuperation?" we argued that survivor speech is

> transgressive first of all in simply challenging conventional speaking arrangements, arrangements in which women and children are not authoritative, where they are often denied the space to speak or be heard, and where their ability to interpret men's speech and to speak against men—to contradict or accuse men—has been severely restricted. (204)

We also felt that survivor speech "presumes objects antithetical to the dominant discourse," such that terms like *father rapist* would challenge the rules of dominant discourses about what constitutes sexual assault and who gets to define the term itself.

Many years later, with many miles now separating us, we both continue our activist work on behalf of survivors of sexual assault. Alcoff is now an internationally known scholar—still at Syracuse University—who remains one of the most well-respected political activists working on any college campus in the United States. Years later I find myself an Associate Professor of English at Northern Arizona University, serving on a community-based Sexual Assault Task Force, now working with young student activists who—like I once did—plan leftist political events that feature the disruptive voices of survivors. Likewise, in my service work I have helped to establish protocols for reporting assaults on campus and been actively involved in starting local, campus-based survivor support groups.

In our various kinds of feminist activist work Alcoff and I continue to maintain that survivor discourses furnish a window into a complex nexus of issues—oftentimes concerns related to race, ethnicity, class, disability, environment, and gender—that can be viewed simultaneously as well as in light of various institutions and privileged ideologies. As we have witnessed, survivors can also put useful pressure upon administrators to take up significant questions about how to better protect women and support women's attempts to seek legal counsel and more viable therapeutic alternatives.

Often in this kind of political work, both the sorts we engaged in years ago as well as now, we have run into major roadblocks dealing with lawyers, administrators, and other sorts of officials. This was and is to be expected. However, as we have been involved in such political activism as well as other kinds of gender-based political work, we realized and experienced that the silencing of gender issues can emerge from some unexpected, more troubling locations. Not only does gender get sidelined by such typically conservative factions but frequently the issue of gender is pushed aside by groups espousing critical political rhetoric, rhetoric that possesses many aims with which we agree. Unfortunately, in both of our experiences, leftist discourse has at times functioned as one more discourse among these. At critical moments when violence against women students, workers, and professionals might have been seen as an issue of great importance to fellow radicals in our activist work, class struggle has sometimes instead been made to stand over and against gender struggle. In the case of one young woman who attended our support group (raped repeatedly over the years by her older cousin)—who identified herself as a lower-class and African American woman—for instance, we believed that class, race, and gender had intersected in powerful ways to force her into silence. And though we saw these forces of oppression as all equally critical to examine and fight against, we felt that there was too little work being done among leftists generally to articulate the commonalties—in a case like hers—between class and gender oppression. We also sensed that too little work was being done to understand how gender can impact other issues such as ethnicity, race, age, the environment, family structure, and disability.

Historically, in both our own experiences as well as in the various scholarly circles in which we have traveled, we have seen that feminists and leftists can experience real difficulties articulating common goals. Instead, sometimes we seem to be working at cross-purposes. For instance, despite the fact that much has changed to alter issues of gender oppression related to survivors since the 1990s—laws that allow for victim compensation, protect a survivor's past sexual history from entering into legal proceedings, and broaden rights for domestic abuse survivors—as well as greater numbers of grassroots groups located in both actual and virtual communities, fractures between feminists and leftists remain. These fractures sometimes make it nearly impossible to talk about the insidious ways in which gender, race, class, and other sorts of oppression collude with and serve to reinforce one another. They also make it hard for us to work together against gender-based oppression in creative, imaginative ways, ways that might seem unorthodox but are politically efficacious.

In the following interview with Linda Martín Alcoff I invite her to speak in more detail about issues such as these that now confront feminists working on the left. She discusses the current state of feminist studies in the United States. Alcoff then explains how antifeminist rhetoric among women, in mainstream television, and by people on the right has been used to further victimize survivors of sexual assault as well as to undermine feminist goals altogether. Alcoff goes on to describe how she views the history of the specific relationship between the women's movement and the left, the ways in which this relationship has played itself out in her own life and scholarship, and what problems, to her mind, have emerged around our attempts at coalition-building. Alcoff concludes by examining the ways in which we might build more productive relationships between feminism(s) and the left. In doing so, Alcoff encourages feminists to reconsider our approaches—what we understand to be "valid" feminist praxis. She also encourages all leftists to see the value of adopting a feminist agenda. Alcoff illuminates how we might deal with leftist politics in productive ways and outlines a positive future for coalition-building, including the critical role of feminism on the left. As such, Alcoff's words offer the most fitting sort of conclusion to this volume—clearly articulating some of the crucial issues that face all left intellectuals and activists as we look toward the future.

> LAURA: This is a complex question. I wonder how you would characterize the current state of feminism(s) in the United States. What do you think are the most significant fractures and problems that are dominating our current landscape?

> LINDA: It is not so difficult to see what the current state of feminism is, but it is certainly difficult to diagnose the most significant problems that are holding it back. The current state is one of paradox: feminism is steadily growing in influence throughout the culture even while it is under increasing attack—and increasingly effective attacks—by powerful elements in the government, the media, and the culture industry. That is, to the extent that feminism can be defined as the belief that women have equal rights over their life choices as men do, and that women are as capable as men in every sphere of life, each successive generation of women shows more and more evidence of holding these beliefs. Women students now outnumber men students in higher education, and women are entering the professions, especially law and medicine, in steadily rising numbers. The high divorce rate which antifeminists blame on feminism may be due to feminism but in a way they won't admit: women are divorcing men when they are in unhappy marriages more often now because we can more easily support ourselves and our children than in the years before equal employment laws gave women any protection against discrimination on the job. Thus, women are widely coming to reject sexist views about our incompetence and inferiority and more often refusing to accept adulterous or abusive husbands. The changes in women's views about ourselves have a necessary impact on the views our children have about women and men, thus influencing the next generation.

But this gradualist cultural evolution is being attacked on many fronts. The media has defined feminism as a victimology and thus represented women who simply believe in their own competence as antifeminists rather than feminists. Thus antifeminists are trying, and often succeeding, to claim that they are the true feminists because they refuse to label women as victims. They characterize the movement against sexual violence as promoting victimization, although our struggle, on behalf of which you and I have both fought, has been to end women's victimization. Instead of supporting this struggle, antifeminists belittle the epidemic of sexist violence women of all ages face, repudiate affirmative action as coddling, attack cultural analysis and criticism as the imposition of political correctness on freedom of thought, and insist that the true victims are white males who are made to feel guilty about their "natural" aggression. The word *feminism* thus continues to carry negative connotations, as it always has; it is just that the specific connotations adapt to the times to maintain their efficacy.

Also important is the erosion of women's reproductive rights, which has a multiplied effect. Women who are forced into motherhood without having the economic and emotional resources or support that motherhood requires are then often bound into a life dictated by the necessary strategies for short-term survival. Their ability to participate in community-building, political leadership, union-organizing, or other social reforms is severely curtailed. Feminism has maintained a slim majority of support in the general population for legal abortion, but has been unable to mobilize this support in order to force medical schools to teach how to perform abortions or to provide free birth control in the schools or to have a full range of reproductive services available to poor women, to rural women, or simply to women in every state.

Thus, the problems here are legion. The culture industry has tried to co-opt feminism to the extent it can sell women running shoes at the same time that it has commodified and exploited women's sexuality for tremendous profit and pushed sexist representations of women to new lows in "The Bachelor" shows and the "The Man Show." The new "cool" is to be "politically incorrect" about women. There is no mainstream equivalent to these shows that promotes feminism: all women are given are the cable networks that give us chick flicks (movies about relationships since women are the ones whose job it is to make relationships work) and fashion advice.

If we look at the ideological landscape, there seems to me to be two critical sites where feminism needs improvement, and both have to do with the domination of a liberal, rather than a left, approach. First, the public face of feminism has all but given up a moral voice. Instead, arguments for reproductive rights and employment opportunities, for example, are all made in the name of freedom of choice, that is, freedom of choice within a private sphere understood as contrasted to the properly public sphere of government regulation. This is because the Republicans have basically won the battle to portray proactive government policy—with the exception of the military, of course—as guilty until proven innocent. Because the private sphere of individual choice is thought to be the only proper arena for moral decisions, liberal feminists cannot make their demands from a moral argument, except to invoke the morality of individualism. But this is both inadequate and unnecessary, as well as wrong! It has been proven woefully inadequate to counter the moral righteousness of the anti-abortion activists with a liberal claim about choice: if one truly believes that abortions are *always* immoral, one will be motivated to thwart them under any conditions or risk losing one's sense of oneself as a moral person.

The kernel of truth in the right-wing Christian movements is that the masses of people want to be moral, and want to believe they are moral, and want a sphere of their life dictated not by selfishness, convenience, or avarice, as the market promotes, but by morality. Liberals have made a huge mistake in ceding the moral ground to the right, and liberal feminist academics have sped this along by trashing moralism or any discourse of the "should." I am not advocating that we opportunistically use moral arguments because that will appeal to people, but that we acknowledge that our best arguments are moral ones, and that we be up-front about it. Religion can be left in the sphere of private choice, but morality cannot be sequestered to the private sphere without contradiction, since the very argument for privatizing morality is itself an argument based on giving the highest moral valuation to individual autonomy. Here, I think a left social analysis is much more persuasive than the liberal one. Liberals believe that we can keep the government out of the business of legislating morality, but, as Marx argued, governments and economic forms of organization are what make morality possible, and will make some moral choices possible and others impossible or nearly so. Since the promotion of some moral value is impossible to avoid, what we need to do is make this process democratic and accountable, rather than trying to avoid it altogether.

LAURA: What critical examples of gendered labor divisions do you see as being part of this landscape as well?

LINDA: Yes, this is a really important issue. The second critical site I would mention actually concerns the sphere of gendered labor. The primary reason why women remain so far behind men economically is because of the gendered division of jobs and the devaluation of those jobs deemed female. With around 80% of women working in jobs associated as female—such as sewing, caring, healing, teaching, and cleaning—there will never be pay equity until either these job descriptions are radically revised or the true value and difficulty of these jobs is recognized in their pay scale. The liberal plan to open up the professions to women is having an impact only on a small minority of middle- and upper-middle-class women. In contrast, workers in nursing homes and daycare centers—two of the sites where women without degrees can readily obtain jobs—are generally paid so low that they will qualify for government assistance if they are doing the jobs as single moms. These jobs are as dangerous as coal mining—nursing home workers are routinely bit and infected with bacteria, and must lift large amounts of weight on a constant basis—and as difficult as any factory manager's job—can you imagine caring for fifteen two- and three-year-olds for ten or eleven hours a day, five days a week?

Here, the left is sometimes as big of a problem as the liberals in redressing such difficulties that millions of women face. The left continues to tend toward a class reductionism that undercuts its ability to develop the kind of cultural analysis one needs to understand a gendered ideology operating to structure the work force. Thus mainstream feminist activists who are almost always liberal are focusing on the upper strata of women workers, and leftists are focusing on an undifferentiated class, leaving the majority of women workers out. I would make two exceptions here: in the academy, there has emerged a tremendous amount of excellent research and analysis on gender and work, such as on the ways in which transnationals make use of sexist ideology and socialization patterns to increase levels of exploitation, and on how immigrant sweatshop workers are fighting back. Second, a significant sector of the labor movement has also caught on to the ways in which race, sex, and immigration status operate to produce what are called "ascriptive class segments," which dictate one's position within the working class. Some unions have thus begun targeted organizational drives and focused on developing contract specifics that can redress some of the existing hierarchies of pay among workers.

So I would suggest that these two arenas—the need for a moral discourse of feminism and the importance of addressing the reforms needed where most women actually work—are the most critical sites for work if we want feminism to advance beyond some of its current stalemates.

LAURA: These are not easy, comfortable arenas for many intellectuals who consider themselves feminists or leftists. This may be why too little work has been done in these areas. But your call to us to do so will be crucial to the future of feminism altogether. We simply cannot afford to rest in our intellectual cocoons anymore. Now I want to ask you a more specific question related to the state of feminism(s). How would you describe the current and historical relationship between the women's movement and the left?

LINDA: As you know, this question, of course, depends heavily on how we define the "women's movement" and "the left." Both have been too often located in white majority groups and never in minority-majority organizations. Most scholars of the history of the women's movement, for example, still tend to locate it as a white women's movement, thus neglecting the black women struggling within SNCC or the Urban League, for example, on issues and programs that address women's and girl's empowerment, or the Latinas of Mecha who put fighting sexism on the agenda of the organization. Such "minority" groups are not the primary ones understood as part of the left in this country either. Moreover, we often don't include within our understanding of the women's movement the labor organizations that are struggling for the empowerment of traditionally female-associated jobs, like nursing or teaching for example, even though these organizations reach out to hundreds of thousands of working-class women, helping them to become organizers and leaders, and engaging in collective struggle to demand a fair valuation of such derided jobs as nursing home care or day care. Instead, the media focuses on feminists who are working to integrate the elite golf clubs.

And it is precisely because of these mistaken characterizations that good working relations among groups, and the collective understanding about how our various agendas might be united, is held back. So the first thing we have to do is rethink how we sometimes think about *where* "the left" and "feminism" exist. I think we need to look simply at where women are engaging in struggle, even if it is not in an organization devoted solely to women's concerns, in order to make a fair assessment of where feminism is at these days. And similarly, we need to look at where challenges to the current economic hierarchy are taking place—wherever these are—to make a fair assessment of the left.

LAURA: You are saying that we need to look beyond leftist and feminist groups and their practices, then? In other words, our best models for effective political change may be emerging from places that we are in danger of overlooking precisely because they do not espouse our politics?

LINDA: Yes, academics sometimes want to justify ignoring such a broader range of groups and activities on the grounds that these groups do not have a left or feminist articulation of their aims. They may not be self-identified as leftist or feminist, but this does not mean that they are not quite aware in sometimes very sophisticated and detailed ways about who is in charge in this country, how this group exerts its will over the population, and what it will take to make social change. I strongly believe in the importance of theory and the need for some people to spend some serious amount of time doing theory; I am, after all, a philosopher. But I also believe that political theory can be found in many places beyond the books named as such. And not just political aspirations; I do mean theory here. For example, look at Horace Campbell's book *Rasta and Resistance* and Tony Bogues's new book *Black Heretics, Black*

Prophets on the black radical tradition in which he draws from Ida B. Wells and popular cultural movements.

So in this sense feminism and the left can be traced through organizations but can also be thought of as a social movement or cultural revolution well beyond any institutional location. The women's movement, in any case, has always been comparatively decentralized as a point of principle. In thinking about the important question you raise—on the relationship between feminism and the left—we will have to give a variegated answer contextualized to *which* left and *which* feminism, and explore a variety of relationships between a variety of locations of class and gender struggles.

> LAURA: I agree with you completely. So, let me situate this question within a very particular, local context. How has your own relationship between feminism(s) or the women's movement and the left played itself out in your own life and work? How has it impacted you personally, politically?

> LINDA: I believe my experience is quite representative of many women of my generation who became politically active in the early 1970s, having been profoundly influenced and radicalized by the social turmoil and collective action we witnessed as we were growing up in the 1950s and 1960s. As soon as I left home, I became involved in both feminist and broader left-wing activity.

When I left my small town in Florida and went to college in 1973, there was a real mass movement still, with many different kinds of organizations on and around the campus. Much of what we called the "organized left," which meant the variety of Marxist-based groups, was castigating the women's movement in those days as "bourgeois feminism." I remember many long arguments we had over whether women such as Golda Meir or Indira Gandhi could be oppressed, or whether the struggle for women's rights so formulated was in essence a struggle for a bigger piece of the pie at the capitalist table. The arguments were about whether bourgeois women suffered sexism, in which case sexism was not reducible to class. Leftist men from the New Left often thought that the only women who were oppressed were working-class women, so there was no reason to focus specifically on women's rights. Feminism was also termed "bourgeois" because it was not calling for the overthrow of the state, and instead it was focused mainly on reformist demands like legal abortion and equal pay. And self-defined feminists were engaged in a lot of local work around the creation of women's healthcare centers with a feminist orientation toward educating and empowering women in regard to our reproductive lives, or battered women's shelters or rape crisis centers to provide a safe space for women suffering from the so-called random male violence that still dominates the news.

These reform efforts at institution-building were responses to the very real crises that were happening in our communities, but some of the privileged student leftists, both white and of color, looked down their noses at such work for not being radical enough. While these leftists were critiquing us in meetings, these feminist college students or ex-students were going into working class communities to provide critical services that no one else would provide.

I don't mean to disparage the critique here too much—one could argue, rightfully, that the state *still* does not provide such services in most communities. Feminist reform efforts can become like the tradition of women's volunteerism—serious work done without much recompense to clean up the ills of the current patriarchal oligarchy. Indeed, our focus must be changing the nature of the power structure in this country or we will be forever working to clean up the disastrous effects of low wages, underemployment, materialist greed, and other problems endemic to the current social system. But male leftists were too often in those days belittling of feminist reformist work, and the charge of "bourgeois feminism" was certainly not applicable to most local women's groups who were not devoting their time to integrating the elite golf clubs. Moreover, in the work accomplished by the Feminist Women's Health Centers, the Rape Crisis Shelters, and the Shelters for Battered Women, feminists were retrieving women from an oblivion of oppression who could then become more fully active in leading their families and communities. Leftists used to ask where the women were when they called meetings; if they had opened their eyes, they would have seen that the women were at home struggling with the difficulties of daily life in a woman-hating society.

LAURA: Absolutely. So where did you choose to put your activist energies during this time?

LINDA: Well, at that time there was still quite a lot of overt sexism on much of the left: masculinist leadership styles, a gendered division of labor in the organizations, and campus programming by the self-identified left rarely focused on gender oppression. I was on the Advisory Board of the Center for Participant Education, a free university such as were springing up in several places around the country, where the goal was to make the intellectual resources of the university free for people from the community. I was a campus activist and assumed that I had been invited onto the Board to help run the organization, but I mainly was asked to do filing, answer the phones, and put up posters. The only program I was asked to organize was for International Women's Day (I brought three different female left-wing leaders to campus). I also used to sell left-wing pamphlets regularly on campus at a table set up in the student center, and among those that we sold were pamphlets from the socialist republic of Albania that talked about the glorious contribution women could make to socialism in reproducing the next generation of socialist workers. At that time, that was the sorry state of the left.

In this context it was understandable that many women who were galva-nized by a dawning recognition of women's oppression began to drop out of male-lead groups and joined, or created, feminist groups, bookstores, health-care centers, and abortion rights organizations, where they could avoid having daily arguments about the legitimacy of these demands and where they could avoid having to deal with sexist men. These were probably mostly white women but not all were white or middle-class: there was a variety of class politics rep-resented in various feminist groups, for example, between NARAL (National Abortion Right Action League), which at that time took a very narrow focus on maintaining legal abortion, to R2N2 (the Reproductive Right National Net-work), which had a broader agenda of reproductive rights so they could fight against sterilization abuses of poor women of color and the right to have chil-dren as well as the right not to. Rather than lumping all the feminist groups together, we need to do a class analysis.

Although I was active in some of these feminist groups, I myself moved toward more broad-based organizations whose announced aims were radical social change in every arena of U.S. society. I wanted to have a sense that I was engaged in a larger struggle against interrelated problems. I was very angry about U.S. imperialism in Central America, which moved straight from Vietnam to El Salvador using non-U.S. ground personnel to avoid an antidraft movement at home. And I was very motivated to fight the antiblack racism in the South where I had grown up, a racism one could feel every day. I was also concerned about class exploitation, and these concerns no doubt had to do with my own particular history—being related to poor rural southerners, being half-Latina and connected to a country with its own legacy of U.S. imperial domination (Panama), having had the experience of being not-quite-white within a fam-ily where there were some white racists, and having grown up during the period when the ugliest Jim Crow one could imagine transitioned into a partial inte-gration with limited results.

But the left-wing organizations that I was drawn toward took the posi-tion that women's oppression had to be dealt with *now*. While some radical groups in those days believed that raising issues of racism and sexism were "divi-sive" if one wanted to focus on uniting the working class, and we needed to basically wait until "after the revolution," there were also groups that argued for making the struggle against the oppression of women a central feature of all struggles. And in one group, for example, the leader of the entire southern organization was a white working-class woman, Lyn Wells, a former SNCC and SSOC organizer, and the leader in Atlanta where I was living at this time was an African American working-class woman, Betty Bryant, who came out of the Mead Strike. These women were very clear about the need to oppose sexism and criticize masculinist styles of leadership, and this was the leadership that the men of the organization had to answer to. This demonstrated to me that the organization took "the woman question" quite seriously.

Like many other young feminists, I was attracted to the left organizations that had broken with the traditional Communist Party USA, which had historically been the largest socialist organization and which had played such a powerful role especially in the 1930s in organizing for unemployment benefits and for racial solidarity, because I was disturbed by the CP's uncritical support of the Soviet Union. The USSR, it seemed to many of us, did not pursue women's equality very vigorously except to get women into the workforce, thus doing nothing about the double day the women then faced or about male chauvinist attitudes and lack of participation in housework, and they also did not push female political leadership in a significant way (Cuba was a better example, we believed, but few of the satellite socialist states in Eastern Europe seemed any better on issues of gender than the USSR).

In the 1970s and early 1980s, at least some of the radical groups were trying to engage in serious large-scale efforts that would unite labor and antiracist and community-based poor people's struggles into a common agenda. Many, many mistakes were made in this effort which we should now learn from (there is a great new book by Max Elbaum, *Revolution in the Air*, finally doing just this). But most important was that some of these radical groups, unlike others then and now, were trying to break out of their political marginalization. They were more interested in widespread political mobilization than maintaining the absolutely pure "correct line." Such groups were well worth our energy and commitment, despite their shortcomings.

> LAURA: These are very useful examples, I think, ones that really contextualize the complexity of feminists' historical relationship to leftist work. I also believe that coalition-building across leftist interests remains one of our greatest problems and poses some of our greatest possibilities for political change. What particular problems do you think have emerged around our various attempts at coalition-building along these lines—in both activist and scholarly circles?

> LINDA: I would say that there are two main problems that have stymied coalition building: (1) sexism on the self-identified left, and (2) a co-optation of feminist demands toward less radical reforms. Let me speak about both of these in turn.

Progressive and socialist groups have been largely unable to theoretically articulate a persuasive account of the oppression of women or the steps needed for our liberation, and have not spent much effort at doing so. The standard accounts of the past—Engels, most especially—have few adherents today. There has always been, and today there is a strong revival, of what we used to call class reductionism: the idea that class exploitation causes women's oppression and therefore we don't need to talk about sexism directly. Mobilizations around class issues will take care of sexism. As you know, very few feminists believe this, for one thing because of the example of socialist states (and there are of course arguments about whether they were ever really socialist, but I'll put that aside) in which women's condition was not improved much if at all. And most of the theorists who have been working on class have realized that one cannot approach class as an undifferentiated grouping—class position is always mediated by race and gender, the work force is totally stratified by race and gender, and thus we need a much more sophisticated analysis that will be responsive to the particular conditions of a former slave society and a patriarchal society that adapted itself to capitalism.

Feminist theorists and activists have had two very positive influences on the left today. First, they have persuaded most people that organizational structure is a political issue and in particular a gendered issue. In other words, the sexism of an organization may be found not in its mission statement but in its organizational style. Certain organizational leadership styles value male abilities over female and render women's leadership styles invisible. So women may be the absolute backbone of an organization and receive no credit for being so (see Karen Sachs' excellent work on this). The contribution of radical feminism and lesbian feminism has been especially important in experimenting with different forms of organization, developing consensus models, small groups, affinity groups, nonhierarchical structures, and promoting decentralization. The current movement against global capitalism has clearly learned a great deal from this about the benefits of decentralization and small group efforts, and their successes in closing down parts of cities during meetings of the IMF and World Bank have been directly due to learning these feminist lessons. Decentralization works brilliantly to maintain a project because there is no "head" to cut off, no "body" that will wither when the head is cut. Multiple sites of struggles with multiple styles, methods, focal points, and even political priorities is a strength, not a weakness. But seeing this requires that we attack directly the old style male aggression of internal competition for leadership, and call it out for what it is.

Also, feminists focused on concrete practice and personal life where sexism is often so manifest that women are barred from effective participation because of their unequal burdens in the home. Sometimes, of course, this political critique of the personal sphere became excessively narrow, as if there was only one right way for a household to be organized or for people to act, dress, and even speak. This spawned the original critique of Political Correctness, which was an internal self-critique within the left before the right-wing ever took this up and distorted it. But the original claim that "the personal is political" had a core of important truth in pointing out that men who espoused social justice and never did the cooking and cleaning at home were politically bankrupt, and that our practice communicates our theory better than theory alone ever can.

Thus I credit these radical feminist efforts at organizational reform and political analysis of the personal with having a wide influence that has yet to be acknowledged. Today in the antiwar movements the affinity group is the norm, and there is almost always an effort to pay attention to process and not just outcomes. Even the right-wing militia movement has discovered the advantages of radical decentralization and small groups! To some extent this is just old-style anarchism in the tradition of the Narodniki in Russia or the Bakuninists in France, but this tradition has been adopted and adapted as well as developed and used more effectively by women's groups than anyone else in the recent past. There have been the Lesbian Avengers and the Guerilla Girls, who avoided having public leaders and instead maintained their anonymity, and many, many smaller local-based groups who are experimenting with truly democratizing styles of work. The point is that these are all lessons that some of the left has learned from women's groups and need to learn more of if they want to transcend the sexism within.

In regard to class reductionism, I think the theoretical contributions of feminist social theorists and social scientists have been very important and have become very influential. What this work has shown is that, although women's oppression is certainly beneficial to capitalism, still, it cannot be explained entirely in reference to the economic forces of capitalism (as if it were an ideal type), but needs to be explained also in reference to a precapitalist sexual division of labor. It is not clear, e.g., that the so-called family wage, wherein women workers are paid less than men on the theory that their wages are not supporting a family, is necessary to capitalism; in so-called free enterprise zones like the maquilladores, we are seeing women workers hired first and given more cash income than their male partners. Capitalists are trying here not to overcome sexism but use it for their own ends once again, viewing women workers as more pliable, less resistant to bad working conditions, and more vulnerable because of their family obligations. Class reductionists can neither adequately explain these patterns nor propose ways to address them: we need an analysis that will make sexism and racism and colonialism as important as class in understanding current forms of oppression.

I would also suggest that the ideological power of the nuclear, patriarchal family which is enjoying such a comeback cannot be explained entirely in terms of its functionality for capitalism alone. Capitalism is always embedded in specific cultural and historical conditions. There are some real benefits for working-class men which have to be faced such that their opposition to sexism will not be entirely supported by their class position. In academic work many feminists have consequently turned to explorations of history and culture to unravel the seeds of sexism; I constantly hear some leftist men saying "where's class?"

This question usually indicates an implicit class reductionism and their inability to think about what class is in these more complex ways.

LAURA: Earlier you mentioned that feminism has been co-opted in various ways. Could you talk more about how and where this is happening?

LINDA: Yes, clearly another main problem between feminism and the left concerns the co-optation of feminist demands. Without a doubt, there are class politics among much of organized feminism, and we need a class analysis of how various groups articulate their agenda and their priorities. Mainstream women's groups of the 1960s demanded entry into professions, the elimination of sexism in hiring and promotion and wages, a relief from the double shift at home and work, legal access to abortion, more daycare, more social supports for raising children, and an end to discrimination against lesbians in the workforce and the terror perpetrated against lesbians on the streets.

Most of these demands have been largely won for upper-class and upper-middle-class women. These groups have entered into many of the main professions in substantial numbers, such as law and medicine. There are federal protections of equal pay when women are doing the same exact type of work as men. Abortion remains legal and it remains accessible for women with money. Relief from the double day can be gained by upper- and upper-middle-class career women through paying for very expensive daycare, by bringing in live-in au pairs from Sweden or El Salvador, and by paying working-class women to clean their homes for terribly low wages.

This kind of co-optation, in which the demands of the 60s are allowed for the upper classes and the restriction of these benefits to the lower classes is justified on the basis of market conditions or the incompetence of the poor has also occurred with other demands from the 1960s such as environmental and quality-of-life-demands: if you are rich enough, you can buy clean water, air filters, organic range-fed chickens, travel to scenic parks, and send your child to a school with lots of money for the arts.

But this isn't feminism and it shouldn't be called such. As bell hooks says, if feminism is for all women, then it has to be about revolution. It has to be left. Teaching this lesson to young women today who are serious about wanting a feminist future can be an uphill battle. The struggle against the global oligarchy seems completely utopian and unrealistic to most of them, and thus they will sometimes settle for a feminism that replicates social stratifications as long as it integrates women fully at each level. And while the left remains sexist, young women will not be attracted to left organizations and movements, and they may find the sexism on the left only confirms their fatalism about significant social change. We must fight this fatalism.

LAURA: Altogether you sound fairly optimistic about our ability to build more effective, long-lasting bridges between feminism(s) and the left. Your positive vision is an important one for all of us who hold feminist agendas to keep in mind. I would like to hear more—and I know others would as well—about your thoughts on where leftists need to concentrate our efforts as we envision the future.

LINDA: I am not so fatalistic first of all because I have great hopes for the labor movement in this country. The AFL-CIO has largely learned its lessons about racism and sexism: the new work force is variegated, and the union movement must adapt or die. Many of the activists in the labor movement today have realized this, and have incorporated antisexist, and antiracist and antihomophobic workshops in their shop steward training, have enforced an affirmative action that preferences hiring women and people of color as new organizers, have enforced a quota system to ensure racial and gender representation at their conferences and national meetings, and are aggressively pursuing the unionization of traditionally female and nonwhite sectors of the labor force. The labor unions have clout, organization, resources, and the ability to reach out to millions of regular working folks. It is not all rosy—the struggles against sexism and racism within are still often very difficult, and there are losses as well as gains. But the old union movement led exclusively by white male craft unions answering to the needs of only the top strata of workers is increasingly becoming a relic of the past.

Unions are not the panacea: they do not put forward a socialist agenda. But they do what is today much more important, in my view: they help to bring out the truly rich and untapped resources of democratization through creating new leadership and ensuring enough of a standard of living that people are not so desperate that they can do nothing else but focus on survival. We who are left-wing and feminist intellectuals, almost always middle-class, will not be the leaders who will show this country how to fulfill its promise of social justice: those who can show us the way are emerging today out of these local struggles, like the Justice for Janitors campaign, the campaign for nursing home workers—so many of whom are women of color—and other local but significant campaigns.

I am also very hopeful about the newly emerging and growing antiwar and antiglobal capital movements. There are better organizational structures than before in these groups, there are many women in leadership, there is an awareness of the problems of sectarianism, and there is often good communication between U.S. groups and groups outside the U.S. who share a common agenda.

Now is not a time for fatalism but a time for action.

WORKS CITED

Alcoff, Linda Martín, and Laura A. Gray-Rosendale. "Survivor Discourse: Transgression or Recuperation?" *Getting a Life: Autobiography and Postmodernism*. Ed. Sidonie Smith and Julia Watson. Minneapolis: U of Minnesota P, 1996. 198–225.

Barrett, Michele. *Women's Oppression Today: Problems in Marxist Feminist Analysis*. London: NLB Verso Editions, 1980.

Bogues, Anthony. *Black Heretics, Black Prophets: Radical Political Intellectuals*. New York: Routledge, Taylor, and Francis, 2003.

Campbell, Horace. *Rasta and Resistance: From Marcus Garvey to Walter Rodney*. Preface by Eusi Kwayana. Trenton, N.J.: Africa World Press, 1987.

Elbaum, Max. *Revolution in the Air: Sixties Radicals Turn to Lenin, Mao, and Che*. London: Verso, 2002.

hooks, bell. *Feminism Is for Everybody: Passionate Politics*. Cambridge: South End, 2000.

———. *Feminist Theory: From Margin to Center*. 2nd ed. Cambridge: South End 2000.

Moorti, Sujata. *Color of Rape: Gender and Race in Television's Public Spheres*. Albany: State U of New York P, 2002.

Sacks, Karen Brodkin. *Caring by the Hour: Women, Work, and Organizing at Duke Medical Center*. Urbana: U of Illinois P, 1988.

Sacks, Karen Brodkin, and Dorothy Remy, eds. *My Troubles Are Going to Have Trouble With Me: Everyday Trials and Triumphs of Women Workers*. New Brunswick: Rutgers University Press, 1984.

Sacks, Karen Brodkin, Kathleen A. Staudt, and James P. Marshall. *Women, Development, and Population: Revising Theories and Approaches*. Tucson: Southwest Institute for Research on Women, 1987.

Vogel, Lise. *Woman Questions: Essays for a Materialist Feminism*. London: Pluto, 1995.

CONTRIBUTORS

EDITOR BIOGRAPHIES

Laura Gray-Rosendale: Laura Gray-Rosendale is Associate Professor of English specializing in Rhetoric and Composition at Northern Arizona University. She teaches graduate and undergraduate classes in cultural studies and politics, visual rhetoric, history of rhetoric, gender studies, identity theory, and autobiography, as well as literacy studies. Along with over thirty articles and book chapters, Gray-Rosendale has published *Rethinking Basic Writing: Exploring Identity, Politics, and Community in Interaction* (Lawrence Erlbaum Associates, 2000), *Alternative Rhetorics: Challenges to the Rhetorical Tradition* with Sibylle Gruber (State U of New York P, 2001), and *Fractured Feminisms: Rhetoric, Context, and Contestation* with Gil Harootunian (State U of New York P, 2003). Her textbook on rhetoric and popular culture, *The [Next] Reader*, is forthcoming from McGraw-Hill Publishers (2006). Much of her activist work involves the struggle for the rights of two survivor groups, survivors of sexual assault and survivors of breast cancer. Gray-Rosendale is currently working on several projects aimed at both scholarly and popular audiences, combining personal narrative with studies on literacy acquisition, gender, class, and identity.

Steven Rosendale: Steven Rosendale is Associate Professor of English specializing in Radical Literature and Theory, American Literature, and Literature in the Environment at Northern Arizona University. He teaches graduate and undergraduate courses in radical literature, literature in the environment, and traditional American literary genres. Rosendale has published *The Greening of Literary Scholarship, and the Dictionary of Literary Biography 303: American Radicaland Reform Writers* with Gale (2004). Rosendale's current project is his monograph *The City Wilderness: Political Ecology on the American Literary Left.*

AUTHOR BIOGRAPHIES

Linda Martín Alcoff: Linda Martín Alcoff is Professor of Philosophy, Political Science, and Women's Studies at Syracuse University. Her books include *Feminist Epistemologies*, co-edited with Elizabeth Potter (Routledge); *Real Knowing: New Versions of the Coherence Theory of Knowledge* (Cornell); *Epistemology: The Big Questions* (Blackwell); *Thinking From the Underside of History*, co-edited with Eduardo Mendieta (Rowman and Littlefield); and *Identities*, co-edited with Eduardo Mendieta (Blackwell 2002). Her book, *Visible Identities: Race, Gender and the Self*, is forthcoming from Oxford Press.

Michael Bennett: Michael Bennett is Associate Professor of English at Long Island University (Brooklyn), where he also teaches in Urban Studies, Gender Studies, and the Honors Program. He is the co-editor of *The Nature of Cities: Ecocriticism and Urban Environments* and *Recovering the Black Female Body: Self-Representations by African American Women* and the author of the forthcoming *Democratic Discourses: Antebellum American Literature and the Radical Abolition Movement*. Bennett is on the Steering Committee of the Radical Caucus of the Modern Language Association and on the Executive Committee of the Long Island University Faculty Federation—AFL-CIO (AFT).

Brenda Jo Brueggemann: Brenda Jo Brueggemann is an Associate Professor of English. She has developed both an American Sign Language program and an interdisciplinary minor in Disability Studies at The Ohio State University. She is the author of *Lend Me Your Ear: Rhetorical Constructions of Deafness* (Gallaudet UP), co-editor and contributor for a collection, *Disability Studies: Enabling the Humanities* (MLA), editor and contributor of another forthcoming collection, *Perspectives on Language, Literacy and Deafness* (Gallaudet UP), co-author with Wendy Hesford of a forthcoming textbook, *Visual Culture: Reading its Rhetoric* (Prentice-Hall), series editor for "Deaf Lives: Autobiography and Biography" (Gallaudet UP), and writer of essays and articles in other edited collections, scholarly journals, and literary journals.

Wendy L. Chrisman: Wendy L. Chrisman is an English Ph.D. student at The Ohio State University, focusing on critical theory and disability studies (inflected with feminisms, performance theory, and a dash of rhetorical theories of the mind/body). Her projected dissertation is an "emerge-*agency*" reconciliation of the medical, legal, theoretical, literary, and social models of madness and disorder, and how these intersect with cyberspace(s). Chrisman was working as a teaching apprentice (part of the Ph.D. requirements) for the course featured in this essay.

Noah De Lissovoy: Noah De Lissovoy is a doctoral student in Urban Schooling at U.C.L.A. His work focuses on hegemony and resistance within public schools. "Educational 'Accountability' and the Violence of Capital," co-authored with Peter McLaren, is forthcoming in *The Journal of Education Policy* (England) "Paulo Freire," co-authored with Peter McLaren, is forthcoming in *The Encyclopedia of Education*, edited by J. J. Chambliss.

Barbara Foley: Barbara Foley is Professor of English at Rutgers University, Newark Campus. She is the author of *Telling the Truth: The Theory and Practice of Documentary Fiction* (1986), *Radical Representations: Politics and Form in U.S. Proletarian Fiction, 1929–1941* (1993), and numerous articles on Marxist theory, African American literature, and U. S. literary radicalism. She is currently at work on two books, both dealing with African American writers and the left: one on Jean Toomer and one on Ralph Ellison. Foley became involved in left politics in the context of the antiwar movement in the late 1960s, and has remained active ever since. She is currently working on the grassroots level in the Combatting Racism Task Force of New Jersey NOW, and she is on the steering committee of the Radical Caucus of the Modern Languages Association. Foley lives in Newark, where both of her kids went through the public school system and where she and her husband are involved in various community projects.

Henry A. Giroux: Henry A. Giroux holds the Waterbury Chair Professorship and is currently the Director of the Waterbury Forum in Education and Cultural Studies at Pennsylvania State University. His most recent books include: *Beyond the Corporate University*, edited with Kostas Myrsiadis (Rowman and Littlefield, 2001); *Public Spaces, Private Lives: Beyond the Culture of Cynicism* (Rowman and Littlefield, 2001); a revised edition of *Theory and Resistance in Education* (Bergin and Garvey, 2001); *Impure Acts: The Practical Politics of Cultural Studies* (Routledge, 2000); *The Mouse That Roared: Disney and the End of Innocence* (Rowman and Littlefield, 2000); *Stealing Innocence: Corporate's Culture's War on Children* (St. Martin's, 2000), *Channel Surfing: Racism, the Media, and the Destruction of Today's Youth* (St. Martin's and Macmillan, England, 1998), and the forthcoming: *Breaking in to the Movies: Film and the Politics of Representation* (Basil Blackwell). His primary research areas are cultural studies, youth studies, critical pedagogy, popular culture, social theory, and the politics of higher education.

Wendy S. Hesford: Wendy Hesford is Associate Professor at The Ohio State University. She is author of *Framing Identities: Autobiography and the Politics of Pedagogy* (University of Minnesota Press, 1999), winner of the 1999 Winterowd Book Award. Hesford has also edited *Haunting Violations: Feminist Criticism and the Crisis of the Real* (University of Illinois Press, 2001) with Wendy Kozol. She has published in various journals, including *Journal of Advanced Composition* and *College English*. Her work can also be found in a number of edited collections, including *Feminism and Composition Studies* and *Writing in Multicultural Settings*, among others.

Marian E. Lupo: Marian E. Lupo is a doctoral student in Rhetoric and Composition at The Ohio State University. Her research interests include disability studies, cultural studies, globalization, and critical feminist pedagogy. Her current research focuses on the rhetoric of the corporate body in early modern England in law and literature. Lupo is chair of committee for the Ohio Conference AAUP and a member of the steering committee for the contract faculty association (CFA)-UAW at Columbus State Community College. She enrolled in the class featured in this essay for independent study credits as a graduate student.

Scott Richard Lyons: Scott Richard Lyons (Leech Lake Ojibwe) is Assistant Professor of Writing and Rhetoric at Syracuse University, where he also teaches in the Native American Studies program. Scott worked at Leech Lake Tribal College from 1999 to 2002.

Peter McLaren: Peter McLaren is a Professor at the Graduate School of Education and Information Studies, University of California, Los Angeles. He has authored and edited over thirty-five books on topics that range from Marxist social theory, sociology of education, critical ethnography, cultural studies, critical pedagogy and critical literacy. His most recent books include *Critical Pedagogy and Predatory Culture* (Routledge, 1995); *Revolutionary Multiculturalism* (Westview, 1997); *Counternarratives*, with Henry Giroux, Colin Lankshear, and Michael Peters (Routledge, 1997); *Che Guevara, Paulo Freire, and the Pedagogy of Revolution* (Rowman and Littlefield , 2000); and *Marxism against Postmodernism in Education*, with Dave Hill, Glenn Rikowski, and Mike Peters (Lexington P, in press). McLaren lectures worldwide on the politics of liberation. His work has been translated into fifteen languages.

Derek Owens: Derek Owens is Associate Professor of English and Director of the Writing Center at St. John's University in Queens, NYC. Author of *Composition and Sustainability: Teaching for a Threatened Generation* (NCTE) and *Resisting Writings (and the Boundaries of Composition)* (Southern Methodist UP), Owens lives with his wife Teresa Hewitt and son Ryan somewhere in the heart of Long Island.

Victor Villanueva: Victor Villanueva is Professor and Chair of the English Department at Washington State University, where he also teaches rhetoric and composition studies. He is the winner of two national awards on research and scholarship for his *Bootstraps: From an American Academic of Color*, and the editor of *Cross-Talk in Comp Theory: A Reader*. Among his current book projects, his *Of Color* five-book series due in 2004 promises to be the first set of disciplinary crossover books, spanning composition studies, ethnic studies, and American literature. Frequently anthologized, Villanueva is the writer of numerous articles. He has delivered nearly sixty oral presentations, more than thirty-five of which have been in keynote or featured speaking roles, bringing him the honor of Rhetorician of the Year for 1999, conferred by the Young Rhetoricians Conference. He is also the former chair of The Conference on College Composition and Communication and has twice co-chaired the organization's Winter Workshop. Villanueva's concern is always with racism and with the political more generally as embodied in rhetoric and literacy.

Alan Wald: Alan Wald is Professor of English and Director of the Program in American Culture at the University of Michigan. He is the author of *The Revolutionary Imagination*, *The New York Intellectuals*, *Writing From the Left*, *The Responsibility of Intellectuals*, *Exiles From a Future Time*, and other books; and he is on the editorial boards of *Science and Society*, *Against the Current*, and *American Literature*.

Evan Watkins: Evan Watkins is Professor of English at University of California-Davis. He has published numerous articles and book chapters on Marxism, education, capitalism, and labor relations. His books include *Everyday Exchanges: Market Work and Capitalist Sense*, *Throwaways: Work Culture and Consumer Education*, *Work Time: English Departments and the Circulation of Cultural Value*, and *The Critical Act: Criticism and Community*. Watkins is currently at work on two other books, *Class Degrees* and *Rhetoric, Gender, and Science*.

Mark Wood: Mark Wood, Professor, has a joint appointment in Religious Studies and African American Studies at Virginia Commonwealth University. He teaches courses on religion, ethics, and politics. He has written on race, class, politics, and education in the United States. His book, *Cornel West and the Politics of Prophetic Pragmatism* (U of Illinois P, 2000), articulates a Marxist critique of Cornel West's progressive pragmatism. Wood has also published essays and reviews on teaching for democratic globalization and is an active participant of local and global struggles for social justice, human rights, and ecological sustainability.

INDEX